FOUNDATION PRESS

ANTITRUST STORIES

Edited By

ELEANOR M. FOX

Walter J. Derenberg Professor of Trade Regulation
New York University School of Law

and

DANIEL A. CRANE

Associate Professor of Law
Benjamin Cardozo School of Law

FOUNDATION PRESS
2007

THOMSON

WEST

© 2007 By FOUNDATION PRESS
        395 Hudson Street
        New York, NY 10014
        Phone Toll Free 1–877–888–1330
        Fax (212) 367–6799
        foundation–press.com
Printed in the United States of America

ISBN 978–1–59941–092–0

 TEXT IS PRINTED ON 10% POST CONSUMER RECYCLED PAPER

ANTITRUST STORIES

FOUNDATION PRESS

ANTITRUST STORIES

*

Introduction

Antitrust stories are the tall tales of American capitalism. David and Goliath. Paul Bunyan. Gulliver. J.P. Morgan. John D. Rockefeller. Bill Gates.

This is a volume of antitrust stories. They are stories of power or imagined power. The storytellers of *Microsoft* see real power in a corporate giant plundering Americans. The storyteller of the case of the striking lawyers sees real power on the side of the FTC Goliath attacking the legal service Davids who are trying to help the poor.

This volume attempts to bring a baker's dozen of great antitrust cases to life in the story-telling tradition. At least sometimes, the story is in the eyes and mind of the teller; for story-telling depends on perspective and in nearly all of the great cases there are the proverbial two sides to the story. We have assembled an exciting group of authors—historians, legal scholars, economists, scholarly litigators, and former antitrust officials; and we let them tell their stories.

The cases on which they write are casebook opinions—some interesting; many dense (as in *Standard Oil*) and give little hint of the humanity that lies behind them. We have encouraged our authors to scratch the legalistic surface and unveil the human dimension.

We have chosen thirteen cases that are not only among the canon of the greats but that also reflect the ebb and flow of antitrust attitudes and assumptions. We hope that our case selection will provide a snapshot of thirteen particular moments in the evolution of antitrust and that the composite of emerging pictures will allow the reader to see the formation of patterns and themes that emerge over time and will surely continue in the future. We hope that reading these stories side-by-side the case opinions will add a depth to the casebook study of antitrust law.

The stories in this book span cartels, monopolies, and mergers, and they venture into the shifting landscape of world markets and jurisdiction. There were several ways to organize the cases. We chose chronological sequence, more or less, since an understanding of the evolution of antitrust is an important part of learning antitrust. However, casebooks are almost universally organized by subject matters. Therefore, we call your attention to subject matter clusters. For cartels, you will want to read the stories of *Standard Oil*, *Socony*, *Superior Court Trial Lawyers*, and *Empagran*; and read *Topco* for a twist you may not see in your casebook. For competitor collaborations that are not hard core cartels, including joint ventures: *Topco* and *BMI*. For monopoly and abuse: *Standard Oil*, *Alcoa*, *Aspen*, and *Microsoft*. For vertical restraints: *Dr.*

Miles, *Schwinn/Sylvania*, *Topco*, and *BMI*. For mergers: *Standard Oil*, *Staples*, and *GE/Honeywell*. For intellectual property: *Dr. Miles*, *BMI*, and *Microsoft*. For global problems—jurisdiction, enforcement, divergence, and convergence: *Alcoa*, *GE/Honeywell*, and *Empagran*.

We start, aptly, with a legal historian's story of perhaps the most renowned antitrust case in history—the case of the Rockefeller Standard Oil Trust. Much ink has been spilled over Rockefeller and his trust, but Jim May provides a fresh account that is highly attentive to the litigation strategies and rhetorical positions of the government and defendants in the litigation. Given the richness of the issues teased out in the lawyers' briefs and the lower courts' opinions, the Supreme Court's *Standard Oil* decision may be as notable for the questions it left unanswered as those it answered.

Monopolies are the tallest tales of antitrust and no monopolization case has cast a longer shadow over the discipline than the great *Alcoa* case that Spencer Waller tackles for us. Spencer shows how the injection of vigor into the newly-formed Antitrust Division under Robert Jackson and Thurman Arnold helped to set up the longest trial in U.S. history. But, as Spencer shows, perhaps the most interesting aspect of the case is not the litigation but the post-litigation decision of the Government to inject competition into the aluminum market by strategically divesting its own aluminum plants.

Looking for monopolistic conduct in a swankier locale, George Priest and Jonathan Lewinsohn head west to the elite skiing slopes of the Rockies and the *Aspen Skiing* case. In that case, the Aspen Highlands ski mountain convinced the Supreme Court that its Aspen rival, Ski Co., which operated three ski mountains, violated the Sherman Act by discontinuing a previous joint venture arrangement in which the parties had sold four-mountain ski passes. George and Jonathan show that Ski Co.'s decision to discontinue the four-mountain arrangement was not based on any monopolistic plan (since, indeed, the Aspen ski area was not a proper relevant market) but was instead motivated by Highlands's abysmal quality and efforts to free-ride on Ski Co.'s far greater investments in its mountains.

Since the famous *Alcoa* decision of 1945, the enterprise of challenging monopolies or their abuse has faced a rocky road. The deep suspicion of monopoly voiced by Judge Learned Hand in *Alcoa* was challenged; conduct, not structure, became the rod for antitrust lightning. As IBM and other well-heeled defendants taught litigators, the trial against giant firms was a war, and not for the faint-hearted. Eventually a new complication clouded the trust-busters' skies: intense market changes; a dynamic new economy had arrived. Therefore it was big news when the Department of Justice threw down its gauntlet to challenge the reputedly ruthless Microsoft. Was this a war that could not be won? Doug Melamed, who was a top Antitrust Division lawyer, and Dan Rubinfeld, who was the top Antitrust Division economist, tell the story of how the war was won.

We move next into cartels and other agreements in restraint of trade. Rudy Peritz kicks off this set of cases with a fascinating history of patent medicines and trademark protection in the early twentieth century, which explains the real basis for the now jettisoned *Dr. Miles* decision prohibiting vertical resale price maintenance. Rudy re-tells *Dr. Miles* as the story of a ferocious fight over intellectual property rights between a branded firm using downstream contractual controls to stimulate brand differentiation and a cut-rate distributor seeking to expand its market share through drastic price discounting.

Next, Dan Crane analyzes the *Socony–Vacuum* decision as emblematic of the political and rapidly shifting nature of antitrust enforcement. To contemporary readers, the *Socony* story may be surprising: The very administration that encouraged and virtually compelled a price-fixing cartel during the first half of the New Deal turned around and criminally prosecuted the members of the cartel for price-fixing when attitudes toward industrial competition shifted abruptly during the second half of the New Deal.

Antitrust law is full of stories and also, some would say, myths. Peter Carstensen and Harry First dismantle the free rider story—or perhaps myth—which today is viewed nearly universally as justifying the exclusive territory system condemned in *Topco*. They conclude that *Topco* should not be understood, as it often is, as a rigidly rule-based holding, but rather as a transitional case in the direction of a more flexible mode of antitrust adjudication.

Dr. Miles started our examination of vertical price restraints and Warren Grimes picks up a similar thread by walking us through the ten-year turn-about from *Schwinn* to *Sylvania* and the law of non-price vertical restraints. He shows that the Schwinn bicycle company was an insecure brand seller that used vertical restraints to confer downstream market power on its retailers. By examining the market positions of both Schwinn and Sylvania, Warren shows that the Supreme Court's ideologically-driven *Sylvania* decision misunderstood the potential of such vertical restraints to harm both interbrand and intrabrand competition.

Steve Calkins introduces us to the entertaining world of music, performance rights, and blanket licensing in CBS's failed lawsuit against BMI and ASCAP. The case, which could easily have been a sleeper, set the stage for a revolution in the way that collaborative restraints of trade are analyzed in large part because of the participation of sophisticated amicus curiae.

In our next cartel case, Don Baker takes us into the strategy war rooms of the lawyers for the Superior Court Trial Lawyers, who were accused of price-fixing and a boycott when they rebelled against the pitifully low fees paid to lawyers who represented indigent defendants. He shows that the FTC's action against a small, competitively insignificant group of criminal defense lawyers grew out of a conservative agency's desire to turn antitrust enforcement away from business interests and toward a traditionally left-leaning constituency. Like the *Socony* defendants, the trial lawyers had reason to understand the antitrust enterprise as a nakedly ideological assertion of political power, albeit in very different circumstances.

Our final set of stories concern mergers and the transnational reach of antitrust law. Since *Standard Oil*, mergers to increase market power have been condemned. But when does a merger increase market power, and how is this effect proved? These questions have bedeviled the law—not just in the United States but also abroad.

U.S. merger law has taken twists and turns. The big twist was the passage of the Celler–Kefauver Act in 1950 against a background of fear of industrial concentration lest the nation fall into communism or fascism. *Brown Shoe*, the first Supreme Court merger case thereunder, broadly assumed that slight increases in concentration harmed competition. But by the 1980s and well before the 1990s, assumptions had changed and the law focused on consumers. We now ask: Does this merger hurt consumers? Will this merger cause prices to rise? Or is it efficient? Will it increase competition? Will prices fall? Beginning in the 1980s, we entered a period of calm on the merger front. This was particularly true at the Federal Trade Commission, which was seen as a sleepy agency. Then along came the appointment of Bob Pitofsky as Chair of the FTC, the appointment of Jon Baker as Director of the FTC's Bureau of Economics, and the announcement that Office Depot and Staples, the first and second largest of the three office supply superstore chains in the United States, planned to merge. This was a challenge, to which the FTC rose. What was the market? Did it include all retail sellers of office supplies? Could the FTC prove that the merger would raise prices? Well, it did, and here is the story of how the FTC won.

We include one additional—and quite different—merger story. This is a case of transAtlantic intrigue and politics: the case of the failed merger plan of General Electric and Honeywell, two U.S. firms that operate in world markets. The story of GE/Honeywell is a story of two jurisdictions: the United States, which cleared the merger, and the European Union, which enjoined it. The story, as told by Eleanor Fox, involved a divergence between U.S. and EU law regarding when a merger is anticompetitive. Is a merger anticompetitive when the merging firms, leaders in their concentrated fields, produce complements (jet engines and avionic equipment for jet aircraft) and the merged firm may have leverage to induce its buyers of one product to buy the other? The story unfolds as the European Commission answers "yes" to the question to which the U.S. Department of Justice answered "no." GE CEO Jack Welch and a coterie of American politicians became incensed. How could Europe stop "their" merger? Meanwhile, just at this time, the European court was scrutinizing and reversing European Commission merger prohibitions for insufficiency of proof, and in some ways European merger law was becoming more American. In the end, Eleanor calls this story, which begins on a note of divergence, a story of how laws converge.

GE/Honeywell segués into our last chapter, which is also a story for the world. This is *Empagran*—the case of the worldwide vitamins cartel and the question whether purchasers of the price-fixed vitamins who buy abroad can recover treble damages in U.S. courts. To answer this question, the Supreme Court construes one of the worst drafted statutes in history, and (applying policy in the face of statutory ambiguity) it answers, "no." The chapter on *Empagran* is an analysis by two economist/law professors, Al Klevorick and Alan Sykes, who remind us that cartel deterrence is a global problem, and who argue that the Supreme Court failed to ask the right questions to determine the optimal path for increasing either national welfare or global welfare. The *Empagran* chapter gives perspective on the place of national enforcement in a world of global markets and transnational wrongs.

Thus draws to an end these stories of antitrust; from the great combination that stamped out competition during the ecomonic transformation that transpired between the Civil War and World War I to the great world vitamins cartel on the wave of globalization. The book ends with the implicit suggestion that globalization, comity, convergence, and efficiency are likely to be threads of the antitrust stories of the second century of antitrust.

Eleanor M. Fox

Daniel A. Crane

*

1

James May[1]

The Story of *Standard Oil Co. v. United States*

Background

The antimonopoly concerns that became a central part of American public life in the late nineteenth and early twentieth centuries had both ancient and recent origins. In Anglo–American experience, anxieties over Crown grants of monopoly to favored enterprisers led Parliament in the seventeenth century to restrict the power of the Crown to make such grants, while the common law over time had evolved doctrines making various private contractual restraints of trade legally unenforceable as against public policy. Animating these developments were concerns that monopolies and private restraints of trade could deprive individuals of a common right to engage in trade and that the public could be deprived of the benefits of competition and thereby face higher prices and a reduced availability or lower quality of goods and services.

Such concerns were heightened for many Americans during the crisis with Great Britain that led to the American Revolution. In the minds of radical opposition writers in England and many American revolutionaries, crown corruption of English politics and the British Constitution was linked with a simultaneous corruption of English economic and social life and a disturbing increase in commercialization through crown favors to rising commercial and manufacturing interests in Britain. As an aspect of increasingly resented British mercantile regulation, monopoly privilege became a focal point of American protest as well.

In the same year as the American Declaration of Independence, Adam Smith in *The Wealth of Nations* provided a deeper theoretical

---

[1] This chapter is derived from a forthcoming book on the case of *Standard Oil Co. v. United States* to be published by the University Press of Kansas.

basis for a moral as well as efficiency-based belief in the virtues of competition and the evils of monopoly. His work provided a foundation for understanding economics as based on discoverable, fundamental natural laws, a foundation that would be elaborated on thereafter by a host of scholarly, political, and popular writers and continue to influence American thinking through the period of the Standard Oil litigation. Within the new American republic, dominant political thinking heavily stressed ideas of liberty and equality that centrally encompassed the protection of property rights and robust and equal opportunity for free white males to pursue their own happiness as well as the public good. Widely-embraced contemporary political ideals stressed the importance of a broad and not too uneven distribution of property, in order to ensure both economic independence and a high level of civic virtue. Guided by such ideals, Americans soon began to consider the proper role of government in promoting or regulating economic life in the New Republic.

In the early decades of the nineteenth century, Americans witnessed the beginnings of an industrial revolution in the North, particularly in New England, simultaneously with the expansion of a slave-based economy in the South. The tremendous expansion of the American territorial domain during the antebellum decades helped to spur an explosion of publicly-supported efforts to interconnect regions within the expanding nation through the establishment of new roads, canals, railroad lines, and steamboat connections. Expansion of this transportation network in turn boosted enthusiasm and opportunities for the development of not just American trade and commerce, but also larger-scale, specialized manufacturing of goods for shipment to consumers over a wider geographic area than previously had been economically feasible. Such efforts were spurred, too, by important new technological and organizational developments in both the United States and Great Britain.

Even in the North, however, the accelerated development of transportation and manufacturing, particularly in expanded, factory settings, generated not only substantial enthusiasm, but also popular and political anxiety. Antebellum economic change occurred within an overwhelmingly agrarian nation characterized by a widely-embraced antipathy to government-granted privileges for some at the expense of others and a widespread belief, particularly in the North, in the importance of assured equality of opportunity for small, independent, self-employed free producers. Such producers were commonly seen as the great foundation of American society.

In this political and cultural context, the increasing state grant of privileges of incorporation to a minority of enterprising individuals, primarily, in the early years, for transportation and banking projects, but later with growing frequency for manufacturing endeavors as well, prominently began to raise economic, social, and political concerns. These concerns would expand greatly in the later nineteenth century with the tremendous growth in the number and size of corporations and what a great many Americans would perceive as a dramatic and dangerous increase in the prevalence and severity of corporate misconduct.

A somewhat more encompassing producer-centered outlook combined with Protestant evangelical morality and anti-slavery sentiment to form the free labor ideology of the Republican Party established in 1854. This ideology would inform the actions of Republicans through the Civil War and Reconstruction in seeking to secure for the freedmen equal civil rights of free labor, property, and contract, along with equal protection of the laws. In later decades, this ideology, and variations upon it, strongly would influence the understanding of many Americans grappling with issues of anticompetitive behavior and monopoly, even as newer economic and political perspectives became increasingly prominent.

In the decades following the Civil War, substantial further expansion of the national transportation and communications network facilitated the greater geographic extension of markets. The ability to reach ever larger numbers of purchasers at greater and greater distances prompted a growing number of firms in many industries increasingly to take advantage of greater economies of scale and other efficiencies made possible by the multitude of technological breakthroughs of the later nineteenth century. The feasibility and profitability of such larger-scale mass production was facilitated as well by an increasing demand for a wide variety of goods and an increased supply of labor. These, in turn, largely resulted from a burgeoning American population and accelerating urbanization, boosted in substantial part by large-scale immigration in the late nineteenth century. In this setting, American output of goods and services increased five-fold between the start of the Civil War and the close of World War I, making the United States the leading industrial nation on earth.

Expanded production and sale over wider geographic areas brought increasing numbers of firms into direct competition with one another. While this often offered immediate benefits for purchasers in terms of greater variety and lower prices, such expanded economic activity and intensified competition soon contributed greatly to pronounced economic volatility and widespread changes in national patterns of business behavior and market structure. These consequent changes seemed not merely to pose a danger of higher or discriminatory prices. For a great many Americans, these changes appeared to threaten the viability of traditional, seemingly natural, patterns of small-scale competitive market capitalism and the economic, social, and political values associated with them.

Post–Civil War economic conditions periodically led to severe temporary "overproduction" in many lines of business. This led to intense price wars, resulting bankruptcies and a recurring pattern of severe economic boom and bust. This proved particularly true where railroads and manufacturing firms with a high percentage of fixed investments in assets not easily transferred to other uses fought to maintain market share in the face of collapsing prices, in order to recoup as much as they could beyond at least their variable expenses.

Particularly, but not exclusively, in these circumstances, late nineteenth-century American firms in large numbers sought protection and better returns through various forms of mutual cooperation, ranging from such "loose" combinations as simple cartels or pools, to such tighter combinations as trusts, holding companies, and mergers, entered into with willing or coerced partners. Such tighter combinations at least theoretically offered possibilities of new productive or managerial efficiencies not achievable through simple "loose" arrangements. At the same time, large firms, now increasingly organized as managerially run corporations, repeatedly employed at times ruthless predatory tactics to eliminate or undercut existing rivals or to exclude potential new entrants from their markets. With unsettling frequency during the Gilded Age and the Progressive Era, powerful firms such as Standard Oil also sought to gain advantage over their rivals in the political realm, by bribing legislators or otherwise corrupting the political process in order to obtain new benefits or to establish new hurdles for would-be rivals.

Americans witnessing these developments widely agreed that they raised fundamental questions about the future of economic, political, and social life in America.[2] Yet, at the very same time, Americans widely and enthusiastically heralded the tremendous increase in American productivity, innovation and output occurring between the Civil War and the turn of the century and marveled at the achievements of entrepreneurial giants like John D. Rockefeller and Andrew Carnegie. Many Americans also approved of the widespread rise of combinations and the substantially increasing level of concentration in many important American industries, seeing such changes as a progressive outcome of ongoing, natural economic evolution. As John D. Rockefeller himself declared: "The day of combination is here to stay. Individualism has gone, never to return." A great many other Americans, however, became alarmed at the spread of cartels, combinations, and apparently predatory behavior

---

[2] E.g., Martin J. Sklar, The Corporate Reconstruction of American Capitalism, 1890–1916: The Market, The Law, and Politics 34 (1988); James May, *Antitrust in the Formative Era: Political and Economic Theory in Constitutional and Antitrust Analysis, 1880–1918*, 50 Ohio St. L.J. 257, 283–84 (1989).

by firms possessing economic wealth and power on a scale undreamt of just a few short decades before.

Early on, farmers charged that as a result of such activities, railroads and grain elevators charged them exorbitant and discriminatory prices for their services, while suppliers of needed equipment exacted excessive prices and food distributors and processors paid them pitiably little for what they produced. Many small businesses came to feel similarly threatened and joined with farmers to push successfully for Granger legislation in a number of Midwestern states to set limits on the rates and terms that railroads and grain elevators could charge. As time went on, farmers, small businesses, consumers and others became more and more anxious over the spread of cartels, combinations, and predatory conduct in the American economy in general, occurring at the same time that workers fought increasingly powerful corporations in stark, large-scale confrontations. They commonly believed that cartels, combinations, and predatory activity threatened fundamental, interrelated natural rights of individual economic opportunity, property, and contract, while ultimately undercutting the maximization and fair distribution of social wealth, social harmony, and the vitality of liberal republican government in America that the unimpeded, legitimate exercise of those rights produced.

Growing public alarm prompted not only new state and federal legislative investigations of anticompetitive behavior, but also the passage of state antitrust laws beginning in the late 1880's. By the 1888 presidential election, both political parties adopted antimonopoly planks in their party platforms and both presidential candidates spoke out against anticompetitive business conduct. The push for legislative action culminated in 1890 with the passage of the Sherman Antitrust Act, which, like state antitrust legislation, built upon common law doctrines addressing anticompetitive conduct.[3]

Following passage of the Sherman Act, antitrust litigation became prominent in a number of states and the federal government began to challenge business conduct under the act. In the two decades following passage of the Sherman Act, three general approaches became prominent in federal court interpretation of the broad language of section 1 of the act. Circuit court of appeals Judge, and later President, William Howard Taft, in his 1898 opinion in *United States v. Addyston Pipe & Steel Company*,[4] proposed a fundamental distinction between naked restraints, to be summarily condemned, and ancillary restraints, potentially sus-

---

[3] Section 1 of the Sherman Act banned contracts, combinations, and conspiracies in restraint of interstate or foreign commerce, while section 2 prohibited monopolization or attempted monopolization of that commerce.

[4] 85 F. 271 (6th Cir. 1898), *modified and aff'd*, 175 U.S. 211 (1899).

tainable if they were reasonable in the sense of supporting some main, beneficial transaction and not more sweeping than necessary to do so. None of the Justices on the United States Supreme Court, however, explicitly embraced Judge Taft's formula. Instead, Supreme Court debate from 1897 until 1911 centered largely around two other well-known, alternative formulations. Justice Rufus Peckham announced and subsequently refined a standard under which section 1 of the Sherman Act banned all contracts, combinations, and conspiracies directly and substantially restraining interstate or foreign commerce. In a dissenting opinion in the 1897 case of *United States v. Trans–Missouri Freight Association*,[5] Justice, later Chief Justice, Edward Douglass White instead urged an interpretation of section 1 of the act banning only "unreasonable restraints of trade."

The issue of a possible "unreasonableness" standard for judging restraints of trade challenged under section 1 of the Sherman Act came to be a central issue in broader public and political antitrust debate from the late 1890's to the eve of the First World War. This debate went far beyond the question of the meaning of Justice White's dissenting opinion in *Trans–Missouri*. In some common law cases prior to the passage of the Sherman Act, some state courts had departed from mainstream common law precedent and had adopted a reasonableness standard that countenanced even naked cartels on the ground that they set only "reasonable" prices, thus, in the eyes of circuit court of appeals Judge Taft, setting sail on a "sea of doubt." After 1897, proposals repeatedly were made unsuccessfully in Congress to amend the Sherman Act explicitly to ban only "unreasonable" restraints. Taft, however, continued to oppose the adoption of any such amendment right up to the time that the Supreme Court decided the *Standard Oil* case.

In this setting, the Standard Oil Company, along with those who led it, became the leading symbol of rising corporate power, concentration, and abuse in late-nineteenth- and early-twentieth-century America. The subject of both intense praise and condemnation in those decades, Standard Oil ultimately became the preeminent target of antitrust efforts to check anticompetitive conduct and concentration. Concern over its activities significantly contributed to the passage of both state antitrust laws and the Sherman Antitrust Act.

The American oil industry that Standard Oil came to dominate had gotten its start with the drilling of the first successful oil well in 1859 in northwestern Pennsylvania, the only area of the country then known to have substantial crude oil deposits. The industry thereafter had boomed as thousands of persons flooded into the area to pursue their American

---

[5] 166 U.S. 290 (1897).

dream of economic self-sufficiency and, beyond that, wealth, through individual enterprise in the production of crude oil to be refined, primarily, into kerosene, a vastly superior affordable product for illuminating homes and businesses.

These developments caught the eye of the earnest young John D. Rockefeller, who had made a fortune in commodities trading during the Civil War. Rockefeller invested funds in a new small refinery in Cleveland and rapidly became increasingly involved in events in the new oil industry. Aided by agreements with the railroads, Rockefeller and his associates advanced from early efforts to help organize cartels among competing refiners to efforts to acquire them, first in Cleveland and then around the country. By the end of the 1870's, the scores of firms acquired by Rockefeller and his associates were coordinated through the first industrial trust arrangement in America.That trust secretly was established in 1879 and was not known to the government when it filed its case against Standard Oil in 1906. Its existence only became public during litigation of that suit. The 1879 trust was succeeded by a more formal and public trust in 1882. This second trust inspired the establishment of trusts in a number of other industries. The 1882 trust, in turn, was succeeded by the reorganization of the Standard Oil Company of New Jersey as a holding company to coordinate the large number of firms that had come to a be a part of the Standard organization.

That reorganization occurred in 1899, in the midst of a new explosion of corporate consolidations that intensified antitrust concerns. The great merger waves of the late 1890's and the early years of the twentieth century took on astounding proportions for contemporary Americans. An estimated 1800 separate firms went out of independent existence and became a part of great new multi-firm consolidations in these few years. As a result, in many important American industries the number of active competitors plummeted.

A little over two years after the reorganization of the Standard Oil Company of New Jersey, Vice–President Theodore Roosevelt, the former progressive governor of New York, became President of the United States in the wake of the September, 1901 assassination of President William McKinley. Roosevelt was particularly interested in government investigation and publicity concerning business, and pushed for the establishment of a Bureau of Corporations within the new Department of Commerce and Labor to pursue such efforts. Roosevelt, however, also supported the reinvigoration of federal antitrust efforts, substantially increasing the number and importance of antitrust cases brought by the government as compared with his predecessor. Antitrust efforts were enhanced in 1903 with the first specific appropriation for Department of Justice antitrust efforts and the passage of the Expediting Act.[6] That act provided for resolution before a four-judge circuit court panel of anti-trust cases the Attorney General certified to be of "general public importance," as well as direct, expedited appeal thereafter to the United States Supreme Court. The year before these developments, Roosevelt's administration had filed the *Northern Securities* case[7] challenging under the Sherman Act the establishment of a holding company combining two parallel interstate railroad lines. That case was decided in the govern-ment's favor by the Supreme Court in 1904. In a four-Justice plurality opinion, Justice John Marshall Harlan found the holding company combination illegal under the direct and substantial effect on interstate commerce test. The needed fifth vote was supplied by Justice David Brewer who, instead, found a violation of the Sherman Act on the ground that the holding company "unreasonably" restrained interstate commerce, thereby raising anew the question of the status of the "unreasonable restraint" test in the Supreme Court.

During Roosevelt's administration, pressure mounted for federal action against Standard Oil. Numerous state actions brought against the Standard Oil combination had not effectively checked the combination's power or ongoing, seemingly anticompetitive activity. A major new exposé by the prominent muckraking journalist Ida Tarbell appeared, first in serial form in *McClure's Magazine*. Tarbell had grown up in the Pennsylvania Oil Regions with a pronounced wariness of Standard Oil and John D. Rockefeller. Her father had been involved in the oil industry in its early days, and her brother was prominently connected with a leading independent refiner in the early years of the twentieth century. Her detailed study of the rise of Standard Oil and its tactics, later published as a book, was a sensation that attracted the attention of, among others, President Roosevelt himself. Tarbell concluded that while Standard Oil had been a force for much technological efficiency and progress in the industry, it had engaged massively in misconduct to achieve its dominance, particularly by repeatedly obtaining discriminato-ry railroad rates that gave it an important advantage over its competi-tors. Pressure for federal antitrust action also came from new complaints to the Department of Justice from rival independent oil producers and refiners and the release of a new Bureau of Corporations report review-ing the oil industry.

All this led to a government preliminary investigation conducted by Frank B. Kellogg, a corporate attorney involved in a prior government antitrust investigation, who was brought in as special counsel, and

---

[6] Act of February 11, 1903, ch. 544, §§ 1, 2, 32 Stat. 823 (repealed 1984).

[7] *Northern Securities Co. v. United States*, 193 U.S. 197 (1904).

Charles B. Morrison, the federal district attorney for the Northern District of Illinois.[8] In the wake of this preliminary investigation, Attorney General William H. Moody directed the filing of a federal antitrust suit against the Standard Oil combination. The case was filed on November 15, 1906 under the provisions of the Expediting Act in the federal Circuit Court for the Eastern District of Missouri. The government's lengthy bill of complaint charged the defendants with violations of sections 1 and 2 of the Sherman Act, largely as a result of the defendants' acquisition of other firms and the combination of those firms in the 1882 trust and 1899 holding company. The bill also, however, charged that the defendants had violated the Sherman Act through various bad acts, including: the obtaining of favorable but discriminatory railroad rates, rebates, and drawbacks; predatory pricing; spying on competitors' shipments; the operation of bogus independents; the obstruction of competing pipe line construction; and cartel and market division agreements. By far the most lengthy and detailed attention in the bill of complaint was paid to numerous alleged instances of improper railroad rates, rebates, and drawbacks.

The circuit court appointed a special master to take evidence in the case, and his voluminous report was filed on March 22, 1909, just a few weeks after William Howard Taft became President. From April 5–10, 1909, arguments based on the parties' briefs were heard before a four-judge panel. The panel consisted of Circuit Judges Walter H. Sanborn, who had found for the defendants on appeal in *United States v. Trans-Missouri Freight Association*, only to be reversed by the Supreme Court,[9] William C. Hook, Elmer B. Adams and Willis Van Devanter,[10] who, subsequent to the circuit court's decision, would be elevated to the United States Supreme Court and participate in the Supreme Court's decision on appeal. Presiding Judge Sanborn announced the unanimous opinion of the circuit court panel in favor of the government on November 20, 1909, just over three years after the government filed its bill of complaint. One and a half years later, Chief Justice Edward Douglass White would announce the opinion of the Supreme Court on appeal, affirming the circuit court's judgment but modifying its decree.

Contemporary Perception of the Importance of the Case

The federal litigation against Standard Oil widely was perceived at the time to be one of the most important cases ever brought to the

---

[8] Bruce Bringhurst, Antitrust and the Oil Monopoly: The Standard Oil Cases, 1880–1911, at 132 (1979).

[9] 58 F. 58 (8th Cir. 1893), *rev'd* 166 U.S. 290 (1897).

[10] Bruce Bringhurst, Antitrust and the Oil Monopoly: The Standard Oil Cases, 1880–1911, at 145–46 (1979).

United States Supreme Court.[11] In the course of his Supreme Court oral argument, for example, Attorney General George W. Wickersham declared that "never in the history of this country have there been presented to any tribunal controversies in which the issues were more momentous than those in the case against the American Tobacco Company and in the case at bar."[12] The Justices of the Supreme Court themselves believed that the stakes in the *Standard Oil* case were unusually high and treated the litigation as considerably more important, for example, than such other well-known cases of the time as *Lochner v. New York*.[13] Thus, it was not at all surprising that the case was argued for and against the government by some of the very most eminent attorneys of the time.

The Briefs and Issues in the Case

The immense factual record in the *Standard Oil* case repeatedly has been examined at length, and economists and others continue to invoke it and other evidence to debate the degree of market power actually achieved by the Standard Oil combination and the manner in which it was attained.[14] The legal briefs in the case, however, have received far

---

[11] *See, e.g.*, Rudolph J.R. Peritz, Competition Policy in America, 1888–1992: History, Rhetoric, Law 61 (1996).

[12] Transcript of Oral Argument of Hon. George W. Wickersham at 44, *Standard Oil Co. v. United States*, 221 U.S. 1 (1911).

[13] 198 U.S. 45 (1905). *See also* Owen M. Fiss, Troubled Beginnings of the Modern State, 1888–1910, at 107 (noting that the Justices placed much greater importance on *Northern Securities* and other antitrust cases in this period than on *Lochner*).

[14] For example, many scholars continue to believe that Standard Oil attained a near monopoly and therefore great market power in production and sale of refined oil products. Others, such as Dominick Armentano, have argued that Standard Oil never restricted supply or set monopoly prices even when it had a high market share and remained "a large, competitive firm in an open, competitive market." Dominick Armentano, Antitrust and Monopoly: Anatomy of a Policy Failure 66 (1990). In a much-discussed recent article, economists Elizabeth Granitz and Benjamin Klein concur that Standard Oil never monopolized oil refining, a market they believe lacked significant barriers to entry, but conclude that Standard shared greatly in monopoly profits generated in the transportation of oil products. See Elizabeth Granitz and Benjamin Klein, *Monopolization by "Raising Rivals' Costs": The Standard Oil Case*, 39 J.L. & Econ. 1 (1996). As to the reasons for Standard's success, some scholars contend, for example, that the combination achieved its preeminence largely on the basis of superior technical or managerial efficiency. See, e.g., Alfred Chandler, Jr., Scale and Scope: The Dynamics of Industrial Capitalism 92 (1990). Other modern accounts focus, as did the government in the original case, on Standard's large-scale acquisition of independent firms and the relative importance of predatory pricing in the establishment of Standard's preeminence. *Compare, e.g.,* John S. McGee, *Predatory Price Cutting: the Standard Oil (N.J.) Case*, 1 Journal of Law and Economics 137 (1958) (concluding that claims of predatory pricing in the *Standard Oil* case are supportable neither by economic theory nor by the record evidence in the case) *with* Richard A. Posner, Antitrust Law 208–09, 211 (2d ed. 2001) (concluding that it is at least possible that

less detailed attention. In part this is due to their voluminousness. The attorneys for the government and for the Standard Oil defendants submitted not only very extended reviews of the evidence in the case, but also over 1,800 pages of separate briefs on the law or on both the law and the facts. The briefs reveal the lawyers' perceptions of the issues at stake in the case, the choices they made in litigating it, and the manner in which they framed the issues for the circuit court judges and the Justices of the Supreme Court. Simultaneously, the briefs reveal the extent to which the circuit court and Supreme Court opinions followed or departed from the arguments of counsel. Finally, the briefs shine important additional light on contemporary economic and legal outlooks more generally on the issues posed by the Standard Oil litigation.

More than fifteen years passed between the time the Sherman Act was enacted, substantially in response to concerns over Standard Oil and similar combinations, and the time that the government finally filed suit against this most famous of the late-nineteenth and early-twentieth century trusts. More than two decades elapsed between the Sherman Act's passage and the Supreme Court's decision in the case. Yet, despite a series of landmark Supreme Court decisions interpreting and applying the act during these years, a host of basic antitrust issues still remained very much open for debate and definitive resolution; and these questions were vigorously contested in the litigation of the case. The resolution of many of these issues in the *Standard Oil* litigation strongly would influence not only the future development of American antitrust law, but also the broader national adjustment to the new patterns and more concentrated structure of a transformed American economy at the end of the Progressive Era.[15]

What should the fundamental goals of antitrust law be deemed to be in this initial and most dramatic period of national antitrust concern? What harms should the Sherman Act primarily seek to prevent—higher prices, lower output, degradations in product quality? Was there a priority of importance among these? Were other values equally or more important—for example, the preservation of robust, widespread entre-

Standard may have engaged in effective predatory pricing). In their landmark 1996 article, Granitz and Klein emphasize the early importance of Standard's relations with the railroads transporting oil products. Instead of attributing the favorable but discriminatory rates the railroads granted to Standard Oil to Standard's purchasing power, however, Granitz and Klein find that a mutually-beneficial arrangement was established between Standard and the railroads. In return for Standard's assistance in maintaining a cartel among the railroads, made possible by Standard's predominant position as a shipper, the railroads helped Standard to maintain its dominant position by charging much higher rates to rival refiners, repeatedly forcing them to fail or to sell out to the Standard combination. Granitz & Klein, *supra*.

[15] *See, e.g.*, MARTIN J. SKLAR, THE CORPORATE RECONSTRUCTION OF AMERICAN CAPITALISM, 1890–1916: THE MARKET, THE LAW, AND POLITICS (1988).

preneurial opportunity, the freedom for all to trade and to compete as they saw fit, the protection of a not too uneven distribution of wealth in society, the safeguarding of democratic government from corruption by concentrated economic power, the maintenance of a proper division between state and federal regulatory power and responsibility? How was the nature and importance of competition itself to be understood and on what basis was legitimate to be distinguished from illegitimate forms of business rivalry? Might this be done through the delineation of fundamental economic rights and their limits as in contemporary constitutional jurisprudence? Would interpretation of the Sherman Act be influenced strongly by related, long-established political-economic principles contrasting natural and normal economic behavior with unnatural and abnormal business activity? Alternatively, would Sherman Act analysis strongly embrace the early stirrings of neoclassical economics and foreshadow more modern antitrust analysis?

A second major set of issues dealt with the appropriate general methodology for further interpretation of the Sherman Act. Should this be guided, for example, by explicit invocation of congressional comments in the debates preceding passage of the Sherman Act, by reference to the general historical circumstances out of which the act arose, or by reference to the "plain" or "ordinary" meaning of the language of the statute? Should interpretation be guided by a detailed doctrinal understanding of the common law terms the act incorporated or, perhaps, by an evolving application of the statute, guided by perceived basic congressional purposes, to take advantage of developing understandings of various forms of business behavior over time? In all of this, how much discretion should federal judges have in deciding concrete antitrust cases?

A third set of issues dealt with the more specific elaboration of antitrust doctrine, particularly with regard to mergers, consolidations, and monopolization. Would the Court revisit the controversial issue of a "rule of reason" interpretation of the Sherman Act or maintain Justice Peckham's "direct and substantial effect" test?

The first time that the Court found a merger unlawful under the Sherman Act was in the *Northern Securities* case, decided just two years before the Standard Oil case was filed. It remained to be seen whether the Court would continue to embrace the approach of the plurality, rather than the dissenters, in that case and find the opinion entirely applicable to the differing facts of the *Standard Oil* case. The issue remained, when were mergers and holding company combinations banned, if not in all cases? If common ownership of multiple companies was permissible in some cases, to what extent would centralized coordination of those firms be deemed legitimate activity akin to the operation of a partnership or, alternatively, be analogized to unlawful cartel activity?

Much remained to be determined, as well, about the general meaning and application of Section Two's ban on monopolization. What was the legal definition of monopoly and of monopolizing? Could a violation of section 2 be established in the absence of mergers collectively establishing a near-monopoly position in a particular industry? Could a firm's overwhelming market power alone be the basis for finding a violation? How was such market power to be proved? If market power alone was not enough, what more would have to be shown?

Would the Court interpret the Sherman Act so as to make it a powerful tool to roll back existing economic concentration and check future movement in that direction? Or, might the Court's interpretation and application of the act reflect the view held by many at the time that rising economic concentration largely should be tolerated as either an unstoppable product of inevitable industrial evolution or as the socially beneficial outgrowth of superior economic efficiency? Where unlawful monopolization was found, what relief would be appropriate and effective?

The Circuit Court Brief for the United States

The government's 196–page brief was filed by then-Attorney General George W. Wickersham and special assistants Frank B. Kellogg, Charles B. Morrison, Cordenio A. Severance, and J. Harwood Graves. The brief argued that more than 35 years earlier, in 1870, John D. Rockefeller, his brother William, and their early associate Henry M. Flagler had entered into a scheme to monopolize both the domestic and export petroleum business. The government charged that the three later were joined in the conspiracy by the other individual defendants, Henry H. Rogers, Oliver H. Payne, Charles Pratt, and John D. Archbold.

The government contended that the conspiracy was carried out largely through the establishment and operation of a series of multi-firm combinations over three distinct time periods: 1870–1882; 1882–1899; and 1899 to the time the case was filed on November 15, 1906. The government noted that the Standard Oil Company of Ohio was established in 1870 as the corporate successor to a Cleveland partnership through which the Rockefellers and Flagler had become involved in the new oil industry. The government alleged that the railroads serving the northwest Pennsylvania area where almost all crude oil then was being produced had granted Standard Oil preferential rates. This advantage had helped Standard Oil to acquire substantially all of the competing refineries in Cleveland in the early months of 1872.[16] The government

---

[16] Brief of the Law for the United States at 6–7, *United States v. Standard Oil Co.*, 173 F. 177 (C.C.E.D. Mo. 1909).

charged that those associated with Standard soon thereafter moved on to acquire controlling stock or partnership interests in large numbers of independent refineries and related facilities in other cities. Although Standard of Ohio stock often was given in payment for such interests, thereby increasing the number of shareholders in that company,[17] the stock of other companies typically was acquired not by Standard of Ohio itself, but by "various individuals, who held the stock for the benefit of the shareholders of Standard Oil of Ohio."[18]

In 1879, the stock of all of the thirty separate companies by then amassed was secretly turned over to three individuals—George H.Vilas, Myron R. Keith and George F. Chester—to hold and manage as trustees for the benefit of all of the shareholders of the Standard Oil Company of Ohio.[19] In 1882, the stock of all of the acquired corporations, along with the interests acquired in various limited partnerships, was turned over to a new group of nine trustees, with the individual defendants constituting a majority of the group.[20] The new trustees were given management authority over the various companies and the right to elect directors and officers of the firms.[21] In exchange for the stock and partnership interests they received, the trustees issued new trust certificates to the individual equitable owners of such stock and interests, equal in value to the appraised worth of the interests transferred.[22] As a result, the government charged, by 1892, the trust included eighty-four corporations, including those who had entered ten years before, and the total value of outstanding trust certificates was $97,250,000.[23]

In 1890, the Attorney General of Ohio challenged the legality of Standard of Ohio's participation in the 1882 trust, in a so-called *"quo warranto"* proceeding in the Ohio Supreme Court. In this proceeding, the Attorney General of Ohio sought to bar that company from doing intrastate business, "on the ground that it had become a party to this trust agreement, which was alleged to be void as tending to monopoly."[24]

---

[17] *Id.* at 8.

[18] *Id.*

[19] The existence of the 1879 trust only was revealed during the course of litigation of the government's antitrust case against Standard Oil. Originally, the only trust the government attacked was the publicly-known one established 1882.

[20] Brief of the Law for the United States at 10, *United States v. Standard Oil Co.*, 173 F. 177 (C.C.E.D. Mo. 1909).

[21] *Id.* at 11.

[22] *Id.*

[23] *Id.* at 11–12.

[24] *Id.* at 12.

In March of 1892, the Ohio Supreme Court declared the 1882 trust void and forbade Standard of Ohio to continue as a member of it.[25] As a result, a resolution was passed officially dissolving the trust and a plan was adopted for the trustees proportionately to distribute the stocks they held to the various holders of trust certificates, who by this point had come to number several thousand. First, however, the stock of sixty-four of the eighty-four companies whose stock was held by the trustees was transferred to the remaining twenty firms, including the Standard Oil Company of New Jersey.[26] Thereafter, each holder of a trust certificate who wished to cancel his or her certificate was entitled to receive, for each certificate held, 1/972,500 of the stock of each of the twenty corporations still held by the trustees.[27]

Over the next six years, practically the only certificate holders who turned in their certificates and received shares of stock under this plan were "the nine trustees who were liquidating the trust and who had been themselves the largest certificate holders, together with the members of their immediate families and their immediate associates."[28] This relatively small group came to control a "majority of the stock of each of the constituent companies."[29] The rest of the stock remained in the possession of the liquidating trustees and was not voted.[30]

In 1897, the Attorney General of Ohio filed a contempt petition in the Ohio Supreme Court, claiming that the trust combination never had been effectively dissolved. In that proceeding, the government noted, John D. Rockefeller "testified that the trust had been dissolved, that each of the companies was competing with the other and each company managed by its own stockholders and directors."[31] On the basis of this testimony, the contempt proceeding had been dismissed.

The government charged that this proceeding sparked the third chapter in the conspiracy. In 1899, the men dominating the Standard Oil interests reorganized the Standard Oil Company of New Jersey to allow

---

[25] *Id.* State *ex rel.* Attorney General v. Standard Oil Co., 49 Ohio St. 137, 30 N.E. 279 (1892). More precisely, the court entered a judgment "ousting the defendant from the right to make the agreement set forth in the petition and of the power to perform the same." 49 Ohio St. at 189, 30 N.E. at 291.

[26] Brief of the Law for the United States at 12, *United States v. Standard Oil Co.*, 173 F. 177 (C.C.E.D. Mo. 1909).

[27] *Id.*

[28] *Id.* at 13–14.

[29] *Id.* at 14.

[30] *Id.*

[31] *Id.* The government asserted that "Rockefeller testified substantially to the same thing in the case at bar." *Id.*

it "to hold the stocks previously held by the trustees"[32] and to engage in all of the activities engaged in by the firms whose stocks the trustees had held. The former trustees became directors of the reorganized company and its adopted by-laws largely duplicated the by-laws under which the trustees had operated.[33] After the remaining outstanding trust certificates were turned in, in exchange for shares of stock in the various firms encompassed by the trust, each of the now several thousand owners of stock in those companies turned their shares over to the Standard Oil Company of New Jersey in return for a proportionate share of $97,250,000 of the common stock of Standard of New Jersey.[34]

Through this process, the government charged, Standard of New Jersey came to control not only the other nineteen principal companies, but also the dozens of other companies whose stock was held by those nineteen firms.[35] Standard of New Jersey thereafter acquired the stock of still more companies and organized some new firms itself. As a result, it came to control "directly by stock ownership 65 corporations, which companies in turn control about 49 other corporations, domestic and foreign, making about 114 in all."[36] When added to the many other previously-competing firms that New Jersey Standard had purchased directly,[37] said the government, the total number of firms New Jersey Standard had come to control was at least 215. This was not just a matter of efficient capacity expansion, the government argued, because a large number of the acquired refining plants subsequently were dismantled rather than used.

The government contended that the defendants had used further improper means to monopolize commerce besides acquisition and combination of previously-competing firms. It stressed particularly the defendants' abusive control of the pipe-line transportation of crude oil,[38] their continued securing of favorable but discriminatory railroad rate discounts,[39] and their use of unfair methods of competition against rivals.[40] The government asserted that such unfair methods had

---

[32] *Id.* at 15.

[33] *Id.* at 16.

[34] *Id.*

[35] *Id.*

[36] *Id.*

[37] *Id.* at 17.

[38] *Id.* at 31–34.

[39] *Id.* at 35–38.

[40] *Id.* at 39–45.

taken the form of price cutting in particular localities while keeping up high prices, or raising them still higher, in other localities where no competition exists; ... of obtaining secret information as to competitive business largely through bribing railway employees, and using said secret information to procure the countermanding of orders of independents, and to facilitate the price-cutting policy; of the use of so-called bogus independent companies—that is, companies held out by the Standard Oil Company as independent which are engaged in price cutting, while the Standard Oil Company maintains the prices through its well-known companies, and other abusive competitive methods against the independents.[41]

All of this activity, the government contended, resulted in Standard controlling "from seven-eighths to more than nine-tenths of the different branches of the oil business in the United States."[42] This allowed the defendants to control crude and refined oil prices throughout the country,[43] charging inflated prices to retailers[44] while reaping tremendous profits and paying very high corporate dividends.[45]

The government vigorously asserted that the acts of the conspirators before as well as after the Sherman Antitrust Act became law on July 2, 1890 were relevant to show the history of the conspiracy and the intent behind its later stages.[46] It contended that common law principles applied to all interstate transactions except where Congress had indicated otherwise and that "unreasonable restraints and monopolies of interstate commerce" like the 1879 and 1882 trusts were void at common law.[47] These trusts had inspired not only public alarm but the establishment of later trusts, each of which subsequently had been challenged and declared void in state courts.[48]

In bringing suit against the holding company successor to the most prominent of all the late-nineteenth century trusts, the government emphasized not only the adverse effect such combinations had on prices and the quality of goods, but also the threat they posed to the freedom and opportunity of others to trade, a more even distribution of wealth in society, and, ultimately, the vitality of republican government. In this

[41] *Id.* at 39.

[42] *Id.* at 25.

[43] *Id.* at 25.

[44] *Id.* at 30.

[45] *Id.* at 26.

[46] *Id.* at 46.

[47] *Id.* at 67.

[48] *Id.* at 69, 74.

regard, the government quoted at considerable length, for example, the description of such dangers set out in the Ohio Supreme Court's opinion in the *quo warranto* case against Standard Oil.[49]

The government insisted that condemnation of industrial trusts did not unconstitutionally infringe the freedom of their developers to contract, but was simply a legitimate exercise of government regulation for the public good.[50] The government pointedly rejected arguments then commonly made in defense of trusts, for example, that new entry could be counted on to correct any dangers posed by their market power,[51] that condemnation of trusts was an interference with natural industrial development,[52] and that a holding company was simply a single entity free to engage in competition along with other corporations and partnerships.[53] In making its arguments, the government invoked, among a

---

[49] *Id.* at 69–72. In the extended passage quoted, Judge Minshall, for the court, noted that in English case law monopoly had been condemned not only for raising prices and degrading product quality, but also for impoverishing others barred from practicing their trade. He explained:

> The third objection, though frequently overlooked, is none the less important. A society in which a few men are the employers and the great body are merely employees or servants is not the most desirable in a republic; and it should be as much the policy of the laws to multiply the numbers engaged in independent pursuits or in the profits of production as to cheapen the price to the consumer. Such policy would tend to an equality of fortunes among its citizens, thought to be so desirable in a republic, and lessen the amount of pauperism and crime....

Id. at 72. Later in its brief, the government approvingly quoted a similar extended passage from the then well-known opinion of the Michigan Supreme Court in *Richardson v. Buhl*, 77 Mich. 632, 43 N.W. 1102 (Mich. 1889) (the "Diamond Match Case"). As quoted in the government's brief at 136–37, the Michigan Supreme Court starkly declared:

> Monopoly in trade or in any kind of business in this country is odious to our form of government.... Its tendency is ... destructive of free institutions, and repugnant to the instincts of a free people, and contrary to the whole scope and spirit of the Federal Constitution, and is not allowed to exist under express provisions in several of our state constitutions. Indeed, it is doubtful if free government can long exist in a country where such enormous amounts of money are allowed to be accumulated in the vaults of corporations, to be used at discretion in controlling the property and business of the country against the interest of the public and that of the people, for the personal gain and aggrandizement of a few individuals. It is always destructive of individual rights, and of that free competition which is the life of business, and it revives and perpetuates one of the great evils which it was the object of the framers of our form of government to eradicate and prevent.

77 Mich. at 658, 43 N.W. at 1110.

[50] Brief of the Law for the United States at 74, *United States v. Standard Oil Co.*, 173 F. 177 (C.C.E.D. Mo. 1909).

[51] *Id.* at 77.

[52] *Id.*

[53] *Id.* at 77–83.

great many other authorities, Judge (and at that moment, President) Taft's 1898 opinion for the Sixth Circuit Court of Appeals in *United States v. Addyston Pipe & Steel Co.*[54] The government noted that the Standard Oil combination did not come within any of the categories of reasonable restraint that Judge Taft had mentioned. Indeed, the government pointed out, Judge Taft had stated that purchases of property for the purpose of suppressing competition were void and had cited approvingly many of the trust cases the government invoked in its brief, including the 1892 Ohio Supreme Court opinion condemning the Standard Oil trust itself.[55]

The government declared that continuance of the trust agreement of 1882 after the Sherman Act became law violated that statute.[56] Even if this were not the case, the defendants violated the act when they "voluntarily dissolved the Standard Oil Trust, segregated all of these corporations, and thereafter combined them again in the Standard Oil Company of New Jersey."[57] The government emphasized that John D. Rockefeller and the then-operational head of the combination, John D. Archbold, had testified that the trust had been dissolved and the firms had been separated before 1899.[58]

The Supreme Court's 1904 opinion in *Northern Securities*, as well as other prior Supreme Court decisions, the government argued, made it clear that the 1899 amalgamation of stocks in New Jersey Standard constituted a combination in restraint of interstate and foreign trade[59] in violation of section 1 of the Sherman Act, whether or not the firms in the combination were competing with each other at the time the holding company was formed.[60] The government contended that in *Northern Securities*, the firms combined in a holding company were themselves commonly-owned prior to the establishment of the holding company. The fact that railroads happened to be involved in that case did not matter, because the Sherman Act applied in the same way to both railways and other companies.[61] The government rejected the defendants' reliance on

---

[54] 85 F. 271 (6th Cir. 1898), *aff'd*, 175 U.S. 211 (1899).

[55] Brief of the Law for the United States at 6–7, 98–100, *United States v. Standard Oil Co.*, 173 F. 177 (C.C.E.D. Mo. 1909).

[56] *Id.* at 114.

[57] *Id.* at 116.

[58] *Id.* at 116–17.

[59] *Id.* at 122–24.

[60] *Id.* at 69, 74.

[61] *Id.* at 128.

the Supreme Court's 1895 opinion in *E.C. Knight*[62] to assert that the defendants' combination and other improper acts were beyond the reach of congressional commerce clause power.[63]

The government asserted that New Jersey Standard's control of interstate and foreign commerce also constituted an unlawful monopoly under section 2 of the Sherman Act.[64] Congress and the public very much had Standard Oil and similar combinations in mind when section 2 of the Sherman Act was passed to prohibit corporations from using any means to monopolize or attempt to monopolize interstate or foreign commerce.[65] Any conduct violating section 1, the government argued, violates section 2 if it tends to monopoly. Any combination amalgamating multiple corporations into a single concern violates both sections if it is of sufficient magnitude to tend to that result.[66] The government declared it "unnecessary . . . to discuss . . . whether mere size of corporation, mere aggregation of wealth, acquired in the usual, ordinary growth of a business enterprise, is sufficient to constitute a monopoly."[67] Whether or not that was true, it was safe to conclude "that a monopoly exists where a great aggregation of capital, like the Standard Oil, is coupled with oppressive use of the power such wealth gives in driving out competitors or controlling the market, by means which may or may not be unlawful or criminal in themselves."[68]

The government asserted that the Standard Oil combination was more dangerous than a cartel[69] and that in every one of the numerous instances "where the Standard Oil combination has come before the state courts it has been held invalid as a monopoly or tending to monopoly."[70] If the combination was in violation of state law where it affected intrastate commerce, the government argued, it similarly should

---

[62] *United States v. E.C. Knight Co.*, 156 U.S. 1 (1895). In that case, the Supreme Court held the Sherman Act inapplicable to a combination of manufacturing companies enjoying an overwhelmingly large market share of American sugar refining.

[63] The government noted that *E.C. Knight* had been limited by later decisions emphasizing that the Sherman Act did reach firms who not only engaged in manufacturing but also transported and sold their products in various states. Brief of the Law for the United States at 148, *United States v. Standard Oil Co.*, 173 F. 177 (C.C.E.D. Mo. 1909).

[64] *Id.* at 120.

[65] *Id.* at 149–150.

[66] *Id.* at 159.

[67] *Id.* at 160.

[68] *Id.*

[69] *Id.* at 161–62.

[70] *Id.* at 157.

be deemed to be in violation of federal antitrust law "when restricting or monopolizing interstate commerce."[71]

The government called for a broad and reasonable construction of the Sherman Act.[72] While recognizing the importance of freedom of contract, such a construction simultaneously would recognize that private efforts to amass wealth can "go to that extent where the individual right and freedom of the citizen may be in danger."[73] "We are not invoking a new principle against an old device," the government emphasized, "but an old principle against a new device. Principles are everlasting; devices change."[74]

To remedy the defendants' violations of the Sherman Act, the government called upon the court to exercise its power under the Sherman Act to do more than simply enjoin continuation of the unlawful amalgamation of stock in New Jersey Standard. The government urged the court to bar the defendants from participating in interstate commerce until the holding company arrangement was discontinued and to enjoin the defendants from again agreeing in any form to end competition among themselves.[75]

The Circuit Court Briefs for the Defendants

In opposition to the government suit, John G. Johnson and John G. Milburn submitted a 188–page brief, as attorneys for the Standard Oil Company and other defendants, while D.T. Watson, John M. Freeman, and Ernest C. Irwin submitted an equally long and more complex brief primarily, but not exclusively, on behalf of the seven individual defendants. More than half of Johnson and Milburn's brief summarized the facts of the case, while the brief submitted by Watson, Freeman, and Irwin analyzed more extensively the legal issues in the case. The two briefs, not surprisingly, presented a very different picture of Standard Oil's rise to preeminence, the state of law before and after passage of the Sherman Act in 1890, and the stakes in the litigation, than had been presented by the government.

Johnson and Milburn portrayed John D. Rockefeller and his earliest associates as "young, vigorous and able men" who had the resources and insight to bring progress out of the chaos of overproduction and wildly fluctuating prices prevailing in the early years of the oil industry.[76] At

---

[71] *Id.* at 158.

[72] *Id.* at 162.

[73] *Id.* at 163.

[74] *Id.* at 162.

[75] *Id.* at 184–98.

[76] Brief for Standard Oil Company and Others at 17–22, *United States v. Standard Oil Co.*, 173 F. 177 (C.C.E.D. Mo. 1909).

that time, Johnson and Milburn related, all branches of the oil business were demoralized and "in an abnormal state"[77] and "the oil business was threatened with ruin."[78] In the early 1870's, most of the Cleveland refiners were in a difficult situation. To improve matters, they voluntarily decided to consolidate their efforts through sales of their operations to the Standard Oil Company of Ohio. These sales had saved Cleveland as a refining center.[79] The oil industry thereafter followed a natural and necessary course of development and centralization. This development, Johnson and Milburn explained, "would inevitably substitute organization for chaos in each of its branches, and favor the survival of the fittest.... Without concentration there was only the promise of destruction."[80]

Following the Cleveland acquisitions, those associated with Standard of Ohio made uncoerced and unconnected acquisitions of many additional refining firms in Pennsylvania and elsewhere from 1872 to 1879. These increased their capacity to handle the growing production of crude oil and their ability to provide an expanded volume of refined oil products.[81] Refiners like Standard Oil needed an assured, steady supply of crude oil, which in turn necessitated a rationalized system of gathering pipe lines collecting crude oil from the wells and delivering it, in the early days, to the railroads and, in later years, to long-distance pipe lines for shipment to the refineries. When the myriad independent crude oil producers were unable to accomplish the needed rationalization,[82] Standard undertook the risk of stepping in to establish pooling arrangements among gathering lines and then to acquire some of the early independent gathering systems. Although Standard initially obtained pipe lines in this way, by 1908, the great majority of its pipe line mileage had been established by its own construction efforts.[83]

Johnson and Milburn stressed that prior to the establishment of the 1879 trust, the stock and properties previously acquired were held in an undivided common ownership by the shareholders of the Standard Oil Company of Ohio. Accordingly, neither the 1879 trust or its more elaborate 1882 successor combined firms that were then independent or

---

[77] *Id.* at 24.

[78] *Id.* at 25.

[79] *Id.* at 26–27.

[80] *Id.* at 30–31.

[81] *Id.* at 36–37.

[82] *Id.* at 39.

[83] *Id.* at 42.

competitive.[84] The trusts were simply arrangements among common owners "concerning the form in which the legal title to the properties and stocks should be held."[85] "Naturally," Johnson and Milburn explained, "after the acquisition of these properties the main process was one of their unification and integration into a single business to secure efficiency and economy."[86] Only a small number of acquisitions had occurred after 1879. Since then, Standard's growth overwhelmingly resulted from internal expansion. Neither the formal dissolution of the trust in 1892 nor the 1899 transfers of stock to Standard of New Jersey changed the long-established common ownership of the various properties and the "conduct of the business as a unit."[87] The 1899 transfers were no more an amalgamation of independent companies than the 1879 and 1882 trusts had been.

Johnson and Milburn insisted that the Standard Oil combination never constituted a monopoly because the oil industry always had remained wide open for new entrants.[88] Other firms had competed successfully against Standard Oil when they became equally efficient. In general, those rivals now were "prosperous and growing" and Standard's market position had been declining as competition intensified in recent years.[89]

The briefs for the defendants did not minimize the importance of the right of all Americans to engage in trade; nor did they argue that it sometimes was good to limit the extent of marketplace competition. On the contrary, the briefs argued that the government cared too little about protecting the right to trade and the vitality of the competitive process. Johnson and Milburn argued that common ownership of the various acquired properties prior to 1890 was not an illegal combination because "[t]he right freely to buy and sell property is a fundamental civil right" protected by the United States and state constitutions.[90] Watson, Freeman, and Irwin added that the right to own property necessarily entails the essential right to use it.[91] Freedom to use and sell property, in turn, includes freedom to choose the method of holding title to property,

---

[84] *Id.* at 63.

[85] *Id.* at 64.

[86] *Id.*

[87] *Id.* at 69–71.

[88] *Id.* at 76.

[89] *Id.* at 92–95.

[90] *Id.* at 105.

[91] Brief on Behalf of the Defendants at 60, *United States v. Standard Oil Co.*, 173 F. 177 (C.C.E.D. Mo. 1909).

"whether as tenants in common or joint tenants" or merely as beneficiaries of a trust.

It was important that state and federal regulation not exceed their proper bounds and infringe upon the "fundamental and indefeasible rights" of each citizen to trade, compete, and unite "to secure community of interest in carrying on business."[92] State and federal regulatory authority operated within separate and distinct spheres. Congress, and not the states, could regulate interstate and foreign commerce, which consisted only of the actual transit of goods between states or between a state and a foreign country, along with bargaining leading to such movement and sale of goods.[93] Federal power did not extend to the "acquisition and the use of manufacturing or producing properties in the States"[94] even if the products made by those properties were sold in interstate or foreign commerce.[95] The states, on the other hand, had power to regulate the acquisition and intrastate use of property, but could not limit the federal constitutional rights of American citizens "to engage in competition for interstate trade."[96]

The federal government had to base its case against Standard Oil solely on federal law and it was irrelevant whether any of the defendants' acts might have violated state law.[97] Before 1890, no federal statute restricted private individuals in their rights to engage in interstate trade[98] and the Sherman Act of that year did not apply retroactively to activity before its enactment.[99] No federal common law,[100] and particularly no federal common law of crimes,[101] existed that restricted private interstate trading activity.[102] As a result, nothing the defendants did prior to 1890 was legally relevant. Nearly all of the defendants' challenged activity *after* 1890 was legally irrelevant as well. When, as in the case at bar, the government did not seek to impose any criminal penalties for prior conduct, but instead sought only injunctive relief to

---

[92] *Id.* at 59–60.

[93] *Id.* at 33.

[94] *Id.* at 171.

[95] *Id.* at 172.

[96] *Id.* at 70.

[97] *Id.* at 36.

[98] *Id.* at 182.

[99] *Id.* at 26, 40, 70, 132, 145.

[100] *Id.* at 135, 136.

[101] *Id.* at 136, 138–39.

[102] *Id.* at 135.

restrain ongoing violations, the only pertinent question was what the defendants were doing when the government filed its petition.[103]

Despite their assertion that the legal issue in the case was a narrow one, the attorneys for the defendants went on to discuss at length the nature of competition, the details of common law restraint of trade and monopoly doctrine, and the meaning of the Sherman Act itself. Competition, the lawyers contended, "denotes strife–struggles with others. It means warfare for the same thing. . . ."[104] Everyone tries to gain as much of a given trade as possible up to the whole amount, and "the law does not limit the extent of the reward for each."[105] The briefs strongly denied both the existence and feasibility of any legal standard judging the means used to compete according to their reasonableness or fairness.[106] Watson, Freeman, and Irwin, for example, noted that a "reasonableness" standard would not be workable:

> If you say that the limitation of competition is that which is unlawful, you have a definite, clear boundary defined. If you say, however, that the competition must be fair and the competition must be reasonable, who will determine what is fair and what is reasonable? Will each jury in each case have its own standard? Will each judge in each case set up his separate standard? If so, how can the trader regulate his competition, and how can he tell what he may do tomorrow. . . .?[107]

What restrictions, if any, then, did common law impose on business activity affecting competition? Common law prohibitions on contracts, combinations, and conspiracies in restraint of trade, Johnson and Milburn explained, referred only to contracts or arrangements restricting the liberty of the parties to them or the freedom of others in the future conduct of their independent businesses.[108] The common law had never considered business expansion by either internal growth or the acquisition of others' property to constitute a prohibited restraint of trade,[109] nor had it sought to limit the activity or rights of an acquirer with

---

[103] *Id.* at 40.

[104] *Id.* at 65. See also Brief for Standard Oil Company and Others at 170, *United States v. Standard Oil Co.*, 173 F. 177 (C.C.E.D. Mo. 1909).

[105] Brief on Behalf of the Defendants at 66, *United States v. Standard Oil Co.*, 173 F. 177 (C.C.E.D. Mo. 1909).

[106] Brief for Standard Oil Company and others at 171–72, *United States v. Standard Oil Co.*, 173 F. 177 (C.C.E.D. Mo. 1909).

[107] Brief on Behalf of the Defendants at 69, *United States v. Standard Oil Co.*, 173 F. 177 (C.C.E.D. Mo. 1909).

[108] Brief for Standard Oil Company and others at 108, 132, *United States v. Standard Oil Co.*, 173 F. 177 (C.C.E.D. Mo. 1909).

[109] *Id.* at 110.

respect to acquired property.[110] Even acquisitions undertaken as part of a scheme to obtain almost all of the properties in a line of business, Johnson and Milburn asserted, did not constitute an illegal combination at common law.[111] The contrary state cases the government invoked either were distinguishable or in conflict with other, better-reasoned cases. The Ohio Supreme Court's 1892 comments on restraint of trade and monopoly were merely dicta.[112]

The lawyers for the defendants contended that the common law had never equated large size and monopoly. Originally, monopoly meant an exclusive license or privilege granted by the King. In modern times, exclusivity remained an essential element of monopoly.[113] The term, however, had been broadened to cover situations of private exclusionary "restraint on the liberty of others"[114] for example, through "contracts, combinations and conspiracies excluding individuals and capital on a comprehensive scale . . . from participation in a particular business"[115] or criminal or tortious acts having that effect.[116] Watson, Freeman, and Irwin went even further and insisted that at common law the only limit on the exclusion of others was "that the means used must be lawful."[117]

When Congress banned contracts, combinations, and conspiracies in restraint of interstate or foreign trade in section 1 of the Sherman Act, it had adopted the common law meaning of those terms.[118] The Sherman Act thus did not "prohibit partnerships or corporations or trusts from engaging in interstate trade"[119] provided they did not themselves make "contracts directly, substantially and immediately restraining such trade or attempt[] by unlawful means to monopolize the same."[120]

---

[110] *Id.* at 117.

[111] *Id.*

[112] *Id.* at 120.

[113] *Id.* at 29, 94–95.

[114] *Id.* at 156.

[115] *Id.* at 157.

[116] *Id.* at 158.

[117] Brief on Behalf of the Defendants at 28, 66, *United States v. Standard Oil Co.*, 173 F. 177 (C.C.E.D. Mo. 1909).

[118] Brief for Standard Oil Company and Others at 132, *United States v. Standard Oil Co.*, 173 F. 177 (C.C.E.D. Mo. 1909).

[119] Brief on Behalf of the Defendants at 101, *United States v. Standard Oil Co.*, 173 F. 177 (C.C.E.D. Mo. 1909).

[120] *Id.* at 28.

Watson, Freeman, and Irwin contended that Congress also had followed common law when it enacted section 2 of the Sherman Act. Accordingly, that section only condemned independently-unlawful private action that excluded would-be new entrants into a trade or business.[121] As long as no means violating another federal statute were used, it was irrelevant whether competitive tactics were "fair or unfair, due or undue, or reasonable or unreasonable."[122] Reflecting their slightly different view of common law, Johnson and Milburn declared that section 2 prohibited the exclusion of other firms through sufficiently serious violations of section 1 or other unlawful or tortious acts.[123] Echoing common law, the Sherman Act had not set any limit on the size a firm could become through internal growth or the lawful acquisition of other firms[124] and to set such a limit would destroy the incentive to compete.[125] Watson, Freeman, and Irwin firmly rejected any "literal" interpretation of section 2, on the theory that every trader is a monopolist because "he has the exclusive use and control of that certain portion, and he allows no one to interfere with that exclusive use and control if he can help it, and this is a necessary law of trade, without which trade could not be carried on."[126]

Both briefs for the defendants argued strongly that even if the government proved that a Sherman Act violation was in progress when the government filed suit on November 15, 1906, the Court could grant only narrowly tailored relief to prevent the continuation of the violation.[127] A decree barring the defendants from participating in interstate trade would be indefensible.[128]

The briefs argued vigorously, however, that there was no reason to reach such questions of relief, because the defendants not only were not violating the Sherman Act in mid-November of 1906, but never at any time had achieved their success through anything but laudable means. The many acquisitions of other firms that began in the early 1870's were

---

[121] *Id.* at 97. See also, e.g., *id.* at 181.

[122] *Id.* at 27, 181–82.

[123] Brief for Standard Oil Company and Others at 168, *United States v. Standard Oil Co.*, 173 F. 177 (C.C.E.D. Mo. 1909).

[124] Brief on Behalf of the Defendants at 24, *United States v. Standard Oil Co.*, 173 F. 177 (C.C.E.D. Mo. 1909).

[125] *Id.* at 101.

[126] *Id.* at 104.

[127] Brief for Standard Oil Company and Others at 177, *United States v. Standard Oil Co.*, 173 F. 177 (C.C.E.D. Mo. 1909).

[128] Brief on Behalf of the Defendants at 52, *United States v. Standard Oil Co.*, 173 F. 177 (C.C.E.D. Mo. 1909).

entirely lawful when they occurred[129] and gave the common owners valid, legal title to the properties.[130] The acquisitions allowed Standard efficiently to expand its capacity. The owners of the firms that sold out to Standard had their own uncoerced reasons for wanting to sell.[131] Even if the various properties had been purchased and had come to be commonly owned after the Sherman Act was passed, their acquisition would not have violated that statute.[132]

Establishment of the 1879 and 1882 trusts lawfully combined non-competing, commonly-owned properties to create a convenient evidence of each person's interest in those properties. Because the trust agreements were lawful, the government had no basis to claim that their alleged 1899 perpetuation through the Standard Oil Company of New Jersey, acting as a holding company, violated the Sherman Act.[133] The briefs rejected the government's alternative argument that the non-competitive properties joined in the 1882 trust had become competitive and independent following the trust's formal dissolution in 1892, thus making their 1899 conveyance to New Jersey Standard "a combination in restraint of trade and a monopoly."[134] Watson, Freeman, and Irwin argued that the government's claim was factually unfounded and "directly contrary to the whole theory of the Government's case as set forth in its petition."[135] In seeking to support this claim, moreover, the government badly had misconstrued the testimony of John D. Rockefeller, which they asserted was the only testimony the government invoked to buttress its claim that the companies had become independently competitive between 1892 and 1899.[136]

Watson, Freeman, and Irwin emphasized that the method of managing the long commonly-owned properties did not dramatically change

---

[129] Brief for Standard Oil Company and Others at 161, *United States v. Standard Oil Co.*, 173 F. 177 (C.C.E.D. Mo. 1909).

[130] *Id.* at 139.

[131] Johnson and Milburn explained that, in some cases, other successful men sold their businesses to further their own interests by uniting with Standard, which they were free to do because "once a competitor always a competitor has never been, and is not now, a maxim of legal compulsion." *Id.* at 128. In many other cases, they noted, small refiners wanted to sell out to Standard Oil because they could not compete successfully or find the capital to make needed improvements as the industry progressed. *Id.* at 60.

[132] *Id.* at 141, 143, 146–48.

[133] Brief on Behalf of the Defendants at 30, *United States v. Standard Oil Co.*, 173 F. 177 (C.C.E.D. Mo. 1909).

[134] *Id.* at 179.

[135] *Id.*

[136] *Id.*

because of the transfer of their legal ownership to Standard of New Jersey.[137] Both briefs for the defendants stressed that the 1899 efficiency-motivated transfer of commonly-owned stock in ordinary, non-competing companies, by the persons who already owned the stock of Standard of New Jersey,[138] was sharply distinguishable from the situation in the *Northern Securities* case of 1904.[139] In that case, they argued, the holding company condemned by the Supreme Court had been designed to smother existing competition between two transcontinental railroad lines that, contrary to the government's assertion, each had its own separate set of shareholders. That holding company arrangement, moreover, had violated a special legal obligation each of those quasi-public corporations had to remain independently competitive.[140] The ordinary manufacturing and trading properties conveyed to Standard of New Jersey "being jointly owned and in a common interest, were not required by any law to compete with each other any more than the members of a partnership could be required so to do."[141]

The defendants had not used unlawful tactics against their rivals. "The joint group did engage in a war of competition," Watson, Freeman, and Irwin, conceded, "but its warfare, and its means of warfare, and the weapons that it used, were not different from or other than those used by its adversaries when opportunity offered."[142] For the government to prove its case, it had to do more than merely show sporadic, occasional acts of excessive competition, favorable rebates,[143] or other improper acts

---

[137] *Id.* at 174.

[138] *Id.* at 31, 152.

[139] *Northern Securities Co. v. United States*, 193 U.S. 197 (1904).

[140] Brief on Behalf of the Defendants at 173, *United States v. Standard Oil Co.*, 173 F. 177 (C.C.E.D. Mo. 1909); Brief for Standard Oil Company and Others at 124–25, *United States v. Standard Oil Co.*, 173 F. 177 (C.C.E.D. Mo. 1909).

[141] Brief on Behalf of the Defendants at 166, *United States v. Standard Oil Co.*, 173 F. 177 (C.C.E.D. Mo. 1909).

[142] *Id.* at 166.

[143] Johnson and Milburn dismissed as utterly baseless claims that favorable rebates on shipping rates from the railroads gave Standard Oil the ability to defeat and acquire its rivals. Brief for Standard Oil Company and Others at 47–49, 59, *United States v. Standard Oil Co.*, 173 F. 177 (C.C.E.D. Mo. 1909). They went on to explain certain contracts between Standard Oil and particular railroads that the government had annexed to its bill of complaint. For example, one of the annexed documents was a contract from 1877 between the Standard Oil Company and the Pennsylvania Railroad, which the government contended was similar to other contracts between Standard Oil and the New York Central and Erie railroads, respectively. Johnson and Milburn calmly explained how under the contract, Standard Oil had taken on the role of enforcer for a railroad cartel:

These contracts were what is known as "evener" contracts and were common in the railroad practice of that time. One of the methods then in vogue to avoid the enormous

prior to 1906.[144] Johnson and Milburn declared that prices and profits
were irrelevant by themselves to prove the existence of unlawful monopoly in the absence of improper exclusionary conduct. In any case,
Standard Oil's prices were not unusually high[145] and its profits were not
excessive given the level of risk involved in the oil business.[146]

Thus, the government completely had failed to "show an active
violation of the Sherman Act when the Petition was filed"[147] that would
entitle it to injunctive relief.[148] As for the seven individual defendants,
Watson, Freeman, and Irwin went on to note, the evidence demonstrated
that they did not even "control either the defendant corporations or the
New Jersey Standard Oil Company or the Trust of 1882."[149] At the time
the bill was filed, Watson, Freeman, and Irwin related, they collectively
owned only a little more than one third of the shares of the Standard Oil
Company of New Jersey and they constituted only a minority of the 15–
member board of directors.

In summing up the case, Watson, Freeman, and Irwin emphasized
that the rise and success of the Standard Oil organization was a story of
natural development and unparalleled skill and innovation that had
benefited American consumers tremendously.[150] Johnson and Milburn
found absurd the government's claim of a conspiracy to monopolize the
oil industry originating just a few years after the close of the Civil War.

---

losses from rate wars among the railroads was an agreement apportioning the heaviest
kinds of traffic, such as grain, cattle, and oil, between them in fixed proportions; and to
make such an agreement effective one or more of the heaviest shippers were selected
to so arrange their business and apportion their shipments as to maintain the
proportions fixed. For that service they were paid a commission. The Standard Oil
Company as the heaviest shipper of oil was made the "evener" in connection with the
pooling agreement between the railroads of October, 1877, and that was the purpose of
this agreement, Exhibit 7, and the agreements of similar tenor with the other trunk
lines. *Id.* at 56–57.

This brief thus openly conceded Standard's role in enforcing a railroad cartel, a type of
activity at the heart of the explanation for Standard's success that, as previously noted,
recently has been urged by the economists Elizabeth Granitz and Benjamin Klein.

[144] Brief on Behalf of the Defendants at 107, *United States v. Standard Oil Co.*, 173 F.
177 (C.C.E.D. Mo. 1909).

[145] Brief for Standard Oil Company and Others at 101–02, *United States v. Standard
Oil Co.*, 173 F. 177 (C.C.E.D. Mo. 1909).

[146] *Id.* at 102.

[147] Brief on Behalf of the Defendants at 188, *United States v. Standard Oil Co.*, 173 F.
177 (C.C.E.D. Mo. 1909).

[148] *Id.* at 179–180.

[149] *Id.* at 21.

[150] *Id.* at 181, 188.

They stressed that the growth of Standard Oil instead was due to remarkable intelligence, energy, and courage on the part of its developers.[151]

The Circuit Court Opinion[152]

In delivering the opinion for the four-judge panel, Judge Sanborn declared that the test of illegality under section 1 of the Sherman Act was whether the necessary effect of a contract, combination, or conspiracy was "to stifle, or directly and substantially to restrict, free competition in commerce among the states or with foreign nations."[153] If this was so, the actual intent of the parties involved was irrelevant, as was the reasonableness of the restraint.[154] The Sherman Act did not apply retroactively to conduct prior to its enactment and it was unnecessary to decide whether or not the defendants' actions prior to that time violated common law.[155] He declared, however, that actions prior to the enactment of the Sherman Act that would have violated the act if done thereafter were relevant evidence with regard to the "purpose and probable effect" of later similar activity.[156]

Judge Sanborn found that from 1899 to 1907, New Jersey Standard and the subsidiary companies collectively controlled overwhelming shares of various branches of the oil business.[157] He further found that New Jersey Standard, under the direction of the seven named defendants, had obtained and was exercising the power to prevent interstate and international competition among the subsidiary companies and between those companies and itself. Under the Supreme Court's holding in *Northern Securities Co. v. United States*,[158] Judge Sanborn declared, such a "stockholding trust" constituted a violation of section 1 of the Sherman Act.[159] Judge Sanborn stressed that many of these companies "were capable of competing with each other ... and would have been actively competitive if they had been owned by different individuals or

---

[151] Brief for Standard Oil Company and Others at 129, *United States v. Standard Oil Co.*, 173 F. 177 (C.C.E.D. Mo. 1909).

[152] *United States v. Standard Oil Co. of New Jersey*, 173 F. 177 (C.C. E.D. Mo.), *modified and aff'd* 221 U.S. 1 (1911).

[153] *Id.* at 179.

[154] *Id.* at 179.

[155] *Id.* at 184.

[156] *Id.* at 184.

[157] *Id.* at 183.

[158] 193 U.S. 197 (1904).

[159] *United States v. Standard Oil Co. of New Jersey*, 173 F. 177, 183–84 (C.C. E.D. Mo.), *modified and aff'd* 221 U.S. 1 (1911).

groups of individuals.''[160] The Sherman Act applied to private manufacturing, trading, and transportation companies in the same way that it
applied to railroad companies. In *Northern Securities*, a single group of
persons similarly had gained control of both railroads involved in the
challenged holding company combination "long before they placed their
stock in the Securities Company in 1901.''[161] It was immaterial that in
the Standard Oil situation, "natural competition" had been prevented
among the subsidiary firms for a much longer time prior to the establishment of a holding company than had been the case in *Northern Securities*.[162] The Supreme Court's opinion in *Northern Securities* foreclosed
the defendants' argument that because "the stockholders of the principal
company were the joint owners of the stock of the subsidiary companies," they "had the right to convey their stock in the latter to the
former in trust for themselves.''[163]

The 1899 stock transfers to New Jersey Standard substantially
restricted competition even though the companies whose stock was
transferred had not competed with each other for a long time. Consolidation of the stock in the hands of New Jersey Standard created greater
and more effective power to coordinate prices and other details of the
business operations of the subsidiary firms and thereby to prevent
competition among them. The consolidation, moreover, made such power
more permanent and less liable to disintegrate. "There is much more
probability that corporations potentially competitive will separate and
compete," the court explained, "when each of their stockholders has a
separate certificate of his shares of stock in each corporation, which he is
free to sell, then when a majority of the stock of each of the corporations
is held by a single corporation, which has the power to vote the stock and
to operate them.''[164] In basing its holding on the more effective and
permanent elimination of potential future competition among what the
court saw as naturally competing firms, the circuit court adopted a
rationale distinct from both of the two theories that the government had
urged. Those two contentions had been: first, that establishment of New
Jersey Standard as a holding company was the perpetuation of an
earlier-established trust combination that itself violated the Sherman
Act when it continued after that act became law; and, second, that the
establishment of the holding company violated the Sherman Act by

---

[160] *Id.* at 185.

[161] *Id.* at 186.

[162] Judge Sanborn declared, "in all other respects the facts of the two cases regarding
competition are practically identical." *Id.* at 186.

[163] *Id.* at 186.

[164] *Id.* at 189.

combining firms that had become independently competitive after 1892. In the circuit court's view, it was not necessary for the government to prove either of these two core claims. The post-Sherman Act establishment of a holding company to control a group of commonly-owned firms long not in competition with each other violated the Sherman Act even in the absence of any earlier trust combination, as long as the commonly owned firms "naturally" would come to compete with each other in the absence of such holding company control.

Judge Sanborn rejected the defendants' contention that no relief could be granted because no continuing violation existed when the government filed its petition on November 15, 1906. He declared that Standard of New Jersey was continuing to exercise the power illegally given it in 1899 to "vote the stock, to elect the officers of the subsidiary corporations, to control and operate them, and thereby to restrict their competition."[165] At the same time, Judge Sanborn related, "the seven individual defendants are dominating and directing its exercise of this power, the subsidiary corporations are knowingly submitting to and assisting that exercise, and all of them are participating in the fruits of it."[166]

Noting, as Watson, Freeman, and Irwin had done in their brief, that everyone "engaged in interstate commerce necessarily attempts to draw to himself to the exclusion of others, and thereby to monopolize a part of that trade," Judge Sanborn rejected a "literal" interpretation of section 2.[167] The act did not condemn monopolies, however successful, if achieved through legitimate competition. It only banned the use of unlawful means to monopolize or perpetuate a monopoly.[168] In the case at bar, the establishment of more effective and permanent control of the combination through the holding company violated section 1 and thereby constituted an unlawful means of monopolization in violation of section 2.[169] Accordingly, it would be enjoined. It therefore became unnecessary to comment on the other means of monopolization alleged by the government.[170]

The circuit court entered a decree barring New Jersey Standard from voting the stock of any of the subsidiary companies found to have

---

[165] *Id.* at 190.

[166] *Id.* at 190.

[167] *Id.* at 191.

[168] *Id.* at 191.

[169] *Id.* at 191.

[170] *Id.* at 192.

participated in the combination[171] or otherwise exercising any control over their actions. Simultaneously, the decree prohibited those subsidiary companies from paying any dividends to New Jersey Standard on account of its ownership of their stock. It also prevented them from allowing New Jersey Standard to vote such stock or exercise control over them. The defendants found to have been members of the combination further were enjoined "from entering into or performing any like combination or conspiracy" in restraint of interstate or foreign commerce.[172] In connection with its order requiring dissolution of the holding company, however, the decree declared that "the defendants are not prohibited by this decree from distributing ratably to the shareholders of the principal company the shares to which they are equitably entitled in the stocks of the defendant corporations that are parties to the combination."[173] The circuit court decree enjoined the defendants covered by it from engaging in interstate commerce until the illegal combination was discontinued. Finally, the court stipulated that its decree would take effect thirty days after its entry, or thirty days after a final decision in the Supreme Court if the case was appealed and the Supreme Court did not reverse or modify it.[174]

The Case on Appeal

The defendants appealed the circuit court's judgment and decree directly to the Supreme Court. As Chief Justice Edward Douglass White would note in his opinion for the Court, the record on appeal was "inordinately voluminous, consisting of twenty-three volumes of printed matter, aggregating about twelve thousand pages, containing a vast

---

[171] In Section Three of the decree, the court found that 33 of the corporate defendants, many of them natural gas companies, had "not been proved to be engaged in the operation or carrying out of the combination" and dismissed the bill as to them. *Id.* at 198.

[172] *Id.* at 199–200.

[173] *Id.* at 199.

[174] *Id.* at 200. In his concurring opinion, Judge Hook stated that the controlling principle in the case, on which all the judges on the panel agreed, was:

A holding company, owning the stocks of other concerns whose commercial activities, if free and independent of a common control, would naturally bring them into competition with each other, is a form of trust or combination prohibited by section 1 of the Sherman antitrust act. The Standard Oil Company of New Jersey is such a holding company. *Id.* at 193.

Judge Hook went on to explain that the test of legality under Section One of the Sherman Act was "not whether the restraint upon competition imposed by the contract or combination in question should be regarded as reasonable or unreasonable, but whether it is direct and appreciable." 173 F. at 194. Judge Hook noted that what activities directly and appreciably restrain trade changed over time with changing economic conditions. He noted, however, that "[v]ital principles ... have not changed; the change is merely in the conditions upon which they operate." *Id.* at 195.

amount of confusing and conflicting testimony relating to innumerable, complex and varied business transactions, extending over a period of nearly forty years."[175]

The Briefs for the Appellants

The appellants submitted three lengthy briefs on the law to the Supreme Court. In the October, 1909 term of the Court, Johnson and Milburn, now joined by Frank L. Crawford, submitted a two-volume brief.[176] Volume one, running to a length of 181 pages, was devoted to the legal issues in the case, while Volume two discussed in detail the facts. In the same term of the Court, Watson, Freeman, and Irwin submitted a 289–page brief supplemented by an additional 38–page appendix. Finally, in the following, October, 1910, term of the court, D.T. Watson alone submitted an even longer, 351–page revised brief, the appellants' final written statement of their argument. Notwithstanding the distinctly different and more limited analysis set out by Judge Sanborn for the circuit court panel, the Supreme Court briefs for both the appellants and the government largely clarified and expanded rather than fundamentally changed the arguments made in the circuit court. The briefs for the defendants, however, went on to criticize severely the circuit court's analysis and related decree.

As they had in the circuit court, the appellants again argued that the circuit court did not have jurisdiction over the appellants because it had not had power to authorize service of process on any of the many defendants in the case except for the single marketing affiliate that was resident in the district where the court sat.[177] They also reiterated that "for many years" the seven individual defendants had held only a minority stock interest and were merely the most active shareholders.[178] In any case, the briefs stressed again, the appellants were not violating the Sherman Act when the case was filed[179] and had not violated it at any previous time.[180]

---

[175] *Standard Oil Co. v. United States*, 221 U.S. 1, 30–31 (1911).

[176] M.F. Elliott and Martin Carey were also listed on the brief as solicitors for appellants.

[177] Brief for Appellants, Volume 1, Law at 167–80, *Standard Oil Co. v. United States*, 221 U.S. 1 (1911).

[178] *Id.* at 78.

[179] *Id.* at 26; Brief on the Law on Part of Appellants at 105–08, *Standard Oil Co. v. United States*, 221 U.S. 1 (1911); Revised Brief on the Law on Part of Appellants on Reargument at 122–31, *Standard Oil Co. v. United States*, 221 U.S. 1 (1911).

[180] Brief on the Law on Part of Appellants at 128, 134–35, *Standard Oil Co. v. United States*, 221 U.S. 1 (1911); Revised Brief on the Law on Part of Appellants on Reargument at 146, *Standard Oil Co. v. United States*, 221 U.S. 1 (1911).

The appellants again argued that the Sherman Act did not incorporate any reasonableness test for challenged conduct.[181] The briefs emphasized the great freedom the appellants had to choose how to compete:

> We could lawfully compete for and seek to monopolize all or any part of the interstate or international trade in oil. We could make that competition fierce, aggressive, and unrelenting. Could depress prices to drive out competitors and raise them afterwards. Could give away oil to drive out a competitor. We could buy out a competitor to get rid of him. We could join the competitor with us in our business. We could use all the shifts and devices of traders to succeed, except that we could not, by unlawful, fraudulent means, deprive any competitor of his equal, lawful right to fight for the trade.[182]

The briefs insisted again on the legality of ongoing, large-scale joint ownership of aggregated properties used together to increase production and trade.[183] They stressed once more that any danger of monopoly power would be checked by new entry.[184] They reiterated that the acquisitions made by the defendants overwhelmingly had occurred thirty to forty years before and had contributed far less to Standard's expansion than had its own internal growth. Such acquisitions could not be a reason now to break apart the entire Standard Oil business.[185] The Sherman Act, they urged, never was intended to be a radical measure to limit business size or to restructure economic life.[186]

Through tremendous ingenuity, skill, and courage those associated with Standard Oil systematically developed "a new and unique industry whereby a new product (crude oil) has been handled in a masterly manner and the world at large furnished, among other things, with the

---

[181] Brief for Appellants, Volume 1, Law at 90, *Standard Oil Co. v. United States*, 221 U.S. 1 (1911).

[182] Brief on the Law on Part of Appellants at 260, *Standard Oil Co. v. United States*, 221 U.S. 1 (1911). See also Brief for Appellants, Volume 1, Law at 90, *Standard Oil Co. v. United States*, 221 U.S. 1 (1911); Revised Brief on the Law on Part of Appellants on Reargument at 330, *Standard Oil Co. v. United States*, 221 U.S. 1 (1911).

[183] Brief on the Law on Part of Appellants at 108–12, *Standard Oil Co. v. United States*, 221 U.S. 1 (1911); Revised Brief on the Law on Part of Appellants on Reargument at 123–26, *Standard Oil Co. v. United States*, 221 U.S. 1 (1911).

[184] Brief for Appellants, Volume 1, Law at 110, 113, 122–25, 130–45, *Standard Oil Co. v. United States*, 221 U.S. 1 (1911).

[185] Brief for Appellants, Volume 1, Law at 106, *Standard Oil Co. v. United States*, 221 U.S. 1 (1911).

[186] Brief for Appellants, Volume 1, Law at 109, *Standard Oil Co. v. United States*, 221 U.S. 1 (1911).

best and cheapest light it has ever known."[187] The defendants who
achieved this now had been condemned, not for actually doing any
unlawful acts, but "simply because they made a mistake as to the
method in which they could the better hold their combined properties."[188]

Turning to the circuit court opinion, the appellants argued that
Judge Sanborn badly had misunderstood both the facts and the legal
implications of the *Northern Securities* case.[189] Accordingly, the circuit
court erred when it based its decision on the Supreme Court's *Northern
Securities* opinion. The circuit court also erred in finding that the 1899
stock transfers were unlawful because they eliminated potential future
rivalry among the commonly owned firms rather than ending existing
competition among the Standard Oil affiliates. This was an entirely new
and unwarranted interpretation of the Sherman Act.[190] Even if the
circuit court's potential competition doctrine were valid in the abstract,
the court erred in finding that the transformation of New Jersey
Standard into a holding company had made the combination more
powerful and permanent than it had been previously.[191] Watson, Freeman, and Irwin argued that the court's approach penalized a business
for simply adopting a more efficient management structure to coordinate
its various parts.[192] Because the circuit court based its finding of a
violation solely on its unsustainable assessment of the 1899 stock transfers to New Jersey Standard, and never addressed other actions challenged by the government, there was no basis on appeal for finding a
Sherman Act violation. Accordingly, the judgment and decree of the
court had to be reversed and vacated.[193]

---

[187] Revised Brief on the Law on Part of Appellants on Reargument at 319, *Standard
Oil Co. v. United States*, 221 U.S. 1 (1911).

[188] *Id.* at 351.

[189] Brief for Appellants, Volume 1, Law at 69, 72, 84, *Standard Oil Co. v. United States*,
221 U.S. 1 (1911); Brief on the Law on Part of Appellants at 13, 55–58, 239, *Standard Oil
Co. v. United States*, 221 U.S. 1 (1911); Revised Brief on the Law on Part of Appellants on
Reargument at 54–55, 71–73, *Standard Oil Co. v. United States*, 221 U.S. 1 (1911).

[190] Brief for Appellants, Volume 1, Law at 175–76, *Standard Oil Co. v. United States*,
221 U.S. 1 (1911); Brief on the Law on Part of Appellants at 47–55, 67, *Standard Oil Co. v.
United States*, 221 U.S. 1 (1911); Revised Brief on the Law on Part of Appellants on
Reargument at 47, 68–70, *Standard Oil Co. v. United States*, 221 U.S. 1 (1911).

[191] Brief on the Law on Part of Appellants at 74–75, *Standard Oil Co. v. United States*,
221 U.S. 1 (1911); Revised Brief on the Law on Part of Appellants on Reargument at 62–71,
Standard Oil Co. v. United States, 221 U.S. 1 (1911).

[192] Brief for Appellants, Volume 1, Law at 66, *Standard Oil Co. v. United States*, 221
U.S. 1 (1911); Revised Brief on the Law on Part of Appellants on Reargument at 64, 67,
Standard Oil Co. v. United States, 221 U.S. 1 (1911).

[193] Brief for Appellants, Volume 1, Law at 181, *Standard Oil Co. v. United States*, 221
U.S. 1 (1911). The briefs argued that the government, not having appealed, could not ask

The lawyers for the appellants contended that the circuit court's decree was not supported even by the facts found by the circuit court itself. Moreover, the decree's sweeping and onerous provisions went beyond the relief authorized by the Sherman Act, which gave courts power only to restrain specific ongoing or threatened illegal acts.[194] The statute did not give federal courts the authority to break apart an ongoing, integrated manufacturing business like the one operated by the defendants.[195] The decree established an overly broad and unduly vague restriction on future interaction among the defendants covered by it,[196] amounting to inappropriate and impractical judicial legislation.[197] Additional corporate defendants should have been excluded from the decree in addition to those the circuit court excluded.[198] It was highly improper, moreover, for the decree to enjoin the appellants from engaging in interstate commerce until New Jersey Standard distributed to its shareholders the stock it held in the subsidiary companies.[199] The decree would be counterproductive. It would ruin much property and force inefficient new duplication of facilities.[200] It would harm myriad Standard

---

for any new facts to be found on appeal in the Supreme Court. Brief on the Law on Part of Appellants at 128, 256, 262, *Standard Oil Co. v. United States*, 221 U.S. 1 (1911); Revised Brief on the Law on Part of Appellants on Reargument at 27, 28, 74–77, *Standard Oil Co. v. United States*, 221 U.S. 1 (1911).

[194] Brief for Appellants, Volume 1, Law at 98–99, *Standard Oil Co. v. United States*, 221 U.S. 1 (1911); Brief on the Law on Part of Appellants at 88–95, 105, 262, *Standard Oil Co. v. United States*, 221 U.S. 1 (1911); Revised Brief on the Law on Part of Appellants on Reargument at 77–80, 119–22, 284, *Standard Oil Co. v. United States*, 221 U.S. 1 (1911).

[195] Brief for Appellants, Volume 1, Law at 157, *Standard Oil Co. v. United States*, 221 U.S. 1 (1911); Brief on the Law on Part of Appellants at 102–05, 262, *Standard Oil Co. v. United States*, 221 U.S. 1 (1911); Revised Brief on the Law on Part of Appellants on Reargument at 78, 102, 118, 120, *Standard Oil Co. v. United States*, 221 U.S. 1 (1911).

[196] Brief on the Law on Part of Appellants at 95–97, 101, 112, *Standard Oil Co. v. United States*, 221 U.S. 1 (1911); Revised Brief on the Law on Part of Appellants on Reargument at 78, 96, 354, *Standard Oil Co. v. United States*, 221 U.S. 1 (1911).

[197] Brief for Appellants, Volume 1, Law at 162, 165–66, *Standard Oil Co. v. United States*, 221 U.S. 1 (1911).

[198] *Id.* at 160, *Standard Oil Co. v. United States*, 221 U.S. 1 (1911).

[199] Brief on the Law on Part of Appellants at 262, *Standard Oil Co. v. United States*, 221 U.S. 1 (1911): Brief for Appellants, Volume 1, Law at 23–25, *Standard Oil Co. v. United States*, 221 U.S. 1 (1911); Revised Brief on the Law on Part of Appellants on Reargument at 78, *Standard Oil Co. v. United States*, 221 U.S. 1 (1911).

[200] Brief on the Law on Part of Appellants at 119, 127, *Standard Oil Co. v. United States*, 221 U.S. 1 (1911); Revised Brief on the Law on Part of Appellants on Reargument at 78, 118, 132–41, *Standard Oil Co. v. United States*, 221 U.S. 1 (1911). D.T. Watson, in the revised brief submitted "that there are no precedents in the books nor logical reason justifying such a confiscatory, such a ruinous decree as entered in this case; that such a decree if carried to its logical conclusion attacks the very foundations of the modern

Oil shareholders who were not parties to the litigation,[201] especially small shareholders.[202] If imposed, the decree was not even likely to accomplish its stated objective. Watson, Freeman, and Irwin in their brief and Watson in his later revised brief clearly suggested that the contemplated proportional distribution of stock in *all* of the affiliated companies to each New Jersey Standard shareholder would not in fact eliminate common control of the companies.[203]

The Briefs for the United States

In the October, 1909 term of the Supreme Court, Attorney General George W. Wickersham and special assistants Frank B. Kellogg, Charles B. Morrison, and Cordenio A. Severance submitted a 413–page "Summary of the Facts and Brief of the Law." This brief largely expanded upon the brief the government had submitted in the circuit court. It also, however, provided a much more detailed summary of the evolution of the Standard Oil conspiracy than the government had provided in its circuit court brief.[204] In the following term of the Court, in response to D.T. Watson's lengthy revised brief, the government submitted a final 64–page reply brief for the United States.[205]

In its main brief, the government again stressed the interstate nature of the oil business and Standard's operations. It noted once more the defendants' very high shares of various branches of the petroleum industry[206] and Standard's allegedly high prices and exorbitant profits.[207] The government continued to assert that "the combination of previously independent concerns" was the main means the defendants used to monopolize and restrain trade.[208] The government reiterated, however,

---

business world." Revised Brief on the Law on Part of Appellants on Reargument at 146, *Standard Oil Co. v. United States*, 221 U.S. 1 (1911).

[201] Revised Brief on the Law on Part of Appellants on Reargument at 11–13, *Standard Oil Co. v. United States*, 221 U.S. 1 (1911).

[202] Revised Brief on the Law on Part of Appellants on Reargument at 141–42, *Standard Oil Co. v. United States*, 221 U.S. 1 (1911).

[203] Brief on the Law on Part of Appellants at 120, *Standard Oil Co. v. United States*, 221 U.S. 1 (1911).

[204] Brief for the United States, Volume 1, Summary of the Facts and Brief of the Law, at 22, 33–44, 46, 54, 57–61, 76, *Standard Oil Co. v. United States*, 221 U.S. 1 (1911).

[205] In addition to the 64–page body of the brief, the reply brief also contained a 21–page appendix.

[206] Brief for the United States, Volume 1, Summary of the Facts and Brief of the Law, at 139, 145–50, *Standard Oil Co. v. United States*, 221 U.S. 1 (1911).

[207] *Id.* at 150, 154–63.

[208] *Id.* at 169.

that the defendants had strengthened their market power through the use of other improper means involving: control of pipelines and abuse of that control, including obstruction of competing pipe line development;[209] railroad rate discrimination;[210] unfair competition;[211] and contracts in restraint of trade entered into with other firms[212] outside the Standard combination.[213] The government contended that such means independently violated section 2 while illuminating the monopolistic intent of the combination.[214]

The most striking new aspect of the government's legal argument was its enlarged discussion of the legislative history of the Sherman Act. Noting the relevance to statutory interpretation of conditions prevailing when a statute was passed,[215] the brief recited extended passages from the congressional debates preceding the Sherman Act's passage. Before 1890, the government noted, great public concern had arisen about Standard Oil and other industrial combinations that "the people believed approached such a degree of monopoly as to threaten the industrial independence of the country."[216] The congressional debates revealed that Congress largely had the Standard Oil trust and other trusts in mind in passing the Sherman Act.[217] Specifically mentioning the Standard Oil trust, Senator Sherman, for example, had urged that new federal legislation was needed to deal with such combinations, which had been void at common law.[218] Similarly, Senator Edmunds, "after mentioning the Standard Oil and the Sugar trusts," declared himself to be "most earnestly in favor, of doing everything that the Constitution of the United States has given Congress power to do, to repress and break up and destroy forever the monopolies of that character."[219] The government argued that in light of Congress' pointed concern over the Standard Oil combination and similar trusts, and its long and careful

---

[209] *Id.* at 169–76.

[210] *Id.* at 177–78, 184.

[211] *Id.* at 187–95.

[212] *Id.* at 186.

[213] *Id.* at 169.

[214] *Id.*

[215] *Id.* at 288.

[216] *Id.*

[217] *Id.* at 289–91; Reply Brief for the United States at 2, *Standard Oil Co. v. United States*, 221 U.S. 1 (1911).

[218] Brief for the United States, Volume 1, Summary of the Facts and Brief of the Law, at 292–93, *Standard Oil Co. v. United States*, 221 U.S. 1 (1911).

[219] *Id.* at 293.

consideration of the broad language of the Sherman Act, it was not possible that Congress did not intend to ban successor holding companies like New Jersey Standard as well as the trusts themselves.[220]

The government declared that section 2 of the Sherman Act, interpreted according to the "fundamental principle of construction that language is to be given its ordinary meaning," banned monopolizing or attempting to monopolize by any means.[221] The government now stressed Justice Joseph McKenna's explanation of the meaning of monopoly in *National Cotton Oil Co. v. Texas:*[222] "Its dominant thought now is . . . the suppression of competition by the unification of interest or management, or it may be through agreement and concert of action. And the purpose is so definitely the control of prices that monopoly has been defined to be 'unified tactics with regard to prices.' "[223] The government also, however, again called special attention to the Ohio Supreme Court's 1892 statement of the multiple political-economic dangers of monopoly.[224] Toward the end of its main brief, the government offered the following statement of the meaning of the Sherman Act as applied to the defendants' activity:

> every contract, combination, or conspiracy, in whatever form, whereby competing corporations or individuals are amalgamated into one concern and brought under a single control, either by purchase of properties or of stock of corporations, if it results in giving to such controlling agency the power to fix prices, determine the amount of production, and suppress competition, and thus effect a monopoly or control of interstate trade and commerce, is also prohibited by the second section of the act as well as by the first.[225]

Illegal monopoly also existed where dominant control was exercised oppressively, as was the case, for example, with Standard Oil's use of its national monopoly position to engage in local predatory pricing.[226] It was

---

[220] *Id.* at 296. See also Reply Brief for the United States at 2–3, *Standard Oil Co. v. United States*, 221 1 U.S. (1911).

[221] Brief for the United States, Volume 1, Summary of the Facts and Brief of the Law, at 336, *Standard Oil Co. v. United States*, 221 U.S. 1 (1911).

[222] 197 U.S. 115 (1905).

[223] Brief for the United States, Volume 1, Summary of the Facts and Brief of the Law, at 336, *Standard Oil Co. v. United States*, 221 U.S. 1 (1911).

[224] *Id.* at 345–46.

[225] *Id.* at 348. In its reply brief, the government, echoing more closely the position of the circuit court, declared that section 1 bans "any form or device employed to hold together corporations or *naturally competing* business establishments so as to eliminate competition." (emphasis added) Reply Brief for the United States at 3, *Standard Oil Co. v. United States*, 221 U.S. 1(1911).

[226] Brief for the United States, Volume 1, Summary of the Facts and Brief of the Law, at 349, *Standard Oil Co. v. United States*, 221 U.S. 1 (1911). See also, Reply Brief for the

unnecessary, the government again declared, to address whether the great size of a business by itself might ever violate section 2.[227]

Appealing to the Supreme Court to adopt a "a broad and reasonable construction of this act," the government declared:

> Congress has declared for freedom of trade against all restraints and monopolies; but the effectiveness of laws depends upon their interpretation and execution. The people have expressed their will, and Congress has exercised its power by declaring that all monopolies in restraint of trade shall be void. It is as it always has been, for the courts to construe this language and to enforce this law.[228]

In its reply brief, the government sought to buttress its case, in substantial part, by invoking a number of state cases decided since the submission of its main Supreme Court brief. In these cases the courts had held the appellants' holding company and similar combinations unlawful under state antitrust laws. The government declared that those laws were substantially similar to the Sherman Act, except that they applied to intrastate rather than interstate commerce.[229] The government noted that antitrust statutes and constitutional provisions had been adopted in 36 states and asserted that "[t]hey evince a great public policy of this nation, which is a material consideration in this court."[230] The government observed that state courts had declared the 1882 Standard Oil trust, the 1899 establishment of New Jersey Standard as a holding company, and similar combinations invalid under state antitrust laws like the Sherman Act in every case in which the issue of their validity had arisen.[231] In light of this, the government argued, it would be anomalous to allow the same and similar combinations to "continue to do business under the shield of Federal authority."[232]

United States at 40, *Standard Oil Co. v. United States*, 221 U.S. 1 (1911). The government in *Standard Oil* thus in substance already articulated what today is the prevailing legal test for finding illegal monopolization. That test, from the Supreme Court's opinion in *United States v. Grinnell Corp.*, 384 U.S. 563, 570–71 (1966), requires proof of "(1) the possession of monopoly power in the relevant market and (2) the willful acquisition or maintenance of that power as distinguished from growth or development as a consequence of a superior product, business acumen, or historic accident."

[227] Brief for the United States, Volume 1, Summary of the Facts and Brief of the Law, at 351, *Standard Oil Co. v. United States*, 221 U.S. 1 (1911).

[228] Brief for the United States, Volume 1, Summary of the Facts and Brief of the Law, at 354, *Standard Oil Co. v. United States*, 221 U.S. 1 (1911).

[229] Reply Brief for the United States at 3–14, *Standard Oil Co. v. United States*, 221 U.S. 1 (1911).

[230] *Id.* at 3 and Appendix A.

[231] *Id.* at 4–5, 6.

[232] *Id.* at 4.

In both its initial and reply briefs, the government strongly supported the legitimacy and appropriateness of the circuit court's decree, embracing that court's view that elimination of the artificial and more powerful constraint created by the holding company would lead over time to the reemergence of competition among the Standard Oil affiliates. Accordingly, the government requested no modification to the decree.[233]

The Supreme Court Opinion

1. The Overall Importance of the Opinion

In his opinion for the Court, Chief Justice White addressed a great many of the key issues debated in the briefs. He discussed the historical concerns and circumstances that had prompted passage of the Sherman Act, the evolving meaning of the common law terms Congress had incorporated into it, and the importance and limits of freedom of contract and its relationship to monopoly and impermissible restraints of trade. He announced the proper methodology for determining the meaning of the Sherman Act. He articulated a new overall approach for judging conduct under the Sherman Act, invoking the controversial phrase "rule of reason," without necessarily still embracing the outlook animating the "reasonableness" test he had urged in his 1897 dissent in the *Trans–Missouri* case. The Chief Justice went on to suggest a somewhat more specific, common-law-inspired guide for identifying unreasonably restrictive contracts or acts, based on their inherent nature or character or, alternatively, their surrounding circumstances. This laid an early foundation for the later, central distinction between *per se* (or summary) and more extended analysis in antitrust law. Chief Justice White's opinion looked to the future in describing rather narrowly the specific harm or harms that the Sherman Act was intended to prevent. At the same time, however, his opinion heavily relied upon and reflected the central distinction between natural, or normal, and unnatural, or abnormal, economic activity that was at the heart of then-longstanding academic and popular variants of classical political-economic thought.

Chief Justice White's opinion for the Court reinforced an evolving, broader conception of the reach of federal commerce clause power in Sherman Act cases. This view contrasted strikingly with the view the Court had articulated in *United States v. E.C. Knight Co.*,[234] the Court's first opinion considering the act. Simultaneously, Chief Justice White's opinion sought to answer concerns over the magnitude of future judicial discretion and judicial "legislation" in antitrust cases. The Chief Justice, for the Court, ultimately resolved the *Standard Oil* litigation by applying

---

[233] *Id.* at 40–42; Brief for the United States, Volume 1, Summary of the Facts and Brief of the Law, at 347, *Standard Oil Co. v. United States*, 221 U.S. 1 (1911).

[234] 156 U.S. 1 (1895).

his newly articulated Sherman Act approach to the established facts of the case. In so doing, he highlighted, among other important issues, the role of bad purpose and of intent inferred from exclusionary conduct. Finally, the Chief Justice evaluated and largely affirmed the relief decreed by the circuit court in this greatest of all early antitrust cases.

2. The Opinion

On May 15, 1911, Chief Justice Edward Douglass White delivered the opinion for the Supreme Court.[235] He began by noting the allegations made by the government, the proceedings in the circuit court and the scope of the record on appeal. Preliminarily, he also stated that it was not prejudicial error for the circuit court to have overruled the defendants' exceptions to those portions of the government's bill that related to actions prior to passage of the Sherman Act. This was because "the court, as we shall do, gave no weight to the testimony adduced under the averments complained of except insofar as it tended to throw light upon the acts done after the passage of the Anti-trust Act and the results of which it was charged were being participated in and enjoyed by the alleged combination at the time of the filing of the bill."[236] Turning to the merits of the case, Chief Justice White emphasized how challenging the case was.[237] He found that the government and the appellants had taken polar opposite positions with regard to both the facts of the case and the meaning of the Sherman Act.[238] Chief Justice White declared that evaluation of these competing contentions called "for the analysis and weighing . . . of a jungle of conflicting testimony covering a period of forty years, a duty difficult to rightly perform and, even if satisfactorily accomplished, almost impossible to state with any reasonable regard to brevity."[239] Chief Justice White noted that the only point of agreement between the contending sides was that disposition of the case turned on a correct interpretation of sections 1 and 2 of the Sherman Act.[240] Accordingly, he began the Court's analysis there.

The Chief Justice declared that while passage of the Sherman Act was influenced by doubts as to whether a federal common law existed governing restraints of trade,

---

[235] *Standard Oil Co. v. United States*, 221 U.S. 1 (1911). As an initial matter, the Chief Justice declared that the circuit court "rightly took jurisdiction over the cause and properly ordered notice to be served upon the non-resident defendants." *Id.* at 46.

[236] *Id.* at 46–47.

[237] *Id.* at 47.

[238] *Id.* at 47–48.

[239] *Id.* at 48.

[240] *Id.* at 48.

the main cause which led to the legislation was the thought that it was required by the economic condition of the times, that is, the vast accumulation of wealth in the hands of corporations and individuals, the enormous development of corporate organization, the facility for combination which such organizations afforded, the fact that the facility was being used, and that combinations known as trusts were being multiplied, and the widespread impression that their power had been and would be exerted to oppress individuals and injure the public generally.[241]

Chief Justice White noted that congressional debates could be looked to in order to determine the historical environment out of which legislation arose, although not directly to interpret a statute.[242]

He then noted that the Sherman Act's key terms were taken from common law and that they had evolved in meaning over time. Contracts in restraint of trade had referred to contractual restrictions an individual voluntarily placed on his own right to carry on his trade. Originally, all such restraints were illegal as harmful to the public and injurious to the freedom of contract of the individual involved. Later, such a restraint was deemed to be lawful "if the restraint was partial in its operation and was otherwise reasonable."[243] A monopoly originally was an exclusive grant from the English King to carry on a particular trade. Parliament later restricted crown authority to grant monopolies because of public outcry over the evils they caused by way of increased prices, reduced output, and a degradation in product quality.[244] It came to be believed that purchase and resale, at least of necessaries of life, by private individuals could generate one of the harms of monopoly, specifically, an artificial increase in prices. As a result, in England, laws relating to the offenses of forestalling, engrossing, and rebating were passed to restrict such conduct and they came be thought of as an example of monopoly as well as restraint of trade, even in the absence of a showing that a predominant part of a given trade had been affected.[245]

Later, improved economic thinking and social change led to the repeal in England of laws against forestalling, engrossing, and regrating, based on a new understanding that the conduct they targeted promoted rather than harmed trade.[246] The common law never banned the private

---

[241] *Id.* at 50.

[242] *Id.*

[243] *Id.* at 51.

[244] *Id.* at 51–52.

[245] *Id.* at 53–55.

[246] *Id.* at 55.

creation of a monopoly per se, in recognition of the fact that so long as government creation of monopoly was banned, "the inevitable operation of economic forces" set in motion by the unimpeded individual exercise of freedom of contract would prevent the harms of monopoly from arising, provided that specific types of private actions threatening to produce such harms were not permitted.[247] Except for contracts in restraint of trade unreasonably restricting a person's own right to trade and conduct restraining "the free course of trade by contracts or acts which implied a wrongful purpose," unrestricted freedom of contract "became the rule in the English law."[248]

Chief Justice White related that the same general evolution had occurred over time in American as well as English thinking. Private conduct thought potentially to generate the evils associated with monopoly came to be spoken of as in restraint of trade and "as amounting to monopoly" and was targeted by state constitutional provisions, statutes, and judicial decisions.[249] In more recent times, legislation and case law evolved to cover additional, newer types of conduct that seemingly manifested the same wrongful intent.[250] Chief Justice White summarized:

> the dread of enhancement of prices and of other wrongs which it was thought would flow from the undue limitation on competitive conditions caused by contract or other acts of individuals or corporations, led, as a matter of public policy, to the prohibition or treating as illegal all contracts or acts which were unreasonably restrictive of competitive conditions, either from the nature or character of the contract or act or where the surrounding circumstances were such as to justify the conclusion that they had not been entered into or performed with the legitimate purpose of reasonably forwarding personal interest and developing trade, but on the contrary were of such a character as to give rise to the inference or presumption that they had been entered into or done with the intent to do wrong to the general public and to limit the right of individuals, thus restraining the free flow of commerce and tending to bring about the evils, such as enhancement of prices, which were considered to be against public policy.[251]

Chief Justice White concluded that the Sherman Act had been drafted in light of this "existing practical conception of the law of

---

[247] *Id.* at 55–56.

[248] *Id.* at 56.

[249] *Id.* at 57.

[250] *Id.* at 57–58.

[251] *Id.* at 58–59.

restraint of trade."[252] At a time when the proliferation of new types of contracts and combinations had become prominent, Congress believed it "essential by an all-embracing enumeration to make sure that no form of contract or combination by which an undue restraint of interstate or foreign commerce was brought about could save such restraint from condemnation."[253] Congress had not expressly defined the agreements covered by section 1, but instead had invoked the categories of "contracts, combinations, and conspiracies in restraint of trade," which were "broad enough to embrace every conceivable contract or combination which could be made concerning trade or commerce . . . if in restraint of trade." Accordingly,

> the provision necessarily called for the exercise of judgment which required that some standard should be resorted to for the purpose of determining whether the prohibitions contained in the statute had or had not in any given case been violated. . . . [I]t follows that it was intended that the standard of reason which had been applied at the common law and in this country in dealing with subjects of the character embraced by the statute, was intended to be the measure used for the purpose of determining whether in a given case a particular act had or had not brought about the wrong against which the statute provided.[254]

Section 2 of the Sherman Act "was intended to supplement the first and to make sure that by no possible guise could the public policy embodied in the first section be frustrated or evaded,"[255] even if acts not covered by section 1 were used to monopolize or attempt to monopolize trade.[256] The criteria to be used to determine whether section 2 was violated was again "the rule of reason guided by the established law and by the plain duty to enforce the prohibitions of the act and thus the public policy which its restrictions were obviously enacted to subserve."[257] Section 2 did not ban monopoly per se ("monopoly in the concrete") for the same reason that English common law did not.[258] That is, Congress believed that in the absence of improper restraint of trade, the legitimate, unimpeded competitive exercise of freedom of contract could be counted on to prevent the harmful exercise of monopoly power.

---

[252] *Id.* at 59.

[253] *Id.* at 59–60.

[254] *Id.* at 60.

[255] *Id.*

[256] *Id.* at 61.

[257] *Id.* at 62.

[258] *Id.*

Chief Justice White presented the Court's view of the Sherman Act as a middle path between what he characterized as more extreme positions urged by the government and the appellants. He asserted that the government in effect urged a mechanical, literal application of the language of the Sherman Act.[259] Such an approach, he said, was untenable. The exercise of judgment was needed to determine whether a challenged act is a contract, combination, or conspiracy and, if so, whether it is "a restraint of trade within the intendment of the act."[260] In taking this position, Chief Justice White, for the Court, embraced a belief in the need for "purposive" interpretation and adjudication guided by the Court's perception of Congress' basic goals in passing the Sherman Act.[261]

Chief Justice White insisted that this approach did not conflict with the approach the Supreme Court had taken in earlier Sherman Act cases, beginning with Justice Peckham's opinions for the Court in *United States v. Trans–Missouri Freight Association*,[262] and *United States v. Joint Traffic Association*.[263] The Chief Justice conceded that general language in those opinions seemed to reject an appeal to reason to determine whether the Sherman Act condemned the challenged conduct. He explained, however, that Justice Peckham actually had resorted to reason for that purpose not only in those cases,[264] but also in the case of *Hopkins v. United States*,[265] in which Justice Peckham held that "[t]here must be some direct and immediate effect upon interstate commerce in order to come within the act."[266] The Chief Justice insisted that there ultimately was no difference between the rule of reason and the direct or indirect effect test.[267]

---

[259] *Id.* at 63.

[260] *Id.* at 63. Otherwise, the act either would have to be interpreted to condemn "every contract, act or combination of any kind" or enforcement of the act would become impossible because of uncertainty. *Id.*

[261] *See, e.g.,* In so doing, Chief Justice White adopted an approach prominently urged by contemporary legal progressives and, even more so, by later legal realists. See, e.g., AMERICAN LEGAL REALISM 167 (W. Fisher III, M. Horwitz, & T. Reed, eds., 1993).

[262] 166 U.S. 290 (1897).

[263] 171 U.S. 505 (1898).

[264] 221 U.S. at 65.

[265] 171 U.S. 578 (1898).

[266] 221 U.S. at 66.

[267] *Id.* The Chief Justice declared, however, that to the extent that divorced from its context, any general language in the two early railroad cartel cases appeared to conflict with the interpretation of the statute now announced, those earlier opinions "are necessarily now limited and qualified." *Id.* at 68.

Chief Justice White also rejected what he asserted were the defendants' two key statutory claims. The first of these, he said, was that the Sherman Act constitutionally could not be applied to the appellants' conduct because, under the Court's decision in *United States v. E.C. Knight Co.*,[268] that conduct was beyond the reach of congressional commerce clause power.[269] The appellants' second basic claim, said the Chief Justice, was that to apply the Sherman Act in this case would unconstitutionally infringe property rights and the freedom of contract or trade.[270] This, he stated, assumed wrongly that "reason may not be resorted to in interpreting and applying the statute, and therefore that the statute unreasonably restricts the right to contract and unreasonably operates upon the right to acquire and hold property."[271] That is, as now interpreted, the act would ban only undue restraints of competition, and such restraints were not within the bounds of constitutionally protected freedom of contract.[272]

Chief Justice White also rejected the proposition that, given the generality of the Sherman Act's language, it could not "be carried out without a judicial exertion of the legislative power."[273] It did not violate due process for courts to decide whether particular acts fell within a generic statutory provision.[274]

Having established the proper approach to interpreting the Sherman Act, the Chief Justice applied the statute to the facts of the case. He concluded that the vast amount of property put under the control of the Standard Oil Company of New Jersey gave it "an enlarged and more perfect sway and control over the trade and commerce in petroleum and its products."[275] He found no reason to doubt the correctness of the lower court's conclusion that the defendants had violated both section 1 and 2 of the Sherman Act by destroying the "potentiality of competition" that otherwise would have prevailed among the various companies controlled by New Jersey Standard.[276] The unification of power and control over crude and refined oil that inevitably had resulted gave rise to a

---

[268] 156 U.S. 1 (1895).

[269] This claim, he said, was foreclosed by subsequent Supreme Court Sherman Act decisions. 221 U.S. at 68.

[270] *Id.* at 69.

[271] *Id.* at 69.

[272] See OWEN M. FISS, TROUBLED BEGINNINGS OF THE MODERN STATE, 1888–1910, at 149 (1993).

[273] 221 U.S. at 69.

[274] *Id.* at 69.

[275] *Id.* at 71.

[276] *Id.* at 72.

prima facie presumption of intent and purpose to maintain the
dominancy over the oil industry, not as a result of normal methods
of industrial development, but by new means of combination which
were resorted to in order that greater power might be added than
would otherwise have arisen had normal methods been followed, the
whole with the purpose of excluding others from the trade and thus
centralizing in the combination a perpetual control of the movements of petroleum and its products in the channels of interstate
commerce.[277]

This presumption was made conclusive, first, by evidence of the
appellants' other actions prior to the formation of the trust agreements
and the establishment of the holding company and, second, by evidence
of how New Jersey Standard had exercised its power after 1899.[278] Even
before the rise of the trusts of 1879 and 1882, the Chief Justice declared,
"an intent and purpose to exclude others ... was frequently manifested
by acts and dealings wholly inconsistent with the theory that they were
made with the single conception of advancing the development of business by usual methods, but which on the contrary necessarily involved
the intent to drive others from the field and to exclude them from their
right to trade and thus accomplish the mastery which was the end in
view."[279] The defendants' actions from 1882 up to 1899 also demonstrated such bad intent.[280] New Jersey Standard's exercise of the power it
attained through its 1899 transformation into a holding company did so
as well because

> the acquisition here and there which ensued of every efficient means
> by which competition could have been asserted, the slow but resist-
> less methods which followed by which means of transportation were
> absorbed and brought under control, the system of marketing which
> was adopted by which the country was divided into districts and the
> trade in each district in oil was turned over to a designated corpora-
> tion within the combination and all others were excluded, all lead
> the mind up to a conviction of a purpose and intent which we think
> is so certain as practically to cause the subject not to be within the
> domain of reasonable contention.[281]

---

[277] *Id.* at 75.

[278] The Court stressed that the evidence of events before the Sherman Act was passed
was considered "not for the purpose of weighing the substantial merit of the numerous
charges of wrongdoing ... but solely as an aid for discovering intent and purpose." *Id.* at
76.

[279] *Id.* at 76.

[280] *Id.*

[281] *Id.* at 76–77.

Chief Justice White, for the Court, then finally turned to the question of the appropriate relief to be granted and approved the circuit court's decree almost in its entirety. In response to the appellants' concerns that the decree was overly sweeping and could prohibit legitimate, publicly-beneficial contracts between various of the subsidiaries after the dissolution of the holding company, the Chief Justice construed the decree "not as depriving the stockholders of the corporations, after the dissolution of the combination, of the power to make normal and lawful contracts or agreements, but as restraining them from, by any device whatever, recreating directly or indirectly the illegal combination which the decree dissolved."[282] The Court also extended the time allowed for dissolving the holding company from thirty days to at least six months. Finally, out of concern for potential harm to the public, the Court eliminated the decree's ban on the defendants' participation in interstate commerce until New Jersey Standard distributed to its shareholders the stock it held in the subsidiary companies.[283]

Justice Harlan's Separate Opinion

Justice John Marshall Harlan filed a separate opinion concurring in part and dissenting in part. He declared that the decree should not have been modified and strongly objected that the Court in effect had told the subsidiary companies that in the future "they may join in an agreement to restrain commerce among the States if such restraint be not 'undue.' "[284] Justice Harlan contended that this upset a long-standing interpretation of the Sherman Act and usurped legislative functions.[285] He noted that attempts repeatedly had been made and rebuffed in Congress to amend section 1 of the Sherman Act to ban only "unreasonable" restraints.[286] Incorporation of a test of unreasonableness into that section, Justice Harlan contended, effectively would make the statute too indefinite to enforce as a criminal statute and create tremendous uncertainty for civil enforcement.[287] Justice Harlan declared:

> When counsel in the present case insisted upon a reversal of the former rulings of this court, and asked such an interpretation of the Anti-trust Act as would allow reasonable restraints of interstate commerce, this court, in deference to established practice, should, I submit, have said to them: "That question, according to our practice, is not open for further discussion here...."[288]

---

[282] *Id.* at 81.

[283] *Id.*

[284] *Id.* at 82.

[285] *Id.* at 83.

[286] *Id.* at 90.

[287] *Id.* at 97.

[288] *Id.* at 101–02.

Justice Harlan's opinion became a rallying point for criticism of the Court's opinion by Progressive Senators and others concerned about the tenor of Chief Justice White's opinion and the potential ineffectiveness of the decree the Court approved. At the same time, other commentators in 1911 and since have seen Justice Harlan's opinion as an overreaction to the Chief Justice's opinion.

Notwithstanding Justice Harlan's criticism, Chief Justice White's opinion did not simply reassert the more ambiguous position he had taken when he argued in dissent in *Trans–Missouri* that section 1 of the Sherman Act banned only unreasonable restraints and seemed willing to countenance at least some cartels.[289] In his 1911 opinion, White stressed much more heavily that the primary focus of Sherman Act analysis should be on whether challenged conduct threatened to produce the harms associated with monopoly, especially an increase in price. Justice Harlan also problematically equated Chief Justice White's position in *Standard Oil* with the many controversial efforts that had been made to amend the Sherman Act explicitly to ban only contracts, combinations, and conspiracies in "unreasonable" restraint of trade, sometimes by persons who wished to allow room, for example, for "reasonable" price-boosting cartels. Additionally striking was Justice Harlan's assertion that the Court had embraced a reasonableness test for challenged conduct at the urging of the lawyers in the case. The government, in line with President Taft's publicly-announced opposition to such a reason-ableness test, never argued for any such interpretation of the act, while the lawyers for the Standard Oil defendants, in both their circuit court and Supreme Court briefs, vigorously had opposed the idea of judging business tactics by any "reasonableness" or "fairness" test.[290]

More than just the wording of Chief Justice White's opinion or the source of its emphasis on judicial reason, however, animated Justice Harlan. Nearing the end of his life, this most fervent of antitrust supporters on the Court feared that the Court's opinion at the very least might encourage the type of "rule of reason" interpretation of the Sherman Act that he vigorously had opposed for years and that he

---

[289] *United States v. Trans–Missouri Freight Association*, 166 U.S. 290, at 343–74 (1897) (White, J., dissenting).

[290] It was the lawyers for the defendants who most strongly rejected a reasonableness or fairness test for alleged exclusionary conduct. In large part, they sought to avoid liability for the acquisition and combination of other firms by insistence upon fixed, traditional common law meanings of contract, combination, or conspiracy in restraint of trade, understood to allow tremendous freedom for exclusionary conduct not independently unlawful and categorically to permit acquisitions of rivals no matter how high the acquiring firm's market share consequently became.

believed would make it excessively hard to hold defendants accountable in future antitrust cases.

Conclusion

The Supreme Court's opinion in *Standard Oil*, together with its opinion two weeks later in *United States v. American Tobacco Company*,[291] proved to be one of the great landmarks in Supreme Court history. It substantially helped to bring to a close a quarter-century of intense national debate over the causes and implications of late-nineteenth and early-twentieth century economic transformation. It synthesized, reformulated, and brought to a climax the early, formative era of Sherman Act interpretation. It ordered the dissolution, effectively or not, of the most prominent industrial combination of the time. It revitalized debate over antitrust policy in national politics and soon would spur the 1914 passage of two new federal antitrust acts, the Federal Trade Commission Act and the Clayton Act. In the longer run, Chief Justice White's "rule of reason" framework would establish an enduring foundation for subsequent doctrinal development and application of the Sherman Act over the next 100 years. It thereby substantially helped to establish the rules and character of market capitalism in modern America. Finally, for the next century, Standard Oil and the *Standard Oil* case would remain powerful and enduring, if variously interpreted, symbols of big business and the extent of its public accountability.

---

[291] 221 U.S. 106 (1911).

*

2

Rudolph J.R. Peritz

"Nervine" and Knavery: The Life and Times of *Dr. Miles Medical Company*

... for nervousness or nervous exhaustion, sleeplessness, hysteria, headache, neuralgia, backache, pain, epilepsy, spasms, fits, and St. Vitus' dance.

Dr. Miles "Restorative Nervine" Label

I cannot believe that in the long run the public will profit by this court permitting knaves to cut reasonable prices for some ulterior purpose.

Justice Oliver Wendell Holmes, Jr.

INTRODUCTION

In the spring of 1911, the Supreme Court issued four opinions involving the Sherman Act, all of them landmark decisions and each in its own way reflective of the era. The *Standard Oil* and *American Tobacco* decisions affirmed dissolution of the notorious oil and tobacco trusts, the first controlled by John D. Rockefeller and the latter by J. B. Duke. The cases confirmed congressional power to impose a statutory regime of competition in the public interest. The Court adopted a rule of reason that would later evolve into the microeconomic logic of modern antitrust analysis. In *Gompers*, the Court sanctioned the issuance of contempt citations to enforce the judicial practice of enjoining labor union strikes. Three years later, Congress would pass the Clayton Act in an effort to limit the broad judicial discretion seen in the rule of reason and to curb the widespread use of injunctions against labor unions.[1]

---

[1] Standard Oil Co. v. U.S., 221 U.S. 1 (1911); U.S. v. American Tobacco Co., 221 U.S. 106 (1911); Gompers v. Buck's Stove & Range Co., 221 U.S. 418 (1911) (holding criminal

The fourth decision was *Dr. Miles Medical Company*. Justice Charles Evans Hughes, writing for the Court, not only pronounced the doctrine that resale price maintenance was *per se* illegal but set in motion the analytical dynamics of modern vertical restraints doctrine.[2] Moreover, the underlying controversy offers a striking picture of the era's swirling cultural and economic currents. *Dr. Miles* arose at the confluence of three federal statutes emblematic of Progressive Era responses to entrepreneurial excess. As every antitrust student knows, the Sherman Act grounded Park's successful defense that the resale price provisions in Miles' form contract were unenforceable. The context was also framed by the Trademark Act of 1905[3] and the Pure Food & Drug Act of 1906,[4] both of which collided with the dominant marketing strategies of patent medicine firms. Because the costs of market entry and product imitation were low, supply tended to exceed demand, spurring intense brand competition.[5] But the trademark statute's stronger protection of nationwide brands in the patent medicine industry, the first market driven by mass advertising, enabled large manufacturers to distance themselves from smaller firms and discourage upstarts.[6] Moreover, the food and drug act's ingredient disclosure requirements and its ban on ill-founded therapeutic claims tended to benefit well-established firms as well as consumers.[7]

---

sanctions for contempt improperly issued but inherently part of court powers in proper proceedings). Clayton Act, ch. 323, 38 Stat. 730, (1914) (current version at 15 U.S.C. § 18). For description of that era, *see* RUDOLPH J.R. PERITZ, COMPETITION POLICY IN AMERICA: HISTORY, RHETORIC, LAW at Chs. 1 & 2 (2001) (hereinafter PERITZ, COMPETITION POLICY).

[2] Dr. Miles Medical Co. v. John D. Park & Sons Co., 220 U.S. 373 (1911); Peritz, *A Genealogy of Vertical Restraints*, 40 HASTINGS L.J. 511 (1989) (hereinafter Peritz, *Genealogy*); State Oil v. Khan, 522 U.S. 3 (1997) (applying rule of reason to maximum resale price maintenance). Over Justice Breyer's sharp dissent, a deeply divided Supreme Court recently overruled Dr. Miles and held vertical price restraints are to be judged by the rule of reason. Leegin Creative Leather Products, Inc. v. PSKS, Inc., 127 S.Ct. 2705 (2007) (U.S.). Writing for the Court, Justice Kennedy declared that economic analysis supports the abandonment of Dr. Miles' outdated common law logic of restraints on alienation of property, which prohibited minimum price restraints. The chapter corrects this misreading of Dr. Miles, showing that the common law logic actually supported the legality of vertical price restraints and, moreover, continues to support their legality in modern cases involving manufacturers' property rights in trademarked goods.

[3] Act of Feb. 20, 1905, ch. 592, § 5, 33 Stat. 724. The prior Trademark Act of 1871, ch. 230, 16 Stat. 198 (1871), was declared unconstitutional in U.S. v. Steffens, 100 U.S. 82, 97 (1879).

[4] Pure Food and Drug Act of 1906, Pub. L. No. 59-384, 34 Stat. 768, 768–70 (1906) (repealed 1938).

[5] JAMES YOUNG, THE TOADSTOOL MILLIONAIRES 165–66 (Princeton Univ. Press 1961) (hereinafter TOADSTOOL).

[6] On rising economies of scale in not only production and distribution but advertising, see ALFRED CHANDLER, JR., SCALE AND SCOPE: THE DYNAMICS OF INDUSTRIAL CAPITALISM 63–65, 168–70 (1990).

[7] See, e.g., Susan Foote & Robert Berlin, *Can Regulation Be as Innovative as Science and Technology? The FDA's Regulation of Combination Products*, 6 MINN. J. L. SCI. & TECH. 619, 624 (2005). Market participants practiced highly sophisticated forms of product

The chapter's first section describes the era's patent medicine markets and pays close attention to the commercial importance of trademarks and advertising. In this light, the second section analyzes *Dr. Miles* through the prism of prior litigation in the industry, an analysis that uncovers the centrality of property rights in the Court's competition policy. That policy is misunderstood today, particularly its underlying classical economics, which informed the twin common law competition doctrines of contracts in restraint of trade and restraints on alienation of property. The chapter concludes with an afterword about modern vertical restraints doctrine and its common law underpinnings.

I. PATENT MEDICINE MARKETS IN THE PROGRESSIVE ERA

The term "patent medicine" was largely a misnomer. Very few of them were actually patented.[8] The vast majority—whether celery bitters, sarsaparilla tonics or bone liniments—boasted the therapeutic value of secret ingredients and thus were more accurately called proprietary medicines. A number of today's mouthwashes, cough syrups and cold medications began as patent medicines and retain their brand popularity as well as their core ingredient—alcohol. Other products that began as patent medicines have migrated to twenty-first century kitchens: Today the vegetarian cure first known as "Dr. Miles' Compound Extract of Tomato" is likely kept in bottles labeled HEINZ KETCHUP.[9] COCA COLA contained narcotic cocaine until 1903 and was advertised as a "brain tonic and intellectual beverage" under the name of "Beverage Moxie Nerve Food."[10]

The predominant business strategy for patent medicine makers involved not patents but trade secrecy, intended to conceal the identity of ingredients from both rivals and customers. Relentless advertising of trademarked names and images sought success in overcrowded and highly contested markets. This volatile mixture of secrecy and publicity, catalyzed by low production costs, yielded differentiated product markets

---

differentiation long before economists developed the tools to describe and analyze them. See generally, PERITZ, COMPETITION POLICY at 106–110; Peritz, *Dynamic Efficiency*, in POST-CHICAGO DEVELOPMENTS IN ANTITRUST LAW 108 (2002) (Cuccinota, A., et al., eds.).

[8] In 1796 the first and one of the few actual patents for a patent medicine was issued to a Dr. Samuel Lee for his "Bilious Pills." TOADSTOOL at 31–35. Patents were more often issued for therapeutic devices. The first was issued in 1796 to a Dr. Elisha Perkins, a founder of the Connecticut Medical Society, for "Metallic Tractors," which were recommended for "Rheumatism, Pleurisy, Some Gouty Affections, etc., etc." TOADSTOOL at 21–27; STEWART HOLBROOK, THE GOLDEN AGE OF QUACKERY 34–36 (1959) (hereinafter QUACKERY).

[9] TOADSTOOL at 171; DAVID ARMSTRONG AND ELIZABETH ARMSTRONG, THE GREAT AMERICAN MEDICINE SHOW 167 (1991). (hereinafter MEDICINE SHOW).

[10] MEDICINE SHOW at 161; JAMES GRAY, WHY OUR DRUG LAWS HAVE FAILED AND WHAT WE CAN DO ABOUT IT 21 (2001).

rife with multiple asymmetries of product information, market failures that improved conditions for widespread entrepreneurial excesses that bordered on fraud. The section describes those markets by plotting the product and demographic dimensions of differentiation. Thereafter, the section turns to congressional legislation that can be understood in retrospect as Progressive Era responses to correct the informational asymmetries resulting from the business model of trade secrecy and trademark publicity. The *Dr. Miles* case resolved questions of competition policy and property rights in these cultural, economic and legal circumstances.

A. *Highly Differentiated Markets*

Proprietary medicine brands such as DR. HARTMAN'S PERUNA, KICKAPOO INDIAN COUGH CURE, and LLOYD'S COCAINE TOOTHACHE DROPS were just as recognizable to consumers a century ago as their modern counterparts—VICKS NYQUIL, ROBITUSSIN, and BAYER aspirin—are today. The ante-bellum period saw a sharp rise in consumption of patent medicines that has been attributed to several factors, including distrust and short supply of doctors, self-medication as a reflection of American individualism, and thinly veiled alcohol and narcotic use in an era of increasing pressure for temperance.[11]

Production and consumption profiles reflected intense product differentiation in two dimensions: product flavors and ingredients; and consumer demographics, particularly along gender lines. As one historian observed:

> [T]he big-scale patent medicine maker ... blazed a merchandizing trail. He was the first American manufacturer to seek out a national market.... the first producer to help merchants who retailed his wares by going directly to consumers with a message about the product.... the first promoter to test out a multitude of psychological lures by which people might be enticed to buy his wares. While other advertising in the press was drab, his was vivid....[12]

The combinations and permutations of ingredients were endless. And so were the flavors. Some recipes used sarsaparilla or cherry, others swamp root or celery teas. They were sweetened with molasses, soured with vinegar, or braced with bitters. Whatever the mix, most patent medicines began with alcohol or an opiate, although LUNGARDIA started with turpentine and kerosene, while TUBERCULENE contained

---

[11] Cf. QUACKERY at 15–17 ("Temperance Drinkers"); TOADSTOOL at 165; Joseph Kennedy, *Drug Wars in Black and White*, 66 LAW AND CONTEMP. PROBS. 153, 160 (2003).

[12] JAMES YOUNG, THE MEDICAL MESSIAHS 21 (1974).

creosote.[13] DR. BATEMAN'S PECTORAL DROPS, a popular choice since the revolutionary war era, contained laudanum—both opium and alcohol.[14] Federal law did not ban most opiates until the second decade of the twentieth century, allowing BAYER and JAMES SOOTHING SYRUP, among others, to sell heroin as a pain killer over-the-counter.[15]

Production costs were low. One reliable estimate put the cost of a dollar bottle of PERUNA, the period's most popular patent medicine, at fifteen to twenty cents.[16] Because manufacturing costs were low and recipes readily available despite the obstacles of trade secrecy, the patent medicine market was enticing to would-be entrepreneurs. According to one observer, their number was as "formidable . . . as were the frogs of Egypt." A prominent trade journal listed more than 28,000 nostrums in 1905. The great majority of producers were small struggling firms. The large manufacturers, like their contemporaries in other sectors of intense competition, sought to consolidate their market positions. But their vehicle was not merger or outright cartel. It was the Proprietary Association, founded in 1881. A. R. Beardsley, treasurer of Dr. Miles Medical, was an active and influential leader of the Association, which protected the interests of large manufacturers by lobbying at both state and federal levels, drafting standard form contracts for newspaper advertising and for product distribution, and coordinating efforts to protect trademarks and maintain retail prices.[17]

In the crowded patent medicine business the most significant cost was marketing. Whatever the chosen ingredients or the favored channels of advertising, success in product differentiation depended upon establishing a distinctive trademark, which was "the fixed star in a universe of flux":

> The ownership of medicines might change again and again, and so might the formulas. The diseases for which medicines were adver-

---

[13] ANN ANDERSON, SNAKE OIL, HUSTLERS AND HAMBONES at 29 (2000). The raw petroleum contaminating someone's salt wells was sold as "The Most Wonderful Remedy Ever Discovered." TOADSTOOL at 171.

[14] Three popular patent medicines were found to have a range of alcoholic content: HOSTETTER'S STOMACH BITTERS (44%), HARTMAN'S PERUNA (28%), PINKHAM'S VEGETABLE COMPOUND (18%). Samuel Adams, "Peruna and the Bracers," COLLIER'S WEEKLY, Oct. 28, 1905, one in Adams' series of ten widely read and influential exposés, available at http://www.bottlebooks.com/Peruna_reprinted_from_collier.htm. TOADSTOOL at 129–30, 220–21; QUACKERY at 56, 85–87, 98–100, 110; MEDICINE SHOW at 167–69.

[15] Harrison Act of 1914, ch. 1, 38 Stat. 785 (1914).

[16] Adams, *supra* note 14.

[17] TOADSTOOL at 109, 238. See discussion *infra* Part II. Regarding trade associations, see PERITZ, COMPETITION POLICY at 62–63, 75–78.

tised might vary over time, and sometimes even names were altered. Trade-marks, however, . . . endured forever.[18]

No trademark was more recognizable than the figure of LYDIA PINKHAM, whose marketers were confident enough to make public the ingredients for her Vegetable Compound long before the Pure Food and Drug Act of 1906 required it. Nor was there a brand with stronger customer loyalty than PERUNA, though its steps were dogged by P–RU–NA, PERINA, ANUREP and other pretenders loosed by the period's weaker trademark protection. But few customers switched to PERUNA sound-alikes or to PINKHAM "generics," at least in part because the first movers did not sit on their laurels. The leading firms recognized, as did their rivals, that brand strength was brittle and depended upon continuing efforts to bolster distinctiveness. In the decades bracketing the turn of the twentieth century, PINKHAM's annual advertising budget exceeded one million dollars. And no patent medicine maker bought as much newspaper columnage as PERUNA.[19] On those efforts PERUNA for decades reigned as the most popular brand and the PINKHAM visage was as recognizable as those of Teddy Roosevelt and John D. Rockefeller.

While PERUNA gained a wide following largely through newspaper and circular advertising, PINKHAM early aimed its marketing at women and, it seems, at men who worried about them. One of its initial advertisements read:

> A FEARFUL TRAGEDY, a Clergyman of Stratford, Connecticut, KILLED BY HIS OWN WIFE, Insanity Brought on by 16 Years of Suffering with FEMALE COMPLAINTS THE CAUSE. Lydia E. Pinkham's Vegetable Compound, The Sure Cure for These Complaints, Would Have Prevented the Direful Deed.[20]

But it was not long before PINKHAM's advertising adopted a softer tone, most effectively in an informational pamphlet entitled *Guide for Women*, which described in plain language female physiology and disorders. It was distributed to drugstores and then door-to-door, first in Boston and in time nationwide. By 1901 the pamphlet had grown into a sixty-two page booklet. A successful national marketing program would subsequently include newspaper advertising but the foundation remained her *Guide*. For many years Pinkham's death remained secret and answers to questions from loyal readers continued to bear her name—until her demise was publicized in "The Great American Fraud,"

---

[18] TOADSTOOL at 167.

[19] TOADSTOOL at 104; QUACKERY at 96.

[20] QUACKERY at 60.

COLLIERS WEEKLY's series of articles about the patent medicine industry that helped stir Congress to pass the Pure Food & Drug Act.[21]

Many other patent remedies were also aimed at women. They were successful, some scholars have suggested, because they supplied alcohol or narcotics to women who were kept from frequenting taverns by an emerging middle-class code of proper conduct. One category of patent medicines was bitters, which effectively flavored large doses of alcohol. Another product category was catarrh, which typically contained cocaine. There are estimates that by 1885 over seventy per cent of those addicted to opiates were middle-class and upper-class white women who had purchased the drug legally.[22]

Of course there were special nostrums for "Secret Diseases of Men." In the Midwestern states, a large chain of medical institutes offered a "Wonderful Prolongation of the Attributes of Manhood." For those who could not afford the entire treatment, there was "Dr. Raphael's Cordial Invigorant" or from Armour & Company, the Chicago slaughter house and meat packer, there was "Orchis Extract," advertised as the "Greatest Known Treatment for Weak Men," and, from parts unknown, the exotic but hardly less subtle "Dr. Crane's Turkish Wafers For Men Only/Turkish Method/The Sultans/and Harems."[23]

Medical institutes were not limited to the diseases of men. In 1890, for example, Dr. Miles opened his "Grand Dispensary" in Elkhart, Indiana, to join a growing number of medical infirmaries offering free advice while selling patent remedies. Miles had begun publishing his free *Medical News* a few years earlier. Though the publication's subject matter was not limited to women's maladies, the era's most successful product for Dr. Miles became "Restorative Nervine" on the promise of relief from "hysteria, blues, melancholy." "Typical" advertisements in 1906 for the cure were aimed at its "large female following."[24]

Trademark familiarity and, with it, successful brand development were often built upon the mass distribution of gift publications that informed, advised or entertained—hand outs such as calendars, almanacs and books.[25] Repetition for brand recognition in mass markets,

---

[21] *Id.* at 62–65.

[22] TOADSTOOL at 221. At the time, the overall rate of addiction was almost five persons per thousand, compared with the more recent rate of about two persons per thousand. HUMBERTO FERNANDEZ, HEROIN 20 (1998).

[23] QUACKERY at 69–84; TOADSTOOL at 175, 200–01.

[24] WILLIAM CRAY, MILES: A CENTENNIAL HISTORY 7, 24 (1984). Congress would pass legislation to prohibit mail-order medical treatment in 1922. *Id.* at 33.

[25] Traveling medicine shows were long the advertising medium of choice in rural areas until Rural Free Delivery became an official postal service in 1902, bringing mail order

whether national or regional, required significant expenditures. James C. Ayer, for example, called attention to AYER CHERRY PECTORAL in his *American Almanac*, printed in his own publishing plant. By 1900, Ayer was spending an average of $120,000 annually to print 16 million copies in 21 languages.[26] Dr. Miles was another of the period's leading firms that published its own materials. In that time period, it spent in the neighborhood of $200,000 annually on advertising and printed 6.5 million almanacs in addition to its calendars and "Little Books" series.[27]

Patent medicine marketers also inundated urban markets with flyers and press advertisements. Some of the larger manufacturers, including Miles, reduced their advertising costs by using their presses to print local newspapers in exchange for advertising space. Indeed, Miles centennial biography would characterize the old firm as "more pressmen than chemists."[28]

Brand recognition was promoted through endless advertising—whether splashed across rural barns or crammed into the columns of metropolitan news dailies. Although roadway signage and building broadsides were condemned as despoiling the countryside, newspaper advertising most provoked critics and reformers. It was not just the volume and character of the ads. As newspapers and magazines came to depend on patent medicines for their primary source of advertising revenue, the advertisers began to assert their economic power over the press to make demands that corrupted editorial independence.

The most insidious example of corruption was the "red clause" in standard advertising contracts. The red-inked clause voided the contract "if any law is enacted by your State restricting or prohibiting the manufacture or sale of proprietary medicines." At a meeting of the Proprietary Association, a leading member confidently announced that the clause was "pretty near a sure thing." And he was right. They were effective.[29] When state legislatures considered bills inimical to the patent medicine industry, editors, upon receiving letters that merely referred to these "muzzle-clauses," would print articles or editorials supporting the industry. In fact, the Proprietary Association credited its many successes

---

catalogues to the countryside. Parcel post service was introduced in 1913, giving rise to mail order houses. Magaera Harris, "Postal Service," in A HISTORICAL GUIDE TO THE U.S. GOVERNMENT 469 (George Kurian, ed. 1998). The 1906 Sears catalogue included twenty pages of patent medicines. QUACKERY at 6.

[26] TOADSTOOL at 140–42.

[27] MARTHA PICKRELL, DR. MILES 48, 56 (1997); CRAY, *supra* note 26, at 19–21. The number of almanacs would reach 16.5 million in 1930. *Id.*

[28] *Id.*

[29] TOADSTOOL at 173, 205–25; QUACKERY at 1–41, 242–43; MEDICINE SHOW at 167–69.

in quashing reform legislation to aid from the American Newspaper Association as well as individual papers. Even more egregious were the many advertising contracts that brazenly took a direct approach with provisions calling for cancellation if any detrimental matter "is permitted to appear in the reading columns or elsewhere in the paper." Too often the result was either silence or praise of patent medicines.[30]

Few newspapers and magazines dared run articles critical of their benefactors, despite growing concern among physicians, including the American Medical Association, and agitation by progressive reformers. For example, only one newspaper, the *Springfield Republican*, even reported on debate in the Massachusetts legislature over a labeling bill. By the 1890s, the *Chicago Tribune, New York Post* and a only few others reported patent medicine abuses; even fewer refused to take their advertising. The *Ladies' Home Journal* in 1904 was the first popular periodical to take a step beyond occasional exposés and critiques when it launched a full-fledged campaign against the patent medicine industry. *Colliers Weekly* soon followed with ten articles by Samuel Hopkins Adams, entitled "The Great American Fraud." The series remains the gold standard for investigative journalism calling for legal reform. Its tone of social and moral disapproval is captured in a still-renowned cover cartoon entitled "Death's Laboratory." The cover displays a skull with patent medicine bottles for teeth and an inscription on the forehead that reads "The patent medicine trust / palatable poison for the poor."[31] Each article focused on specific companies and products, in total attacking well over two hundred firms and individuals. The article that provoked public outrage reported that the coroner in Cincinnati, Ohio, determined the death of a two-year old child was caused "by the poisonous effects of opium [in] a bottle of DR. BULL's COUGH SYRUP."[32] The pure food and drug act was still over the horizon, and the label did not list ingredients.

B. *Federal Legislation: Progressive Era Responses to Informational Asymmetries*

In the Progressive era, Congress and several states enacted legislation aimed at improving the lot of those whose health, safety or rights were imperiled by commercial practices in unregulated markets. Two federal statutes had particular impact on the patent medicine industry and, thus, influenced the commercial setting for the controversies mir-

---

[30] See Mark Sullivan, *The Patent Medicine Conspiracy Against Freedom of the Press*, in THE MUCKRAKERS 182–87, 189–91 (Arthur Weinberg et al., eds., 1961). Cf. Edwin Baker, *Advertising and a Democratic Press*, 140 U. PENN L.R. 2097 (1992).

[31] See sources cited *supra* note 35; http://www.fda.gov/cder/about/history/Gallery/galleryintro.htm (cartoon); http://www.mtn.org/quack/ephemera/oct7–01.htm (articles).

[32] QUACKERY at 23–24.

rored in the *Dr. Miles* case. They were the Pure Food & Drug Act and the Trademark Act.

1. The Pure Food & Drug Act of 1906

Public concern about the safety of food processing and patent medicines exploded into countrywide uproar with publication of *The Jungle*, Upton Sinclair's 1906 novel. The story was set in fictionalized "Packingtown" but was taken as an indictment of Chicago's meat packers, an indictment that quickly broadened into condemnation of the entire food processing industry. President Teddy Roosevelt was infuriated over the dismal failure of inspectors in the Department of Agriculture and bullied Congress to act quickly. Sinclair's book together with investigative journalism about the patent medicine industry mobilized public opinion to overcome the well-organized lobbying efforts of the Proprietary Association, the American Newspaper Association, and their food industry allies. After years of dilatory debate, a reluctant Congress swiftly passed the Pure Food & Drug Act before the New Year.[33]

Unlike the 1938 law that would establish the Food & Drug Administration, the 1906 statute did not regulate ingredients in patent medicines. Nor did it call for government inspection of drug products. Neither alcoholic nor narcotic content was prohibited.[34] The statute sought only to remedy what we today would call informational asymmetries—patent medicine's combination of secret ingredients and unsupported therapeutic claims. What the 1906 statute required was accurate labeling of ingredients, and therapeutic claims free of fraudulent and misleading statements. Of the two requirements, the obligation to list ingredients had the greater impact.[35]

---

[33] Pure Food and Drug Act of 1906, Pub. L. No. 59–384, 34 Stat. 768, 768–70 (1906); http://www.fda.gov/oc/history/resourceguide/background.html. The press strenuously opposed the statute. GEORGE SELDES, FREEDOM OF THE PRESS (1935); JAMES YOUNG, PURE FOOD (1989); TOADSTOOL at Ch. 14; Wallace Janssen, *Outline of the History of U.S. Drug Regulation and Labeling*, 36 FOOD DRUG COSM. L.J. 420, 421–422 (1981); OSCAR ANDERSON, THE HEALTH OF A NATION 1–16 (1958). In 1848, Congress banned "the Importation of Adulterated and Spurious Drugs and Medicines," 9 Stat. 237. Vincent Kleinfeld, *Legislative History of the Federal Food, Drug, and Cosmetic Act*, 50 FOOD & DRUG L.J. 65 at n. 2 (1995). My colleague Ed Purcell reminded me that Sinclair's novel was intended as an indictment of working conditions.

[34] The Smoking Opium Exclusion Act of 1909, 21 U.S.C. §§ 176–185 (1909) banned opium imported for smoking purposes. The Harrison Act of 1914, ch. 1, 38 Stat. 785 (1914), prohibited distribution of opiates, including morphine and heroin, and cocaine outside medical channels. http://www.druglibrary.org/schaffer/Library/studies/cu/cu8.html. FRANKLIN ZIMRING & GORDON HAWKINS, THE SEARCH FOR RATIONAL DRUG CONTROL 57 (1992); CAROLINE ACKER, CREATING THE AMERICAN JUNKIE 13 (2002).

[35] The Department of Agriculture, Division of Chemistry, was charged with enforcing the new law by seizing adulterated or misbranded articles on the market. John Swan,

Congress intended to rein in false or misleading therapeutic claims by prohibiting product misbranding. But a surprising Supreme Court decision would give a narrow reading to the statute's crucial language of "misbranded" that excluded false or misleading statements about the drug's curative effect. Although Congress quickly passed an amendment which expanded the definition, the Agriculture Department continued to lose enforcement actions because courts required proof of fraudulent intent.[36] In consequence, the statute had limited deterrent effect on unsupported therapeutic claims.[37]

The 1906 statute's requirement to list ingredients had greater impact because it turned unwanted light onto the substantial amounts of alcohol and narcotics in patent medicines.[38] The new labels informed not only the consuming public but also the Treasury Department, which collected excise taxes. Soon hundreds of patent medicines could be sold only as alcoholic beverages. Some of the most popular curatives, each for their own reasons, quickly lowered alcohol content. PINKHAM'S VEGE-TABLE COMPOUND did so to retain its reputation as a gentle restorative for women, and remained the leading brand in its large demographic niche. But PERUNA was not so fortunate. As one large distributor lamented, "Peruna is nowhere. We used to get a [train] carload, even two carloads a month. Now we hardly handle a carload in a year." After the new label revealed that it was nothing more than alcohol and flavored water, herbal content was added and alcohol level lowered to avoid the category of alcoholic beverage. Sales of the long-time market leader plummeted, apparently because less alcohol together with herbs having "slight laxative" qualities gave the new potion an unappealing flavor and undesired effect. PERUNA never recovered its popularity.[39]

For the most part, the ingredient labeling requirement weeded small and marginal firms out of the market, in consequence reducing the competition of mavericks and price discounters. Although the market became more concentrated, numerous firms remained and consumers

---

"Food and Drug Administration," in A HISTORICAL GUIDE TO THE U.S. GOVERNMENT at 248, 250 (George Kurian, ed., 1998).

[36] U.S. v. Johnson, 221 U. S. 488 (1911). The term "misbranded ... shall apply to ... any *statement*, design, or device regarding such article, or the ingredients or substances contained therein which shall be false *or* misleading ..." [emphasis added] The 1912 amendment would require statements to be false *and* misleading. Pub. L. No. 62–301, 37 Stat. 416, 21 U.S.C. § 10 (1912); Swan, *supra* note 35.

[37] MEDICINE SHOW at 169–70.

[38] Under separate authority, the Treasury Department was charged with collecting taxes on alcoholic beverages and, for some periods, on patent medicines. QUACKERY at 99–101, 162–63.

[39] QUACKERY at 101. TOADSTOOL at 125–30.

benefited from better market information. Moreover, a growing number of the larger firms had already begun to produce more "ethical" drugs— that is, they were already disclosing the ingredients in over-the-counter medicines and developing prescription drugs marketed directly to physicians.[40]

Passage of the food and drug law seemed to rein in the excesses of trade secrecy and product puffery and, with them, the dangerous extremes of competition in the patent medicine business that threatened health and safety of consumers. The statute did change producer behavior, although questions remained about the degree of benefit when weighing actual improvements in product information and in the products themselves against harm associated with increased market concentration. A second piece of legislation, the new trademark statute, had less obvious but nonetheless significant effect on product information and market concentration.

2. The Trademark Act of 1905[41]

Large consumer-product firms that developed national distribution networks together with strong brand identities had been lobbying Congress to pass a federal trademark law since the late 1860s. Until Congress passed the Trademark Act of 1881, brand protection rested entirely within the province of state law. On the surface, the 1881 legislation seemed to change little because Congress enacted a narrowly written statute that applied only to international commerce. Thus patent medicine marketing and the industry dynamics of product differentiation had to make do, for the most part, with state common law protections. Still, the 1881 statute did provide for federal registration and, with it, a Trademark Office available for settling domestic priority disputes between rival claimants. And there was even a bit more to the story: Because federal judges were still breathing the air of *Swift v. Tyson*, the common law doctrines of trademark and trade-name protection rested comfortably in the interstices of the new federal registration scheme.[42]

---

[40] *Id*. at 206–07, 248–49. "Ethical" drug manufacturers voluntarily listed their ingredients. Direct marketing to physicians raised its own problems, whether the courting of physicians with financial incentives, their dependency on drug company literature for information or their reliance on recommendations of salesmen in the face of overwhelming amounts of information or inadequate training. Moreover, many medical journals, including the AMA Journal, continued to accept their advertising. *Id*. at 206–210; QUACKERY at 27, 207.

[41] Act of Feb. 20, 1905, 33 Stat. 724, 15 U.S.C. §§ 81–134 (1905).

[42] *See, e.g.*, L.E. Daniels, *The U.S. Trade–Mark Association*, 33 TRADE MARK REP. 3 (1943); Robert Merges, *One Hundred Years of Solicitude*, 1900–2000, 88 CAL. L. REV. 2187 (2000). PERITZ, COMPETITION POLICY at 29; Swift v. Tyson, 41 U.S. (19 Pet.) 1 (1842). Congress was timid because the Supreme Court had struck down its first trademark statute as unconstitutionally founded on the Progress Clause, U.S. Const'n, Art. I, sec. 8, par. 8.

Moreover, national registration saved trademark owners the time and expense of successive state registrations. In this respect, federal registration was particularly valuable to leading patent medicine makers because it gave constructive notice to all would-be competitors that nationwide trademark rights were claimed. In practical effect, federal registration changed the fundamental doctrine of state common law that trademark protection required commercial use in a particular locale. With the national system, registration plus use in any locale was enough for national exclusivity. Once again, the new federal system was particularly valuable to leading firms because registration itself extended their brands into all states and locales.[43]

The 1905 statute altered the landscape of trademark protection in a second significant respect: It effectively lowered the owner's burden of proving trademark infringement. Under the prevailing common law standard, the owner had to prove not only that the registered and accused marks were virtually identical but also that the infringement was intentional. In place of these stringent elements, the new statute merely required the owner to show that buyers were likely to confuse the two marks.[44] At the time, the use of copycat marks was a common practice in the patent medicine industry. The new law would prohibit the practice by allowing trademark owners to enjoin a broader array of similar marks. Both changes—the nationalization of mark effectiveness and the broader notion of mark similarity—provided conditions for increased concentration in the patent medicine industry by strengthening the exclusionary power of established trademarks. But a growing group of mavericks, the discount drug wholesalers and retailers, were raising the temperature of price competition.

II. *THE DR. MILES MEDICAL CASE*: "THE CUT–RATE BUSINESS" CHALLENGES "THE DIRECT CONTRACT PLAN"

The litigants were fierce commercial adversaries. While Dr. Miles employed strategies to maintain prices and differentiate its brand in the

---

Trade–Mark Cases, 100 U.S. 82 (1879). Subsequent legislation was enacted under the Commerce Clause.

[43] United Drug Co. v. Theodore Rectanus Co., 248 U.S. 90 (1918) (constructive notice). Prior local trademarks remained effective but could not expand into other locales. See generally MERGES ET AL., INTELLECTUAL PROPERTY IN THE NEW TECHNOLOGICAL AGE 628–31 (2004).

[44] The statutory burden of proof tracked the state common law action for unfair competition, which was used to good effect by Nabisco, Coca Cola, and other leaders in the emerging national markets for consumer goods. See, e.g., National Biscuit Co. v. Baker, 95 F. 135 (C.C.N.Y. 1899) ("Iwanta" and "Uneeda" biscuits); Moxie Nerve Food Co. v. Beach, 33 F. 248 (C.C. Mass. 1888) ("Noxie" and "Moxie"); ALFRED CHANDLER, JR., SCALE AND SCOPE 63–65, 168–70 (1990); MERGES, *supra* note 42, at 2205–10.

densely populated market for proprietary medicines, Park & Sons fought to expand its discount wholesaling business. A producer and wholesaler since the 1840s, Park become a leader in the "cut-rate business" that employed the increasingly efficient networks for distributing patent medicines.[45] At the same time, Miles, in concert with other large patent medicine makers, sought to stem the growth of discounters by adopting standard form contracts to control product distribution and pricing, and by refusing to deal with discounters. The procession of cases seeking to enforce the form contract and its resale price maintenance provision evidences widespread if not universal use orchestrated by the Proprietary Association, which also organized the large manufacturers' standard advertising contract. Miles and Park were courtroom veterans well-versed in the era's legal battles over mass distribution and retailing. It was inevitable that their paths would cross and more than coincidence that their rivalry would lead to the Supreme Court.

A. The Doctrinal Framework: Property Rights and Restraints of Trade

The case arose in the early years of the Sherman Act, a time when the relationship between the statute and the preceding common law of trade restraints was still in flux. On the one hand, Supreme Court decisions such as *Trans–Missouri Freight Association* (1897) and *Northern Securities* (1905) had announced that the statute was not to be interpreted as a codification of the common law. On the other, the Supreme Court in *Addyston Pipe* (1899) had approved the approach taken in Judge William Howard Taft's opinion below, which portrayed common law doctrine as consistent with the Anti–Trust Act. Taft had written his influential opinion for the Sixth Circuit, the site for the two leading patent medicine cases, including *Dr. Miles*, although Taft would not author those opinions. But federal judges, embedded in the common law mind-set of *Swift v. Tyson,* found Taft's approach attractive because it permitted them to address trade restraint claims in corresponding terms of the statute and the common law. The section places *Dr. Miles* in this jurisprudential context by examining the parties' participation in prior litigation involving the industry-wide "direct contract plan of marketing proprietary preparations."[46] With that framework set in place, the section turns to the *Dr. Miles* case.

1. Standard form contracts and Dr. Miles

Miles would file suit against Park with a confidence borne of success in three prior cases that upheld the contract plan for maintaining resale

---

[45] See *Fowle v. Park*, 131 U.S. 88 (1889).

[46] Dr. Miles Medical Co. v. Platt, 142 F. 606, 607 (N.D. Ill. 1906) ("direct contract plan"). U.S. v. Trans–Missouri Freight Association, 166 U.S. 290 (1897); Northern Securities Co. v. U.S., 193 U.S. 197 (1904); Addyston Pipe & Steel Co. v. U.S., 175 U.S. 211 (1899), *aff'g* 85 Fed. 271 (6th Cir. 1898).

prices. The triplets offer valuable insights into both industry practices and the era's competition policy. In the first case, Miles sued a discounter to enforce the "direct contract plan," describing itself as a company that

> ... manufactures proprietary medicines ... under formulas which are secret, and ... under trade-names, and ... possesses, as far as it legally may, an exclusive monopoly. The company has adopted an elaborate system to control the prices, at wholesale and retail, of its articles, and insure sales of its articles at uniform prices.[47]

By "exclusive monopoly," Miles was asserting its trade secrets and trade-names as the ground for immunizing its contract system for setting resale prices from the common law of trade restraints. Its "elaborate system" was portrayed as the contractual exercise of a lawful monopoly embodied in its intellectual property rights. The court agreed and issued a permanent injunction.[48]

In the two subsequent cases, Miles would make the same argument with the same result. The first consolidated three suits against Platt, a retail druggist who discounted not only Miles patent medicines but also those of Hartman's PERUNA, the largest selling patent medicine, and those produced by members of World's Dispensary Medical Association, a national trade association. All three plaintiffs sought injunctions to enforce "what is known as the direct contract plan of marketing proprietary preparations."[49] They alleged that Platt tortiously "caused complainant's ... agents to violate their contracts and supply the goods to him."[50] Platt asserted the antitrust defense that the plaintiffs "conspired ... with a number of druggists to ... fix and maintain an exhorbitant [sic] and arbitrary price for all kinds of medicines ... and [to] restrict ... competition in the sale thereof, with intent thereby to compel the public to pay a higher price ..."[51]

The court rejected Platt's antitrust defense, citing the common law doctrine that "trade secrets ... owners ... may sell them on such terms as they please, may withhold them from one person while selling to

---

[47] Miles Medical Co. v. Goldthwaite, 133 F. 794, 795 (C.C.D. Mass. 1904).

[48] *Id.* On the dephysicalization of property, see PERITZ, COMPETITION POLICY 69–72; MORTON HORWITZ, THE TRANSFORMATION OF AMERICAN LAW 145–68 (1992); Kenneth Vandevelde, *The New Property of the Nineteenth Century*, 29 BUFF. L. REV. 325 1980; John Nockelby, *Tortious Interference with Contractual Relations in the Nineteenth Century*, 93 HARV. L. REV. 1510 (1980).

[49] Miles Medical Co. v. Platt, World's Dispensary Medical Ass'n v. Same, Hartman v. Same, 142 F. 606 (N.D. Ill. 1906).

[50] *Id.* at 607.

[51] *Id.* at 608.

others, and may fix any price in their sole and exclusive discretion."[52]
The underlying policy was protection of "the property right ... in the
secret process.... The right of a patentee, owner of a copyright, or
owner of a secret process is merely the right of exclusion or debarment."
The resale price maintenance provision was a "lawful and proper"
exercise of *property* rights denominated "exclusive monopolies."[53] The
contract question of trade restraints was "collateral." It was collateral
because Miles and the others did "not in any way claim through or
under the unlawful combination in this action."[54]

Thus the court drew a formal distinction between common law
contract and property rights, and thus between restraints of trade and
restraints on alienation, although both restrained competition. The court
treated Platt's defense as turning on whether the plaintiffs' intellectual
property rights fell into the recognized category of "exclusive monopoly," which would permit them to impose downstream restraints on
alienation that would run with the goods. No contractual restraints were
necessary and so the common law contracts doctrines of trade restraints
would not come into play. Argument over the relationship between these
two threads of common law competition policy would re-appear in
subsequent cases involving the industry-wide contract system.

In the third case, Miles sued Jaynes Drug Company, again seeking
an injunction to enforce its contract system.[55] Here, the court did take up
the contract issue of whether the resale price provision should be
prohibited as a restraint of trade. The outcome was no different. The
court moved without hesitation from the doctrine that IP rights permitted restraints on alienation of property, to the tenet that contract
provisions exercising those IP rights were permitted restraints of trade:

> Contracts ... concerning articles made under trade secrets, the
> same as similar contracts concerning articles made under a patent
> or a copyright, are outside the rule of restraint of trade, whether at
> common law or under the federal statute.[56]

The *Jaynes* court was unconcerned that "[t]hese contracts are in force
between [Miles] and nearly all the wholesale druggists of the country
and over 40,000 retail druggists." In effect, the decision crushed price
competition in the industry by permitting Miles and its rivals to rely on
"the direct contract plan" to restrain the "knavery" of price discounters.

---

[52] *Id*. at 609.

[53] *Id*. at 610–11.

[54] *Id*.

[55] Dr. Miles Medical Co. v. Jaynes Drug Co., 149 F. 838 (C.C.D. Mass. 1906) (Colt, J.).

[56] *Id*. at 841–42.

2. Standard form contracts and John D. Park & Sons

Park, too, was a veteran of the industry's contract wars. Before its court date with Miles, the discounting wholesaler was party to two major cases that arose from its attempts to sidestep the two complementary standard contracts used in patent medicine markets. In the first, Park sued the National Wholesale Druggists' Association (NWDA) in the New York courts, seeking to enjoin enforcement of the wholesalers' standard contract. In the other, Samuel Hartman sued Park in federal court, asking for an injunction against the discounter's continuing attempts to obtain PERUNA, the industry leader, outside the price-setting provisions in the manufacturers' "system of contracts." Unlike the uniformly narrow view of competition policy expressed in the Dr. Miles cases discussed above, these reflected sharply different positions in the competition policy debate over nationwide standard contracts.

a. The *NWDA* case

In 1896, Park filed suit against the NWDA, which was "formed by the co-operation of [125] wholesale druggists and manufacturers of proprietary medicines for mutual benefit and protection." Manufacturers, who were non-voting members of the association, refused to do business with Park because he did not abide by the contract's pricing provisions. Rather, Park sought to buy at a discount and then sell to retailers in the "cut-rate business." The New York state court initially issued a preliminary injunction[57] on the rationale that the contracts likely were restraints of trade but later withdrew it on a property rights rationale:

> The sacred right of the toiler to earn the means of subsistence . . . always will be recognized. . . . [I]nventive skill, even though applied to medicinal compounds, may yet have protection from outlawry if the inventor reasonably uses his property rights. . . . He may join with others in similar need . . .[58]

After seven years of grinding litigation, the Court of Appeals of New York finally affirmed dismissal of Park's claims. The state's highest court split 4–3 over the imperatives of competition policy and the effect of the standard sales contract on consumers. The majority concluded that the NWDA contract did "not operate against the rights of the general public . . . because wholesale dealers have not secured the authority to . . . restrict either the price or the quantity sold." The concurring judge, the swing vote in this case, emphasized that the contract "attempts no restraint whatever upon the manufacturer in

---

[57] Park & Sons Co. v. NWDA, 50 N.Y.S. 1064 (S.Ct., N.Y.Cnty., 1896) (page numbers not given for lower court opinions because they do not appear in the Westlaw documents).

[58] Park, 64 N.Y.S. 276, 277–78 (S.Ct., N.Y. Cnty., N.Y. 1900).

making prices," the wholesalers' only interest being uniform prices. The dissenting faction sharply disagreed, calling the majority's view "a plain perversion of the complaint to say that it states a claim or cause of action involving merely the right of a manufacturer to sell his goods to whom he will."[59]

The majority configured the contours of its competition policy by aligning the interests of association members and consumers against those of price discounters. The opinion began by adopting the trial court's view that "inventiveness" justified the manufacturers' control over "goods ... covered by patent rights and trademarks, which give the proprietors the exclusive right of specifying prices ... and ... the right also to require dealers to maintain the prices specified." The majority then characterized consumer interests in terms, surprising to modern readers, of "a uniform price in all sections of the country." And it was patent medicine manufacturers' exercise of intellectual property rights that authorized the NWDA as intermediary to satisfy that preference. In the majority's view, "[w]hile public policy demands a healthy competition, it abhors favoritism, secret rebates, and unfair dealing, and commends the conduct of business in such a way as to serve all consumers alike."[60] The danger of unhealthy competition lay in the knavery of discounters like Park, who

> could command large capital, and by reason of this they could purchase proprietary goods in larger quantities and more cheaply than the other wholesale and jobbing druggists.... [T]hus they are enabled to undersell and drive out of business the small merchants in their vicinity.[61]

Apparently, the court dressed all large firms, including discounting wholesalers, in the populist rhetoric of monopoly. It saw them all as villains engaged in the commercial buccaneering associated with the era's "Robber Barons"—Andrew Carnegie in steel, Cornelius Vanderbilt in railroads and, of course, John D. Rockefeller and his Standard Oil Trust.

The opinion reflects a tension in the era's twin rhetorics of monopoly. On the one hand, courts adopted the technical common-law doctrine of legal or exclusive monopoly to permit contracts that exercised intellectual property rights to restrain downstream alienation of goods, although clearly anticompetitive. On the other hand, a populist discourse of monopoly gave voice to widespread concerns about the power of large

---

[59] 175 N.Y. 1, 19, 22, 31 (N.Y. 1903).

[60] *Id.* at 9–11. It is unclear whether the court recognized that the patent medicines were not actually patented.

[61] *Id.*

firms to corrupt politics and to harm both consumers and the small independent firms that were seen as the country's economic and political backbone. The New York court's populist rhetoric did not, however, invite inquiry into whether lower wholesale prices were attributable to favoritism and secret rebates or to quantity discounts and other legitimate efficiencies. It was enough that Park was seen as "command[ing] large capital."

In this view, consumers benefited because the NWDA enabled the "little storekeeper" to compete on equal footing with the "great merchants." But this approach did not take account of the market reality that the NWDA contract worked hand-in-glove with the manufacturers' own contract system, which "fix[ed] . . . a selling price by the druggists." Caught in this economic web of restraints, consumers would uniformly pay more than the discount prices Park's druggists wanted to charge. But lowering prices was less important to the court than remedying the unhealthy competition associated with the populist vision of monopoly's political and economic power to corrupt and control. Still, Park was not a large firm like Standard Oil or American Tobacco, not even in comparison to manufacturers such as Miles and Hartman. Moreover, political and economic power could reside in trade associations of small firms as well as large firms: Indeed, the NWDA who sold to "little storekeepers" actually "represented 90 per cent. of the wholesale jobbing trade of the United States."[62]

At bottom, the NWDA, "little storekeepers" and patent medicine manufacturers shared two economic interests. As the concurring opinion put it, they were all concerned, first, about keeping large-volume discount wholesalers like Park from introducing price competition and, second, about immunizing full-price wholesalers from the pressures of large-volume discount retailers.[63] In short, they all wanted to protect their profits from price competition. And so, while the NWDA enforced price uniformity, the manufacturers set the price levels. The two standard contracts worked in tandem to restrain price competition and protect not only "little storekeepers" but also branded manufacturers and the network of distributors that linked them.

The New York court majority confined its analysis to the NWDA wholesalers contract directly at issue in the case. In passing, however, it recognized both the manufacturers' power to set prices and its broader implications:

---

[62] *Id.* at 14, 21. Such market relations currently spur debate over the impact of WALMART stores.

[63] *Id.* at 15–16.

> This plan ... is not one confined to the sale of proprietary medi-
> cines, but is one that has been adopted by many manufacturers of
> merchandise and other goods where manufacturers have established
> a trade-mark, and have gained a reputation which they wish to
> maintain throughout the country ... They have consequently estab-
> lished prices at which their goods shall be sold to the consumer, and
> require all wholesale and retail dealers to supply the consumer at
> the price list established. The decision, therefore, reached herein,
> may largely affect the plan of conducting business in other articles
> of commerce.[64]

The broader implication, largely unrecognized in modern accounts of the
era, was that the industry standard contract was a widespread method
for restraining trade, no less effective than industry consolidation by
merger and cartel.

Although the pleadings also confined the New York court's dissenters to the NWDA wholesale contract, that was enough for them to
conclude that

> ... the association was organized ... for the purpose of monopoliz-
> ing and controlling the business of wholesale druggists and jobbers
> in the sale of proprietary articles or patent medicines in the entire
> United States, [and] to prevent competition therein.[65]

After pointing to the long line of cases that prohibited such restraints of
trade, the dissenting faction insisted that the evidence offered no basis
for special dispensation from the common law, even if patent medicines
were actually patented, because the patent rights were owned not by the
wholesalers but the manufacturers.[66]

Although New York's high court was unanimous in seeing the broad
anticompetitive effects of the two standard contracts' combined impact,
the case produced two sharply different views of the commercial logic
driving the industry—the majority's intellectual property logic of manufacturers rightfully exploiting the fruits of their "inventiveness" and, in
the process, benefiting citizens, consumers and small business; and the
dissenters' competition logic of wholesalers and distributors, in concert
with manufacturers, wrongfully restraining trade to the detriment of
consumers.

b.   The *Hartman* case

In litigation that would directly influence the *Dr. Miles* case, Dr.
Samuel Hartman, the leading patent medicine maker, sued Park to stop

---

[64] *Id.* at 8.

[65] *Id.* at 31.

[66] *Id.* at 44.

it from acquiring PERUNA outside the price restraints of the standard sales contract. Park's answer reprised its antitrust challenge to the nationwide system of contracts.

The lower court rejected Park's antitrust challenge and issued a preliminary injunction. But the appeals court would accept the antitrust defense, find the contract system unenforceable, and dissolve the injunction. This case, like the subsequent *Dr. Miles* litigation, passed through the Sixth Circuit. Both opinions were written by Circuit Judge Lurton,[67] who would write in *Dr. Miles* that "[t]he acts and conduct against which complainant seeks relief are identically the conduct complained of in the Hartman Case, and the opinion in that case may be referred to for a more detailed statement of the case."[68]

Hartman sought to enjoin Park from tortious interference with the system of contracts, alleging that Park obtained

> ... 'Peruna the Great Tonic' ... from complainant's wholesalers and retailers by ... dishonest methods and persuading them to break their contracts with him, and [sold] same to retailers operating 'cut rate drug stores' at less than the wholesale prices fixed by him, who in turn sell to consumers at less than the retail prices so fixed.[69]

Park responded that the antitrust laws prohibited Hartman from setting the resale prices of patent medicines that were sold outright. The argument's foundation was the established common law tenet that once ownership of goods passed to the buyer, control over the goods passed with it. This argument was asserted in several cases discussed above but without success because the courts recognized an exception for contracts that exercised intellectual property rights in the goods.[70] In sum, Park's

---

[67] Hartman v. Park & Sons, 145 F. 358 (C.C.E.D. Ky 1906), overruled,153 Fed. 24 (6th Cir. 1907), cert. dismissed on petition of counsel, 212 U.S. 588 (1908). See Hill Co. v. Gray & Worcester, 127 N.W. 803, 807 (Mich. 1910) (describing dismissal requested by Hartman's counsel). Lurton was soon appointed to the Supreme Court and promptly recused himself from participating in *Dr. Miles*.

[68] *Miles*, 164 Fed. 803, 804 (6th Cir. 1908).

[69] *Id.* at 359.

[70] But the very core of the property-based exception to free trade was controversial. The Supreme Court earlier showed reluctance in permitting restraints to run with patented goods. Keeler v. Standard Folding–Bed Co., 157 U.S. 659 (1895). Moreover, the Court would soon hold that copyright ownership itself did not allow the seller to "qualify the title of a future purchaser." That is, restraints on alienation would not run with copyrighted goods. Bobbs–Merrill Co. v. Straus, 210 U.S. 339, 351 (1908). Finally, the Court would conclude that notice of restraints affixed to patented goods exceeded the statutory grant of legal monopoly. Motion Picture Patents Co. v. Universal Film Mnfg. Co., 243 U.S. 502 (1917). These limits on restraints on alienation are known as the first-sale or exhaustion doctrine and remain part of modern patent and copyright law.

claim was simply that, without an intellectual property exception, the standard contract's resale price provision stood on its own as an illegal restraint of trade.

Park advanced the argument in two stages. First, he asserted that the standard contract was an illegal trade restraint unless a patent or copyright brought the special exception into play; here, PERUNA enjoyed only trade secret protection. Judge Cochran rejected Park's argument: "As applied to things made under a secret process, it lacks this favoring circumstance. But it would be illogical to argue therefrom that so applied it was unlawful."[71] In short, falling outside the patent and copyright exception made the Hartman contracts open to scrutiny but not unreasonable restraints of trade *per se*.

Park moved to the second stage of argument—that the contract system, even if not categorically illegal, "contravenes the common-law rule invalidating contracts in restraint of trade." For guidance in determining whether the Hartman contracts were unreasonable restraints, the court turned to Judge Taft's opinion for the Sixth Circuit in *Addyston Pipe* (1898), an opinion whose harmonization of common law and Sherman Act doctrines had been approved by the Supreme Court.[72] Taft had developed the common-law distinction between direct and ancillary restraints, a distinction that depended on the contract's main purpose. If the main purpose was to restrain trade by, for example, fixing prices, then the restraint was deemed direct and thus *per se* illegal. But if the contractual restraint was ancillary to a lawful purpose, then the court would determine whether the particular restraint was reasonable in the circumstances.

Cochran turned first to prior cases and determined that "the whole trend of authority is favorable to the validity of the system." Then applying Judge Taft's approach, the judge concluded that the resale price provision, like a seller's covenant not to compete in the sale of a business, was "ancillary or collateral to the main purpose of a lawful contract, to wit, a sale of the medicine. . . . The sweeping principle which has taken form in Judge Taft's [analysis] . . . upholds it."[73] The contract system was a permissible restraint of trade.

Hartman's victory, however, was short-lived. On appeal, Judge Lurton wrote for the Sixth Circuit:

---

[71] 145 Fed. at 359–70. Chadwick v. Covell, 151 Mass. 190, 191 (1890) (Holmes, J.).

[72] *Addyston Pipe*, note 53, *supra*, 145 Fed. at 387.

[73] *Id.* at 381–83. Although *Addyston Pipe* involved what current readers call horizontal restraints, the modern distinction between vertical and horizontal was not yet part of competition policy, whose foundation of classical economics derived from freedom of contract, regardless of the parties' relationship.

> Even if the lower court is right in characterizing the restraint as
> ancillary to a contract for sale, the restraint is unreasonable....
> The single covenant might in no way affect the public interest, when
> a large number might. The plain effect of the 'system of contracts,'
> is ... first, to destroy all competition between jobbers or wholesale
> dealers in selling complainant's preparations.... Next, all competi-
> tion between retailers is destroyed....[74]

Hartman's industry-wide contract system had broad anticompetitive
effects that rendered it an unreasonable restraint of trade. Moreover,
Lurton rejected the lower court's view that patent protection holds no
special purchase in the analysis of trade restraints. His approach applied
the technical common-law doctrine of "legal monopoly," which is sharply
different from the modern conception of economic monopoly: "So far as
the machine was the subject of patent its use was lawfully a monopoly,
and therefore no contract relating to it could be condemned as creating a
monopoly."[75] That is, a patent was a legal monopoly in the technical
sense that it granted the holder an immunity from common law prohibition of contracts in restraint of trade. But the dispensation derived from
trade secrecy was more limited:

> To say that the owner of this secret need not make the medi-
> cine, nor sell it when made, unless it suits his convenience, is true.
> But the same thing may be said of the man who grows potatoes. He
> need not grow them, and need not sell them when grown. But, if
> something be conceded in favor of an article which no one can
> produce except the owner of the formula over one which any one can
> produce, what shall it be? There is no statute creating a lawful
> monopoly such as seems to take articles made thereunder without
> the rule against illegal restraint.... None of the reasons which
> apply to patented articles, copyrighted productions, or to restricted
> disclosure of the secret formula itself apply to the product of the
> formula.[76]

Federal legislation granted an immunity from liability for restraints of
trade to contracts for the sale of patented and copyrighted goods. But
where the goods were protected only by trade secrecy, the dispensation
was limited to the secret information. Goods produced by secret formula
were treated no differently than potatoes. The court of appeals concluded
that Hartman's system of contracts was an unreasonable restraint.[77] The
opinion explained:

---

[74] *Hartman*, 153 Fed. 24, 41–42 (6th Cir. 1906).

[75] *Id.* at 40.

[76] *Id.* at 33.

[77] *Id.* at 46.

[Hartman's counsel] averred that the "system" had and will accomplish the suppression of "the competition plan" and "greatly benefit your orator in his business by increasing the sales of and demand for his remedies." . . . [But] the whole economic system which has made our civilization is founded upon the theory that competition is desirable, and the common-law rules against restraints of trade rest upon that foundation.[78]

Counsel for Hartman petitioned the Supreme Court but subsequently asked for dismissal because the company stopped using the sales contract at issue in the case. It switched to a consignment contract, which the federal courts were already scrutinizing in the *Dr. Miles* litigation. Hartman and others in the patent medicine industry would wait for the federal courts to rule on their new standard consignment contracts.

Why did the patent medicine manufacturers switch to consignment? Miles and the others would adapt the old consignment form, a centuries-old means of retaining a security interest in goods sold on credit, for the new purpose of allowing the manufacturer to retain title in the goods and thereby hold on to property rights that re-defined resale price maintenance as nothing more than setting prices for *its* goods. The consignment form was, they hoped, a stroke of legal ingenuity that would immunize resale price maintenance from the twin common law strands of competition policy: The property doctrine against restraints on alienation would not apply because the retention of ownership meant no goods would be alienated until consumer sales. Moreover, retention of title would avoid the contracts doctrine of trade restraints because the resale price restraint would run with the goods. Finally, ownership in the goods themselves would provide a more stable legal foundation than the shifting boundaries of "legal monopoly" associated with intellectual property rights. It would be the Supreme Court that ultimately decided the success of the consignment strategy.

B.   Dr. Miles Medical v. John D. Park & Sons in the Lower Courts

In 1908, Dr. Miles Medical filed the fourth in a series of tort actions for malicious interference with its contract plan, this one against John D. Park, the discount drug wholesaler. Park replied by demurrer, which was summarily sustained. Writing for the Sixth Circuit Court of Appeals, Judge Lurton affirmed dismissal. Just as he had in Hartman's case against Park, Lurton struck down the standard contract system as an unreasonable restraint of trade—even though the new contract was a consignment.[79] Revision from sale to consignment made no difference because, in the court's view,

---

[78] *Id.* at 44.

[79] 164 F. 803, 807 (6th Cir. 1908).

> The scheme is one to enhance or maintain prices by eliminating all possibility of competing rates between either jobbers or retailers, and is quite as effectual in its results as if the contract with the jobber was plainly one of sale.[80]

By Judge Taft's lights in *Addyston Pipe*, the consignment was not an ancillary restraint, but a direct one whose main purpose remained price fixing and whose effects were equally anticompetitive. The new contract was unreasonable *per se*.

Perhaps recognizing the appeal of the consignment strategy's property logic, Judge Lurton proceeded to evaluate the consignment on its own terms and found that it was ill-scrivened: Miles' contract had "too many features which seem inconsistent with a mere agency or commission agreement. All the responsibility of an owner seems cast upon the so-called 'consignee.'" Despite the best lawyerly intentions, the new form remained a sales contract. Still, the opinion sent a clear message to Miles as well as Hartman and the other patent medicine producers that consignments, even if properly drafted, would not receive special treatment under the antitrust laws.[81]

> This case must, after all, turn upon whether there is such identity of character between the statutory monopoly of articles made under a valid patent or copyright and articles made according to some private formula as to exempt them from the principles which apply to contracts which tend to create a monopoly or restrain trade when the subject is an article not made under a patent or copyright or secret formula.[82]

Were the policies underlying common-law property rights, Judge Lurton asked, close enough to those underlying statutory copyright and patent to treat them as "legal monopolies" and, thus, as special exceptions to the dictates of competition policy? The answer would be No. Lurton had already concluded that the ownership rights retained under consignment contracts did not stand up to such scrutiny. Turning to trade secrecy, he reiterated the view expressed in *Hartman* that trade secrets were no more exceptional than potatoes.[83] The question was answered: Common-law property rights did not merit special treatment under the antitrust laws.

---

[80] *Id.* at 804. Justice Lewis Powell would adopt this rationale in Continental TV, Inc. v. GTE Sylvania Inc., 433 U.S. 36 (1977).

[81] *Id.*

[82] *Id.* at 805.

[83] *Id.*

The opinion affirmed the trial court's refusal to enjoin Park from purchasing and reselling at discounted prices DR. MILES 'RESTORA-TIVE NERVINE' and other potions. The new system of consignment contracts was a direct restraint of trade that eliminated competition among wholesalers and among retailers and, thus, was a *per se* violation of the antitrust laws. But Miles would carry the question to the Supreme Court.

C. Dr. Miles in the Supreme Court

Writing for the Court, Justice Charles Evans Hughes noted Miles' statement that the contract plan was adopted by "over four hundred jobbers and wholesalers and twenty-five thousand retail dealers in proprietary medicines in the United States."[84] Hughes observed that the contract system was "carefully devised . . . to maintain certain prices fixed by it for all the sales of its products, both at wholesale and retail." "The principal question," he announced, "was the validity of the restrictive agreements."[85] The Court would invalidate the new contract following the approach taken by Judge Lurton in the case below and in the *Hartman* case, but with one crucial difference: The Court would not declare consignments categorically illegal restraints of trade.

Justice Hughes resolved the issue by scrutinizing the document and finding that the language in Miles' pleadings as well as in the contract betrayed it as a sale rather than a consignment. Miles offered two well-trod grounds for its validity under the common law as well as the Sherman Act. The first was trade secrecy and its claimed equivalence to letters patent as a special exception to the competition policy embodied in restraints of trade doctrine. The Court rejected the analogy, as did Judge Lurton below, on the rationale that patents are exclusionary rights that Congress rewarded special treatment in exchange "for the advantages derived by the public for the exertions of the individual." Trade secrecy was not a congressional grant: "The complainant has no statutory grant." Nor did trade secrecy offer comparable public benefits of encouraging innovation. There was no special property-based exception to the "public interest in maintaining freedom of trade with respect to future sales." The Court carried forward the common law policy favoring free trade that limited restrictions that run with real property or chattels after sale.[86] "A general restraint on alienation is ordinarily invalid" because "it is against trade and traffic and bargaining and contracting." Without a "legal monopoly" of patent and copyright, there

---

[84] 220 U.S. 373, 374–5, 381 (1911).

[85] *Id.* at 382.

[86] Cf. Zechariah Chafee, Equitable Servitudes on Chattels, 41 Harv. L. Rev. 945 (1928).

was no special property right that trumped competition policy as the default rule for commercial markets.[87]

Miles' second argument shifted ground from the property doctrine against restraints on alienation to the contract doctrine that the "liberty of the producer [to] make and sell, or not, as he chooses" should not be limited because the new standard form, even if treated as a contract for sale, was not an unreasonable restraint of trade. Citing a string of sources from the English common law to *Addyston Pipe*, Justice Hughes invalidated the resale price restraint because it was not ancillary to "a sale of good will, or of an interest in a business, or of a grant of a right to use a process of manufacture." Its main purpose was "to prevent competition among those who trade in" the patent medicines. "[T]he restrictions ... were invalid both at common law and under the act of Congress.... We think that [Judge Lurton] was right"[88] because

> ... the public interest is still the first consideration.... [T]he restraint ... must be found reasonable both with respect to the public and to the parties.... [T]he public is entitled to whatever advantage may be derived from competition in the subsequent traffic.[89]

But unlike Lurton's opinion, the Court maintained a studied silence toward the question of whether a valid consignment contract would provide a safe harbor from antitrust liability. Instead, Justice Hughes found contract provisions, loopholes, that permitted outright sales to discounters like Park. The implication was that the property right retained in a proper consignment could have shielded the price restraints from antitrust scrutiny.[90]

Justice Holmes dissented, opining that the Court majority "greatly exaggerate the importance to the public of competition in the production and distribution of an article ... as fixing a fair price." There were other criticisms along the way that led him to characterize Park and his ilk as "knaves [who] cut reasonable prices for some ulterior motive of their own."[91] But in both practical and jurisprudential terms, what was most salient was Holmes' observation that

> ... by a slight change in the form of the contract the plaintiff can accomplish the result in a way that would be beyond successful

---

[87] *Id.* at 383.

[88] *Id.*

[89] *Id.* at 383–84.

[90] *Id.* at 382–83; *id.* 386 (Holmes). U.S. v. General Electric, 272 U.S. 476 (1926) (validating resale price maintenance in consignment).

[91] *Id.* at 386.

attack, if it should make the retail dealers also agents in law as well as in name, and retain title until the goods left their hands ...[92]

Holmes made plain what the majority only implied—that Miles and fellow members of the Proprietary Association could easily close loopholes and strengthen infirmities to draft a proper consignment contract that would allow them to maintain resale prices. Park, it seems, won the battle but lost the war.

In the end, Holmes got it right—although for the wrong reasons. He got it right not because competition was over-rated but because price competition would be restrained as a result of the powerful immunity reserved for consignment contracts. Indeed, the price restraints would be *per se* legal once the manufacturer retained title to the goods. Holmes recognized that the loopholes would be closed before the ink dried on the majority opinion.[93]

Afterword

The consignment form was a stroke of lawyerly brilliance, no less than the invention of the commercial trust form first adopted by Standard Oil, because it allowed Miles in concert with other patent medicine manufacturers to avoid the imperatives of price competition. The property logic of a consignment exception to competition policy would hold until the latter half of the twentieth century, when the Supreme Court would close it, re-open it, and close it emphatically in *GTE Sylvania*, only to suggest later that it was open yet again.[94] Regardless of its current status, the consignment form sheds light on the property logics that shape antitrust policy.

Indeed, another powerful property logic drives the current antitrust jurisprudence of vertical restraints. It is the logic of trademark ownership. Although asserted unsuccessfully in the *Dr. Miles* era, trademark ownership and the commercial strategy of branding would later influence the Supreme Court to view markets as bifurcated, as working at distinct levels of intra-brand and inter-brand competition. Trademark ownership would draw a bright line across the terrain of competition

---

[92] *Id.*

[93] The consignment device had unspoken impact on the market: Only firms with financial resources could do business on a consignment, the traditional instrument for securing credit sales. Consignment was attractive to resellers because they paid only after the goods were sold. The prospect of delayed payment and associated costs of financing distributors and retailers raised financial difficulties for small firms seeking entry or expansion in addition to the high advertising costs. They faced entry barriers in the strictest sense insofar as their borrowing costs were typically higher because they carried greater risk of default.

[94] *GTE Sylvania, supra* note 80; Bus. Electronics Corp. v. Sharp Electronics Corp., 485 U.S. 717, 733 (1988), see Peritz, *Genealogy* at 511–16, 531–37, 550, 562–67.

with the result that manufacturers were increasingly permitted to impose restraints on downstream alienation of their trademarked goods.

In *White Motor* (1963), the Court declared that a small branded manufacturer could impose non-price restraints on its dealers, on intra-brand competition, when it offered to show that the restraints enhanced competition against General Motors, Chrysler or Ford, when they enhanced inter-brand competition. The implicit economic logic was that White Motor could not compete on price because it could not match the larger firms' economies of scale. Without dealer restraints to enforce its plan to compete on quality against other brands, White Motors would fail.[95] If the original impulse was a special solicitude toward small firms often attributed to that era, it dissipated long ago.

GTE Sylvania (1977) would adopt Judge Lurton's view that consignments did not provide a special exception to competition policy at the very moment it announced that inter-brand competition was simply more important than intra-brand. In effect, it was an exchange of property logics—trademark ownership for chattel ownership under consignment. For twenty years, the Court declined to extend the trademark logic of brand competition to price restraints. But in the last decade of the century, Court extended the special dispensation for intra-brand restraints to maintenance of maximum resale prices.[96] And as this chapter is written, the Supreme Court will likely reconsider the issue in *Dr. Miles*—the *per se* illegality of minimum resale price maintenance.[97]

Much has changed since the heyday of patent medicines. Dr. Miles Medical became Miles Laboratories and found commercial success in the mid-twentieth century with its popular over-the-counter remedy ALKA–SELTZER. In the latter part of the century, Miles merged into the corporate confines of Bayer Laboratories. But what has not changed is that one property logic or another has always provided special dispensation from competition policy. Despite current orthodoxy, branding is not a natural barrier across the terrain of competition; nor is inter-brand competition inherently preferable to intra-brand. It is the property logic of trademark ownership that makes it so by portraying a discounter as a free rider or knave rather than a free trader.[98]

A century after antitrust battles over industry standard contracts that manufacturers used to control the prices of RESTORATIVE NERVINE, PERUNA and other patent medicines, at least two things are

---

[95] White Motor Co. v. U.S., 372 U.S. 253 (1963).

[96] *Khan, supra* note 2.

[97] See note 2 *supra*.

[98] EDWARD CHAMBERLIN, THE THEORY OF MONOPOLISTIC COMPETITION (1933) (Appendix on Trade Marks); Peritz, *supra* note 7.

clear amidst whirlwinds of change. First, the property logic of trademark protection shapes the modern vertical restraints jurisprudence that allows branded manufacturers broad power to restrain competition in consumer product markets. Second, technologies of distribution and marketing are changing dramatically, as they did a century ago. Indeed, some say the Internet changes everything, as others believed of railroads in their time. That remains to be seen. While new technologies promise wider access to markets and more information about them, technological advances and accepted licensing practices have extended manufacturers' capabilities to retain control over their products by what the common law called restraints on alienation and restraints of trade, the twin doctrines that still define competition policy. Moreover, in today's economy, to the extent that brands organize systems of complementary products strategically developed around technological incompatibilities, the property logic of trademarks immunizes a pervasive structure of trade restraints, as did the widespread use of direct marketing contracts a century ago. We close then with an old question: What role should competition play in shaping consumer product markets driven by new technologies and organized by the exclusionary rights of property holders?

3

Daniel A. Crane*

The Story of *United States v. Socony–Vacuum*: Hot Oil and Antitrust in the Two New Deals

INTRODUCTION

The 27 oil companies and 56 of their employees were shocked to be criminally indicted in Madison, Wisconsin for violating Section 1 of the Sherman Act. After all, the misconduct alleged was participating in a petroleum stabilization program that had originated in the highest echelons of the very federal government that was now bringing the indictment. But such is the political nature of antitrust enforcement. Today's dogma is tomorrow's relic.

The historical volatility of antitrust may come a surprise to those weaned on the Chicago School consensus of the past thirty years, which has largely driven dissenting voices to the margins of the antitrust conversation. With few exceptions, competition policy has come to be perceived as technocratic, conservative, and incremental. But it was not always this way. The Sherman Act's history is Hegelian, a history of clashing paradigms, ideologically dominated epochs, and sharp departures from preexisting norms.[1] One can never get too comfortable with the status quo, for the rug is quickly pulled out from under it.

---

* Thanks to Anna Brickman and Ken Lashins for outstanding research assistance on this chapter.

[1] *See generally* Robert Pitofsky, *The Political Content of Antitrust*, 127 U. Pa. L. Rev. 1051 (1979) for a generally sympathetic view of the need to accommodate political values in antitrust. For a more pessimistic view of political intervention in antitrust, see THE CAUSES AND CONSEQUENCES OF ANTITRUST: THE PUBLIC CHOICE PERSPECTIVE, Fred S. McChesney & William F. Shugart II, eds. (1995).

No case better illustrates this reality than the "Madison Oil" case—
United States v. Socony–Vaccum.[2] Today, *Socony* is known for its articulation of the rule of per se illegality for price fixing agreements, but that doctrinal aspect of the case is perhaps less interesting than the story it tells about how quickly antitrust paradigms can shift. *Socony's* story begins in the depth of the Depression in a depressed oil industry plagued by overproduction and volatility. Seeking to rationalize and manage the industry, the Roosevelt administration set out on an ambitious regulatory program that involved a combination of central planning by government administrators and a guild-like association of industry executives. After the Supreme Court invalidated key portions of Roosevelt's National Industrial Recovery Act, the oil association voluntarily continued the stabilization program initiated by the government. Next thing they knew, the members of the association were criminally indicted for price fixing in violation of the Sherman Act. The very government that prompted the cartel was now calling it a criminal conspiracy. When the jury returned a verdict against the defendant oil companies and executives, the defendants were stunned. An editorial in the *New York Times* summed up popular sentiment: "For proceeding to stabilize price conditions in the demoralized crude-petroleum fields under the powerful pressure of one branch of the Roosevelt Administration, thirty oil-company managers now stand as convicted criminals, a result of a prosecution by another branch."[3]

How could this have happened? If competition policy were merely a rationalistic, expertized, and managerial bureaucratic task as we commonly assume today, the story of *Socony* would be bewildering. But if antitrust is understood as a sometimes naked expression of powerful ideological impulses, the story makes perfect sense. And so the *Socony* defendants learned.

I. HOT OIL AND THE NIRA EXPERIMENT

A. *The Oil Industry in the Great Depression*

The *Socony* saga has its roots in another great antitrust case—
Standard Oil Co. of NJ v. United States,[4] whose divestiture decree reshaped the oil industry thirty years before *Socony*. The *Standard Oil* decree fractured John D. Rockefeller's empire into 34 operating units

---

[2] 310 U.S. 150 (1940).

[3] Arthur Krock, *How One Attorney General Dealt with Business*, N.Y. Times, Jan. 27, 1938 (In the Nation) at 20.

[4] 221 U.S. 1 (1911).

and 9 principal petroleum marketers. Among the surviving companies was the Standard Oil Company of New York—SO–CO–NY—the first named defendant[5] whose name attaches indelibly to the case studied in this chapter.[6]

The effectiveness of the Standard Oil decree has been the subject of much historical debate. Standard Oil was already losing some of its dominance by 1911 and the decrees may have done little more than to transform Standard Oil from a national monopoly into a series of regional monopolies.[7] The break-up had no measurable effect on petroleum production or prices. By the booming twenties, however, oil production surged as the automobile replaced the horse and buggy as the common person's means of transportation.

Beginning in about 1926, there was an unprecedented surge in oil production. But capital could not have been poured into the oil industry at a worse time. In October 1929, the stock market crashed. Stocks that had quadrupled in the preceding decade lost 80% of their value in the next three years. Demand for consumer and industrial goods plummeted, businesses shut their doors, banks failed by the hundreds, and millions of people lost their jobs. The Great Depression was on.

The petroleum industry was hard hit. Just when millions of dollars had been sunk into drilling new wells, demand for oil fell precipitously. Oil producers were reluctant to abandon their wells because, once abandoned, subsurface changes made it difficult or impossible to bring the wells back into operation if demand rose again. Further compounding the overproduction problem, the largest oil field in history was discovered in East Texas in 1930. Crude oil prices sank to 10 to 15 cents per barrel and gasoline was selling in Texas for $2\frac{1}{8}$ cents per gallon.

In the early 1930s, several state governments tried to curtail overproduction through proration laws. In 1931, with the Great Depression looming as a true economic emergency, the governors of Texas and Oklahoma even declared martial law and seized oil wells to curb production. But production was not easily curbed, particularly given the structure of the industry.

---

[5] The indictment named Standard Oil of Indiana as the first defendant, but a post-conviction decision by the district court granted Standard a new trial, leaving Socony as the first named defendant for appellate purposes. *U.S. v. Standard Oil Co. (Indiana)*, 23 F. Supp. 937 (1938).

[6] *See* WAYNE HENDERSON & SCOTT BENJAMIN, STANDARD OIL: THE FIRST 125 YEARS 15, 22 (1996).

[7] E. Thomas Sullivan, *The Jurisprudence of Antitrust Divestiture: The Path Less Traveled*, 86 Minn. L. Rev. 565, 578–79 (2002).

The players in the oil industry fell into two categories. First, there were the "majors," large vertically integrated companies that operated at every level of production and distribution. These were the descendents of the Standard Oil company, like Socony, Standard of Indiana, and Continental Oil, and other large oil companies like Gulf, Shell, and Phillips. They took oil from the ground, refined it, and sold it to consumers at their own retail outlets. The second category of industry player consisted of "independents," much smaller firms that operated in only one segment of the production and distribution chain. There were independent refiners, independent jobbers (or wholesalers, as we say today), and independent retailers. In addition to producing on their own account, the majors sold gasoline to the jobbers under long-term wholesale contracts. The jobbers paid the majors a price that was indexed to the spot market price, which fluctuated based on the supply from the independent refiners. Thus, in addition to being concerned about the effect of depressed retail prices, the majors had to be concerned about spot market prices at wholesale.

Meanwhile, the independent refiners were stuck between a rock and a hard place. If they shut down operations during the glut to wait for industry conditions to improve, they would irretrievably lose their wells and their industry connections. Conversely, they would lose money if they tried to produce at the levels mandated by the state proration laws. Nor was storing oil until demand improved an option, since the independents did not have much bulk storage capacity.

As a result, independent East Texas refiners were constantly flooding the market with illegal or "hot" oil, which they unloaded at whatever price they could fetch. Although the hot oil represented only about 5% of the gasoline marketed in the Midwestern region, it significantly depressed both the wholesale and retail prices of gasoline. By March of 1933, when Franklin Delano Roosevelt was inaugurated President, the wholesale price of gasoline was below the cost of production. The oil industry, like many others, appeared to be in a death spiral where it paid neither to be in business nor to shut down.

B. Roosevelt's Response: The NIRA

Roosevelt swept into office with a control of both houses of Congress and tremendous political capital. Intent upon reversing the passivity of the Hoover administration, the President promised decisive economic action within his "first hundred days." The centerpiece of his economic reform agenda was the National Industrial Recovery Act, which passed Congress in June 1933, barely a hundred days after Roosevelt's inauguration.

The NIRA grew out of wide-spread perception that much of the fault for the Depression lay at the feet of "chiselers," industrial price-cutters akin to the "scabs" of labor who chiseled the price of goods down to ruinous levels.[8] Too much competition was thus to blame. Greater cooperation between industry and government—or "associationalism"— was needed.[9]

Two sections of the NIRA are significant for present purposes. Section 9 related specifically to the oil industry. It empowered the President to prohibit the transportation in interstate commerce of hot oil marketed in violation of state proration laws. Section 3 was considerably broader. It empowered the President, upon application of any industrial association, to approve "codes of fair competition" for industry. Although the Act provided that "such codes shall not permit monopolies or monopolistic practices," a provision that would also have made price-fixing illegal was defeated in Congress. Further, the Act conferred antitrust immunity on industry groups to agree on codes of fair competition and operate under them if ratified by the President and made violation of any code of fair competition a misdemeanor, thus compelling industry to live by the industry codes.

Roosevelt immediately issued an executive order prohibiting interstate shipments of hot oil. Shortly afterwards, on August 19, 1933, Roosevelt approved a code of fair competition for the petroleum industry. Among other things, it set maximum hours of work and minimum wages, forbade petroleum sales below cost, required vertically integrated companies to conduct each branch of their business on a profitable basis (in order to avoid internal cost and revenue allocations that would have masked unprofitable production), established a fixed relationship between crude oil and refined gasoline prices, and authorized refiners to engage in retail price maintenance. Roosevelt also appointed his Secretary of the Interior, Harold Ickes, administrator of the code.

Ickes was one of the liberal icons of the New Deal. Roosevelt had appointed him Interior Secretary immediately upon his election in 1933 and added various important titles over the years, including Administrator of the Public Works Administration and, now, Petroleum Administrator. Ickes, a Midwesterner, populist, and committed environmentalist, was one of the most outspoken anticorporatists in the Roosevelt administration and frequently lambasted the monopolistic power of corporations.[10] He once described the oil industry as "ruthless, arrogant and

---

[8] ELLIS W. HAWLEY, THE NEW DEAL AND THE PROBLEM OF MONOPOLY: A STUDY IN ECONOMIC AMBIVALENCE 37 (2d ed. Fordham Press 1995).

[9] The associationalist strand of New Deal thinking picked up on ideas that became popular during the 1920s. See RUDOLPH J.R. PERITZ, COMPETITION POLICY IN AMERICA, 1888–1992: HISTORY, RHETORIC, LAW 78 (1996).

[10] See Spencer Weber Waller, The Antitrust Legacy of Thurman Arnold, 78 St. John's L. Rev. 569, 574 (2004).

haughty,"[11] publicly demanded that an oil dictator be appointed, and threatened to turn the oil industry into a public utility.[12]

Yet, during the early New Deal, Ickes reacted with sympathy to the large oil producers' desire to curb excess production. This was partly attributable to his environmental leanings. In a 1935 *Saturday Evening Post* article, Ickes raised the specter of "burning oil wells, billions of feet of natural gas escaping into the air, insane competition ... [and] wasteful methods of capture."[13] Until World War II at least, his primary concern was eliminating wasteful overproduction. So closely did Ickes cooperate with industry executives to curb production that an anonymous detractor wrote him poison pen letters accusing Ickes of selling out to oil interests.[14] (Ickes later discovered that the perpetrator was one of his Department of the Interior subordinates with whose wife Ickes was having an affair and promptly had the perpetrator fired.)[15]

One of Ickes's first acts as Petroleum Administrator was to establish a Petroleum Administrative Board that was tasked with making recommendations to Ickes "to stabilize the oil industry upon a profitable basis." Separately, Ickes created a petroleum Planning & Coordination Committee to aid in the administration of the petroleum code of fair competition. An organizational chart of the petroleum industry under the code of fair competition shows the Planning and Coordination Committee with a direct line reporting relationship to Ickes and Ickes with a direct line reporting relationship to Roosevelt. One of the leading members of the Committee was Charles E. Arnott, a vice-president of Socony whose first job was answering the telephone for John D. Rockefeller, who could claim that he acted with the direct authority of the Secretary of the Interior and only one step removed from the President.

The Committee immediately turned to the problem of hot oil. In April of 1934, at the Committee's behest, Roosevelt approved an amendment to the code of fair competition that permitted vertically integrated refiners to buy excess oil from the small, non-vertically integrated refiners that lacked sufficient storage capacity and were dumping oil on the market. The Petroleum Administration Board also sought commitments from the largest oil companies to buy up large stocks of crude oil and hold them off the market.

---

[11] Graham White & John Maze, Harold Ickes of the New Deal: His Private Life and Public Career 220 (1985).

[12] *Id.*

[13] *Id.* at 159.

[14] *Id.* at 123.

[15] *Id.* at 123–25.

But despite Ickes's efforts, oil prices remained depressed and hot oil continued to flow, particularly out of East Texas. A price war at the retail level further compounded the problem. In July of 1934, the PBA asked Arnott to head up a voluntary cooperative movement to deal with the price war. Ickes wrote Arnott a letter authorizing him to take actions "necessary to stabilize the price level to conform to that normally prevailing in contiguous areas where marketing conditions are similar." In effect, Ickes was asking Arnott to run a government-sponsored price-fixing cartel.

C. The Dancing Partner Program

And so he did. In late 1934, Arnott established a General Stabilization Committee with headquarters in Washington, D.C. and fifty state and local committees. At a meeting in Chicago on January 4, 1935, the Committee agreed that nothing could be done about the retail level price war so long as conditions remained volatile in the tank car market—the level at which independent refiners unloaded hot oil. A Tank Car Stabilization Committee was appointed to study the problem of refined hot oil.

The Committee first set its sights on the Mid–Continent Oil Field, a vast geological region including Oklahoma, northern and western portions of Texas, the southern and eastern portions of Kansas, the southern portion of Arkansas, and the northern portion of Louisiana. This was the oil-producing region closest to Midwestern markets and therefore of most concern to the Midwestern oil executives meeting in Chicago. The Committee estimated that between 600 and 700 tank cars of distress oil flooded the Midwestern spot market every month from 17 independent refiners in the mid-continent field. If this inconvenient excess inventory could be removed from the market, prices could be stabilized.

But whose job was it to buy up the excess oil? There was an obvious collective action problem—none of the large producers wanted to buy up oil that it could not sell, for the benefit of the market as a whole. At a February meeting in Chicago, H.T. Ashton, a Socony division manager, gave a speech that created a lasting metaphor for the Madison Oil case. The oil industry was like "a great economic ball." The majors had each asked some of the larger independent refiners to dance. But there were seven or eight smaller independent refiners—"wallflowers" at an "old country dance"—that no one wanted to dance with. Ashton summed up his proposal: "I think it is going to be one of the jobs of this Committee to introduce some of these wallflowers to some of the strong dancers, so that everybody can dance."

So was born the "dancing partner" metaphor that came to symbolize the Socony conspiracy. The basic idea was to match the majors with small independent refiners. Whenever the small refiner had hot oil that it was prepared to dump on the market, its dancing partner would buy up the oil and squirrel it away. Now, yet another committee was formed, the Mechanical Sub–Committee (of the Tank Car Stabilization Committee). The Sub–Committee was supposed to see that the majors were paying a sufficiently high price at wholesale to their dancing partners to prevent the dancing partners from unloading the oil on the open market.

It quickly became clear that dealing with hot oil from the Mid–Continent field would be insufficient to stabilize the Midwestern market. As Mid–Continent spot market prices stabilized, East Texas prices were about 1/8 cents per gallon lower, which presented the prospect that Mid–Continent prices would become depressed again. In early 1935, independent Texas refiners formed the East Texas Refiner's Marketing Association to coordinate efforts to dispose of surplus gasoline. The majors quickly availed themselves of the East Texas association to replicate the dancing partner arrangement. Every Monday morning the secretary of the East Texas association would ascertain each member's surplus oil quantity, obtain a consensus asking price, and find buyers from the major oil retailers.

There was conflicting evidence at trial about the effect of the dancing partner program on prices, but there is no doubt that gas prices in the Midwestern region began to rise in March of 1935, just when the Mid–Continent dancing partner program went into effect. Between March and June, prices rose from about 3 ½ cents per gallon to about 4 ¾. By the middle of January, 1936, prices were above 5 cents. Although some volatility in price continued into 1936, the oil industry had largely achieved Ickes's stabilization mandate.

D.   The End of the NIRA Experiment

Unfortunately for the Midwestern majors, Ickes's mandate soon lost its legs. Five days after the Chicago meeting where the General Stabilization Committee agreed that something had to be done to deal with the hot oil problem, the United States Supreme Court handed down *Panama Refining Co. v. Amazon Petroleum Corp.*,[16] one of two significant decisions that dealt a severe blow to Roosevelt's first New Deal. At issue was the constitutionality of Section 9 of the NIRA, which authorized the President to prohibit the interstate shipment of hot oil. In an opinion by Chief Justice Hughes, who was like Roosevelt a former governor of New York, the Supreme Court invalidated Section 9 as an unconstitutional delegation of legislative power to the executive branch of government.

Then, on May 27, 1935—just as the Mechanical Sub–Committee was achieving progress on stabilizing prices—the Supreme Court dealt a fatal blow to Roosevelt's NIRA. In the famous (or infamous) "sick chicken"

---

[16] 293 U.S. 388 (1935).

case—*A.L.A. Schechter v. United States*[17]—the Court invalidated Section 3 of the NIRA. Again per Chief Justice Hughes, the Court held that the Act exceeded Congress' regulatory power under the commerce clause and unconstitutionally delegated legislative power to the executive branch and to the industry associations that promulgated codes of fair trade for the President's approval.

Panama Refining and *Schechter* had no immediate impact on Arnott's dancing partner program. The program had always been voluntary and persuasion-oriented and not coercive. It is in the interest of any cartel to cooperate to achieve higher prices and no governmental coercion is usually required if other effective self-policing mechanisms are in place. At trial, the oil companies stressed that there was never any agreement on prices or even on commitments to dancing partners. Everything was done on a voluntary basis under gentlemen's agreements, both before and after the Supreme Court decisions. By the time of *Panama Refining* and *Schechter*, the Mechanical Subcommittee had cobbled together a sufficient infrastructure that running the dancing partner program had become almost automatic. Shortly after the Supreme Court handed down *Schechter*, the Tank Car Stabilization Committee met and decided that things should proceed as before.

Panama Refining and *Schechter* were also to have a relatively short legacy as a matter of constitutional law. By 1937, in the face of Roosevelt's proposal to "pack" the Supreme Court with more progressive Justices, the Supreme Court began to reverse ground on the commerce clause powers of the federal government and to uphold the Roosevelt administration's socio-economic programs.[18] Similarly, the non-delegation doctrine fell into disuse and the Supreme Court finally put it out of its misery in 2001.[19]

Nonetheless, the cases had a significant impact on the shape of Roosevelt's New Deal programs. Historians often classify the New Deal into two halves.[20] The first half, from 1933 to 1935, was marked by associationalism—legislative and executive efforts at centralized planning of the economy through industrial codes derived from guild-like

---

[17] 295 U.S. 495 (1935).

[18] Although it is commonly thought that Justice Roberts's switch to voting to uphold progressive legislation was prompted by Roosevelt's court-packing plan, it now seems likely that Roberts switched his vote before Roosevelt announced his plan. Richard D. Friedman, *Switching Time and Other Thought Experiments: The Hughes Court and Constitutional Transformation*, 142 U. Pa. L. Rev. 1891, 1896 (1994).

[19] *See Whitman v. American Trucking Ass'n*, 531 U.S. 457 (2001).

[20] See, *e.g.*, ARTHUR M. SCHLESINGER, JR., THE POLITICS OF UPHEAVAL 393–95 (1960); ERIC GOLDMAN, RENDEZVOUS WITH DESTINY 333–42, 361–67 (1953); MICHAEL E. PARRISH, ANXIOUS DECADES: AMERICA IN PROSPERITY AND DEPRESSION 1920–1941, 297–99, 338–39 (1992).

associations closely supervised by governmental administrators. The second half of the New Deal, prompted in substantial measure by *Panama Refining* and *Schechter* but also by the failure of the NIRA model to improve industrial conditions,[21] involved more modest and targeted efforts at market regulation. As constitutional historian Bruce Ackerman has pointed out, the central organizing concept of the first New Deal was "planning" while that of the second half was "liberty."[22]

This shift would have critical implications for antitrust enforcement. On business matters, the New Deal was really an uneasy alliance of at least three major ideological impulses. First, there were adherents to a "business commonwealth" vision who wanted "a rational, cartelized business order in which the industrialists would plan and direct the economy, profits would be insured, and the government would take care of recalcitrant chiselers."[23] A second group favored "cooperative, collectivist democracy" in which all relevant interests—business, labor, consumers, etc.—were given a seat at the bargaining table.[24] During the short tenure of the NIRA, the first two groups prevailed. But with *Schechter* and the failure of the NIRA in 1935, a third leg of the New Deal coalition began to grow in influence. This third group believed in old-fashioned, atomistic competition "in which basic decisions were made in an impersonal market and the pursuit of self-interest produced the greatest social good."[25] They were adherents of Louis Brandeis, the champion of small business and author of *The Curse of Bigness*, and found their modern captain in Harvard law professor and New Dealer extraordinaire Felix Frankfurter. And they counted among their numbers William O. Douglas, Robert Jackson, and Thurman Arnold, three of the most important players in the *Socony* saga.

A recession in 1937 that was generally blamed on price-gouging by monopolists (who had apparently forgotten that they were supposed to be "chiselers" on price) strengthened the Brandeisians' hands. On April 29, 1938, Roosevelt gave a speech complaining that the American economy had become a "concealed cartel system."[26] A substantial ideological shift had taken place within the Roosevelt administration.

---

[21] By the time of *Schechter*, the NIRA process and Hugh Johnson, the top NIRA administrator, had become very politically unpopular and the program would likely have collapsed under its own weight even without *Schechter* and *Panama Refining*. *See* HAWLEY, *supra* n. 8 at 72–90.

[22] BRUCE ACKERMAN, WE THE PEOPLE: TRANSFORMATIONS 310 (1998).

[23] HAWLEY, *supra* n. 8 at 35.

[24] *Id.*

[25] *Id.*

[26] *Id.* at 412.

Arnott and his colleagues did not see it coming. Even while the Brandeisians were consolidating their power in Washington, the dancing partner program continued, reflexively and automatically, until the trouble began.

II. THE *SOCONY* LITIGATION

A. *The New Antitrust Division*

In 1933, at the time that Harold Ickes was frantically trying to curb excess oil production, the Antitrust Division of the United States Department of Justice was a sleepy backwater in the Roosevelt Administration. Antitrust had fallen into desuetude since the trustbusting days of Teddy Roosevelt. The Hoover administration preferred industry cooperation to competition and, initially, the Roosevelt administration showed little propensity to reverse course. Between 1933 and 1938, antitrust enforcement was sporadic and, ironically, often centered on enforcing the anticompetitive NIRA and Agricultural Adjustment Act codes.[27] Even after *Panama Refining* and *Schechter* drove a stake through the heart of the first New Deal, the Antitrust Division showed few signs of life despite the growing influence of the Brandeisians in the higher levels of the administration.

But then along came Robert Jackson and Thurman Arnold, two New Deal giants who would place enduring stamps on the Antitrust Division. Jackson took charge of the Division on January 18, 1937 after serving as Assistant Attorney General in charge of the Tax Division. In his draft autobiography, Jackson describes the Division as "somewhat moribund" on his arrival, largely because the National Recovery Administration "was based on the philosophy almost exactly opposite to that of the antitrust laws."[28] Jackson recounts that "during the N.R.A. experiment, here had been a pretty general suspension of antitrust law activity. Businessmen were encouraged to meet and cooperate and particularly in the oil industry they were encouraged to enter into agreements which might have been considered as violative of the antitrust laws."[29]

Jackson believed it was a time for a sharp change in the administration's view toward antitrust. The NRA was gone and the Division must now revert to the philosophy of the last serious antitrust enforcing administration—Woodrow Wilson's—"that free competition is the wisest and most liberal measure of business regulation."[30]

---

[27] *See* SPENCER WEBER WALLER, THURMAN ARNOLD: A BIOGRAHY 78–80 (2005).

[28] H. Hewitt Pate, *Robert H. Jackson at the Antitrust Division*, 68 Albany L. Rev. 787, 789 (2005), *citing* Robert H. Jackson, *Draft Autobiography* 85–86 (on file in the Robert H. Jackson Papers, Library of Congress, Manuscript Division).

[29] *Id.*

[30] *Id.* at 789–90.

But Jackson well understood that he would have to be selective in his reinvigorization of antitrust enforcement. Despite the addition of an economics unit by his predecessor, John Dickinson, resources in the Division were still quite limited. More importantly, despite the failure of the first New Deal, it was not yet clear that the Roosevelt administration as a whole had much of an appetite for vigorous antitrust enforcement. So Jackson resolved "to select for intensive investigation those complaints which show the most flagrant cases of antitrust violation and in which the greatest public interest is involved."[31] Unfortunately for Arnott and the other *Socony* defendants, there was no case that better fit the bill of "flagrant" antitrust violation and "greatest public interest" than the Midwestern dancing partner program.

For some time, independent jobbers had been complaining about the dancing partner program.[32] Although the vertically integrated majors and small independent refiners both benefited from the arrangement, the wholesalers did not. Their compensation was usually on a cost-plus basis—retailers paid the jobbers a two cent per gallon premium over the spot market wholesale price. Unlike the retailers and refiners, the jobbers were indifferent to the spot market price of gasoline, except insofar as it affected demand and hence the volume of gasoline they could sell. When prices were depressed and there was therefore greater demand, the jobbers alone did quite well by selling a larger volume. Conversely, by increasing the spot market price and hence lessening demand, the dancing partner program hurt the jobbers.

It is not clear why the Department of Justice focused its attack on the Midwestern region, except perhaps in the hopes of finding a prairie, populist, anti-big-business jury. Certainly, the dancing partner program was not unique. In California the oil companies hired an oil umpire to allocate production quotas,[33] an even more explicit market allocation scheme than the dancing partner agreement. But, for whatever reasons, by late 1936, the Justice Department staff was eager to proceed against the Midwestern oil companies.

The proposed indictment set off a storm of controversy at the highest levels of the Roosevelt administration. Attorney General Homer Cummings supported it but Ickes, who was largely responsible for instigating the alleged conspiracy, argued that "the oil men were being unjustly prosecuted."[34] (Ironically, Ickes had been at the forefront of the post-*Schechter* antitrust revival, repeatedly prodding Roosevelt to go

---

[31] *Id.* at 790–91.

[32] Hawley, *supra* n. 8 at 374.

[33] *Id.* at 318.

[34] Pate, *supra* n. 28 at 791.

after big capital in other industries). After a review of the facts, Jackson concluded that the defendants "had clearly violated the law and proceeded to prosecute them vigorously."[35]

The indictment, filed just in time to ruin the defendants' Christmas on December 22, 1936,[36] alleged an elaborate conspiracy resulting in monopolistic control over the oil industry and artificially inflated prices. 27 corporations and 56 individuals were named. The defendants were the majors that participated in the dancing partner program, their executives, and three Midwestern trade journals that published the spot market prices of gasoline. Generally, the indictment claimed that the defendants "combined and conspired together for the purpose of artificially raising and fixing the tank car prices of gasoline in the aforementioned spot markets, and [intentionally] . . . have maintained said prices at artificially high and non-competitive levels." Curiously, the government chose to assert February of 1935 as the starting date of the conspiracy, even though Arnott was acting under Ickes's orders at that point and Supreme Court did not invalidate Section 3 of the NIRA until May of 1935. The indictment alleged that the gasoline exchanged among dancing partners constituted almost 50% of the gas sold by independent refiners and, because of the majors' burgeoning control over the market, were "made at uniform, high, arbitrary, and non-competitive prices. . . ."

B. The Trial

On October 4, 1937, the *Socony* trial began in Madison, Wisconsin. 101 lawyers showed up to represent the defendants, leasing an entire hotel during the trial.[37] The two lead trial lawyers for the government were from the Antitrust Division. Robert Jackson, himself a former trial lawyer from upstate New York, was concerned that the Antitrust Division lawyers had never tried a case before a "country jury" so he hired W.P. Crawford, a country lawyer from Superior, Wisconsin, to assist with the case. Jackson told Crawford that he "did not want him ever to bother to learn the law or the facts of the case, but [that Jackson] wanted him to keep the case on a level such that the jury would understand it."[38] As we shall see, Crawford took Jackson a little bit too literally.

---

[35] *Id.* at 792.

[36] A grand jury returned an earlier indictment against the same defendants on November 6, 1936. It was challenged due to alleged irregularities in the drawing of the grand jury. Although the district court eventually upheld the indictment, the government proceeded with a new indictment while proceedings with the first indictment were pending. Report of Assistant Attorney General Robert H. Jackson 48.

[37] THURMAN W. ARNOLD, THE BOTTLNECKS OF BUSINESS 208 (1940).

[38] Pate, *supra* n. 28 at 792 (quoting *Jackson Draft Autobiography*, *supra* n. 28 at 88–89).

In his opening argument, Crawford explained that he would favor lay-person analysis as opposed to the "legal phraseology" contained in the indictment. He presented to the "country jury" a morality play between the wealthy and greedy oil companies and the helpless jobbers and consumers who relied on automobile transportation: "Not only, gentlemen of the jury, is this prosecution actuated by the Government because of the injury done to the public, but because of the fact that it is a terrible thing that a group of influential, wealthy millionaires or billionaires should take over the power, take over the control, the power to make prices."

In its case in chief, the government methodically presented the workings of the dancing partner program: the interdependency of tank car prices and retail prices, who directed which aspects of the scheme, and the necessity of the market journals in propping up prices. A key point in the government's argument was establishing that the majors wielded control over the jobbers, specifically, that the jobbers had no other source for oil at market prices. The jobber "has found over a period of years that the public demands a major brand of gasoline,—an advertised brand, that the consumer can depend upon or has been persuaded by advertising to believe is dependable. . . . He must go to one of the defendant major oil companies in this case. . . ." Aware that the jurors would be primarily interested in consumer effects, the government repeatedly stressed that "tank car prices for gasoline obtained in each of the spot markets . . . tend to, and do, directly and substantially influence the retail prices of gasoline."

When it was their turn, the defendants' strategy was to prove that the dancing partner program was sanctioned at the highest levels of the Roosevelt administration and that it was a reasonable response to the market-depressing evil of hot oil. They introduced numerous exhibits showing Ickes's encouragement of their efforts to curb overproduction and hot oil even after the Supreme Court's invalidation of the NIRA. They also argued that the federal government's support of the industry's stabilization initiatives did not end with the Secretary of the Interior. Defense Exhibit 901 was a May 31, 1935 article from the *Tulsa Tribune* that reported on a speech Roosevelt gave in Washington four days after the Supreme Court handed down *Schechter*. Roosevelt lambasted that decision as depriving the federal government of control over national social and economic conditions and "relegat[ing] the interstate commerce clause of the constitution back to the horse and buggy days." Perhaps already contemplating the court-packing plan he would announce the following year or a constitutional amendment, Roosevelt characterized *Schechter* as the most important decision since *Dred Scott*. For the defendants, however, the most significant part of Roosevelt's speech came near the end, when the President turned from his attack on the Supreme Court to his continuing economic agenda. According to the *Tulsa Tribune* article introduced into evidence by defendants, "the president turned to the question of voluntary code adherence [and] expressed hope that all industry would live up to them. . . ." From this, the defendants extracted a challenge by Roosevelt to continue with the necessary work of the industry codes on a voluntary basis.[39]

The one thing the defendants never produced at trial was any formal legal document authorizing the continuation of the dancing partner program after *Schechter*. Indeed, the government introduced a letter from Ickes to Arnott, written shortly after *Schechter*, warning that "when the understandings arrived at a bases of solution of price wars affecting the industry over a considerable area are intended to operate over a definite period of time or involve substantial changes in the policy of the various supply companies made only in consideration of similar action on the part of other companies," formal approval under the NIRA would be required to avoid violating the antitrust laws. The defendants, however, could point to an even later letter from Ickes expressing "the appreciation of the government" for Arnott's work "in the diminution of unfair competitive practices [and] the balancing of crude oil supply with demand."

The defendants also worked to refute the government's assertion that the dancing partners program had had a predominant effect on the sharp increase in the price of oil. Throughout its presentation, the government had highlighted two periods: the spring of 1935, when the price of oil shot up, and the period following January 1936, when the price of oil abruptly stabilized. The defendants tried to show that numerous other factors had caused movements in gasoline prices, including the Connally Act's effective shut down of hot oil, the expansion of refinery allocations as a result of an amendment to the code in 1934, a seasonal increase in national consumption of oil, and crude oil controls.

Additionally, in an effort to convince the jury that the price had not been unnaturally set, the defendants adduced evidence of prices in other

---

[39] The defendants were probably overstating Roosevelt's support for voluntary compliance with the codes. Indeed, the text of Roosevelt's press conference reported in the May 31, 1935 *Tulsa Tribune* article suggests that the president was not so much expressing support for voluntary compliance with industry codes as skepticism that business could be trusted to police itself:

> You and I know human nature. Fundamentally it comes down to this. In the long run can voluntary processes on the part of business bring about the same practical results that were attained under N.R.A.? I mean the good results. Of course there have been some bad ones. But I mean the good results. Can it be done by voluntary action on the part of business? Can we go ahead as a Nation with the beautiful theory, let us say, of some of the press, "At last the rule of Christ is restored. Business can do anything it wants and business is going to live up to the golden rule so marvelously that all of our troubles are ended." It is a school of thought that is so delightful in its naïveté.

regions throughout the country. They showed that for all but four weeks in 1935 the Midwestern area price for crude oil was lower than that outside the area, whereas the Midwestern area price for crude oil had been higher than that of the outside area for 14 weeks in 1934, before the dancing partner program began.

The Government's lawyers seem to have had a hard time behaving themselves during the defendants' case. According to questioning by Senator Warren Austin during Jackson's 1938 confirmation hearings for Solicitor General: "A certain witness named John W. Frey was called to the witness stand. He was under examination, and one of the attorneys representing the Department of Justice, during the course of his answers, said in an audible voice to counsel and to the jury, 'liar.' " Jackson did not deny the charge.

When it came time for the government's closing argument, Crawford thought back to Jackson's admonition that he ignore the facts and the law and play to the prejudices of the country jury. Much of his closing argument was spent in what he himself described as "clowning," where he made personal references to the lawyers involved in the case, the parties, the court and other irrelevant subjects. When he did hit on serious themes, it was often to invoke class prejudice. Crawford argued that the conspiracy involved "the biggest men in the country," that it was a "terrible thing that a group of confidential, wealthy millionaires or billionaires should take over power," and warned that the fallen Roman Empire provided a lesson about what happened when moneyed interests were left unchecked.

He also tackled the defendant's leading defense, that they had acted with the approval of Ickes and Roosevelt. Crawford repeatedly argued that it would be impossible for the Justice Department prosecutors to be prosecuting the case if Ickes did not believe the defendants had committed an antitrust violation. (As noted earlier, Ickes in fact vehemently opposed the indictment). Leaning over toward the jury, he said:

> Now, just between yourselves, do you honestly think that these boys here (indicating counsel at the government table) fired up with the enthusiasm of crusaders, as I say, and having given to this case every ounce of mental and physical strength they have and I myself have contributed, also, would be trying to convict these men unless that was the wish and desire of the highest officials in the government of the United States?[40]

Crawford even went so far as to testify in impeachment of the defendants' witnesses. Referring to the testimony of Sidney Swensrud of Standard of Ohio, Crawford told the jury:

---

[40] 310 U.S. at 265.

I just didn't think much of Swensrud's whole testimony, especially after I found out that he was giving testimony that they could ship gasoline in 1935 and 1936 up the Mississippi River to St. Paul. I happen to be around the Mississippi River quite a lot about it. In 1935 and 1936, you couldn't get a rowboat up the Mississippi River . . .[41]

When the judge sustained an objection to this wildly inappropriate testimony, Crawford carried on with further wildly inappropriate ad hominem attacks and religious references. The *Socony* trial ended with a bang.

C.   Conviction and Aftermath

On January 22, 1938, after a four-month trial, during which the jurors were sequestered for Thanksgiving, Christmas, and New Year's, a very grumpy jury returned a guilty verdict against 46 defendants. Each of the corporate defendants was fined $5,000 and each of the defendants $1,000.

Newspaper sentiment generally expressed sympathy for the convicted defendants. As noted at the outset, an editorial in the *New York Times* pointed out the irony that the very government that instigated the stabilization program was now criminally prosecuting it. On the other hand, the liberal *The Nation* noted many "gross inaccuracies about this case which have flooded the papers" and disputed the idea, purportedly believed by "a large part of the public," that "these officials were prosecuted and convicted for having patriotically done what the government had asked them to do."[42] *The Nation* focused on the secrecy with which the dancing partner program had been carried out, concluding that "[f]or men engaged on a patriotic mission, they certainly spared not pains to cover their tracks."[43]

As in any complicated litigation, the Madison Oil case involved endless procedural skirmishes during and after the trial that cannot be fully recounted here. In response to motions for directed verdict or judgment notwithstanding the verdict, the district court entered judgments of acquittal in favor of all but 12 corporations and 5 individuals for lack of evidence of participation in the conspiracy. Although some newspapers saw these acquittals as major defeats for the government's case, this was scant comfort to Socony, Arnott, and their guilty co-defendants as they grimly prepared for the appeals ahead.

---

[41] *Id.*

[42] Paul Y. Anderson, *F.D.R. Under Two Flags*, 146 The Nation 6, at 147–149, Feb. 5, 1938.

[43] *Id.*

In March of 1938, while post-trial motion practice was proceeding, Jackson was promoted to Solicitor General and Thurman Arnold took over the Antitrust Division. If the *Socony* defendants hoped that the change would bring a more sympathetic hearing from the Roosevelt administration, their hopes were quickly dashed. If anything, Arnold took an even more severe view of the defendants' conduct than Jackson. Arnold was not swayed by the oil companies' arguments that they had simply been following Ickes's orders. In his influential book, *The Bottlenecks of Business*, written shortly after the Supreme Court handed down the *Socony* decision, Arnold argued that executive approval of cartels is insufficient to immunize them from antitrust scrutiny: "The power to approve combinations by restraint of trade, *in general*, cannot be delegated to any administrative tribunal, however laudable the purpose. Only the courts can determine the reasonableness of a combination on such a broad scale as [the Madison Oil cases]."[44] The New New Dealers were firmly in control of the relevant departments of government and were determined to erase the bad memories of the NIRA's associationalist failures.

Hope returned when the United States Court of Appeals for the Seventh Circuit reversed the convictions.[45] The Court of Appeals did not believe that what the majors had done was "price fixing," since they had not agreed on what price would be paid to the independent refiners. Further, even if it was price fixing, the court did not believe that Supreme Court precedent held that all price fixing is illegal. Rather, "the criterion employed in determining whether concerted action is such as to come within the condemnation of the statute, is the effect which the action had upon fair competition."[46] Since the district court had submitted the case to the jury under a "per se illegality" instruction—that they must find guilt if they found price fixing—reversal was required.

The defendants would have been happy to retry the case under Seventh Circuit's "fair competition" norm. What could be "fairer" than a cooperative agreement to remove surplus gasoline from the market, particularly when this had been the objective of the federal and state governments for a number of years? But then the Supreme Court agreed to hear the case, and the defendants had reason to be gloomy once again.

III. THE SUPREME COURT DECISION

Arnott and the other defendants must have been pessimistic going into the Supreme Court. So much had changed since Ickes and Roosevelt

---

[44] ARNOLD, *supra* n. 37 at 105.

[45] U.S. v. Socony–Vacuum Oil Co., 105 F.2d 809 (7th Cir. 1939).

[46] 105 F.2d at 825.

kicked off the petroleum stabilization program in 1933. Not only had the Antitrust Division undergone a radical transformation, but the Supreme Court's old guard had been overtaken by New Dealer Justices appointed between 1937 and 1940. And not just any New Dealers. There was Felix Frankfurter, the dean of the anti-big-business Brandeisians, and Hugo Black, who as a Senator voted against the NIRA in 1933 on the grounds that it diluted the antitrust laws.[47] Stanley Reed, former Solicitor General and leading New Dealer, would almost certainly not override the Justice Department. Frank Murphy, who had just stepped down as Attorney General responsible for the *Socony* prosecution took his seat as Associate Justice on February 5, 1940, the date the Socony argument began, but recused himself.

Murphy's recusal was little help to the defendants. William O. Douglas, a fifth recently appointed New Dealer, was ultimately assigned to write the *Socony* opinion. Douglas and Thurman Arnold were old drinking buddies from their days together on the Yale Law School faculty and addressed each other as "Partner" in their frequent correspondence. Douglas entered the Roosevelt administration as a commissioner on the Securities and Exchange Commission, which was originally conceived as a vehicle for limiting the power and size of monopolistic corporations. Before joining the Court, Douglas served with Arnold on the Temporary National Economic Committee, a commission appointed to study national economic problems and the need for renewed antitrust enforcement. Roosevelt appointed Douglas to the Court a year before *Socony* arrived. It was his first antitrust opinion and his most important.

How things had changed since 1933 when the old guard "Four Horseman" on the Court would reliably slap down the Roosevelt administration!

Thurman Arnold chose to argue *Socony* in the Supreme Court personally to underscore the importance of the case. Seeking to preempt the defendants' leading argument, Arnold told the Justices that the majors were making "an attempt to set up the NRA again without control."[48] Like the trial, the Supreme Court oral argument wasn't lacking for theatrics. "According to press reports, Arnold got carried away and shouted that similar practices were so prevalent in the economy that 'this case represents the most dangerous threat to the enforcement of the antitrust laws ever seriously presented to this court.' "[49] Given the composition of the Court, Arnold probably didn't need these theatrics to prevail.

---

[47] KENNETH FINEGOLD & THEDA SKOCPOL, STATE AND PARTY IN AMERICA'S NEW DEAL 71 (1995).

[48] WALLER, *supra* n. 27 at 97.

[49] *Id.*

A. *Dispatching the Governmental Encouragement Defense*

From the defendants' perspective, the case was all about reasonableness of their conduct in light the ruinous conditions in the petroleum industry and Ickes's mandate to do something about it. But, for Douglas, this theme was merely a distraction. Early in the opinion, Douglas framed the defendants' argument under the heading "Alleged Knowledge and Acquiescence of the Federal Government." The heading itself gave the back of its hand to defendants' key argument. "Alleged," as in not proven; "Knowledge and Acquiescence," as though the NIRA mandate were merely a casual wink and nod by a low-level official; "the Federal Government," as if the alleged acquiescence occurred within a faceless bureaucracy and not in the persons of Harold Ickes and F.D.R.

Having thus been framed, the argument could be easily dispatched. "As to knowledge or acquiescence of officers of the Federal government little need be said"[50]—and little was said. Section 2 of the NIRA provided antitrust immunity for codes approved by the President, and the dancing partner program had never been approved because of *Schechter*. Even though some "employees of the federal government may have known of those programs and winked at them or tacitly approved them," no immunity was obtained.[51] Even if the dancing partner program were generally consistent with the aims of the NIRA, that could not immunize it from illegality since price-fixing agreements are "illegal per se."[52]

The New New Dealers had little patience for these rich oilmen's arguments that it was all the Old New Dealers' fault. The age of associationalism had been misguided and was better forgotten. The future lay in vigorous enforcement of the antitrust laws.

B. *Framing the Absoluteness of the Price Fixing Rule*

1. "Consistently and Without Deviation"

Douglas dedicated the bulk of *Socony* to establishing that price-fixing agreements are per se illegal, that there simply is no defense to such market manipulation. Today, that proposition may seem self-evident, but it was not such an easy point to make in 1940.

Even judges as ruthlessly independent as William O. Douglas prefer to justify their decisions by appealing to precedent. "Because I said so" never reads well in an opinion. Proving continuity with precedent would be particularly important in a case like *Socony* where the defendants could assert, without exaggeration, that their conduct had been prompted, condoned, and indeed virtually compelled by the very executive

---

[50] 310 U.S. at 225.

[51] *Id.* at 226.

[52] *Id.* at 228.

branch of government that was now their antagonist. So Douglas set out to prove a conclusion that would cut through the Gordian knot of the defendants' reasonableness defense: "[F]or over forty years this Court has consistently and without deviation adhered to the principle that price-fixing agreements are unlawful per se under the Sherman Act and that no showing of so-called competitive abuses or evils which those agreements were designed to eliminate or alleviate may be interposed as a defense."[53] If this principle were correct, it would make affirming the convictions a reflexive act of adjudication preordained by a long stream of consistent authority.

But the assertion was questionable at best. The Court had on several occasions entertained reasonableness defenses in cases that involved, quite literally, price fixing. Nonetheless, Douglas patiently explained how each of these decisions did not fall within the per se rule.

His two largest problems were *Chicago Board of Trade ("CBOT")*[54] and *Appalachian Coals*.[55] In *CBOT*, Justice Brandeis had upheld a Board of Trade regulation fixing the price for "to arrive" grain between the closing of a trading session and its opening the next day. This was literally a "price fixing" agreement, since it involved competitors agreeing to adhere to a mutually agreed upon price. Douglas distinguished *CBOT* as a case in which "no attempt was made to that the purpose or effect of the [call] rule was to raise or depress prices."[56]

True enough, but that was because the Government thought that the CBOT's conduct was subject to a per se rule akin to the one that Douglas was about to announce in *Socony* and therefore didn't bother to try and prove anticompetitive effects.[57] Further, as we will see shortly, in his famous footnote 59, Douglas ruled that the power to raise prices, and actual effects on prices, are not necessary for a price-fixing conspiracy to be unlawful. So the distinction of *CBOT* was weak.

Appalachian Coal, was an even more clearly anticompetitive arrangement and Douglas's distinction of it even weaker. In that case, a coalition of Appalachian coal producers accounting for about 64% of the Appalachian market created a joint sales agency that would sell all of their coal, at prices established by the agency. There was little doubt that the effect of this program was to increase coal prices. Nonetheless, the Supreme Court upheld the program as a reasonable means of dealing

---

[53] 310 U.S. at 218.

[54] Chicago Board of Trade v. United States, 246 U.S. 231 (1918).

[55] Appalachian Coals, Inc. v. United States, 288 U.S. 344 (1933).

[56] 310 U.S. at 217.

[57] *See* ROBERT H. BORK, THE ANTITRUST PARADOX 42 (2d ed. 1993).

with overproduction and rationalizing the industry. After all, *Appalachian Coal* was decided in 1933, the very year of NIRA's passage and the push for industry associationalism.

Douglas pretended to be unimpressed with defendants' reliance on *Appalachian Coal*. Unlike the *Socony* dancing partner arrangement, he wrote, "the plan in the *Appalachian Coals* case was not designed to operate vis a vis the general consuming market and to fix prices on that market."[58]

Douglas's effort to distinguish the case was extraordinarily weak. If his point was that the Appalachian Coals participants sold only into the wholesale market and not at retail, that would not distinguish the dancing partner program, which also operated directly only at wholesale. Moreover, there is little doubt that a seller's consortium with a 64% market share will affect prices at retail, and Douglas certainly understood this. A memo to Douglas from one of his law clerks, recommending the grant of *certiorari*, explained that "[t]he Appalachian Coals case upheld a combination which raised prices to a level above [the] cost of production by preventing the sale of surplus coal below the market price." In truth, *Appalachian Coals* should have been a much easier price-fixing case than *Socony*. As more recent cases have recognized, *Appalachian Coals* effectively has been limited to its facts and is no longer followed.[59] But that is not the sort of admission that Douglas wanted to make given the equities of *Socony*. So "consistently and without deviation" it was.

2. Market Power, Causation, and Reasonableness

Now Douglas turned to the heart of his opinion, articulating the absoluteness of the per se rule. Each of the defendants' defenses was raised and rejected. Defendants protested that the price increases in 1934 were caused by many things other than the dancing partner program, such as governmental efforts to control hot oil and an increase in demand, and that they did not have market power. But, wrote Douglas, market power—the power to raise prices—is not required for a restraint of trade to be condemned under the per se rule and the government need not prove an actual affect on prices from the conspiracy. A "conspiracy to fix prices violates [Section 1] of the [Sherman] Act though no overt act is shown, though it is not established that the conspirators had the means available for accomplishment of their objective . . . ."[60]

---

[58] 310 U.S. at 216.

[59] *See, e.g.*, Virginia Excelsior Mills, Inc. v. FTC, 256 F.2d 538, 541 (4th Cir. 1958).

[60] *Id.* at 224 n.59.

Defendants also argued, as they had at trial, that they had been acting reasonably to cure the ruinous competitive evil of overproduction. Douglas responded that "the elimination of so-called competitive evils is no legal justification for such buying programs."[61] Otherwise, "the reasonableness of prices would necessarily become an issue in every price-fixing case."[62]

The *Socony* per se rule was not a complete innovation. It had roots in a number of earlier Supreme Court decisions, including *Trans–Missouri*,[63] *Addyston Pipe*,[64] *Standard Oil*, and *Trenton Potteries*.[65] Those cases, also, had rejected defendants' attempts to argue that their conduct was reasonably designed to eliminate competitive evils. But here there was a difference. The majors were not simply arguing that the prices they charged at retail were reasonable, a line of argument that the Court had squarely rejected in *Trenton Potteries*. They were arguing that their entire course of conduct was reasonable in light of the Depression, NIRA, and the Roosevelt administration's directive. It was the absolute rejection of any reasonableness argument once the "price fixing" label attached that made *Socony* the per se rule's defining case for many years to come.

C.   *Explaining How the Dancing Partner Program Amounted to Price Fixing*

That left only one major issue to be resolved: whether the "price-fixing" label should be attached to the defendants' conduct. Defendants had a pretty good argument that it should not. Unlike in *CBOT* where the exchange's call rule had literally set the price of "to arrive" grain at the previous day's closing price and *Appalachian Coal* where the coal producers had appointed a single agent to set prices on their behalf, the *Socony* defendants had not agreed on what price would be paid to the independent refiners for hot oil or what the spot market wholesale or retail prices of gasoline would be. Indeed, as the Court of Appeals pointed out, there was evidence that the majors paid substantially different prices to their dancing partners. For example, there was a day in March of 1935 when the majors paid three or four different prices to the independent refiners. Overall, more than one price was paid on 72% of the relevant days.[66]

---

[61] *Id.* at 220.

[62] *Id.* at 221.

[63] United States v. Trans–Missouri Freight Association, 166 U.S. 290 (1897).

[64] Addyston Pipe & Steel Co. v. United States, 175 U.S. 211 (1899).

[65] U.S. v. Trenton Potteries Co., 273 U.S. 392 (1927).

[66] 105 F.3d at 819.

But this only gave Douglas an opportunity to announce the sweeping scope of the per se rule. It was unimportant, he wrote, "that the prices paid by the combination were not fixed in the sense that they were uniform and inflexible."[67] Price fixing—this per se unlawful act as to which there are no defenses—consists of things other than the literal fixing of prices. Any "manipulation" or "artificial stimulus" "which prevents the determination of . . . prices by free competition alone" is price fixing.[68] "Any combination which tampers with price structures is engaged in an unlawful activity."[69] Since the dancing partner program was clearly designed to affect the spot market price of gasoline, which in turn was the index for the major's supply contracts with independent retailers, the program amounted to "price fixing."

D. *Other Issues*

Socony is remembered for its articulation of the per se rule of illegality for price fixing, but Douglas had to dispose of several other legal issues raised by the defendants, including the propriety of venue in Madison, Wisconsin and the judgments of acquittal in favor of some of the defendants. Most interesting for present purposes was defendants' argument that the flagrant misconduct of Jackson's "country lawyer" cost them a fair trial. Justice Robert's dissent lambasted the government for Crawford's closing argument. This issue appears to have been the only one to have given the ordinarily decisive Douglas any pause. A handwritten note from Douglas's papers shows that he circulated this portion of the opinion to Justice Black for his comments before he circulated the opinion to the other justices. Still, Douglas would not let Crawford's overly theatrical presentation stand in the way of the per se rule's overpowering coverage and dismissed the prosecution's conduct as harmless error, if error at all. At the end of the day on May 6, 1940, the convictions stood.

IV. THE PER SE RULE IN HISTORICAL CONTEXT

A. *Sixty Years of Dualism*

As with any great legal case, it was not long before *Socony* ceased to be "about" the people and facts involved and became an inert doctrine: the per se rule of illegality for price fixing arrangements. Twenty times over the next sixty years, the Supreme Court cited *Socony* for that proposition, and the lower courts did so hundreds of times. Long after the Depression, NIRA, Harold Ickes, Thurman Arnold, the associationalism of the first half of the New Deal, and the raw unfairness of

---

[67] 310 U.S. at 222.

[68] *Id.* at 223.

[69] *Id.* at 221.

criminally prosecuting defendants who had done the government's bidding had faded from public memory, that much of *Socony* lived on as the staunchest of antitrust principles. Price fixing is per se illegal, reasonableness is no defense, market power by defendants need not be shown.

Of course, *Socony's* per se rule was only half of the doctrinal story. *Socony* had not overruled the *CBOT* principle that some restraints of trade are subject to a rule of reason in which the defendant's market power and the effect on prices are relevant and the defendant is free to justify his conduct on efficiency grounds. After *Socony*, all collaborative restraints of trade would be lumped into two uneasy categories—the rule of per se illegality for price fixing and a few similar categories of misconduct and the rule of reason for all other restraints.

The categories were uneasy because it often was not clear which one applied to a particular defendant's conduct, just as it wasn't in *Socony* itself. To paraphrase Ludwig Wittgenstein, the problem with rules is that they don't tell you when to apply them.[70] So, despite the apparent clarity and absolutism of *Socony*, defendants still found opportunities to defend the reasonableness of their collaborative arrangements with competitors by arguing that they did not amount to "price fixing." Thirty years after *Socony*, in *BMI v. CBS*,[71] the Supreme Court rejected textual "literalism" and held that application of the per se rule against price fixing is not as "simplistic" as "determining whether two or more potential competitors have literally 'fixed' a 'price.'" Rather, "[a]s generally used in the antitrust field, 'price fixing' is a shorthand way of describing certain categories of business behavior to which the *per se* rule has been held applicable."[72] Application of the per se rule turns not on whether the conduct amounts literally to price fixing but on whether the "particular practice is one of those types or that it is 'plainly anticompetitive' and very likely without 'redeeming virtue.'"[73]

So, as things developed, *Socony's* price fixing prohibition became a conclusion rather than a mode of analysis. If a court found a particular collaborative arrangement to be unjustifiably anticompetitive, it would condemn it as a per se illegal price fixing agreement. But the efficiency of the defendant's conduct would generally be admissible to determine whether the conduct was unjustifiably anticompetitive, bringing into the

---

[70] Ludwig Wittengenstein, Philosophical Investigations §§ 143–252 (G.E.M. Anscombe trans., 1953).

[71] Broadcast Music, Inc. v. Columbia Broadcasting System, Inc., 441 U.S. 1 (1979).

[72] *Id.* at 9.

[73] *Id.* Similarly, in its recent decision in *Texaco, Inc. v. Dagher*, 547 U.S. 1 (2006), the Court explained that conduct that is "price fixing in a literal sense, [is not necessarily] price fixing in the antitrust sense."

front end of the analysis the sort of efficiency criteria that *Socony* dictated should not be considered at the back end. In the wake of *BMI*, rule of reason/per se rule dualism survived, but a path was opened to avoid the "price fixing" label by characterizing the relevant conduct as efficient.

B.   Beyond Dualism

In the last few years, even the nominal dualism of Section 1 analysis has begun to fray. In recent opinions, the Federal Trade Commission and United States Court of Appeals for the D.C. Circuit rejected the idea of "dualism" and proclaimed that all antitrust restraints are to be measured on a continuum. The D.C. Circuit explained that "[t]he Supreme Court's approach to evaluating a § 1 claim has gone through a transition over the last twenty-five years, from a dichotomous categorical approach to a more nuanced and case-specific inquiry."[74] Bright-line rules are out, open-ended standards are in.

If we really are seeing the end of post-*Socony* dualism, scholars will doubtlessly argue that it began to unravel in *BMI* and continued its decline in cases like *NCAA v. Board of Regents*[75] and *California Dental v. FTC*,[76] where the Supreme Court recognized that Section 1 analysis is not quite as dualistic as earlier cases might have suggested and that all restraints of trade fall along a continuum from socially desirable to socially harmful. But the better argument will be that *Socony* never really set up a dualistic juridical regime at all. Although Douglas's prose is imminently quotable as legal doctrine, the doctrine itself was too riddled with inconsistencies and loopholes to be outcome-determinative most of the time. The power of *Socony* was never in its doctrine—in its rejection of the reasonableness defense or its disclaimer of the need to show market power or an actual effect on prices. Its power was in its soaring appeal to the norm of competition and its confirmation of the political triumph of the New New Dealers.

V.   POSTSCRIPTS

Even if the Madison defendants were just following orders in the case by which posterity would remember them, it seems that they *were* up to no good independently of the NIRA and Harold Ickes. The Justice Department brought a second indictment against the same defendants in 1936, this time alleging a conspiracy dating back to 1931 to fix the maximum margins of gross profits for gasoline jobbers and the terms of jobber contracts. Socony, Arnott and a number of other corporate and

---

[74] Polygram Holdings, Inc. v. FTC, 416 F.3d 29 (2005).

[75] NCAA v. Board of Regents, 468 U.S. 85 (1984).

[76] California Dental Association v. FTC, 526 U.S. 756 (1999).

individual defendants pled *nolo contendere* (effectively guilty) to those charges in 1938 after their convictions in the main *Socony* case.[77]

In 1939, while Government was preparing its appeal to the Supreme Court, the Justice Department brought a third action against the majors, this time in Danville, Illinois. The government alleged that the majors were still up to the same practices condemned in the Madison cases. This time, the federal grand jury refused to return the indictment. With war brewing in Europe, big oil was beginning to regain its luster.

Ickes's relationship with the oil industry and the Roosevelt administration remained rocky. In 1946, he resigned from the Truman administration over an oil conservation dispute, a staunch conservationist to the end.

Justice Douglas would go on to serve on the Court until 1975, and even attempted to serve after his retirement, prompting his "brethren" to gently push him out.[78] The *Socony* case brought him both scorn and accolades and some correspondence that, shall we say, missed the point. One Elgie MacCloud, a Standard Oil Station operator from Bailey, Michigan, wrote Douglas immediately after the *Socony* decision to complain that Standard Oil had recently cut his commission, which Elgie believed would hurt federal and state tax revenues and therefore required investigation by Douglas personally. Edith Waters, Douglas's secretary, kindly informed Elgie that, as a member of the Court, Justice Douglas was not in a position to dispense legal advice.

Robert Jackson's career path continued to rocket upwards, with appointments as Solicitor General, Attorney General, United States Supreme Court Justice, and chief United States Prosecutor at the Nuremberg war crimes trials. The *Socony* case caused some controversy during his confirmation hearings for Solicitor General in 1938, when Senator Warren Austin of Vermont introduced Ickes's July 20, 1934 letter to Arnott into the record and accused Jackson of an unfair prosecution of oilmen who had only been following Ickes's orders.

Like Ickes, Thurman Arnold would struggle in the Roosevelt Administration. While his aggressive antitrust enforcement could be tolerated in peacetime, once the war began political priorities shifted again. Arnold's indictment of the carpenter's union and its president, William Hutcheson, was a serious political miscalculation because labor was such an important component of the New Deal coalition. Arnold was finally forced out of the DOJ (and into a seat as a federal appeals court judge)

---

[77] *Statement of Grounds of Action—Oil Industry—United States v. Socony-Vacuum Oil Company, Inc., et al.* (U.S. D.C. W.D. Wis.—CR. No. 11364)—Pleas of Nolo Contendere, Dept. of Justice May 25, 1938.

[78] Bob Woodward & Scott Armstrong, The Brethren 396–99 (1979).

after he attempted to indict the railroads (which were essential to the war effort) and political luminary Averell Harriman for price fixing.[79] He eventually founded the law firm that became Arnold & Porter, which today often represents large corporations, including oil companies, in antitrust proceedings.

Socony's conviction did not bring long-term harm to the company. In 1955, its name was changed to Socony Mobil Oil Company, Inc. and in 1966, it dropped the "Socony" and became the Mobil Oil Corporation. In 1999, Exxon and Mobil merged to become Exxon Mobil Corporation, the sixth largest company in the world. In January of 2007, Exxon Mobil announced a record profit for any U.S. company—$39.5 billion on revenue of $377.6 billion in 2006, or more than $75,000 for every minute in the year. Harold Ickes and Thurman Arnold both rolled over in their graves.

CONCLUSION

It is tempting to think of *Socony* as only a case about the fickleness of competition policy. That is doubtlessly how it felt to Charles Arnott and his co-defendants. One cannot help but feel that criminal prosecution of the *Socony* defendants was a harsh way to accomplish a U-turn of federal antitrust enforcement. It bears noting that the government took a much gentler approach with other industries that had been once subject to the NIRA's codes. For example, when Thurman Arnold initiated the Paramount action in 1938 leading up to the famous Paramount decree, he brought only a civil action for injunctive relief aimed at future conduct and generally emoted a conciliatory attitude toward the film industry.[80] One wonders whether the same could not have been done in the Madison Oil case.

Nonetheless, *Socony's* strength as a vehicle for articulating the per se rule lies in the very fact that the equities so overwhelmingly favored the defendants. If reasonableness was not a defense under such circumstances, when could it ever be? For those who favor bright-line, invariable judicial rules even in the face of compelling contrary equities, *Socony* is a pedogically perfect decision.

Still, *Socony* is best remembered not as an articulation of legal doctrine but as a reminder that, despite its dull econometrics and tedious trial records, antitrust enforcement is highly dependent on the ideological commitments of the administration in power in general, and of the leadership of the federal antitrust agencies more particularly. There are many different ways to run an economy other than mandating competi-

---

[79] WALLER, *supra* n. 27 at 109.

[80] HAWLEY, *supra* n. 8 at 436.

tion and many different values that a competition law system can serve. If nothing else, *Socony* should remind us that the legal apparatus of antitrust enforcement—the rules, the culture, and the institutional players—is only as stable as the values on which it is premised. Since the values underlying antitrust—such as competition, efficiency, deconcentration, and individualism—are often contradictory, it should not be surprising that antitrust enforcement tends toward radical shifts as well.

*

4

Spencer Weber Waller

The Story of *Alcoa*: The Enduring Questions of Market Power, Conduct, and Remedy in Monopolization Cases

United States v. Aluminum Company of America[1] remains one of the standard chestnuts of American antitrust law. It appears in one form or another in virtually every antitrust law casebook and industrial organization economics textbook. It represents a lens in which we see what we want to see, either a reasonably efficient and innovative firm that created an entire industry or an aggressive monopolist preserving its position through a web of carefully constructed entry barriers including exclusive contracts, participation in international cartels, relentless expansion, and complete vertical integration.

While the *Alcoa* case is first and foremost the story of aluminum, it is also the story of a quirky chemist who invented a new industry, the investors who joined the inventor in commercializing the new way to smelt aluminum, a diminutive boarding house acquaintance of the inventor who worked his way up from laborer to chairman of the board over nearly sixty years with the company, one of the most prominent financier families in American history who bankrolled Alcoa's development and expansion, a crusading head of the Antitrust Division who finally brought Alcoa to trial for monopolization, and one of the most famous Second Circuit judges who had to step in to author the landmark opinion when the Supreme Court could not muster a quorum to hear the case.

---

[1] 148 F. 2d 416 (2d Cir. 1945).

Alcoa is one of the first cases to crystallize thinking about Section 2 of the Sherman Act. It also analyzed the hard questions concerning how to define a market, what conduct of a monopolist should be prohibited, and what remedy should be imposed to best restore competition, questions that all continue to be debated today.

I. THE STORY OF ALUMINUM

Aluminum is a widely abundant mineral, yet it proved almost impossible to produce in its pure form until the late 1880s. Alumina, the oxide form of the metal, is found in a wide variety of common rocks and clay and comprises almost 8% of the earth's crust. The first techniques for isolating the metal used various chemical processes but were too costly and produced too little of the metal to manufacture anything except prohibitively expensive jewelry, eating utensils, baby rattles, and similar novelties. While the price of aluminum per pound had fallen dramatically by the 1880s, it was still too expensive for mass commercial applications.

Almost simultaneously, two separate inventors changed all that.[2] In France, Paul L.T Heroult invented a method of using electricity to smelt aluminum from its raw oxide mineral state. So did Charles Martin Hall, a twenty-two year old chemist in Oberlin, Ohio. Hall had studied chemistry at Oberlin College and legend has it that he was inspired by a remark by his chemistry professor that great fortune lay ahead for the person who could figure out how to produce aluminum on a commercial scale. After graduation, Hall set up a homemade laboratory in a wood shed next to his parent's kitchen. He then began to tinker with a variety of projects, but eventually focused on aluminum full-time.

After toying with the existing chemical techniques, Hall turned to electrolysis. Hall constructed a series of batteries and applied electrical current to different crucibles containing various solutions of dissolved alumina. On February 23, 1886, he was successful in producing small globules of almost pure metal. Despite the probable earlier invention of a similar technique by Heroult, Hall was able to file the first United States patent application, which gave him legal priority in the United States for one of the most commercially successful inventions of the late 19th century.

---

[2] The story of Charles Martin Hall's discovery of an electro-chemical process to smelt aluminum is set forth in greater detail in an Alcoa commissioned history of the company and numerous other sources. See GEORGE DAVID SMITH, FROM MONOPOLY TO COMPETITION: THE TRANSFORMATION OF ALCOA, 1888–1986 at 1–17 (1988). See also CHARLES W. PARRY, ALCOA: A RETROSPECTION 7–11 (1985); CHARLOTTE FELDMAN MULLER, LIGHT METALS MONOPOLY 98–101 (1946); CHARLES C. CARR, ALCOA: AN AMERICAN ENTERPRISE 1–13 (1952).

Having the exclusive right to make, use, or sell aluminum produced through the Hall method was not, however, the same as having a commercially viable method of smelting aluminum or a way to sell it on the mass market. That required capital, a large scale production facility, and a market for aluminum ingot. Hall worked briefly for a Cleveland smelting company which produced various metals and alloys through electro-chemical processes. This firm obtained an option on the Hall process for a pittance but ultimately let the option expire, and Hall moved on.

Hall then met Alfred Hunt, a consultant in the steel industry in Pittsburgh, who better saw the commercial promise in Hall's technology. Hunt recruited others from the steel industry who invested $20,000, and on October 1, 1888 the Pittsburgh Reduction Company was created. Shortly thereafter, Hall recruited Arthur Vining Davis who lived in the same boarding house as Hall to join the fledgling company.

By Thanksgiving of 1888 a small plant in Pittsburgh began operations. The key was electricity, lots of it, plus quality control of the batches of chemicals heated with the alumina. Hall and Davis each worked twelve hour shifts around the clock. Production rose to 475 pounds a day and the price fell correspondingly as economies of scale emerged. Plans were in the works for a move to an even bigger facility in New Kensington, Pennsylvania which had access to cheaper sources of coal and natural gas as a source of crucial electricity.

The Mellon family in Pittsburgh acquired a significant block of stock in 1890 in exchange for critical financing needed for expansion and to weather a cash shortage.[3] The Mellons were notorious symbols of late 19th century finance capitalism and became even more so during the 1920s and 1930s, but nonetheless remained largely aloof from the day-to-day operations of the company. Day-to-day operations remained in the hands of Hall, Hunt, and Davis. By the time Hunt passed away in 1899, Hall had focused most of his time and energy on company-related research pursuits; thus, Davis became firmly in charge along with Hunt's surviving brother, Roy.

The Hall patent, and another patent acquired through the settlement of infringement litigation, gave the Pittsburgh Reduction Company the exclusive rights to produce aluminum through the only commercially viable method in the United States until the end of 1909.

The Pittsburgh Reduction Company became the Aluminum Company of America, Alcoa for short, in 1907. As Alcoa continued to grow, it began to vertically integrate both backward and forward. To assure itself a source of bauxite, the mineral containing the highest percentage of

---

[3] CARR, ALCOA: AN AMERICAN ENTERPRISE, *supra* note 2, at 40–48.

alumina, Alcoa acquired bauxite mines, first in the United States and later internationally. To guarantee timely and cost effective transportation of the ore to its smelters, it similarly built or acquired steamships and rail lines.

The company's greatest needs remained cheap, plentiful electricity which eventually meant hydroelectricity. It built hydroelectric generating plants at Niagara Falls and in Canada, and sited its smelting plants next to them to take advantage of this critical input. It also entered into long term contracts with public and private hydroelectric power plants, which virtually prohibited the sellers from selling to other aluminum smelters, even though there were no other smelters to sell to at the time. Over time, the Hall patent, and later the vagaries of the business cycle, Alcoa's vertical integration, its economies of scale and scope, the significant tariffs on imports, and the necessary vast capital costs all proved formidable barriers to entry.[4]

None of this guaranteed a market for Alcoa's wares. In order to change aluminum from a novelty into a commodity, Alcoa had to promote its product to a skeptical nation.[5] As part of its process, it vertically integrated downward and entered into fabricating virgin aluminum into new products previously made out of other metals and materials. Plants were added to turn ingot into wire, tubes, sheets, and other castings. Soon Alcoa's fabricating operations became the smelting operation's largest customers.

Alcoa ended up going so far as to acquire and expand manufacturing operations for cookware, kitchen utensils, tea kettles, and coffee pots. More industrial applications included alloys and various shaped aluminum for packaging, bicycles, machine parts, automotive parts, electrical transmission wire and cable, and increasingly aircraft. Aluminum displaced brass, zinc, tin, copper, iron, and steel in the process. While others eventually entered the field at the fabricating level, no one in North America challenged Alcoa in the smelting of aluminum.

II.   EARLY ANTITRUST LITIGATION

The initial government antitrust challenge against Alcoa was filed in 1911 by the Taft Administration as part of the first wave of antitrust enforcement which included the famous *Standard Oil*[6] and *American*

---

[4] Note, *Vertical Integration in Aluminum: A Bar to Effective Competition,* 60 YALE L.J. 294 (1951) (contending that vertical integration was still key entry barrier in industry as late as 1950).

[5] CARR, ALCOA: AN AMERICAN ENTERPRISE, *supra* note 2, at 109–21.

[6] Standard Oil Co. of New Jersey v. United States, 221 U.S. 1 (1911). See chapter one, *infra*, James May, *The Story of Standard Oil*, ANTITRUST STORIES (2007).

Tobacco[7] cases. Unlike its more famous contemporary cases which resulted in Supreme Court opinions affirming orders of divestitures, the first
Alcoa case ended in a relatively modest consent decree barring Alcoa
from participating in an international cartel affecting imports into the
United States. This decree also barred Alcoa from discriminating against
customers based on whether the customer also competed in fabrication
with Alcoa, engaging in boycotts and threats, and further prohibited
Alcoa from enforcing certain covenants not to compete with its suppliers
and customers.[8] During the 1920s, Alcoa was also subject to a prolonged
antitrust investigation by the Federal Trade Commission which ultimately resulted in a published government report, but no further litigation.

During its early years Alcoa also was subject to a number of private
antitrust cases. Most of these cases ended in dismissal of the allegations
or in minor settlements that did not result in any significant change in
the company's operations.[9] Alcoa would not, however, be so lucky in the
next round of government antitrust challenges.

III.   THE CASE THAT BECAME "ALCOA"

The case that culminated in the famous 1945 second circuit opinion
by Learned Hand was filed by the government just as Robert Jackson
became head of the Antitrust Division of the Justice Department. The
Antitrust Division itself had only been created in 1933, and had done
relatively little to enforce the antitrust laws during the early years of the
New Deal. Instead, the New Deal emphasized government-business
planning through various industry codes, akin to the cartels, promulgated under the National Industrial Recovery Act.[10] However things began

---

[7] United States v. American Tobacco Co., 221 U.S. 106 (1911).

[8] United States v. Aluminum Company of Am., Equity No. 159 (W.D. Pa. 1912),
reprinted in DECREES AND JUDGMENT IN FEDERAL ANTI-TRUST CASES, JULY 2,
1890—JANUARY 1, 1918 at 341–350 (1918) *abstract reprinted in* ANTITRUST CONSENT
DECREES 1906–1966 at 217–18 (1968).

[9] Aluminum Co. of Am. v. Thompson Prods., 122 F.2d 796 (6th Cir. 1941) modifying
decree issued in Aluminum Co. of Am. v. Thompson Prods., 25 F. Supp. 175 (N.D. Ohio
1938); Baush Mach. Tool Co. v. Aluminum Co. of Am., 79 F.2d 217 (2d Cir. 1935); Baush
Mach. Tool Co. v. Aluminum Co. of Am., 72 F.2d 236 (2d Cir.), *cert. denied*, Aluminum Co
of Am. v. Bausch Mach. Tool Co., 293 U.S. 589 (1934); Baush Mach. Tool Co. v. Aluminum
Co. of Am., 63 F.2d 778 (2d Cir.), *cert. denied*, Aluminum Co. of Am. v. Baush Mach. Tool
Co., 289 U.S. 739 (1933); Aluminum Co. of Am. v. Sterling Prods. Corp., 66 F.2d 958 (8th
Cir. 1933); Haskell v. Aluminum Co. of Am., 14 F.2d 864 (D. Mass. 1926); Gen. Chem. Co.
v. Aluminum Co. of Am., 11 F.2d 810 (W.D. Pa. 1924), *aff'd*, Gen. Chem. Co. v. Aluminum
Co. of Am., 11 F.2d 813 (3d Cir. 1926).

[10] ALAN BRINKLEY, THE END OF REFORM: NEW DEAL LIBERALISM IN RE-
CESSION AND WAR (1995); ELLIS W. HAWLEY, THE NEW DEAL AND THE PROB-

to change dramatically in 1937. The mild recovery from the Great Depression abruptly ended and the nation slid back into recession. Ever the pragmatist, President Roosevelt began to shift his focus from the approach of the NIRA, which had been declared unconstitutional anyway by the Supreme Court, towards a renewed interest in market competition and antitrust enforcement as a cure for the nation's ills.

Robert Jackson had been the general counsel of the Bureau of Internal Revenue of the Treasury Department, earning a reputation in the process as one of the rising stars of the Administration. He was also a member of the market competition wing of the administration. He restored much needed vigor to the Antitrust Division and enjoyed rapid promotion to Solicitor General, Attorney General, and then was appointed to the United States Supreme Court. He further took a leave of absence to serve as lead prosecutor for the Nuremberg War Crimes Tribunal and then returned to the Supreme Court until his untimely death in 1954.[11]

When Jackson became Solicitor General, Roosevelt turned to an even more unlikely choice to guide the Antitrust Division, Professor Thurman Arnold of Yale Law School. Arnold was born and raised in Laramie, Wyoming and had been a prominent attorney and had served as the mayor of Laramie and as the only Democratic representative in the Wyoming legislature. He entered academia in the late 1920s as the dean of the West Virginia University College of Law and later joined the Yale Law School faculty in the early 1930s. At Yale, Arnold rose to prominence as a member of the Legal Realist movement which sought to analyze the way the law worked in action, as opposed to the law on the books, and to use social science to better achieve the goals of a just society. While on the Yale faculty, Arnold moonlighted part-time for the New Deal by working on projects for the Treasury Department, Securities Exchange Commission, the Justice Department, and the U.S. governor of the Philippines.

Arnold achieved minor fame as the author of the improbable best seller *The Folklore of Capitalism* in which Arnold ridiculed critics of the New Deal who contended that FDR's program for national recovery violated the immutable law of the market and laissez faire.[12] Although Arnold was known to the President both for his writings and his service to the Administration, there is no evidence that FDR actually read any

---

LEM OF MONOPOLY (1966); SPENCER WEBER WALLER, THURMAN ARNOLD: A BIOGRAPHY (2005).

[11] Jackson's life and relationship with President Roosevelt is discussed in his posthumously edited and published memoir, ROBERT H. JACKSON, THAT MAN: AN INSIDER's PORTRAIT OF FRANKLIN D. ROOSEVELT (John Q. Barrett ed. 2003).

[12] THURMAN W. ARNOLD, THE FOLKLORE OF CAPITALISM (1937).

part of *Folklore,* which included an attack on the antitrust laws as empty symbolic vehicles that promised to punish bad people without actually promoting change in the growth of the modern corporation and market economy.[13]

Because of these harsh words and a general reputation for being a smart aleck, Arnold was a controversial choice for the position and endured a tense confirmation hearing conducted by some of the same Senators he had ridiculed in print. At the hearings, Arnold contended that he was being misunderstood, that antitrust could play a meaningful role in reforming the economy, and he would do his utmost to enforce the laws.

Once in office, Arnold confounded his critics and became the most active head of the Antitrust Division in our nation's history. He brought more cases than in the nearly fifty years prior to his assuming office. He revived the criminal enforcement of Section 1 of the Sherman Act, helped establish the *per se* rule against price fixing in the *Socony-Vacuum* case,[14] brought high profile cases in virtually every major industry in the economy, and prosecuted a series of key international cartel cases involving market division schemes between American and German firms which affected US preparations for entering World War II.[15]

IV. THE LONGEST TRIAL IN U.S. HISTORY

The *Alcoa* case was no ordinary trial. The stakes were high. *Alcoa* was the most important case in a generation, rivaling those against *Standard Oil* and *U.S. Steel* in the past and the much later cases against *AT&T* and *Microsoft.* The sheer scope of the case was vast, covering the fifty year history of the industry and included 49 separate corporate and individual defendants all connected with Alcoa or its international operations. Andrew Mellon, the financier and board member of Alcoa, as well as the former Secretary of the Treasury throughout the Republican administrations of the 1920s, had been named as a defendant, but had died before trial began.

The trial commenced on June 1, 1938[16] with Thurman Arnold himself at the counsel table. Alcoa was represented by an enormous legal

---

[13] *Id.* at 207.

[14] United States v. Socony–Vacuum Oil Co., 310 U.S. 150 (1940).

[15] Arnold also enjoyed a remarkable career after leaving the Justice Department in 1943. He served for two years as a judge on the D.C. Circuit and then founded one of the quintessential Washington law firms that is currently known as Arnold & Porter. *See generally* WALLER, THURMAN ARNOLD, *supra* note 10.

[16] The trial would have commenced somewhat sooner but for an entertaining side show in which Alcoa unsuccessfully sought to enjoin the Justice Department from suing

team including Charles Evan Hughes Jr., the son of the former Presidential candidate and Supreme Court Justice.

The Antitrust Division promised to prove that Alcoa had a "100% monopoly in virgin aluminum and bauxite industry throughout the Western Hemisphere" and controlled output throughout the "rest of world" through subsidiaries, affiliates, and a cartel with foreign producers. Alcoa's lawful monopoly on the production of aluminum from bauxite ore through various patents had expired in the early part of the 20th century. The 1912 consent decree had eliminated certain restrictive covenants and cartel arrangements with foreign producers which had further buttressed Alcoa's monopoly of the American aluminum market. Alcoa sold more than 90% of the virgin aluminum ingot in the United States, although a growing amount of recycled ingot was also entering the market. New domestic competition was almost impossible given Alcoa's aggressive expansion and its lock on sources of hydroelectric power, the single most important input for aluminum production after bauxite ore itself. Imports remained next to nothing due to Alcoa's continuing participation in international cartel arrangements.

The trial lasted until August 14, 1940; more than 40,000 pages of testimony were taken and 10,000 pages of exhibits entered into evidence. The *New Yorker* magazine in a famous two part article about the case claimed it was the longest trial in the history of the world and that the trial record was three times heavier than the Encyclopedia Britannica and thirty times longer than *Gone with the Wind*.[17] The judge immediately issued a draft oral opinion dismissing all charges, which itself took nine days to deliver.[18] Judge Caffey's oral and later written opinion exonerated the defendants on every possible matter. He addressed each claim of monopolization or restraint of trade seriatim. He dismissed claims of monopolization of bauxite, alumina, and electrical power on the grounds that Alcoa lacked monopoly power over these commodities. He similarly dismissed charges of monopolization of markets for different fabricated aluminum products also for lack of market power. He dismissed the allegations that Alcoa had monopolized the production of aluminum itself on the grounds that Alcoa had engaged in no exclusionary conduct and lacked market power in a market consisting of both virgin and scrap aluminum sold to customers other than Alcoa subsidiaries.

---

anywhere but Pittsburgh where the 1912 consent decree had been entered. Aluminum Co. of Am. v. United States, 302 U.S. 230 (1937).

[17] Alva Johnson, "Thurman Arnold's Biggest Case," *The New Yorker* 25 (Jan. 24, 1942).

[18] United States v. Aluminum Co. of Am., 44 F. Supp. 97 (S.D.N.Y. 1941).

It was a total defeat for the government. Observers aligned with both the government and the company attributed Alcoa's victory to the superior trial tactics of veteran defense counsel, the scatter shot techniques of Arnold's younger, more zealous courtroom team, and the strong favorable impression that Arthur Vining Davis made on the judge in his more than thirty days of testimony.[19]

When Arnold asked for permission to appeal before the judge finalized his opinion in writing, the exhausted district court judge replied: "If there is any legal way for me to get rid of this case, I'll do it so quick it'll make your head swim." Alas for the trial judge, the final judgment dismissing the case did not appear until July 23, 1942.[20] The government appealed directly to the Supreme Court, as permitted by then existing law, but the Court lacked a quorum of six justices to hear the case. The Court was down to only eight members because Roosevelt had not yet filled the seat formerly held by Justice Byrnes. Justices Jackson, Reed, and Murphy presumably were disqualified for their earlier work on the case for the Roosevelt Justice Department with Chief Justice Stone similarly being disqualified because of his earlier involvement in prosecuting Alcoa while Attorney General under Coolidge. Even if Roosevelt had filled the vacancy, there may not have been a quorum for this critical case given the President's penchant for choosing Justice Department and other New Deal insiders. This left matters in a quandary until Congress stepped in and passed a statute designating the Second Circuit as the court of last resort to hear the government's appeal in the case.[21]

V.   THE FINAL WORD ON LIABILITY, BUT NOT REMEDY

On March 12, 1945, the Second Circuit reversed the district court opinion almost in its entirety and found Alcoa liable for monopolization of aluminum ingot. The resulting opinion created landmark precedent on what constitutes a monopoly, when a monopolist's actions in the market violate the antitrust law, and when anticompetitive conduct outside the United States constitutes a violation of the Sherman Act.[22] Even then, the Court deferred the issue of remedy until after World War II. The case was assigned to a most distinguished panel of Learned Hand, his cousin Augustus Hand, and Thomas Swan. There is considerable irony in Learned Hand emerging as the author of the famous opinion expansively interpreting Alcoa's behavior as unlawful monopolization. Although Hand had been an important part of the Progressive movement early in

---

[19] SMITH, FROM MONOPOLY TO COMPETITION, *supra* note 2, at 206–07; CARR, ALCOA: AN AMERICAN ENTERPRISE, *supra* note 2, at 219.

[20] SMITH, FROM MONOPOLY TO COMPETITION, *supra* note 2, at 206–07.

[21] 58 Stat. 272, 15 U.S.C. § 29.

[22] United States v. Aluminum Co. Of Am., 148 F.2d 416 (2d Cir. 1945).

the century while still in private practice, he had little interest in the judicial enforcement of the Sherman Act on a case-by-case basis. Hand found more appealing Theodore Roosevelt's vision that bigness was inevitable and that some regulatory method was needed to distinguish between the good trusts and the bad trusts. Accordingly, he found little of interest in Taft's aggressive antitrust enforcement campaign or Wilson's proposals for a New Nationalism. Instead, he supported the third party candidacy of Theodore Roosevelt and wrote in support of Roosevelt's antitrust views in an unsigned editorial in *The Outlook* magazine.[23]

a. Market Power: Numerators and Denominators

Judge Hand began by attacking the lower court's conclusion that Alcoa lacked market power and hence could not be liable for monopolization. Everything turned on market definition. The district court had held that Alcoa had approximately a 33% share of a market that included all virgin aluminum and secondary scrap aluminum, but excluded virgin aluminum that Alcoa itself fabricated. In one of the most heavily criticized parts of the opinion, Hand redefined the relevant market as being limited to virgin aluminum, both that sold to outside customers and that used by Alcoa for its own fabrication purposes.

Hand began by including all of Alcoa's virgin ingot production in the relevant market regardless of whether it was sold to outsiders or fabricated internally. In an uncontroversial part of the opinion, he reasoned that all ingot produced could affect demand and therefore should be included in the relevant market.[24]

He then excluded secondary or scrap aluminum even though he acknowledged that, for most purposes, it competed with virgin on a nearly equal basis. Hand relied on the grounds that since Alcoa controlled the production of virgin ingot, it indirectly controlled the amount of secondary aluminum that reentered the market and could thereby predict and account for its impact in setting price and production of virgin ingot.[25]

---

[23] GERALD GUNTHER, LEARNED HAND: THE MAN AND THE JUDGE 206–09 (1994). Antitrust proved to be the defining issue of 1912 Presidential election won by Wilson. The differing positions of the candidates and the campaign itself is recounted in JAMES CHACE, 1912: WILSON, ROOSEVELT, TAFT & DEBS—THE ELECTION THAT CHANGED THE COUNTRY (2004).

[24] 145 F.2d at 424. This portion of the opinion is widely supported by commentators. *See e.g.*, 2A PHILLIP E. AREEDA, HERBERT HOVENKAMP & JOHN L. SOLOW, ANTITRUST LAW § 535E (2d ed. 2002).

[25] 148 F.2d at 425–26. For an earlier opinion by Judge Hand adopting an equally narrow market definition see United States v. Corn Products Refining Co., 234 F. 964 (S.D.N.Y. 1916).

Judge Hand then recalculated Alcoa's market share as the amount of all virgin aluminum ingot produced by Alcoa divided by the total amount of all virgin aluminum sold in the United States. Given that no one else produced virgin aluminum in the United States and that imports were negligible because of tariff levels and Alcoa's participation in various international cartel arrangements, Alcoa had approximately 91% of the market defined in this way.

Hand began his discussion of relevant markets and market shares with the often quoted statement that in excess of 90% of the market is "enough to constitute a monopoly; it is doubtful that sixty or sixty four percent would be enough; and certainly thirty three per cent is not."[26] Given that including secondary aluminum in the relevant market would have produced a market share of 64% and excluding Alcoa's internal consumption of ingot would have produced the 33% share found by the district court, most critics have simply assumed that Hand picked the market share percentages he needed to proceed onto the next stage of the analysis and then worked backwards, gerrymandering the market definition until it produced the desired result.

In particular, excluding secondary aluminum on the grounds cited by Hand is highly debatable on both theoretical and empirical grounds. While it is possible that a producer who knew the fixed percentage of its product that reentered the market as scrap could take that in account in the early years to limit competition from secondary product, such a calculation becomes increasingly complicated and unwieldy as the years pass and the amount of secondary material overhanging the market increases. For example, by the 1930s recycled aluminum amounted to between 20% and 31% of the market.[27] On a more mundane level, there is little if any evidence produced at trial that Alcoa actually behaved in this manner, especially during an era when production was increasing exponentially.[28]

There is the strong possibility, however, that Hand got the market definition correct, albeit for the wrong reasons. Stronger grounds for excluding secondary aluminum from the relevant market consist of the

---

[26] 148 F.2d at 424.

[27] MORTON J. PECK, COMPETITION IN THE ALUMINUM INDUSTRY 1945–58 at 7–8 (1961); Valerie T. Suslow, *Estimating Monopoly Behavior with Competitive Recycling: An Application to Alcoa*, 17 RAND J. ECON. 389, 390 (1986).

[28] Moreover, there is the possibility that the relevant market could have included products besides aluminum itself. The history of Alcoa was to find new uses for aluminum for products previously made from other metals. Although aluminum clearly had unique properties that made it a relevant market onto itself for certain uses, consumers still regarded other metals as reasonably effective substitutes for aluminum for certain purposes like automobile manufacturing.

fact that secondary aluminum is only an imperfect substitute for virgin ingot for a number of product lines, its supply is highly inelastic, and the lag time before secondary aluminum reenters the market is both lengthy and unpredictable.[29]

Hand also addressed the questions of the relationship between Alcoa's profits and its status as a monopolist. Alcoa had argued that its profits were in the range of ten percent a year and this showed that it was not a monopolist since it did not earn extortionate monopoly profits. While economists then and now agree that proof of substantial profits over marginal costs for a substantial period of time would constitute evidence of monopoly power, Hand refused to concede that the converse was true. He questioned whether the courts were in a position to determine whether dominant firms earned a fair or unfair level of profits and held such proof irrelevant under either an economic or broader social reading of the antitrust laws. Even under a strictly economic view of the law, Hand wrote ringing words that resonate even today among those who find the possession of monopoly power a cause, rather than a cure, for the inefficiency that the antitrust laws condemn:

> Many people believe that possession of unchallenged economic power deadens initiative, discourages thrift and depresses energy, that immunity from competition is a narcotic, and rivalry a stimulant, to industrial progress; that the spur of constant stress to counteract an inevitable disposition to let well enough alone.[30]

b.   The Conduct Requirement: When Does a Monopolist Monopolize?

Having concluded that Alcoa was indeed a monopolist, Hand turned to the question of whether Alcoa had acted in a way that violated Section 2's prohibition against "monopolization." Previous case law had relied on finding some morally reprehensible conduct by the monopolist, such as independent violations of Section 1 of the Sherman Act or some acts of predation against its competitors. Standard Oil had been condemned for such conduct and U.S. Steel had been exonerated precisely because the Supreme Court could not find any such bad conduct.

Judge Hand changed the focus of Section 2 in a way that was rapidly endorsed by the Supreme Court and set the ground rules for Section 2 litigation for a generation. He set the tone for the rest of the opinion by stating early on:

> Having proved that "Alcoa" had a monopoly of the domestic ingot market, the plaintiff had gone far enough; if it was an excuse, that "Alcoa" had not abused its power, it lay upon "Alcoa" to prove

---

[29] PECK, *supra* note 27, at 7–8, 11; Suslow, *supra* note 27 at 391, 400.

[30] 148 F.2d at 427.

that it had not. But the whole issue is irrelevant anyway, for it is no excuse for "monopolizing" a market that the monopoly has not been used to extract from the consumer more than a "fair" profit. The Act has wider purposes. Indeed, even though we disregard all but economic considerations, it would by no means follow that such concentration of producing power is to be desired, when it has not been used extortionately.[31]

He dismissed Alcoa's arguments about earning only a "fair" profit, stating that there was "no evidence that a 'fair' profit could not have been made at lower prices."[32] He then rejected any test that would condemn only those monopolies which could not show that they had exercised the highest possible ingenuity, had adopted every possible economy, had anticipated every conceivable improvement, stimulated every possible demand, in essence an efficiency defense for monopolization. He relied on both a literalist interpretation of the Sherman Act condemning all trusts and a political and social justification for the antitrust laws that rejected a world where those engaged in business must accept the direction of a few.[33]

The opinion went on to discuss the *per se* condemnation of certain agreements in restraint of trade under Section 1 of the Sherman Act and argued that such agreements were merely partial monopolies and were condemned whether their power to affect competition was exercised or not. Similarly for Hand, there was no practical distinction between monopoly power and its exercise under the law.[34] Hand then spoke of the social, as well as economic, reasons behind the antitrust laws and stated: "Throughout the history of these statutes it has been constantly assumed that one of their purposes was to perpetuate and preserve, for its own sake and in spite of possible cost, an organization of industry in small units which can effectively compete with each other."[35]

The only possibility of escaping liability was for those monopolists who did not achieve monopoly but where monopoly may have been

---

[31] 148 F.2d at 427.

[32] Id.

[33] 148 F. 2d at 427 (citations omitted).

[34] 148 F.2d at 428. Most contemporary commentators approvingly understood Alcoa to hold that the possession of monopoly power without more was a violation of Section 2. Walter Adams, *The Sherman Act and its Enforcement*, 14 U. PITT. L. REV. 319, 329–30 (1953); Walter Adams, *Dissolution, Divorcement, and Divestiture: The Pyrrhic Victories of Antitrust*, 27 IND. L.J. 1, 6 (1951); Eugene V. Rostow, *The New Sherman Act: A Positive Instrument of Progress*, 14 U. CHI. L. REV. 567, 577 (1947); Robert W. Harbeson, *A New Phase of the Antitrust Law*, 45 MICH. L. REV. 977, 986 (1947); Note, *Enforcement of Section 2 of the Sherman Act*, 54 YALE L.J. 860, 861 (1945).

[35] 148 F.2d at 429.

thrust upon them. The Sherman Act would thus not reach those who
became monopolists by force of accident or through superior foresight,
skill, and industry.[36] This narrow escape route was quickly closed for
Alcoa itself. Hand held that Alcoa was not a passive beneficiary of a
monopoly, but had in fact sought to strengthen and maintain its original
lawful patent monopoly by exclusionary means. In response to one of
Alcoa's defenses that any specifically illegal anticompetitive acts ceased
as of the consent decree of 1912, the court replied:

> The only question is whether it falls within the exception
> established in favor of those who do not seek, but cannot avoid, the
> control of a market. . . . It was not inevitable that it should always
> anticipate increases in the demand for ingot and be prepared to
> supply them. Nothing compelled it to keep doubling and redoubling
> its capacity before others entered the field. . . . [W]e can think of no
> more effective exclusion than progressively to embrace each new
> opportunity as it opened, and to face every newcomer with new
> capacity already geared into a great organization, having the advan-
> tage of experience, trade connections and the elite of personnel.[37]

For Hand and his colleagues on the panel, intent was irrelevant
since "no monopolist monopolizes unconscious of what he is doing."[38]
Hand's formulation of unlawful monopolization, which required little
more than the possession of monopoly power by reason of something
other than an accident, was thus critical. The court went on to affirm
the vast majority of the district court's opinion rejecting most of the
specific allegedly illegal exclusionary acts undertaken by Alcoa.[39]

To understand the broad scope of the ruling in *Alcoa*, step back from
the case for a moment and put yourself in the shoes of the general
counsel or outside counsel for Alcoa or any similar monopolist. How
would you answer the following question from your client: "Following
Alcoa, assuming we are a monopolist, what can we do as a company that
will not violate Section 2?" Any answer seems fraught with peril, absent
the virtually hypothetical defense that monopoly was entirely accidental
or "thrust upon" but not sought.[40]

---

[36] 148 F.2d at 429–30.

[37] 148 F.2d at 431.

[38] 148 F.2d at 432.

[39] 148 F.2d at 432–39.

[40] Even this grudging exception for the "thrust upon" monopolist was criticized by a
number of contemporary commentators as too expansive. Harbeson, *supra* note 34, at 986.
The one contemporary situation which comes closest to Hand's example of the accidental
monopolist may be Microsoft which was the unintended beneficiary of IBM's decision to
sell the fledgling DOS operating system for personal computers when IBM temporarily

c. Establishing the Extraterritorial Application of the Sherman Act

While Alcoa maintained its monopoly in the United States, it did face international competition. Because Hand's opinion artificially separates the domestic and international aspects of the case, the importance of this section is often downplayed and the case is frequently not viewed as an organic whole. However, the existence of an international cartel for aluminum was a critical factor in allowing Alcoa to maintain its unlawful monopoly in the United States. Large European competitors existed which were capable of exporting to the United States, if prices rose enough to make exports profitable given the existing transportation costs and customs tariffs. Nonetheless, imports remained negligible through the World War II era, not counting US–Canada transactions between Alcoa affiliates. Part of the explanation related to the existence of a series of fairly formal international cartels based in Europe in which Alcoa participated indirectly through its Canadian affiliates.

Beginning in 1896, Alcoa entered into a formal cartel agreement with its European competitors which limited exports to the United States market. Although these agreements were spearheaded by Arthur Vining Davis, Alcoa only participated on a formal basis through its Canadian subsidiary because of concerns over U.S. antitrust law. Alcoa and Davis referred to this as doing business "the European way." Alcoa was content to limit its export opportunities in order to protect its core market, but always did so carefully and indirectly because of the United States antitrust laws.[41] Alcoa must have taken comfort in the 1909 Supreme Court opinion in the *American Banana* case which had held that the Sherman Act did not apply to conduct entirely outside the United States.[42] This route quickly was foreclosed through the 1912 consent decree which enjoined Alcoa from directly or indirectly being party to any agreement with competitors relating to the import or export of aluminum.[43]

In 1928, a new company called "Aluminium Limited," also known as just "Limited," was established to take over Alcoa's international prop-

---

decided to exit the software market. The DOS operating system evolved into Windows and became ubiquitous when the clones of the IBM PC came to dominate the desktop and laptop computer market and became the foundation for Microsoft's enduring monopoly for PC based operating systems. *See* Chapter 10 *infra*, A. Douglas Melamed & Daniel L. Rubinfeld, *U.S. v. Microsoft: Lessons Learned and Issues Raised*, ANTITRUST STORIES (2007).

[41] The details of the early formal cartels and the leading role played by Arthur Vining Davis in their creation and operation is set forth in MUELLER, LIGHT METALS MONOPOLY, supra note 2, at 97–119.

[42] American Banana Co. v. United Fruit Co., 213 U.S. 347 (1909).

[43] Consent Decree, *supra* note 8, at § 1.

erties. Limited was then spun off to Alcoa's existing shareholders. Thus, Limited was a separate Canadian corporation, not a subsidiary of Alcoa. Limited's principal shareholders were the same as Alcoa's, Arthur Vining Davis and members of the Mellon family. The officers were similar but not identical.[44] Arthur Vining Davis played a key role in Limited operations, even to the extent of creating, naming, and planning the details of Arvida,[45] the Canadian town where Limited was located.

Limited was not created solely to allow Alcoa to continue doing business in the "European way," but that was one of the principal benefits from Alcoa's point of view. Having a free standing Canadian corporation allowed greater access to sales opportunities in the British Empire which was showing a decidedly "Buy British" predilection. Limited also allowed Alcoa to solve a delicate matter of corporate succession. Edward Davis, Arthur's younger brother, and Roy Hunt, the brother of Alfred Hunt who had created the company, were both in senior positions and needed room to grow in the company. Edward Davis became president of Limited and Hunt became president of Alcoa as part of a grand bargain.[46] However, an equally important part of Limited's attraction was the docile manner it used to coordinate price and production with its American cousin and its foreign corporate structure which shielded Alcoa from liability for Limited's participation in formal cartel agreements with its European competitors.[47]

Limited entered into two such agreements that were international in scope. A 1931 global price, market division, and production agreement called the Alliance appeared to carve out the United States market from its provisions, but a subsequent 1936 revision of the Alliance agreement had the effect of limiting exports to the United States. Although the commencement of World War II in Europe rendered the agreement moot for the duration of hostilities, it technically remained in effect.[48]

The government contended that both Limited and Alcoa were liable for an illegal price fixing agreement in violation of Section 1 of the Sherman Act. The Second Circuit reluctantly held that there was no grounds to overturn the district court's finding that Alcoa and Limited acted independently, at least as of the time of the 1936 agreement which

---

[44] MULLER, LIGHT METALS MONOPOLY, *supra* note 2, at 122–24.

[45] **Ar**thur **Vi**ning **Da**vis = Arvida.

[46] PARRY, ALCOA: A RETROSPECTION, *supra* note 2, at 15–16; SMITH, FROM MONOPOLY TO COMPETITION, *supra* note 2, at 146; CARR, ALCOA: AN AMERICAN ENTERPRISE, *supra* note 2, at 186–91.

[47] MULLER, LIGHT METALS MONOPOLY, *supra* note 2, at 124–29.

[48] *Id.* at 120–46.

included the U.S. market. As a result, the court refused to hold Alcoa itself liable for the illegal international cartel.[49]

The Court, however, held Limited guilty of participating in an illegal price fixing and market division scheme despite its foreign nationality and the tableau of events taking place outside the United States. The Court expanded a line of cases imposing liability when some of the illegal acts took place within the United States and held that the illegal effects of the cartel within the United States were the legal equivalent of physical acts within U.S. territory and were equally condemned by the antitrust laws.[50] The court thus rejected any rule that focused on the physical location of the defendants or the site of the illegal acts. However, the court limited its effects test to those agreements which were intended to and, in fact, did affect the U.S. market. The *Alcoa* intended effects test ushered in the era of the extraterritorial application of the Sherman Act which continues to this day.[51]

d.   Remedy Deferred

The Second Circuit's *Alcoa* decision was as cautious on remedy as it was expansive on liability. The court refused to dissolve Alcoa or even to direct the submission of a plan of divestiture for execution after the war. The court noted that it had been nearly five years since the close of evidence at trial and that nearly everything in the industry had changed because of the advent of World War II. The government had entered the aluminum business in a major way constructing numerous new smelting and fabricating plants, thereby creating the possibility of competition once the war was over. The court cited to recent hearings of the Senate Truman Committee on War Preparedness which showed that Alcoa's own production was now dwarfed by the production of the government plants under lease and the smaller plants of two new entrants, the Reynolds and Olin companies.[52] While the end of the war was in sight in March 1945 when the Second Circuit issued its opinion, no one knew when victory ultimately would be achieved in Europe and Asia or what the state of the industry would be after the war. The court presciently alluded to the government's ability to dispose of its surplus property after the war, to the possibility of new competition inherent in that

---

[49] *Id.* at 440–442.

[50] *Id.* at 444.

[51] The court's holding was even more expansive than the famous intended effects test which the opinion announced. The court also held that once intent was established, the burden shifted to the defendant to show a lack of effect. 148 F.2d at 455. This portion of the opinion is probably not good law today. See note 69 *infra*.

[52] 148 F.2d at 445.

process, and remanded the matter of relief to the district court for further proceedings.[53]

VI.   TURNING MONOPOLY INTO OLIGOPOLY: SELLING SURPLUS GOVERNMENT ALUMINUM PLANTS

After nearly thirty five years of antitrust investigations and litigation, the Government found itself holding the keys to creating competition in the aluminum industry. Despite Alcoa having been judged guilty of monopolization for endless expansion and preempting demand, the company badly underestimated the demand for aluminum during World War II. As late as 1941, the company was confidently assuring Congress and the military that it could meet the needs of both the United States and Great Britain on its own.[54] Even the most ambitious expansion plans could not fill the military's insatiable need for the metal, primarily for aircraft and other armaments needed to fight the Nazi war machine. This miscalculation, more than all the antitrust litigation, may in the end have cost Alcoa its monopoly.

Alcoa itself expanded greatly during wartime although it was heavily subsidized by the government through electric power programs and accelerated depreciation provisions in the tax code. The Defense Plant Corporation ("DPC") financed the rest of the expansion. Alcoa built for the government numerous new plants at all stages of the production process. The only new entrant was Reynolds Metals which built two aluminum plants financed through loans from the Reconstruction Finance Corporation.

Virtually all of the government plants were leased back to Alcoa. As a result of the massive building program of government owned plants, Alcoa now owned less than 40% of the smelting capacity in the industry. The disposition of the leased plants after the war would determine the fate of competition in the industry far more efficaciously than any antitrust decree and with far less muss and fuss. The disposition of such property was governed by the Surplus Property Act of 1944 which directed that these facilities be disposed of in such manner, and with such purpose, as would foster competitive conditions in the aluminum industry of the nation.[55]

---

[53] The Second Circuit further discussed the need to defer the remedy and to reexamine Alcoa's position in the industry after the war in a subsequent opinion when the United States brought a mandamus action challenging the entry of the district court's judgment as inconsistent with the prior opinion by the Second Circuit. United States v. United States District Court for the Southern District of New York, 171 F. 2d 285 (2d Cir. 1948).

[54] *See* Charlotte Muller, *The Aluminum Monopoly and the War*, 60 POL. SC. Q. 14, 16–24 (Mar. 1945).

[55] 58 Stat. 765, 50 U.S.C.A. Appendix § 1611 *et seq. See* Herbert Roback, *Monopoly or Competition Through Surplus Plant Disposal?*, 31 CORNELL L.Q. 302 (1946).

Throughout the war, Alcoa was in an awkward position. On the one hand, it was a major participant in the war effort supplying the lion's share of a vital strategic metal. On the other hand, it was the defendant in one of the most important antitrust trials in the history of the country. While it had prevailed at trial, the case remained on appeal until virtually the end of the war, and the company's monopoly remained vulnerable to either court ordered divestiture or the disposition of the government owned plants at the conclusion of the conflict.

To make matters worse, Alcoa found itself a criminal defendant in a different antitrust case which also had national security implications. Alcoa had acquired an interest in the magnesium industry, also a strategic commodity. Alcoa's magnesium subsidiary had entered into various market division agreements with I.G. Farben, the German conglomerate now firmly part of the Nazi war planning effort. This cartel agreement had potentially important implications on Alcoa's ability to develop magnesium as a strategic commodity for the U.S. military and devastating implications for Alcoa's public relations. The company prudently pled nolo contendere in the case and rededicated itself to the war effort and the far more central matter of the post-war structure of the aluminum industry.

The company was initially intransigent in its negotiations with the government over the disposition of the newly constructed plants. Alcoa wanted to purchase the plants it had built and operated which had played a vital difference in the outcome of the war. But it had little bargaining leverage. The Justice Department took the position that any sale of Government property to Alcoa would compound its illegal monopoly. To make matters worse, Alcoa's long-time chairman, Arthur Vining Davis, had offended Stuart Symington, the Truman appointee in charge of the sale or lease of the now surplus aluminum plants. Nor was help forthcoming from Capitol Hill. The Senate Subcommittee on Surplus Property was chaired by Joseph O'Mahoney, a long-time friend and supporter of former antitrust chief Thurman Arnold, and strong antitrust supporter in his own right. Moreover, all of these negotiations were in the shadow of the final disposition of the government antitrust case which still remained in the district court awaiting a final decision on remedy.[56]

Caught in this whipsaw, Alcoa eventually surrendered its leases early after some public huffing and puffing. The government sold the vast majority of the war time plants at a discount to Reynolds Metal and Kaiser, a new entrant from the steel industry. Toward the end, Alcoa reluctantly even licensed certain key technology to its new competitors royalty free, so the new plants could be run effectively on a stand alone

---

[56] Roback, *Surplus Plant Disposal*, *supra* note 55, at 311–23.

basis. There were now three firms where, for the past sixty years, Alcoa had stood alone.

VII. ENDING WITH A WHIMPER: THE FINAL OPINIONS

While the sale of the government plants was the defining moment for the aluminum industry, the antitrust litigation lingered on. In 1947, Alcoa applied to the district court for a determination that it no longer had a monopoly and that competitive conditions had been restored in the aluminum industry. In response, the Government filed a petition for further divestiture and other relief, contending that competitive conditions in the aluminum industry had not been established.

Chief Judge John C. Knox of the Southern District of New York, who had inherited the case, conducted a separate trial on remedy that lasted approximately fourteen months. In an exhaustive opinion, Judge Knox found that Alcoa had a market share under 50% as a result of the growth of its two new competitors, the increase in imports, and the competition from secondary aluminum and other materials. Judge Knox included secondary aluminum in the relevant market, holding that market conditions, particularly the vast amount of scrap generated during the war years, had substantially changed from those in 1945 when Judge Hand refused to include scrap aluminum in his calculations of Alcoa's market share.[57]

He granted the Government's application for divestiture only to the extent of requiring that the major stockholders of Alcoa divest themselves of either their Alcoa stock or Aluminum Limited stock.[58] This proved to be more than token relief. Over time this key decision created Alcan, as the Canadian firm eventually became known, a truly independent fourth aluminum producer in North America.[59]

The Government's application for all further divestiture was denied. Nevertheless, Judge Knox stated: "[T]he Government, for a period of five years, if conditions so warrant, may petition the Court for further and more complete relief."[60] In dogged pursuit of its long-time foe, the government unsuccessfully sought the extension of the court's jurisdiction at the end of the five year period. The now weary district court

---

[57] U.S. v. Aluminum Co. of Am., 91 F.Supp. 333, 355–364 (S.D.N.Y. 1950). Judge Knox also considered the possibility of competition from steel, copper, zinc, lead, tin, wood, textiles, plastics, paper, clay, glass, leather and cork also without reference to Hand's prior opinion on the subject. *Id.* at 355.

[58] 91 F.Supp. at 392–99, 418–19. Judge Knox also voided grant back provisions in certain patent licenses to Alcoa's competitors. *Id.* at 410–413.

[59] Morton Peck credits the new independent Limit's entry into the United States as contributing to effective competition in the aluminum field. PECK, *supra* note 27, at 215.

[60] 91 F.Supp. at 419.

denied the government's motion based on the continued expansion of Kaiser and Reynold's, Limited's renewed interest in serving the U.S. market, and new entry all suggesting that the original remedial scheme had succeeded.[61] Thus, it was not until 1957 that Alcoa escaped the antitrust journey that began forty-six years before.

VIII. WHAT SURVIVES OF ALCOA AND ITS APPROACH TO MONOPOLIZATION?

Although Alcoa is an iconic opinion, little of its doctrine and holding are probably still good law. Although the Supreme Court quickly endorsed *Alcoa*[62] and has never overruled it, the law of monopolization has moved on. Beginning in the 1970s, critics associated with the Chicago School of Antitrust[63] savagely attacked Hand's opinion for encouraging higher prices and the entry of less efficient firms to the detriment of consumers.[64] By 1990, the Ninth Circuit characterized *Alcoa* as holding that a defendant monopolist could be held liable by being efficient and concluded that this "has been questioned by just about everyone who has taken a close look at it."[65] Antitrust law typically looks for behavior which raises price and limits output, not the converse, which was the gist of the situation in *Alcoa*. The law permits, and indeed encourages, dominant firms and monopolists to compete and compete hard.[66] The courts will only impose liability under Section 2 of the Sherman Act where there is clear harm to competition and not merely competitors. Liability normally is limited to those instances where there does not appear to a readily obvious business or procompetitive justification for

---

[61] U.S. v. Aluminum Co. of Am., 153 F.Supp. 132 (S.D.N.Y. 1957). In contrast, the government antitrust case against IBM lasted from 1968 until 1982, the case against AT & T a similar time frame, and the series of cases in the United States against Microsoft which began in the early 1990s are only now slowly petering out with the district court's jurisdiction under the most recent consent decree set to expire in 2009.

[62] American Tobacco Co. v. United States, 328 U.S. 781 (1946).

[63] Richard A. Posner, *The Chicago School of Antitrust Analysis*, 127 U. PA. L. REV. 925 (1979). For a particularly vigorous critique of Alcoa as a condemnation of efficiency by future chairman of the Federal Reserve, Alan Greenspan, see Alan Greenspan, *Antitrust*, in CAPITALISM: THE UNKNOWN IDEAL 56 (1966).

[64] ROBERT H. BORK, THE ANTITRUST PARADOX 170 (1978); John E. Lopatka & Paul E. Godek, *Another Look at Alcoa: Raising Rivals' Costs Does not Improve the View*, in FAMOUS FABLES OF ECONOMICS: MYTHS OF MARKET FAILURE 246 (Daniel Spulber ed. 2002)(responding to the view that despite faulty reasoning *Alcoa* reached a sound decision based on the defendant's exclusionary acts of denying access to bauxite and electricity to actual and potential rivals).

[65] United States v. Syufy Enters., 903 F.2d 659, 668 (9th Cir. 1990).

[66] *See e.g.* Berkey Photo, Inc. v. Eastman Kodak Co., 603 F. 2d 263 (2d Cir. 1979).

the defendant's behavior.[67] At a minimum, proof of monopoly power represents only the beginning of the inquiry and not basically the end of the matter as it seemed to be for Judge Hand and his colleagues on the Second Circuit.[68]

However, much of *Alcoa* remains good law or the subject for contemporary debate. Hand's rule of thumb, that a 90% market share is probably a monopoly, 60% is doubtful, and 33% cannot be, is one of the most quoted aphorisms in antitrust law. The intended effects test for extraterritorial jurisdiction that Hand used to impose liability in the international portions of the opinion went through some ups and downs but is now entrenched in Supreme Court precedent,[69] is shared by most nations in enforcing their own competition laws, and has become the basic tool in a global war against cartels.[70] One of the most lively debates continues over the relationship between innovation and monopoly power. Some theorists contend that only monopoly power can create the proper environment for the waves of creative destruction that innovation brings.[71] Others contend that Hand got it exactly right—that the rewards of monopoly are the quiet life and only competition best furthers innovation.[72] Still others contend that it all depends on the specific industries and technologies at issue.[73] Here the debate rages on.

Alcoa is also the beginning of the most important debate governing the interpretation of Section 2 of the Sherman Act. What matters most: market structure or the conduct of the defendant? What does it mean to

---

[67] Aspen Skiing Co. v. Aspen Highlands Skiing Corp., 472 U.S. 585 (1985); United States v. Microsoft Corp., 253 F.3d 34 (D.C. Cir.), *cert. denied*, 534 U.S. 952 (2001).

[68] Recently Justice Scalia went so far as to praise monopoly power as "an important element of the free market system." Verizon Communications, Inc. v. Law Offices of Curtis V. Trinko, 540 U.S. 398, 407 (2004).

[69] Hartford Fire Ins. Co. v. California, 509 U.S. 764 (1993).

[70] JAMES ATWOOD, KINGMAN BREWSTER & SPENCER WEBER WALLER, ANTITRUST & AMERICAN BUSINESS ABROAD Ch. 6, 14, 16–18 (West Publishing 3d ed. 1997 & Supp.).

[71] JOSEPH A. SCHUMPETER, CAPITALISM, SOCIALISM AND DEMOCRACY 81–86 (2d ed. 1947).

[72] Kenneth J. Arrow, *Economic Welfare and the Allocation of Resources for Invention*, in THE RATE AND DIRECTION OF INVENTIVE ACTIVITY: ECONOMIC AND SOCIAL FACTORS 609 (1962).

[73] See Jerry Ellig & Daniel Lin, *A Taxonomy of Dynamic Competition Theories*, in DYNAMIC COMPETITION AND PUBLIC POLICY 16 (Jerry Ellig ed. 2001). Alcoa's own record of research and innovation under conditions of both monopoly and then oligopoly is discussed extensively throughout SMITH, FROM MONOPOLY TO COMPETITION, *supra* note 2; CARR, ALCOA: AN AMERICAN ENTERPRISE, *supra* note 2, at 135–45, 167–69. Peck concludes that innovation in the aluminum industry increased following the entry of Kaiser and Reynolds after the war. PECK, *supra* note 27, at 201.

procure a monopoly through foresight as opposed to through anticompetitive practices? Is a firm guilty of monopolization only where its conduct is inexcusable? While virtually everyone agrees that mere monopoly is not a violation, what more is required and the extent of the remedy imposed are the enduring questions of antitrust. *Alcoa* thus began a conversation that continues today and helps us define what we fear most about market power and what we expect from the antitrust laws.

IX. CONCLUSION

To litigate for a nearly half a century is an extraordinary thing. On the other hand, to have an actual monopoly for nearly sixty years is an equally extraordinary thing. But to have the key to competition lie in the disposal of surplus government property is unprecedented.

As one might expect, antitrust was an extremely sensitive subject at Alcoa throughout the 20th century. It was also an extremely personal subject as most of the key players at the trial and the disposition of the war plants had been with the company since its founding. Charles Martin Hall, whose invention started everything, remained with the company until his death in 1914. Arthur Vining Davis joined the company in 1889 and did not formally retire as chairman until 1957. Roy Hunt, Alfred Hunt's brother, worked for the company for nearly sixty years. The Mellon family played a direct role in the company from 1890 onward. One of the original investors in Hall's then untested process for smelting pure aluminum remained with the company until 1949. For them, Alcoa was simply The Aluminum Company, their aluminum company, the only aluminum company there was, and the government was trying to take it away from them. In the end, even they and their heirs in the company ruefully admitted that a little competition was not such a bad thing. As a subsequent president of the company conceded, the injection of competition was a "bum deal" but it "basically stimulated the company."[74]

---

[74] Interview with Fritz Close, *cited in* SMITH, FROM MONOPOLY TO COMPETITION, *supra* note 2, at 276.

*

5

Warren S. Grimes*

From *Schwinn* to *Sylvania* to Where? Historical Roots of Modern Vertical Restraints Policy

A generation of antitrust lawyers has viewed *United States v. Arnold Schwinn & Co.*[1] as the set up pitch for Justice Powell's overruling home run ten years later in *Continental TV Inc. v. GTE Sylvania Inc.*[2] *Schwinn* is perhaps the shortest lived Supreme Court precedent in the century-plus history of the Sherman Act. In contrast, *Sylvania* has provided the paradigm for antitrust treatment of vertical restraints for the past 30 years.

The best reason for revisiting *Schwinn* is that it provides a compelling story that can guide the debate about the future of vertical restraints law. *Schwinn* produced a ruling that the Government neither sought nor expected. The strong reaction to Supreme Court's opinion produced its own imbalanced legacy. *Sylvania's* rule of reason might be viewed as simply a return to the Court's 1963 holding in *White Motor Co. v. United States*[3], which declined to establish a standard for assessing non-price vertical restraints. Still, while *White Motor* was cautious, neutral and noncommital in its response to vertical restraints, *Sylvania* was judgmental and partisan. *Schwinn* begat *Sylvania* and it is the

---

* Irving D. and Florence Rosenberg Professor of Law, Southwestern Law School, Los Angeles.

[1] 388 U.S. 365 (1967).

[2] 433 U.S. 36 (1977).

[3] 372 U.S. 253 (1963).

rhetoric of *Sylvania* that has survived, shaping judicial precedent and policy over the past 30 years.

As the facts of *Schwinn* demonstrate, the reality of most vertical restraints is that they promote a brand selling strategy by stifling *both* intrabrand competition *and* interbrand competition. They limit intrabrand competition directly and intentionally. They limit interbrand competition by creating incentives for retailer brand promotion that, while perhaps channeling valuable information to consumers, run a high risk of exploiting information deficiencies or consumer buying foibles. At least in some instances, the loss of intrabrand competition is telling because it is the most viable remaining mechanism (in light of the reduced interbrand competition) to maintain a competitive and efficient distribution system.

Schwinn and *Sylvania* have left antitrust with a partisan legacy that has obstructed progress toward a coherent and viable strategy for dealing with vertical restraints that substantially undermine intrabrand competition. But revisiting these cases may move this crucial debate forward.

I. THE SCHWINN CORPORATION

In 1895, Ignaz Schwinn and Adolph Arnold (the financier) formed a bicycle manufacturing firm in Chicago.[4] Ignaz, an immigrant with experience in the German bicycle industry, ran the firm; it was to remain in his family's control for four generations, until 1992. The company was an almost instant success. There was vigorous consumer demand for the bicycle as an efficient mode of transportation in the pre-automobile era. Bicycle manufacturers were then and are now assemblers of parts obtained from a variety of suppliers. Schwinn, and other producers, manufactured the bicycle frame while obtaining rims, tires, pedal assemblies, and other parts from outside suppliers.

Early Schwinn success was soon thwarted when the popularity of the automobile greatly diminished demand for bicycles. Despite consolidation, the industry continued to struggle until the 1930s when Schwinn, by then under the creative and aggressive leadership of Ignaz's son, F. W. Schwinn, introduced innovations such as the balloon tire and a redesigned frame which improved performance and durability. Schwinn generated a vigorous market for children's bicycles and established itself as a preeminent bicycle brand known for innovation and quality. Consumers willingly paid more to acquire Schwinn bicycles, leading to highly profitable years that continued through the 1970s.

---

[4] Material on the history of the Schwinn Corporation is largely from Judith Crown & Glenn Coleman, No Hands, The Rise and Fall of the Schwinn Bicycle Company, An American Institution (1996).

Marketing swings in the industry continued. By the 1960s, sleek, thin-tired racing bikes with front and rear derailleurs allowing for 10 or more gears created a new market for adult, recreational bicycles. By the 1980s, there was a market shift to "mountain bikes" with resilient frames, wider tires, shock absorbers, and expanded ranges of gears. Schwinn's failure to respond in a timely fashion to some of these market swings is cited as one of the reasons for the firm's closing of its Chicago factory in 1983 and its bankruptcy in 1992.[5]

The Schwinn Distribution System

Throughout the first 40 years of the 20th century, Schwinn and its manufacturing rivals sold a large percentage of their output through mass retail outlets such as Sears and Montgomery Wards. These large retailers demanded private labels (the "Sears" brand bicycle) and low prices, pushing Schwinn and other manufacturers toward low cost generic components and the low end market. Beginning in the 1930s, when Schwinn began to build its preeminent brand image, Schwinn was able to demand higher prices from retailers and their customers. Schwinn resisted pressures to lower prices and, by the 1950s, had begun to move away from private labels and shun sales through mass retailers. Instead, Schwinn adopted a selective distribution system that created retailer brand promotion incentives. The firm cut retailers from 12,000 to 5,000, and also culled 93 wholesalers from its network. This focused distribution on a relatively small number of retailers that were producing the bulk of Schwinn sales. Over a period of two years, marketing expenses were reportedly cut from 13% to around 7% of sales.[6] As Schwinn implemented its new distribution policies, competition from foreign and domestic rivals increased. Schwinn's market share fell (from 22.5% in 1951 to 12.8% in 1961),[7] but Schwinn managed to recover from the surge of imports and, in 1961, had roughly the same output that it had in 1952.[8]

Schwinn distributors were granted exclusive territories. Authorized retailers, while not granted exclusivity, were assured that a limited number of retailers in their geographic area would be authorized. All retailers were pressed to promote the Schwinn line and devote at least 50% of their floor space to Schwinn bicycles.[9]

---

[5] *Id*. at 164–67.

[6] Robert C. Keck, *The Schwinn Case*, 23 Bus. Law 669, 673 (1968).

[7] United States v. Arnold, Schwinn & Co., 237 F. Supp. 323, 325 (N.D. Ill. 1965).

[8] *Schwinn*, Reply brief of the United States at 13 (reporting Schwinn sales of 478,838 in 1952 and of 471,506 in 1961).

[9] Crown, *supra* note 4, at 69.

Schwinn used a method, known as the Schwinn Plan, to streamline treatment of orders from retailers. When a distributor received a retailer order, Schwinn would ship the bicycles directly to the retailer. The distributor in the retailer's territory was paid a commission for the order, but no title passed to the distributor. Distributors, however, continued to maintain Schwinn inventories for spot or fill-in purchases of a retailer who could not wait for factory delivery.[10] Schwinn also used variations on the Schwinn Plan, including consignment sales to the distributor, where Schwinn held title until a sale was made to a retailer.[11]

Schwinn's shift in marketing strategy in the early 1950s apparently caused substantial ill will among the large number of terminated retailers and distributors. A 1953 FTC investigation of Schwinn's distribution was closed because the information gathered "failed to provide a proper basis for further proceedings."[12] But residual anger with Schwinn's substantial terminations may have stimulated the interest of the Antitrust Division, which convened a grand jury that ultimately led to the civil antitrust complaint filed in 1958.

The Litigation in the Trial Court

Led by Earl Jinkinson, a team of attorneys from the Antitrust Division's Chicago Office filed a Sherman Act civil complaint in June of 1958. The action was filed in the Eastern District of Missouri because that state had no fair trading law and much of the Department's evidence involved Missouri retailers. It was transferred on defendants' motion to the Northern District of Illinois. There were three defendants: Arnold, Schwinn & Co., the Schwinn Cycle Distributors Association (22 Schwinn distributors were members), and the B.F. Goodrich Co. Goodrich, with a declining role as a Schwinn retailer, that reached an out of court settlement with the Government before trial and was not a player in the litigation thereafter.[13]

The complaint alleged a variety of conduct in violation of Section 1 of the Sherman Act, including (1) limiting the number of franchised retailers in each market area; (2) a policy, enforced by Schwinn, of prohibiting distributors and Schwinn retailers from selling Schwinn bicycles to non-franchised retailers; and (3) a refusal to supply Schwinn bicycles to franchised retailers who fail to "adhere to retail prices for

---

[10] Keck, *supra* note 6, at 671–72.

[11] *Id.* at 672.

[12] *Schwinn*, 237 F. Supp. at 331.

[13] *Id.* at 325.

Schwinn products fixed by defendant Schwinn."[14] As in a sister case filed on the same day against the White Motor Co, the Government relied on a per se rule in attacking both the price and non-price vertical restraints.[15]

Schwinn was represented by Robert C. Keck of Spray, Price & Underwood in Chicago. The distributors association was represented by Earl E. Pollock of Chicago's Sonnenschein firm. Early on, the defendants concluded that the Government's claims would not survive a careful factual inquiry and devised a strategy of taking depositions of non-terminated retailers from across the country. The trial judge rejected efforts of the Government to limit the scope of evidence that could be introduced. The prolonged discovery and lengthy trial (73 days) led to a 13,000 page record[16] that, according to then Justice Department attorney Joel Davidow, filled seven file cabinets.[17] Five and one-half years elapsed between the filing of the complaint and issuance of the trial court's opinion in January 1965.

Despite evidence indicating Schwinn was pressuring retailers to adhere to suggested prices in both fair trading and non-fair trading states,[18] Judge Perry concluded that the larger evidentiary picture showed retailers had pricing freedom and that terminations of retailers were for a variety of reasons, never solely because of their discounting activity.[19] The Government also largely failed to prove its claims that the resale limitations on distributors and retailers violated Section 1. At trial, the Government argued that, while Schwinn could pick retailers to whom it would sell when it made direct sales, it could not "lawfully combine with anyone to restrict the customers to whom its purchasers may resell."[20] Judge Perry saw the Government argument as bad policy because it would favor large firms that could afford direct distribution to

---

[14] *Id.*

[15] White Motor proceeded more expeditiously through trial and was decided by the Supreme Court on March 4, 1963, just as the 73–day *Schwinn* trial came to an end. *White Motor*, 372 U.S. at 253.

[16] Keck, *supra* note 6, at 677.

[17] Telephone Interview with former Justice Department attorney Joel Davidow (June 30, 2006) (notes on file with the author).

[18] Fair trading states had enacted statutes to take advantage of the antitrust exemption provided by the Miller–Tydings and the McGuire Acts for qualifying resale price maintenance programs. This history is described in Warren S. Grimes, *The Seven Myths of Vertical Price Fixing: The Politics and Economics of a Century–Long Debate*, 21 Southwestern U. L. Rev. 1285,1287–1291 (1992).

[19] *Schwinn*, 237 F. Supp. at 342.

[20] *Id.* at 333–34.

retailers and prejudice smaller companies that relied on independent distributors.[21] He ruled that Schwinn could, when making direct shipments to retailers, pay a commission only to the distributor in a retailer's territory. Insofar as distributors were acting as agents of Schwinn, Schwinn was free to allocate territory among its distributors.[22]

The Government's sole success was the determination that exclusive territories for distributors were unlawful to the extent that they purchased bicycles from Schwinn for resale to retailers. Judge Perry saw this territorial division as a horizontal restraint.[23] The defendants did not appeal this ruling. By 1961, only 25% of Schwinn bicycles were sold in this manner.[24]

Schwinn in the Supreme Court

The Government made a direct appeal to the Supreme Court under the Expediting Act.[25] Jurisdiction was noted in December 1965, but the case was not argued until April of 1967 (the delay was apparently occasioned by problems in preparing the lengthy typewritten record for printing).[26] The Government chose not to appeal the district judge's ruling on resale price maintenance, addressing only the non-price vertical restraints that Schwinn imposed on its distributors and retailers.

A new team of lawyers now represented the Government. Joel Davidow, then a junior attorney in the Antitrust Division, was given the task of writing the initial draft of the Government's brief. Davidow recalls the lengthy process of reading the trial record and writing a draft that asked the Court to use a "sliding scale" rule of reason to evaluate non-price vertical restraints based on an assessment of the severity of anticompetitive effects. His initial draft was turned over to Richard Posner, then an Assistant to the Solicitor General, who was to argue the case for the United States.[27] The final version of the brief was largely the

---

[21] *Id.* at 334–35.

[22] *Id.* at 342.

[23] *Id.*

[24] *Schwinn*, 388 U.S. at 370 n.3.

[25] Section 2 of the Expediting Act, 32 Stat. 823, as amended, 15 U.S.C. § 29.

[26] Transcript of Oral Argument, United States v Arnold, Schwinn & Co., in ORAL ARGUMENTS OF THE SUPREME COURT OF THE UNITED STATES: THE WARREN COURT, 1953–1968 TERM 49 (1984).

[27] Howard Shapiro, then head of the Antitrust Section's Appellate Division, is also listed on the Government's brief and reply brief. Shapiro has no recollection of involvement. E-mail to the author from Howard Shapiro (June 29, 2006). Davidow recalls that Shapiro "stayed out" of this case, leaving it for Posner and (perhaps) Assistant Attorney

work of Posner,[28] picking up perhaps the statement of facts and brief passages or ideas from Davidow's original draft.

The Government's policy-oriented brief presents a view of vertical restraints that is consistent with the Antitrust Division's experience in the preceding decade. In 1949, the Antitrust Division took the position that rigid territorial and customer restrictions, like vertical price restraints, were per se illegal.[29] Extending through 1963, there were at least sixteen Justice Department prosecutions of such activity, each ending in a consent decree that allowed the use of primary territories but prohibited the use of exclusive territories.[30] In *White Motor*, the Government, for the first time, urged the Supreme Court to accept its view that exclusivity should be per se unlawful. After the Supreme Court rejected the per se rule, the defendant nonetheless settled that case on terms that allowed the assignment of primary, but not exclusive, territories.[31] The Government's position in *Schwinn* reflected a similar approach. Schwinn was to be allowed assignment of primary territories to its distributors. Restrictions that prohibited either Schwinn distributors or authorized retailers from reselling to non-authorized retailers were, however, objectionable. The challenge facing the Government lawyers was that *White Motor*, decided as the *Schwinn* trial was completed, had rejected application of a per se rule to territorial distribution restraints. The Government response was to urge the Supreme Court to adopt a rule of presumptive illegality for the resale restrictions imposed by Schwinn.

Reading the Government's brief today, one is struck by how up-to-date it is. The brief adopted a tone of relative neutrality, tracking language in the Court's opinion in *White Motor*. The brief conceded the benefits of non-price vertical restraints in promoting the sale of an upscale brand. It acknowledged that a new entrant or struggling competitor might, for a limited time, need to impose such restraints to gain a secure foothold in the market.[32] In contrast to many post-*Sylvania* writings, however, the brief unabashedly celebrated the potential bene-

---

General Donald Turner. Telephone interview with Joel Davidow (June 30, 2006)(notes on file with the author).

[28] E-mail to the author from Judge Richard Posner (July 7, 2006) (copy on file with the author).

[29] See Rifkind, *Division of Territories*, in How to Comply with the Antitrust Laws, 127–39 (Van Cise & Dunn eds., 1954).

[30] Charles L. Steart, Jr., *Franchise or Protected Territory Distribution,* 8 Antitrust Bull. 447, 470 n.51 (1963).

[31] United States v. White Motor Co., 1964 Trade Cas. (CCH) ¶ 71,195 (N.D. Ohio 1964).

[32] *Schwinn,* Brief for the United States, at 27–28.

fits of intrabrand competition when a strong brand has insulated itself from interbrand competition.

The Government argued in its brief that "outlet limitations," restrictions on resale to non-franchised retailers, unreasonably restrained trade because non-franchised retailers were an important source of competition that could bring down the price of Schwinn bicycles.[33]

According to the Government's brief:

> Economists teach that, by advertising or other means of stressing real or imagined differences, a manufacturer may be able to persuade a substantial number of consumers that his Brand A is superior to other brands of the same product. In such a case, unless there is effective competition among the retailers of Brand A, each retailer can raise his retail price for that brand to just below the point at which the consumer will switch to other brands despite his initial preference for Brand A. Stated otherwise, retailers of preferred brands who are free from effective intrabrand competition enjoy considerable market power, which they can exploit to increase the price to the consumer.[34]

Although abandoning the Government's claims of resale price maintenance, the Government's brief urged that Schwinn's motivation for the outlet limitations was price-related. "Schwinn evidently believed that its reputation as a producer of quality bicycles, and its ability to charge a premium price for its product, would be enhanced if its bicycles were not discounted or sold through outlets which frequently grant—or are thought to grant—discounts."[35] Because this restraint operated to eliminate a class of competitors and to "inhibit competition in price in the resale of his products," the manufacturer had a "heavy burden" to justify the restraint.[36]

One way in which the outlet restraints might thwart interbrand competition is if the distribution restraint deceives the consumer. On this point, the Government argued:

> Either the Schwinn bicycle is in fact a superior product for which the consumer would willingly pay more, in which event it should be unnecessary to create a quality image by the artificial device of discouraging competition in the price of distributing the product; or it is not of premium quality, and the consumer is being deceived into believing that it is by its high and uniform retail price. In neither

---

[33] *Id*. at 21–23.

[34] *Id*. at 26–37.

[35] *Id*. at 46.

[36] *Id*. at 26.

event would the manufacturer's private interest in maintaining a high-price image justify the serious impairment on competition that results.[37]

These reflections in the Government's brief anticipate future scholarship emphasizing the potential deception inherent in some vertical restraints, particularly those imposed on multi-brand retailers. Hidden incentives that push a retailer of multiple brands to favor a particular brand could be deceptive for consumers who might not recognize that the purchasing advice and promotional material was from a non-neutral source.[38] The extent to which this may have occurred under the Schwinn distribution system is unclear, but Schwinn retailers who carried competing manufacturers' bicycles might have pushed customers to the Schwinn label because of a high retailer mark up, engendered by vertical restraints that limited intrabrand competition and created promotion incentives to limit interbrand competition.[39]

The brief adds to its argument the point, to become central in the Supreme Court's opinion, that Schwinn's restrictions constitute a "restraint on alienation" contrary to common law policy. The argument is mentioned once and developed later only in a short paragraph that suggests that such restraints are most harmful in "restrictions upon distribution that affect price."[40]

Schwinn and the Cycle Distributors filed separate briefs in the Supreme Court. The Schwinn brief was lengthy (106 pages) with extensive recitation and analysis of the facts (argument began only on page 43). Both defendants argued without success that the Court should dismiss the Government's complaint because Schwinn had acted unilaterally.[41]

The Schwinn brief made no effort to argue that the non-price distribution restraints should be judged under the rule of reason. Instead, the brief pointed out that the Government had conceded the applicability of the rule of reason standard and proceeded to argue that the non-price distribution restraints were (repeating the holding of the

---

[37] *Id.* at 47.

[38] These concerns were developed in Warren S. Grimes, *Brand Marketing, Intrabrand Competition, and the Multibrand Retailer: The Antitrust Law of Vertical Restraints*, 64 ANTITRUST L. J. 83, 107–109 (1995).

[39] CROWN, *supra* note 4, at 68 (reporting that Schwinn retailers were advised "never [to] apologize for your price," but to stress the quality and safety of Schwinn bicycles).

[40] *Schwinn*, Brief for the United States, at 26–27, 39.

[41] *Schwinn*, Brief for Schwinn & Co., at 96–100; Brief for Cycle Distributors, at 20–22.

district court) ancillary to a procompetitive franchising distribution system and therefore reasonable.[42]

The brief for the Cycle Distributors more directly joins issue with the Government's brief on policy issues. As the brief points out, the distributors in the association had the most to lose in this litigation. Independent distributors faced loss of their Schwinn distributorships if the case were decided in a manner that limited Schwinn's control over resale by each distributor. Schwinn had begun planning to integrate forward into distribution, and did so after the Supreme Court's opinion was issued.[43]

The distributors argued that the outlet limitations were procompetitive because they ensured the survival of both Schwinn as a manufacturer and of the independent distributors and retailers.[44] Both the Government and the defendants thought that the passing of title should not obscure the fundamental issue of the competitive effects of a restraint. The Government argued that the prohibition on resale to non-franchised retailers should be illegal regardless of who held the title. The Cycle Distributors, joined by Schwinn, argued that the restrictions were, in either case, reasonable and therefore lawful under the rule of reason.[45]

The Cycle distributors directly challenged the restraints on alienation argument that the Government raised as a supplementary point. The brief took a manufacturer's view of distribution restraints, urging that a manufacturer's interest in controlling downstream resale is not meaningfully different depending on whether title has or has not passed to the distributor.[46] In support of this argument, the Distributors relied on the writings of former FTC Commissioner Philip Elman,[47] who had earlier employed both Richard Posner and Joel Davidow as law clerks.

Oral argument before the Court was held on April 20, 1967. The argument was only two days after Schwinn filed its brief and only one day after the Government filed its reply. Only seven justices heard the case: Chief Justice Warren and Associate Justices Black, Douglas, Harlan, Brennan, Stewart, and Fortas. Associate Justices White and Clark did not participate in either *Schwinn* or in *United States v. Sealy, Inc.,*[48]

---

[42] *Id.* at 55–69.

[43] Keck, *supra* note 6, at 685–86.

[44] *Schwinn*, Brief for the Cycle Distributors, at 22–23.

[45] *Id.* at 19.

[46] *Id.* at 57–59.

[47] The Distributors cited passages from Philip Elman, *"Petrified Opinions" and Competitive Realities*, 66 COL. L. REV. 625, 629, 630–31 (1966).

[48] 386 U.S. 989 (1967).

argued the same day. Assistant Attorney General Donald Turner sat at the Government's table, and passed notes to Richard Posner,[49] who argued for the Government. Robert Keck (for Schwinn) and Earl Pollock (for the Distributors) divided time for the defendants. Counsel for both sides were allowed time to present their pre-prepared argument, and there were periods of active questioning.[50]

The 1960s were the high point of the "populist" embrace of anti-trust[51] and the Government was accustomed to success. In the previous term, the Court had decided *United States v. General Motors Corp.*,[52] a case in which the Court found that dealer-initiated efforts to prevent either GM or other dealers from selling to unauthorized dealers were a per se unlawful horizontal restraint. *Sealy* was a horizontal combination of manufacturers who had combined to promote their brand. Both *GM* and *Sealy* involved restraints only on intrabrand competition, but be-cause they were deemed horizontal in origin, the Court invoked the per se rule. Posner, for the Government, stressed that these horizontal cases were distinguishable because Schwinn was the initiator of the restraints in this case.[53] The Government, Posner argued, did not advocate a blanket condemnation of these vertical restraints.[54]

Although oral argument provided no clear sense of where the Court was headed, Posner recalls completing the argument with a sense that the Government would prevail.[55] With the benefit of hindsight, one can perceive in some of the questions (at least those of Justice Fortas) a sense that the Government's proposed rule of presumptive illegality was not deemed a satisfactory way to resolve this case. Some questions, for example, suggested doubt that the *Sealy* or the *GM* cases (applying a per

---

[49] E-mail to the author from Joel Davidow, July 19, 2006.

[50] The transcript sets forth questions by "The Court," without identifying individual justices, but references of counsel suggest that Justices Fortas and Black, joined by Justices Brennan and Harlan, were among the active questioners. *Schwinn* Transcript, *supra* note 27, at 18–19, 22, 42 (Fortas, J.); 22, 35 (Black, J.); 33–34 (Brennan, J.); 17 (Harlan, J.).

[51] The Supreme Court had, in its previous term, decided *United States v. Von's Grocery*, 384 U.S. 270 (1966), in which Richard Posner also argued for the Government. That case had provoked Justice Stewart's frustration that "the Government always wins" in merger cases brought before the Court. *Id.* at 301 (Stewart, J., dissenting).

[52] 384 U.S. 127 (1966).

[53] Posner later criticized efforts to distinguish these cases based on horizontal or vertical origins of the restraint. RICHARD A. POSNER, ANTITRUST LAW, AN ECONOMIC PERSPECTIVE 159–166 (1976).

[54] *Schwinn* Transcript, *supra* note 27, at 4.

[55] E-mail from J. Richard Posner, *supra* note 29.

se rule based on restraints deemed horizontal) were meaningfully distinguishable.[56]

The Supreme Court's Decision

The Supreme Court's 5–2 decision in *Schwinn* gave the Government more than it sought or could reasonably have anticipated. The Government's unsuccessful argument in *White Motor*, that exclusive territories should be per se unlawful, was narrower than the sweeping rule that the *Schwinn* majority announced: that all non-price vertical restraints were per se unlawful when title had passed from the manufacturer. Schwinn remained free to refuse direct sales to non-authorized retailers and to prohibit such sales in cases where the distributor held no title to a bicycle.

Justice Abe Fortas authored both the *Schwinn* opinion and the *Sealy* opinion issued the same day. It seems likely that his antitrust views were respected by colleagues. Fortas had started a law firm with Thurman Arnold, a distinguished former head of the Antitrust Division. As a practicing lawyer, Fortas had experience trying antitrust cases.

An intriguing aspect of the majority opinion is why the Court declined to rule for the Government under its proposed rule of presumptive illegality. The proposal was largely ignored by the Court, which addressed it only in footnote 5:

> The United States, having abandoned its contention that the restraints in the present case are *per se* violations of the Sherman Act, now urges "a standard of presumptive illegality," presumably on the basis of a showing that a product has been distributed by means of arrangements for territorial exclusivity and restricted retail and wholesale customers. We do not consider this additional subtlety which was not advanced in the trial court. The burden of proof in antitrust cases remains with the plaintiff, deriving such help as may be available in the circumstances from particularized rules articulated by law—such as the *per se* doctrine.[57]

The Court was willing to adopt a per se rule for non-price vertical restraints that no party had urged upon it (and that it had rejected in *White Motor*), but was unwilling to adopt a lesser rule of presumptive illegality advocated by the Government. Perhaps Justice Fortas and the majority saw the universe of antitrust rules as consisting only of the polar extremes of the per se rule or an open-ended rule of reason. Whatever validity that view may have had in 1967, it is difficult to sustain today with an antitrust jurisprudence that recognizes a number

---

[56] *Schwinn* Transcript, *supra* note 27, at 5, 11–13.

[57] *Schwinn*, 388 U.S. at 374 n.5.

of hybrid rules, including the modified per se rule governing tying[58] and a narrowed rule of reason inquiry in horizontal cases involving a restraint on output.[59]

Where title remained with Schwinn, the Court applied a rule of reason standard to the prohibition Schwinn imposed on distributor sales to non-authorized dealers (75% of Schwinn's sales). The Court was unwilling to depart from the district court's findings and analysis that territorial and direct sale restrictions were ancillary to an efficient franchise method of distribution. This portion of the Court's opinion reads much like *White Motor*, and might even be mistaken for language in *Sylvania*:

> [W]e are not prepared to introduce the inflexibility which a *per se* rule might bring if it were applied to prohibit all vertical restrictions of territory and all franchising, in the sense of designating specified distributors and retailers as the chosen instruments through which the manufacturer, retaining ownership of the goods, will distribute them to the public. Such a rule might severely hamper small enterprises resorting to reasonable methods of meeting the competition of giants and of merchandising through independent dealers, and it might sharply accelerate the trend towards vertical integration of the distribution process.[60]

But with scant analysis, the Court sounds a different tone in concluding that a per se rule of illegality will attach once the manufacturer has sold its inventory: "Under the Sherman Act, it is unreasonable without more for a manufacturer to seek to restrict and confine areas or persons with whom an article may be traded after the manufacturer has parted with dominion over it." The Court continues in this conclusory tone: "Such restraints are so obviously destructive of competition that there mere existence is enough." The only supporting case law cited is *White Motor* and *Dr. Miles Medical Co. v. John D. Park & Sons*,[61] both in apparent support of the property law doctrine that restraints on alienation are invalid. The Court completes this discussion with the observation that because most goods are sold rather than consigned, to permit such post sale restraints might make them the "ordinary instead of the

---

[58] Jefferson Parish Hosp. Dist. No. 2 v. Hyde, 466 U.S. 2, 12–18 (1984).

[59] FTC v. Indiana Federation of Dentists, 476 U.S. 447, 459 (1986); National Collegiate Athletic Ass'n v. Board of Regents, Univ. of Oklahoma, 468 U.S. 85, 103 (1984). In *California Dental Association v. FTC*, 526 U.S. 756, 781 (1999), a 5–member majority of the Court rejected the Ninth Circuit's "quick look" analysis of a dental association's advertising restrictions, but acknowledged "a sliding scale formula" for rule of reason analysis ("an enquiry meet for the case").

[60] *Schwinn*, 388 U.S. at 379–380.

[61] 220 U.S. 373 (1911).

unusual method" of distribution. At the end of the opinion, the Court concludes that the resale restrictions "would violate the ancient rule against restraints on alienation and open the door to exclusivity of outlets and limitation of territory further than prudence dictates."[62]

Perhaps the Court took comfort from the district court's distinction between outright sales to distributors and direct sales to the retailers. But the district court's condemnation of the territorial division among distributors was, as Justice Stewart's dissent points out, grounded in what the lower court deemed horizontal market division.[63]

Justice Stewart (joined by Justice Harlan) dissented from that portion of the Court's opinion that introduced a per se rule for resales by the distributor or retailer. The Stewart opinion protested that the Court majority, without explanation, had rejected the teaching of *White Motor* (4 years earlier) that there was insufficient basis for establishing a per se rule for non-price vertical restraints. Turning to policy, and anticipating much of what post-*Schwinn* critics and the Court would later say in *Sylvania*, Justice Stewart extolled the procompetitive virtues of selective distribution implemented through non-price vertical restraints, echoing findings of the district court that the limited distribution plan had strengthened Schwinn and its retailers.[64] He then attacked the majority's reliance on restraints on alienation rule, which he found inapposite to modern distribution systems and unresponsive to the "actual impact on the marketplace."[65]

The Reaction to Schwinn

Schwinn provoked a flurry of scholarship, much of it negative and focused on the per se rule that the Court applied to resale transactions. Among those writing critically of *Schwinn* were all three of the attorneys who argued before the high Court, including Richard Posner.[66] Posner was critical of the *Schwinn* majority's reliance on the common law rule of restraints on alienation. In their articles, Keck and Pollack also criticized the decision, but went on to point to various strategies that *Schwinn* left open to manufacturers who wanted to restrict distribution.

---

[62] *Schwinn*, 388 U.S. at 380.

[63] *Id*. at 389.

[64] *Id*. at 383–86.

[65] *Id*. at 391–93.

[66] POSNER, supra note 53, at 163–64; Earl E. Pollock, *Alternative Distribution Methods After Schwinn*, 63 N.W. L. Rev. 595 (1968); Keck, *supra* note 6. Writing after *Sylvania*, Posner indicated that his post-*Schwinn* views on vertical restraints took "a 180–degree turn." Richard A. Posner, *The Rule of Reason and the Economic Approach: Reflections on the Sylvania Decision*, 45 U. Chi. L. Rev. 1, 2 (1977).

After *Schwinn*, Pollack suggested that a manufacturer could still employ location clauses and establish primary territories. More direct circumvention of the resale restrictions could occur through vertical integration or through consignment transactions in which the title stayed with the manufacturer.[67] In 1975, Pollack wrote again to urge reconsideration of *Schwinn*.[68]

There were defenders of *Schwinn*, more than the *Sylvania* Court was to acknowledge.[69] Donald Turner questioned the "broad per se language" of *Schwinn* in a 1977 amicus brief filed in the *Sylvania* case,[70] but Turner had previously defended the result, if not the rule, in the case. In a 1968 response to a characterization of Schwinn's distribution system as procompetitive, Turner said: "[T]hat characterization of the Schwinn Plan is close to hilarious. The people to whom the wholesalers were not allowed to sell were discount houses and anybody who showed a disposition to cut prices. How that could be procompetitive is beyond me."[71]

Some of the scholarship critical of *Schwinn* that the *Sylvania* Court cited[72] would not have favored the *Sylvania* paradigm. Donald Baker, for example, accused the Court of "barren formalism" in its reliance on the common law rule against restraints on alienation, but offered support for the Government's proposed presumption of illegality to attach to certain non-price vertical restraints.[73] This was apparently the view of the Antitrust Division as late as 1974.[74] Another view was that *Schwinn's*

---

[67] Pollack, supra note 66, at 602–610.

[68] Earl E. Pollack, *The Schwinn Per Se Rule: The Case for Reconsideration*, 44 ANTITRUST L.J. 557 (1975)

[69] The *Sylvania* Court, 433 U.S. 36, 48 n.13, cited two articles that defended *Schwinn* but its list was perfunctory and without analysis of the content. Martin B. Louis, *Vertical Distributional Restraints Under* Schwinn *and* Sylvania, *An Argument for the Continuing Use of a Partial* per se *Approach*, 75 MICH. L. REV. 275 (1976); Zimmerman, *Distribution Restraints After* Sealy *and* Schwinn, 12 ANTITRUST BULL. 1181 (1967). Another defender of *Schwinn* not mentioned was Peter C. Carstensen, *Vertical Restraints and the* Schwinn *Doctrine: Rules for the Creation and Dissipation of Economic Power*, 26 CASE W. RES. L. REV. 771 (1976).

[70] Continental T.V. Inc.v. GTE Sylvania, Inc., Amicus Brief of Motor Vehicle Manufacturers Association, 34–47 (1977), available at 1977 WL 1889274.

[71] CCH Trade Regulation Reporter, 1968 N.Y. Bar Ass'n Antitrust L. Symp., at 67.

[72] *Sylvania*, 433 U.S. 36, 48 n. 13 (citing Donald Baker, *Vertical Restraints in Times of Change: From* White *to* Schwinn *to Where?* 44 Antitrust L. J. 537 (1975)).

[73] Baker, *supra* note 72 (proposing a structured analysis of vertical restraints).

[74] Testimony of Deputy Assistant Attorney General Bruce Wilson, Hearings on H.R. 122, S. 978 (and related bills) Before the Subcomm. On Commerce and Finance, House Comm. On Interstate and Foreign Commerce, 93d Cong., 2d Sess. 18 (1974).

per se rule was too sweeping but should be replaced by a "hard-boiled" rule of reason that prohibited some vertical restraints.[75]

An important but less discussed topic is the impact of the decision on the Schwinn corporation and its distributors. The authors of a book on the firm's history describe the case as a "turning point" for Schwinn.[76] The firm acquired two of its distributors during the pendency of the litigation[77] and, within 72 hours of the Supreme Court's decision, announced plans to open regional distribution centers in 4 more states.[78] Ultimately, Schwinn took over all of its own distribution. Some former Schwinn distributors went out of business while others began distributing rival brands to retailers.

The case's longer term impact on Schwinn is unclear. The distributors' lawyer (Earl Pollack) thought the case benefitted Schwinn by expanding "its U.S. parts business" and "establishing direct relations with retailers."[79] Another view is that the loss of independently owned distributors eliminated strong voices that Schwinn management would have heeded, whereas retailers beholden to Schwinn might have spoken less forcefully or with less effect.[80]

Schwinn continued to enjoy banner years through the early 1970s, but the firm's difficulties mounted thereafter, leading to bankruptcy in 1992. The downturn has been attributed to multiple causes, including lack of inspired leadership in the third and fourth generations of the Schwinn family and arrogance in its interaction with dealers. Schwinn failed to maintain its reputation as an innovator and leader in the industry, losing out to American rival Trek in the market for top-of-the-line mountain bikes. The firm also made unproductive investments in a new production facility in Mississippi and in various foreign firms. As its product line lost its appeal, selective distribution methods caused increasing friction with retailers who wanted to promote non-Schwinn lines thought to have more customer appeal. In the end, even *Sylvania*'s

---

[75] F.M. Scherer, Industrial Market Structure and Economic Performance 512 (1970). Yet another view was that the deficiencies of Schwinn could be traced to the Expediting Act which "precludes court of appeals review of government proceedings for equitable relief" and placed the parties and the Court, given the massive record, on an unreasonably short time schedule. Richard W. McLaren, *Territorial and Customer Restrictions, Consignments, Suggested Resale Prices and Refusals to Deal*, 37 Antitrust L.J. 137, 143 (1968).

[76] Crown, *supra* note 4, at 78

[77] Keck, *supra* note 6, at 686.

[78] Crown, *supra* note 4, at 80.

[79] *Id.*

[80] *Id.* at 81.

relaxed paradigm for assessing vertical restraints could not save a century of family ownership of Schwinn.[81]

The *Sylvania* Story

The paradigmatic *Sylvania* case that has governed non-price vertical restraints for three decades grew out of a rather inauspicious distribution dispute. George Shahood, the child of Syrian immigrants, started, built up, and ran a substantial Northern California chain of retail television stores, doing business as Continental TV. Shahood was a strong-willed, independent entrepreneur who fervently embraced the common law rule against restraints on alienation. For Shahood, inventory acquired was inventory owned and to be disposed of solely as the owner willed.[82] One can find acceptance of Shahood's valued entrepreneurial independence in many Sherman Act cases.[83] The 1977 Supreme Court, however, was not to be receptive.

GTE Sylvania was a struggling television producer with a low national market share. There were striking parallels between the Schwinn and Sylvania corporations. Both had sought to reduce the number of retailers to focus on those that would most aggressively promote the firm's brand. Both manufacturers also imposed vertical restraints that limited how a retailer would resell the product. In the case of Schwinn, distributors and retailers were told not to resell to non-authorized retailers. In the case of Sylvainia, retailers were free to resell to anyone, but only from the retailer's approved location.

After Sylvania licensed a competing retailer near Continental's San Francisco store, Continental cut back its purchases of Sylvania products and later attempted to open a new store in a non-approved location in Sacramento. Sylvania terminated Continental's franchise. In the ensuing litigation, Continental claimed a violation of Section 1 of the Sherman Act and invoked the per se rule announced in *Schwinn*.

The case was tried before retired Justice Tom Clark, sitting by designation. When Clark, who did not participate in the *Schwinn* decision, gave the per se instruction requested by Continental, the jury returned a verdict for Continental. The court of appeals affirmed in a split panel decision, but subsequently withdrew that opinion and, after an en banc rehearing, reversed in a 7–4 decision.[84] The majority found

---

[81] This story is told in the final chapters of Crown, *supra* note 4.

[82] I am grateful to Lawrence A. Sullivan, who represented Continental through much of the *Sylvania* litigation, for sharing this information about George Shahood.

[83] Albrecht v. Herald Co., 390 U.S. 145 (1968); *Schwinn*, 388 U.S. 365, United States v. A. Schrader's Son, Inc., 252 U.S. 85 (1922); Dr. Miles Co. v. John D. Parke & Sons Co., 220 U.S. 373 (1911).

[84] 537 F.2d 980 (9th Cir. 1976).

the district court erred in approving a per se instruction to the jury because the location clause employed by Sylvania was distinguishable from the resale restrictions at issue in *Schwinn*.

Continental petitioned the Supreme Court for certiorari. Lawrence Sullivan,[85] who wrote the petition, recalls arguing that if anyone was to limit the *Schwinn* rule, it should be the Supreme Court. The Court accepted this challenge.

On the merits, the briefs for Continental and Sylvania tell a story from strikingly different view points. Continental emphasized its dispute with Sylvania and its efforts to open a new store in Sacramento, an area in which there was only a single authorized Sylvania dealer.[86] There was, in Continental's view, no meaningful distinction between Sylvania's use of the location clause to prevent intrabrand competition in the Sacramento market and Schwinn's use of resale restrictions to prevent intrabrand competition. Continental also vigorously defended the *Schwinn* rule as a sound extension of the common law rule against restraints on alienation and venerable Sherman Act decisions that recognized competition was served by allowing retailers independence in setting the terms and prices of resale. There was, in Continental's view, no basis for drawing a distinction between non-price vertical restraints and resale price restraints.[87]

Sylvania, represented by San Francisco attorney Laurence Popofsky, told the story through the lens of the manufacturer. After struggling with a declining national market share, Sylvania responded by adopting a restricted distribution system that greatly reduced the number of retailers while imposing limits on the location of the retailers' stores (location clause). Sylvania claimed that competing dealerships were still in place in urban markets, although that apparently was not the case for the 500,000 people in the Sacramento area. Sylvania attributed its rebounding national market share to the restricted distribution system. Sylvania defended the Ninth Circuit's distinction between location clauses and Schwinn's resale restrictions, arguing that this narrow reading of *Schwinn* was valid.[88]

The Sylvania brief also strongly urged the Court to reconsider its *Schwinn* holding. In support, the brief cited the success of Sylvania's restricted distribution in improving the firm's national market share, arguing that the location clauses were a tool to increase interbrand

---

[85] Sullivan was then an antitrust professor at the University of California at Berkeley.

[86] *Sylvania*, Brief for Petitioner, at 29–36, available at 1977 WL 189272.

[87] Sylvania, Petitioner's Reply Brief 11–19, available at 1977 WL 189272.

[88] Sylvania, Brief for Respondent, 29–51, available at 1977 WL 181222.

competition. The brief also touted the substantial literature gene_____
Schwinn that criticized the broad sweep of the *Schwinn* rule.[89]

Sylvania came before the Court just 10 years after *Schwinn*. The antitrust climate and the Court had changed markedly in the intervening decade. Robert Bork and Richard Posner had challenged what they and others deemed the excesses of a populist antitrust policy. They argued for a more constricted interpretation of the Sherman Act that emphasized economic analysis and focused on allocation or output injury.[90] These Chicago scholars urged a more tolerant approach to vertical restraints, stressing what they deemed the procompetitive potential for such restraints and equating the manufacturer's interests with consumer interests in maintaining a competitive distribution system. Some lower courts had shown sympathy for these arguments, construing *Schwinn* narrowly to not require application of the per se rule for mild vertical restraints.[91]

The Supreme Court was primed to hear these arguments. Four of the five justices that made up the *Schwinn* majority (Fortas along with Warren, Black, and Douglas) were gone from the Court.[92] Justice Powell, who as an attorney had represented large firms in economic regulatory litigation, was about to write the first of a series of antitrust opinions that showed his strong voice on business and regulatory issues.[93]

The *Sylvania* Court had an opportunity to rule narrowly on the question of location clauses, construing *Schwinn* narrowly (as the Ninth Circuit had done and as Justice White did in his concurring opinion) to apply only to the more restrictive resale controls that *Schwinn* had imposed. The six justices who joined Justice Powell's majority opinion, acting without amicus input from the Government, were looking to make

---

[89] *Id.* at 51–64.

[90] Richard A. Posner, *Antitrust Policy and the Supreme Court: An Analysis of the Restricted Distribution, Horizontal Merger and Potential Competition Decisions*, 75 COLUM. L. REV. 282 (1975); Robert Bork, *Legislative Intent and the Policy of the Sherman Act*, 9 J. LAW & ECON. 7 (1966); Robert Bork, *The Rule of Reason and the Per Se Concept: Price Fixing and Market Division* (I), 74 YALE L. J. 775 (1965); Robert Bork, *The Rule of Reason and the Per Se Concept: Price Fixing and Market Division* (II), 75 YALE L. J. 373 (1966).

[91] E.g., Colorado Pump & Supply Co. v. Febco, Inc., 472 F.2d 637 (10th Cir.), cert. denied, 411 U.S. 987 (1973) (primary responsibility clause for distributor); Superior Bedding Co. v. Serta Associates, Inc., 353 F. Supp. 1143 (N.D. Ill. 1972) (compensation for promotion required when dealer makes sale in neighboring dealer's territory).

[92] The remaining member of the *Schwinn* majority, Justice Brennan (joined by Justice Marshall), dissented in *Sylvania*.

[93] For a discussion of Justice Powell's role in antitrust cases, see E. Thomas Sullivan & Robert B. Thompson, *The Supreme Court and Private Law: The Vanishing Importance of Securities and Antitrust*, 53 EMORY L. J. 1571 (2004).

a broader statement. The *Sylvania* rule that has endured over the past 3 decades is that non-price vertical restraints are to be assessed under the rule of reason. In contrast to *White Motor*'s caution in assessing non-price vertical restraints, Justice Powell's *Sylvania* opinion was a robust brief for the perceived procompetitive benefits of vertical restraints.

Schwinn Reevaluated: An Insecure Brand Seller Imposes Downstream Power Restraints

Contemporary vertical restraints theory draws a distinction between vertical restraints imposed under conditions of upstream or manufacturer power (such as tying or vertical maximum price fixing) and restraints imposed under conditions of downstream or retailer power (such as exclusive territories, location clauses, or vertical minimum price fixing).[94] Downstream power restraints, such as those involved in *Schwinn* and *Sylvania*, may be imposed by the upstream seller, but the seller acts in response to conditions of downstream power. Brand sellers who are insecure in their distribution relationships impose downstream power restraints. These restraints create a downstream incentive (typically by guaranteeing a higher margin for retailers) to carry and promote the seller's products.

Consider the patent medicine being marketed by the Dr. Miles firm in the well known vertical minimum price fixing case of that name.[95] The product was a patent medicine, probably with alcohol as its prime active ingredient, that competed with numerous other similar products in the early 20th century. The Dr. Miles company needed to create an incentive for drug stores to not only carry its brand, but for a pharmacist to affirmatively promote it through store display or by recommendation to customers. That incentive, provided by the vertical minimum price fixing scheme, was the higher margin that the pharmacist would earn whenever a Dr. Miles product was sold. As a brand seller, Dr. Miles had obtained some name recognition—sufficient to make it worthwhile for the discounters of that era to carry the product. But the name recognition was insufficient to ensure that pharmacists would carry the Dr. Miles product or, absent promotion, that consumers would buy it. Dr. Miles, like Schwinn and Sylvania, was an insecure brand seller.

Compare the Dr. Miles product with another patent medicine that apparently had obtained greater brand loyalty and, accordingly, made the manufacturer secure in distribution. Lydia Pinkham's compound had captured much of the women's market for such patent medicines.[96]

---

[94] For an overview of vertical restraints theory, see LAWRENCE A. SULLIVAN & WARREN S. GRIMES, THE LAW OF ANTITRUST: AN INTEGRATED HANDBOOK, Chapter VI (2d ed. 2006).

[95] *Dr. Miles*, 220 U.S. 373 (1911). The *Sylvania* paradigm was the lynchpin in a recent 5–4 decision overturning *Dr. Miles*. Leegin Creative Leather Products, Inc. v. PSKS, Inc., ___ U.S. ___, 127 S.Ct. 2705 (2007).

[96] This example was offered by Robert Steiner, *The Nature of Vertical Restraints*, 30 ANTITRUST BULL. 143, 169 (1985).

Another alcohol based medicine, it was sold prominently during the first 30 years of the 20th century without use of any vertical restraints. Strong brand sellers have no need to impose downstream power vertical restraints because a retailer who does not carry the brand will lose sales to competing retailers. Secure brand sellers also have a disincentive to impose downstream power restraints because they may be costly to impose or enforce and because they limit downstream intrabrand competition in a manner that could reduce sales of the product. Lydia Pinkham's manufacturer finally did attempt to impose resale price maintenance, but only in the 1930s when the brand equity and market share of Lydia Pinkham's began to fall off sharply.

Schwinn's banner years began in the 1930s and extended through the 1970s. Schwinn used no selective distribution in the 1930s or 1940s when its product was on the rise and enjoyed maximum consumer acceptance. In 1952, Schwinn had 22.5% of the market. In the face of competition from lower-priced U.S. and foreign rivals, Schwinn's share fell to 12.8% by 1961.[97] It was precisely during this period that Schwinn was actively implementing a selective distribution system designed to insulate retailers from competition and allow them to charge a higher margin. Schwinn was, at this point, an insecure brand seller. While its brand equity remained high in the 1950s, Schwinn's lower cost rivals were quickly copying improvements that Schwinn brought to the market. Most of the distinguishing features of Schwinn bicycles of the 1950s, their thin tires, front and rear hand brakes, and three speed gearing in the hub of the rear wheel,[98] were obtained from outside suppliers and readily available on lower-priced rival bikes. Schwinn was losing market share because price-sensitive buyers found reasonable and cheaper alternatives.

The district court concluded that the Schwinn selective distribution or "franchise" system of the 1950s saved the firm.[99] While perhaps hyperbole, the district court's view seems justified by the full record, which shows that a smaller number of Schwinn retailers with fewer rivals were able to maintain or increase their per store sales. Selective distribution assured these retailers a higher margin than they would have captured with wide open distribution. Although there is evidence in the record that Schwinn retailers were forced to reduce their margin during the 1950s,[100] the extraordinary efforts that Schwinn made to cull retailers and to prevent resale to non-authorized retailers show an intent

---

[97] *Schwinn*, 237 F. Supp. at 325.

[98] My brother and I rode Schwinn bicycles matching this description during the 1950s.

[99] *Schwinn*, 237 F. Supp. at 355.

[100] Keck, *supra* note 6, at 675.

to limit price competition at the retail level and maintain higher margins for authorized retailers than would be available for sales of rival bicycles.

Some vertical restraints theorists have suggested that if a vertical restraint produces higher output for the seller imposing it, the restraint is presumptively procompetitive.[101] There are two obvious problems with equating brand marketing efficacy with a procompetitive outcome. The first is that brand marketing gains achieved through vertical restraints come at a high risk for consumer deception. As described above,[102] a consumer is likely to give credence to a multi-brand retailer who recommends one brand over another when the consumer is unaware that a vertical restraint has given the retailer an incentive to promote a particular seller's product. Self-interested retailer promotion may or may not involve outright and actionable deception, but its consequences for competition are identical: consumers end up with the wrong product at the wrong price.

The second problem with equating a vertical restraint's output gains with procompetitive results is that, despite an individual seller's short term output gain, overall industry performance may suffer as other firms adopt similar vertical restraints.[103] If vertical restraints are widely employed in the industry, an individual manufacturer's promotion gains from imposing a restraint will tend to be nullified by restraints imposed by rivals. The price of the industry's products will be higher, with the result that demand for the rivals' products goes down. There is no record evidence to support widespread use of Schwinn's exclusive restraints, although the possibility that other manufacturers might adopt similar restraints cannot be excluded.

Given the additional analytical insights of today's vertical restraints theorists, would the Schwinn distribution system of the 1950s survive a structured rule of reason test such as the Government proposed in its *Schwinn* brief? Schwinn could clearly establish its selective distribution system, designate primary territories for distributors, location clauses for distributors and retailers, and suggest resale prices to retailers. These relatively mild vertical restraints may make it easier for a manufacturer to implement efficient selective distribution. But as the vertical restraints operate to clamp down on all possibilities for efficient retailers

---

[101] ROBERT BORK, THE ANTITRUST PARADOX: A POLICY AT WAR WITH ITSELF 295–96 (1978); Richard A. Posner, *The Rule of Reason and the Economic Approach: Reflections on the Sylvania Decision*, 45 U. CHI. L. REV. 1, 18–19 (1977); Frank Easterbrook, *Vertical Arrangements and the Rule of Reason*, 53 ANTITRUST L. J. 135, 154 (1985).

[102] See footnotes 38–39, *supra*, and the accompanying text.

[103] SULLIVAN & GRIMES, *supra* note 94, § 6.3c3. F.M. Scherer, *The Economics of Vertical Restraints*, 52 ANTITRUST L. J. 687, 702–704 (1983).

to lower prices to buyers, the burden of justification on the defendant should rise.

The last steps in Schwinn's effort to wholly restrict distribution to authorized retailers were neither efficient nor procompetitive. To limit any resale to an efficient discount outlet would, for example, entail a substantial enforcement burden in tracing the source of such a resale transaction, investigating it, and incurring the substantial costs of terminating the distributor or retailer who had made the resale. If the enforcement were successful, it would eliminate meaningful intrabrand competition and the benefits that flow from it. Such intrabrand competition will tend to limit the margins that authorized retailers can charge, and lessen their incentives to promote the branded product on false or misleading grounds. If there is no deception involved in the promotion induced by the selective distribution, then the product must possess superior characteristics that would insulate it from *interbrand* competition. In that instance, the producer may have a strong brand that no longer requires the promotion incentives of a vertical restraint. Whether or not the vertical restraint continues, the consumer needs the protection of *intrabrand* competition to maintain an efficient distribution system and ensure that this distinctive product is available at the most competitive price.

The foregoing leads inexorably to the conclusion that the resale restrictions which the Government attacked in its Supreme Court brief were then, and are now, anticompetitive and a proper place for the antitrust law to draw the line. It is a line that allows manufacturers a great deal of freedom to engage in brand promotion activities, even when that promotion is effected by vertical restraints. Only the most constricting of those restraints that would stifle all or nearly all downstream retail price competition would be subject to a per se rule or to a rule of presumptive illegality.

Sylvania Reevaluated: The Need for an Updated Paradigm

The *Sylvania* story illustrates the value of another core element of modern vertical restraints analysis. One of the fundamental insights of post-Chicago learning is that competition occurs not only among firms at the same horizontal level, but also vertically in manufacturer-retailer relationships. The traditional assumption has been that firms in successive vertical stages of distribution are in a complementary relationship. In this one-dimensional world, only horizontal competition would matter. Robert Steiner points out, however, that manufacturers and retailers compete vertically over their respective shares of a brand's consumer price.[104]

---

[104] Robert L. Steiner, *The Inverse Association Between the Margins of Manufacturers and Retailers,* 8 REV. INDUS. ORG. 717, 723–27, 29 (1993).

In consumer goods markets, there is usually an inverse association between markups at the two levels. When the manufacturer's markup is high, the retailer's is low, and vice versa.[105] Steiner points to another inverse association—the tendency of strong or highly advertised brands to have thinner retail gross margins than manufacturers' fringe brands and private labels. Thus, a manufacturer will sell its strong brand at a high mark up to retailers who then are forced by the intensive intra-brand competition to resell at a low retail mark up. That same retailer, however, will offer a store brand, acquired at a much lower factory price, at a much higher retail mark up. The retailer will still sell the store brand for less than the advertised brand due to the latter's superior reputation. Both of Steiner's postulated inverse relationships have now been verified by empirical investigation.[106]

None of these insights would appear to threaten the *Sylvania* Court's ultimate conclusion that location clauses should be assessed under the rule of reason. They add force, however, to the conclusion that retail intrabrand competition is a powerful force to maintain the competitive distribution of strong brands.

When vertical restraints of a non-dominant firm do not severely undercut retail intrabrand competition, they should probably be presumptively lawful. The *Sylvania* majority, however, made no attempt to distinguish among non-price vertical restraints. Instead, it offered sweeping generalizations about the use of such restraints that are misleading, if not incorrect. Among these generalizations are: (1) that vertical restraints promote interbrand competition by allowing a manufacturer to obtain efficiencies in distribution;[107] and (2) that interbrand competition is "the primary concern of antitrust law."[108]

In postulating that vertical restraints promote interbrand competition, the Court also opined that interbrand competition somehow "provides a significant check on the exploitation of intrabrand market power because of ability of consumers to substitute a different brand for the same product."[109] In fact, downstream power vertical restraints promote brand selling. Brand selling is here to stay and no doubt, on balance, more beneficial than harmful to consumers. Among other benefits, brand

---

[105] Id.

[106] Michael P. Lynch, *Why Economists Are Wrong to Neglect Retailing and How Steiner's Theory Provides an Explanation of Important Irregularities*, 49 ANTITRUST BULL. No. 4 (Winter 2004).

[107] Justice Powell's words were that "[v]ertical restraints promote interbrand competition by allowing the manufacturer to achieve certain efficiencies in the distribution of his products." *Sylvania*, 433 U.S. at 54.

[108] *Sylvania*, 433 U.S. at 52, n.19

[109] *Id.* at 52, n.19.

selling can convey valuable quality information to buyers, create an incentive for the manufacturer to maintain quality, and allow a manufacturer to expand production and achieve economies of scale. But brand selling is a way of *reducing, not increasing,* interbrand competition.[110] It is a fallacy to assume that one form of competition could offset the loss of the other because when vertical restraints are used to promote brand selling, both intrabrand and interbrand competition are reduced,. As the Posner-drafted brief for the United States recognized in *Schwinn,* brand selling insulates the seller from interbrand competition and allows the manufacturer and retailer to sell at higher prices.[111] Whether a particular instance of brand selling is beneficial or harmful will depend on whether the consumer is getting a preferred product without deception and whether the distribution system is competitive.

The record in *Schwinn* (and perhaps the record in *Sylvania*) supports the proposition that restrictive distribution can be efficient. Schwinn, for example, greatly reduced its distribution and promotion expenses by eliminating large numbers of low volume wholesalers and retailers. But the efficiency inherent in restrictive distribution may not require the use of any vertical restraints and certainly does not necessitate ending all retail intrabrand competition. If a manufacturer opting for restricted distribution is an insecure brand seller, that manufacturer may well wish to implement brand promotion incentives. Although the efficiencies inherent in restricted distribution may at times be more easily obtainable when the manufacturer can create brand promotion incentives, there are, as the concluding section describes, numerous ways to generate these incentives without ending all retail intrabrand competition.

The *Sylvania* Court's observation that the major goal of the Sherman Act is protecting interbrand competition[112] is also susceptible to much mischief.[113] In a market with many rival brands, interbrand

---

[110] In a footnote, Justice Powell responded to the point that vertical restraints decrease interbrand competition by arguing that vertical restraints "convey socially desirable information about product availability, price, quality and services." Id. at 56 n. 25. To the extent that vertical restraints convey socially useful information about quality and services, the effect may be socially desirable, but this in no way undercuts the point that brand selling differentiates brands and insulates a favored brand from interbrand competition. More recent literature suggests that one of the problems with harmful vertical restraints is that they create incentives for dealers to convey deceptive or misleading information. Grimes, *supra* note 41.

[111] *Schwinn,* Brief for the United States, at 26.

[112] This aphorism was most recently repeated by the Court in *Volvo Truck North America, Inc. v. Reeder–Sinco GMC, Inc.,* 546 U.S. 164, 180–81 (2006).

[113] For additional analysis of the economic reasoning underlying *Sylvania,* see Robert L. Steiner, *Sylvania Economics—A Critique,* 60 ANTITRUST L. J. 41 (1991); Robert L. Steiner, *Intrabrand Competition—Stepchild of Antitrust,* 36 ANTITRUST BULL. 155 (1991).

competition does indeed provide consumers a choice and a means of
checking the abusive power of one brand holder. But the stronger the
brand preference, the weaker the check provided by interbrand competition. The lack of intrabrand competition on a strong brand will invite
anticompetitive behavior in downstream distribution. Because vertical
restraints are tools to increase brand promotion incentives, their use can
decrease cross-elasticity of demand between brands and leave consumers
unprotected from anticompetitive distribution behavior.

The Future of the Law Governing Downstream
Power Vertical Restraints

Downstream power vertical restraints limit downstream intrabrand
competition, so they have an additional negative impact not present
when brand selling is promoted by other means. To win and maintain
retailer loyalty for its product, the insecure brand seller must offer
inducements to retailers. Many of those potential inducements do not
meaningfully limit either interbrand or intrabrand competition. For
example, low factory prices, manufacturer sponsored advertising and
promotion, promotion allowances paid to the retailer, agreements to buy
back unsold retailer inventory, or even some loose form of exclusivity for
retailers (such as a location clause) can generate brand promotion
without substantial harm to competition at any level. In contrast, other
forms of vertical restraints, such as resale price maintenance or strictly
enforced resale restrictions, do substantially undercut both intrabrand
and interbrand competition.

The Supreme Court's sterile policy analysis in *Schwinn* was followed
by *Sylvania's* more in depth but highly partisan and error-ridden policy
analysis. The stories behind these litigations tell a more compelling and
useful story than anything contained in either of the two Supreme Court
decisions. The Government's brief in *Schwinn* speaks to real market
place issues involving downstream power restraints that have yet to be
addressed by the Court. The brief most certainly did not endorse the
Sylvania aphorism that vertical restraints promote interbrand competition. In their casebook, Easterbrook and Posner defend the Government's brief as focused on the risks the Schwinn distribution system
posed for *interbrand* competition.[114] The presumption of illegality advocated in the brief offers a viable approach for those downstream-power
vertical restraints, such as Schwinn's resale restrictions, that severely
limit retail intrabrand competition while also reducing interbrand competition.

---

[114] Richard A. Posner & Frank H. Easterbrook, ANTITRUST 246–47 (2d ed. 1981).

6

Peter C. Carstensen and Harry First[*]

Rambling Through Economic Theory: *Topco*'s Closer Look

Without the *per se* rules, businessmen would be left with little to aid them in predicting in any particular case what courts will find to be legal and illegal under the Sherman Act. Should Congress ultimately determine that predictability is unimportant in this area of the law, it can, of course, make *per se* rules inapplicable in some or all cases, and leave courts free to ramble through the wilds of economic theory in order to maintain a flexible approach.

—*United States v. Topco Associates, Inc.*, 405 U.S. 596. 609 n.10 (1972).

The Oral Argument

On the morning of November 16, 1971, Howard Shapiro stepped into the well of the United States Supreme Court to argue Case No. 70–82, *United States v. Topco Associates, Inc.*[1] Shapiro, dressed in the formal morning coat traditionally worn for Supreme Court arguments by lawyers for the Department of Justice, was the first to argue that day. The government had lost its case at trial below—in those days government

[*] The authors were attorneys in the Antitrust Division of the Department of Justice when the *Topco* case was being argued in the Supreme Court, but did not work directly on the case. For their recollections of the case, we thank Donald Baker, John Dienelt, Kenneth Elzinga, Victor Grimm, Stephen Rubin, Howard Shapiro, and Joseph Tate. We also thank Yookyung Moon and Eric Johnson for their excellent research assistance. Financial assistance for this article was provided in part by a research grant from the Filomen D'Agostino and Max E. Greenberg Research Fund at New York University School of Law.

[1] The transcript of the oral argument is reproduced in 32 Philip B. Kurland & Gerhard Casper, Antitrust Law: Major Briefs and Oral Arguments of the Supreme Court of the United States, 1955 Term–1975 Term 419–450 (1979). All subsequent quotations in the text are from this transcript.

civil antitrust cases were appealed directly from the trial court to the Supreme Court—and Shapiro, representing the appellant, had the task of convincing the Court to ignore the factual findings made by District Court Judge Hubert Will and focus on the government's legal approach.

Shapiro appeared confident as he began. His argument was straightforward. Topco was the vehicle for its owners—twenty-three supermarket chains and two wholesalers—to buy grocery products cooperatively and to sell many of them at retail under brands owned by Topco. Its cooperative buying was not a problem for the government. The problem was that Topco restricted the territories within which its member-supermarket chains could sell Topco-branded goods, which the government felt gave each member the effective right to exclude all other Topco members from its territory. In the government's view, this restriction amounted to a horizontal territorial allocation scheme, long held illegal per se under section 1 of the Sherman Act.

But Shapiro was not as confident of his position as he appeared. Although the Antitrust Division had characterized this case from the start as a "simple" case of horizontal competitors allocating territories,[2] Shapiro actually was dubious about the government's position. Topco's main defense was that the territorial restrictions were necessary to enable the Topco members to provide their customers with a "private-label brand" and thereby compete better with the "Big Three" chains of the day, A&P, Safeway, and Kroger. Shapiro, as Chief of the Antitrust Division's Appellate Section, had to defend the Division's per se approach, but he thought there was some merit to the argument that the better approach would be to balance the pro- and anticompetitive effects of the restrictions—less competition in Topco-branded goods (or even among Topco members) but more competition among supermarkets, just the sort of balancing approach in which the district court judge had engaged.

Shapiro began by laying out the government's legal position—territorial restraints were condemned as long ago as *Addyston Pipe*, decided in 1898, and as recently as *Sealy* and *Schwinn*, decided by the Court on per se grounds only four years earlier.[3] He also advanced the traditional arguments favoring per se rules. Although "once in a while" there might be a case where a horizontal territorial restraint was not

---

[2] *See* Memorandum For the Attorney General, Re: Proposed Complaint Against Topco Associates, Inc., from Donald F. Turner, Ass't Attn'y Gen'l, Dep't of Justice, Antitrust Div., at 3 ("Our theory of the case is a simple one.") (undated) (authors' files). At that time, approval of the Attorney General was required before the Antitrust Division could file a case.

[3] *See* United States v. Addyston Pipe & Steel Co., 85 F. 271 (6th Cir. 1898), *aff'd*, 175 U.S. 211(1899); United States v. Sealy Corp., 388 U.S. 350 (1967); United States v. Arnold, Schwinn & Co., 388 U.S. 365, 390 (1967).

extremely harmful, the per se rule should still be applied because of the benefits of predictability. "Right now any antitrust lawyer in the country can tell a supermarket chain: You may not divide up territories with your competitors. The law is absolutely clear on that." But with the district court's approach, Shapiro argued, the parties won't know the answer until after a "full-scale" trial with an "extremely difficult" rule of reason examination. Referring to the district court's rule of reason effort, Shapiro noted that "you'll find nothing in the record showing what A&P's position is in these fifty-five [local] markets. It's almost impossible to do that kind of vast market analysis."

The heart of Shapiro's argument, though, was not really on the legal principles. Appellate courts, deprived of live witness testimony and dependent on a printed record, are often more concerned that they understand the facts of a dispute. So Shapiro made two important factual points, based on the record but not made explicit in Judge Will's findings of fact.

The points were made in response to questions from the Court about whether Topco would dissolve absent territorial exclusivity.[4] Judge Will had found that it would, but Shapiro disagreed: "Now if they were freed from agreements not to compete, it's quite possible that they could still achieve some of the benefits of individual labeling, for example, by using a joint organization to achieve brands for each of them." In other words, Topco didn't need territorial exclusivity among its members to provide each of its members with their own "private brand." Shapiro also pointed to an example in the record of where two Topco members with a territorial conflict had been forced to compete against each other, with both chains carrying Topco-branded products. The testimony, Shapiro noted, was that these chains competed "all over the place" and that the revenues of the more successful competitor went up. How to explain this result? Shapiro quoted the witness's testimony: "Well, sometimes you get so mad and work so hard that you run past yourself." Surely, Shapiro added, "this is what we think the Sherman Act is about and this is what the *per se* prohibition against market division is intended to achieve."[5]

When Victor Grimm, counsel for Topco, began his argument by stressing the importance of an exclusive private label, the Court picked up the point Shapiro made about creating separate brands for its

---

[4] The transcript of the oral argument refers generally to "the Court" and does not identify the particular Justice who is speaking.

[5] The government had made the same point in its brief on the merits, providing factual support for its argument that Judge Will erred in finding that the elimination of Topco's territorial restraints would lead to its demise. *See* Brief For the United States at 36–37 and n.25, United States v. Topco Assocs., Inc., 405 U.S. 596 (1972) (No. 70–82).

members. The Court posed a hypothetical. Suppose that Giant (a former Topco member with stores in the D.C. area) and Seven–Eleven were competing in the same market, "with Giant having green beans under some private Giant label of green beans, and Seven–Eleven having some private Seven–Eleven green beans, although they're both packed by the same packers. . . . Why doesn't that work?" And more to the point—"Was this possibility explored in the District Court?"

Grimm replied that there was "discussion" of this issue at trial and then paused to find the spot in the record referencing it. Shapiro, perhaps anticipating the question, had the record at the ready. From the government's counsel table he handed the record up to Grimm, open to Government Exhibit 102, so that Grimm could answer the Court's question.

GX 102 was a Topco memorandum titled "A Second Family of Topco Brands" which reported on a study done by three executives of supermarket chains that were Topco members, a study which rejected the creation of a second set of Topco brands.[6] The study estimated the direct cost to develop a second family of brands at about $350,000, a fact noted by Grimm. The Court continued the line of questioning: Assume that such a sum "would not have that much effect" on Giant or Seven–Eleven, "then the private Seven–Eleven label would be competing with the private Giant label." But "that doesn't happen because only Giant or only Seven–Eleven is allowed a Topco private label; isn't that right?" The conclusion quickly followed: "Then the effect of exclusivity in this arrangement is simply to limit competition in private label territories."

Grimm could not agree, of course. He responded that Topco members could find other sources for private labels. Or Topco members could leave Topco and create their own private labels—although only if they had a large enough volume of sales. But if there were no exclusivity, Grimm emphasized, members would no longer be willing "to pour their resources into a private label which would be subject to use by others." Without exclusivity, Topco would "disappear."

On rebuttal, Shapiro pressed the factual points. True, the government presented a per se case. But "on the record that was made" the government did "try to carry the burden that this practice was unreasonable" by showing that Topco's exclusivity agreement "inhibits expansion by members into each other's territories" and "affects price."[7]

---

[6] Government Exhibit 102 was reproduced in the parties' jointly-prepared Appendix, filed with the Court along with their briefs. *See* Appendix at 438–41, *Topco* (hereinafter Joint Appendix).

[7] The government made the same argument in its brief. *See* Brief for the United States, *supra* note 5, at 16–17 (although government did not attempt to prove that Topco's

Topco's own expert witness had testified that the "whole purpose of exclusivity" is to insulate the seller from price competition. As for the alleged need to protect brand loyalty, Shapiro pointed to record testimony indicating that there were no studies about whether there was any brand loyalty to private labels. Whatever it is that "brings the housewife in," Shapiro suggested, it "certainly isn't loyalty to a private label brand." After all, "[p]eople don't travel across a city to get Food Club canned peas."

Shapiro then returned to the argument over developing "a second line of brands." Topco had not developed a second line precisely because that would facilitate competition amongst its members. Referring back to GX 102, Shapiro pointed to one of the reasons given in the memorandum for not establishing a second family of brands—if there were a second line, "the competitive edge" that the Topco program gives its members "against each other" would be "eliminated."[8] Topco wouldn't need to develop a different brand for each of its members for every product, Shapiro added. "They might achieve some real wonders with a smaller line...."

Whether fortuitously or intentionally, Shapiro did not end his rebuttal with a ringing endorsement of the per se rule. In response to the Court's observation that exclusive territorial restraints was one means by which "these independents could hold their own" against A&P and "the other big ones," Shapiro responded simply: "There are ... less restrictive means, let us put it, which is really what the ancillary restriction rule is about. There are less restrictive means by which it can be done, Your Honor." And with that, the case was submitted for decision.

The factual questions raised in oral argument, though, were not decisively answered by either side. Was a second family of labels possible—Giant-brand green beans and Seven–Eleven-brand green beans competing in the same market, to take the Court's example? How much would it cost? Why hadn't Topco provided such a label? If the reasons for

---

practices were illegal under the rule of reason, the record "reveals the kind of adverse economic effects which traditionally have justified application of the per se rules").

[8] The quote to which Shapiro referred was made in the context of discussing whether a second family of brands should be developed for new members joining Topco. The full quote reads as follows:

> There is reason to doubt that Members generally would agree to our licensing *new* Members in their present "prime" territories, if we had a complete second family of brands. Such licensing would give competitors of present Members equal private brand quality and packaging appeal. Thus, in such cases the competitive edge the Topco program gives its Members would be eliminated.

Joint Appendix, *supra* note 6, at 440. Note that the government did not attack Topco's method of deciding whether to admit new members.

private label exclusivity didn't hold up, then was Topco just a cartel of supermarket chains, designed to keep its members out of each other's markets? These questions, of course, are a long way from those apparently relevant under the formal per se rule, but there was little doubt after the oral argument that these were the issues most troubling the Court and that at least some of the Justices were skeptical of Topco's purported justification.

Topco's Economic Context

House Brands and Buying Groups

Economic efficiency in the retail grocery business, necessarily focused on keeping costs down, involves buying at the lowest possible price and getting the goods onto store shelves at the lowest transaction cost. A retailer may have trouble achieving these goals when a producer advertises its goods and establishes substantial consumer goodwill for its brands. Not only is a grocery store usually obliged to carry the brand or loose customers, but the producer with a well-established and popular brand, having differentiated its product, is in a strong bargaining position when it comes to pricing those goods to the retailer.[9]

Starting in the 1920s the emerging national grocery chains, notably A&P, began to develop "house brands" for many popular lines of foods.[10] The house brand provided an important and very attractive alternative to the national brand. The chain store developed its own label and then contracted with a processor to produce the product with the chain's label. In this transaction the processor had little bargaining power. There was no differentiated demand for its particular product; rather, any well equipped food processor could duplicate the product. Hence, the chain with a house brand program could bargain for much lower prices. Moreover, although the chain might do some promotion of these products, the primary selling point was lower price. Positioned on the shelf next to the branded product but with a substantially lower price, the house brand provided a visible alternative for the cost-conscious consumer. Despite the lower retail price, the house brand was usually more profitable to the chain store because of the combination of low acquisition price and limited promotional expenditure.

---

[9] Robert Steiner has focused attention on this aspect of retailing and what he calls "vertical competition" between retailers that seek higher margins and manufacturers that create a differentiated demand that allows them to capture a larger share of the final sales price. *See* Robert Steiner, *The Evolution and Applications of Dual–Stage Thinking*, 49 ANTITRUST BULL. 877 (2004). *See generally, Special Issue: The Implications of the Work of Robert L. Steiner*, 49 ANTITRUST BULL. 821–1042 (2004).

[10] For an account of the rise of house brands, see WILLIAM APPLEBAUM & RAY GOLDBERG, BRAND STRATEGY IN UNITED STATES FOOD MARKETING (1967).

With the growing success of the national chains in the use of house brands, other grocery businesses began to look for ways to imitate this success. Cooperative buying groups, such as Topco, emerged to develop their own labels, as did major food wholesalers. By the 1960s, according to Topco, a grocery chain needed annual sales of about $250 million to support an effective house brand label.[11] Topco also estimated that the direct costs of creating such a label would be about $350,000 (the figure to which Grimm referred in oral argument)—a little over .01% of the minimum $250 million in annual sales, a rather small percentage (thus confirming the Court's intuition that such an amount would not be significant for companies like Giant or 7–Eleven).

Large chains had another important advantage over their smaller rivals. The large chains had substantial buyer power and could, because of the volume of their purchases, negotiate favorable prices from producers. Even heavily advertised national brands could be subject to significant pressure from a buyer that takes a substantial share of total production.[12] Concerns with the impact of such negotiations were central to the government's challenge to A&P in the 1930s that culminated in a decree imposing significant restrictions on its buying practices.[13]

Hence, pooling the buying power of a group of regional chains had significant impact on the ability of the group to negotiate prices. Although Topco was certainly not the only buying group in the grocery world, there is no contemporary evidence of a significant number of alternative groups.[14] Indeed, of the thirty-five chains with reported 1967–

---

[11] This was the estimate given by Topco's witnesses at trial, although it was not supported by any documentary proof. Topco's marketing expert, for example, offered the estimate as a matter of "general judgment" rather than "exact knowledge" and the estimate was somewhat undercut by cross-examination pointing to smaller companies with private label programs. See Joint Appendix, supra note 6, at 201–04 (expert testimony of William Appelbaum). Some Topco-member witnesses testified to a higher number, see, e.g., id. at 300 ($300–$400 million). The district court judge found that annual sales of $250 million "or more" were necessary and that "twice that amount" would "probably" be required "for optimum efficiency." See United States v. Topco Assocs., Inc., 319 F. Supp. 1031, 1036 (N.D. Ill. 1970) (finding of fact 33).

[12] See Paul Dobson, Exploiting Buyer Power: Lessons from the British Grocery Trade, 72 ANTITRUST L. J. 529 (2004) (in the United Kingdom grocery chains buying as little as 9% of a producer's output have substantial buyer power).

[13] See Great Atl. & Pac. Tea Co. v. FTC, 106 F. 2d 667 (3d Cir. 1939) (affirming entry of order). The concerns about A&P's practices are explored in JOEL B. DIRLAM & ALFRED E. KAHN, FAIR COMPETITION: THE LAW AND ECONOMICS OF ANTITRUST POLICY (1954).

[14] A few buying groups were referred to in trial testimony, but without much exploration. See, e.g., Joint Appendix, supra note 6, at 202 (mentioning Staff, Certified, and Roundy), 282–83 (wholesaler brands, but product coverage not as extensive as Topco's), 286 ("alternatives not as good"), 329 (no organization "comparable" to Topco). Staff Supermarket Associates, which provided private labels, was organized similarly to Topco,

sales volumes between $50 million and $200 million, ten were Topco members, including five of the eight chains with sales between $150 million and $200 million.[15] If these data reflect the potential for creating other buying groups with comparable services, then Topco's membership already included many of the most likely potential members, making the formation of such other groups unlikely.

Large grocery wholesalers also had the capacity to engage in similar negotiations and serve smaller stores with a range of products including the wholesaler's house brand. But wholesalers provide a greater variety of services and functions than do buyer groups like Topco. Most notably, wholesalers receive products into their warehouses and then reship them to grocery stores. This costly function would duplicate the warehousing capacity of the mid-sized chains that dominated Topco, likely making wholesaler house brands more expensive to Topco members than the creation of their own brands, allowing them to avoid paying twice for the warehousing function.

The Relative Efficiency of National Chains, Regional Chains, and Mom & Pop Stores

Grocery retailing in the 1950s and 1960s involved three types of retail operations—national chains, regional chains (including some large individual stores whose volume of sales approximated that of smaller regionals), and individual, neighborhood retailers, often referred to as "Mom & Pop" stores.

The small neighborhood stores lacked the scale necessary to achieve very great efficiency. Their competitive advantage lay in location and sometimes hours of operation. Such stores were accessible for a quick purchase, a late night or weekend need, and might carry specialized products such as ethnic foods that were particularly desired in the neighborhood. These advantages allowed these stores to charge customers higher prices that, in the successful stores, offset the higher operating costs. Over the period of the 1950s and 1960s, these stores were the most likely to exit the business as regional and national chains duplicated more of their products and offered lower prices.[16] The increased

---

except that it dealt exclusively with small chains. At the time of the litigation, Staff's 15 members had annual sales of approximately $350 million. *See id.* at 483 (FTC Study) (GX 1).

[15] *See* Joint Appendix, *supra* note 6, at 17–19 (list of 81 chains with sales volumes for 1966 and 1967), 20–21 (list of Topco members, 1964–1967, with sales volumes).

[16] From 1963 to 1972, the number of single store grocery operators in the United States declined from 218,615 to 155,235. GERALD GRINNELL, RUSSELL C. PARKER, & LAWRENCE A. RENS, GROCERY RETAILING CONCENTRATION IN METROPOLITAN AREAS, ECONOMIC CENSUS YEARS 1954–72, 51, Table 4 (1979).

mobility of the American population contributed to this transformation as well. A customer in a car would find it much easier to pass by the neighborhood store and go to the suburban chain grocery with its larger selection and better prices.

At the other end of the spectrum the national chains often suffered diseconomies resulting from their large size and dispersed operations. Of necessity such organizations required many more levels of managerial oversight and more complex systems of record keeping and operation. They had the advantage of greater buyer power in buying groceries, but this was offset by their higher administrative costs. Such chains tended, therefore, to promote their services and general image. In general these chains did not emphasize price competition.[17]

It appears that the regional chains that made up Topco probably had, on average, better operating efficiency than either of the other two general classes of grocery stores.[18] Such chains were usually organized around a central warehouse that could serve all the stores. This model minimized costs by eliminating the need for balancing inventory among warehouses as well as other coordination costs among regional divisions. The use of buying groups like Topco was another source of efficiency. The group supervised the buying process, used their ability to combine the demand of all the participants to negotiate favorable terms, developed the house brands, and provided centralized oversight of the quality of the goods. The food processors would ship products directly to the members' warehouses and bill them for the goods, thereby eliminating any intermediate warehousing and reshipping. These activities created economies of scale and scope to the benefit of the members. Conceptually, this was an integration of the primary activities that contributed to the cost advantages of the national chains. But because the integration was only partial, it avoided the administrative and coordination costs that the fully integrated national chains faced.

Topco's Origins and Activities

In the early 1940s a group of grocery store owners in Wisconsin got together to establish an entity that would act as their purchasing agent in buying products for their stores. Initially focused on dairy products,

---

[17] See In re National Tea, 69 FTC 265 (1966).

[18] An FTC study of profitability data for 1965 to 1974 found that the average profitability for chains with less than $500 million in sales (weighted by sales volume of the chains involved) was approximately comparable to the largest retail chains (sales over $1 billion) and generally higher than chains in the $500 million to $1 billion range. See FTC Staff Report on Food Chain Profits, Rep. No. R–6–15–23 (1975). Given that the smaller chains put greater emphasis on lower prices than did the large chains, and had less buying power, it is reasonable to infer that their operations were more efficient in order to produce the same ultimate level of profitability.

they soon expanded into other product lines and ultimately developed a house brand label, Food Club, that processors affixed to many of these products. This enterprise took the name Topco.

Topco's members were not marginal "Mom & Pop" grocery stores. Rather, the participants were small chains that operated groups of stores in a region, usually served by a single central warehouse. Basically, this allowed the chain to receive carload size shipments of goods that could then be distributed among the stores in the chain. Such chains did not need the full line of services that a standard food wholesaler would provide. But as relatively small buyers, the individual chains lacked the bargaining power of the major national retailers. As a result, they were less able to obtain discounts from processors. In addition, it was relatively costly for such a chain to engage in quality control with respect to any unbranded products they purchased. For this reason, as well as the costs associated with the actual development of a brand, such chains had little ability to offer house brands.

Topco pooled its members demand for products to get better prices. The processor shipped directly to each member the quantity it had ordered and billed that member accordingly. Topco's role was combining the orders to create a stronger bargaining position. For unbranded products including fresh vegetables and meat, Topco provided a level of centralized quality control at low cost that resulted from scale economies inherent in such supervision. The members also had the volume of collective business that made it possible to establish a house brand and provide the oversight needed to ensure consistent quality. An additional feature of the venture was that it provided a source of innovation in grocery products because of its ability to collect and evaluate information from a variety of sources.

Topco's membership experienced turnover as members grew to a size where the efficiency gains from participating in Topco diminished. As members withdrew and established their own house brands (often based on the name of the chain), Topco continued to attract new members, thereby maintaining its volume purchasing ability. Because Topco required a minimum of about $50 million in sales to be eligible for membership, its membership came to be composed of mid-range regional chains.[19] By 1968, Topco had 26 members with total sales of $2.3 billion, more than all but the three largest national chains.[20] Topco's members were located in all parts of the country, with a notable concentration

---

[19] As of 1967, however, six of its twenty-six members had sales below that threshold. *See* Joint Appendix, *supra* note 6, at 20–21 (list of members with their sales volumes for 1964–1967).

[20] *See* United States v. Topco Assocs., Inc., 405 U.S. 596, 600 (1972).

from Virginia to Massachusetts and in some areas of the Midwest.[21] Although there are no complete figures available for member shares of local markets, and no figures available for shares of competitors in those local markets, data presented at trial indicate that some Topco members likely had market shares in the 20 to 35 percent range in a number of markets and that some likely had shares of less than 5 percent in a number of markets.[22]

Topco itself remained a modest organization. Its primary role was to bargain for grocery products on behalf of its members and ensure the quality of the goods. Organized as a not-for profit cooperative under Wisconsin law,[23] Topco members each owned the same amount of voting stock and were also required to purchase non-voting preferred stock based on their sales volume. Topco's income came from an assessment on its members for the services it rendered, but service charges were based on a member's gross annual sales of all products, not just Topco-branded products.[24]

Under Topco's bylaws members had exclusivity with respect to Topco-branded products in an assigned territory, although some territo-

---

[21] See Brief for Topco Assocs., Inc., at A3 (App. B) (map showing exclusive territories), United States v. Topco Assocs., Inc., 405 U.S. 596 (1972) (No. 70–82). Seven members, with sales in excess of $560 million, were located between Boston and Washington; six members, with sales in excess of $830 million, were located within 200 miles of Chicago. See Brief for the United States, supra note 5, at 6. With only one exception, all Topco members operated in states where they were "proximate to a state in which one or more other members operate." Id., n.6.

[22] GX 52, based on 1960 data from Supermarket News, identifies 16 of 61 local markets in which the Topco member's share is 20 percent or more; it also identifies 21 markets in which a member's share is five percent or less, although in 18 of these markets the Topco member also operated in other markets in which the member had larger shares. See Joint Appendix, supra note 6, at 418–19. Judge Will found that the "average" market share for Topco members in 1966 was 5.87 percent, see Topco, 319 F. Supp. at 1033 (finding #12), a figure repeated in the Supreme Court's opinion, see Topco, 405 U.S. at 600 ("approximately 6%"). The shares are not broken out by local markets, but appear to aggregate member sales across local markets. In addition, Will made an arithmetical mistake in his calculation. Based on his data the correct average is 7.7 percent, not 5.87 percent, with the median firm having 8 percent. There was little testimony at trial regarding market shares. See Joint Appendix, supra note 6, at 206 (testimony of Topco's expert marketing witness that he does not know the market shares of individual Topco members); id. at 233 (Penn Fruit president estimates Penn Fruit's market share at 9 percent; competitors were Acme with 22 percent, A&P with 15 percent, and Food Fair with 14 percent); id. at 267–68 (Brockton's president estimates that Brockton had 18 percent of the market in Portland, Maine, and a higher market share than A&P in Brockton, MA); id. at 288 (president of American Community Stores testifies that its Hinky–Dinky stores in Omaha were "nip and tuck" with Safeway in market share).

[23] See Brief for Topco Assocs., supra note 21, at 11.

[24] See 319 F. Supp. at 1033 (finding of fact 14).

ries were shared with specific other members and some territories were open to all. Each year the members reviewed these territorial allocations and revised assignments. Members could and did withdraw from membership. This required a one-year advance notice. The most common reason for a chain to withdraw was that it had become large enough to support its own house brands and had sufficient volume of sales to negotiate good prices with suppliers.

Although house branded products were a modest part of the total groceries that individual members sold, constituting only about six percent of their total sales,[25] access to the Topco house brands was critical to effective competition. Essentially, the retailer needed a consistent and reliable house brand to achieve efficient operation. Moreover, trying to maintain two brands could greatly complicate the warehousing and distribution elements of such businesses and increase their operating expenses. Hence, the territory within which a grocery retailer member could sell the Topco-branded products likely determined the geographic scope of operations for that member. The same reasons that made private labels so critical to effective competition made it extremely unlikely that a Topco member would expand into a new territory without Topco-branded products.

Why Did Topco Allocate Territories?

Two hypotheses could explain the territorial allocation that Topco members embraced. First, the territorial allocation might be a response to perceived risks of free-riding or opportunistic conduct by other members relating to the investment that members made in promoting Topco-brand goods. Second, the territorial allocation might be a cartel's effort to limit actual and potential competition among its participants.

The plausibility of the free-rider hypothesis depends on three key assumptions: 1) The members engage in continuous, expensive investments to promote Topco house brands. 2) Without territorial exclusivity, Topco members would take a free ride on other members' investments by entering another member's territory without incurring the cost of establishing Topco-brand loyalty in consumers' minds. 3) Such conduct, if widely followed, might destroy everyone's incentive to invest in the house brand. If these assumptions hold, then to have a successful venture the parties must assure each other that they will not engage in such opportunistic conduct.[26]

---

[25] *See id.* (finding of fact 10).

[26] The Supreme Court's hypothetical in *Sealy*, discussed *infra* text accompanying note 31, mirrors this model. In that hypothetical the joint venture engaged in collective advertising of its brands much as Sealy promoted its mattresses nationally. This was not true for the Topco participants.

The plausibility of the cartel hypothesis depends on the economic position of the regional chains that owned and ran Topco. Regional chains appear to have had an inherent cost advantage over rival types of grocery retailers, *i.e.*, national chains and local stores, making them generally the lowest-price competitors in the market. Price is an important component of retail grocery competition, but it is not the only component. Location and convenience play major roles in the selection of a primary source for purchasing groceries, and there are limits on the set of customers likely to switch primary shopping stores based on price. As customers who shop at rival types of stores take account of these factors, the incremental gain from price cutting will begin to diminish—at some point, further decreases in price will not lead to an offsetting increase in sales volume. But if a grocery retailer is faced with competition from an equally efficient competitor with a similar retailing strategy, competition between them could lead both to reduce prices as they compete for the same customers, with prices falling to the competitive level. Similarly, a retailer could be faced with an equally efficient potential entrant, leading the incumbent retailer to reduce its prices below the profit-maximizing level so as to reduce or eliminate its potential rival's incentive to enter.

If there are few efficient firms in the market, tacit collusion may be feasible and prices could be kept above competitive levels. Dealing with potential entrants is more complicated. If a potential entrant is to be persuaded not to enter, it would want something in return for withdrawing its entry threat. The parties would need to agree, tacitly or expressly, on some way to allocate markets and to give assurance that each firm would not enter the market assigned to the other firm. Only in this way could an efficient firm in a market of differentiated retailers retain as much as possible of the economic rents associated with its comparative efficiency.

It is inherently difficult to engage in tacit collusion with potential competitors, of course. Hence the need for an express agreement among the Topco members, a group of regional chains that appeared to be likely potential entrants into each other's markets. Each participant would get freedom from the potential competition of equally-efficient rivals. Each would then be able better to exploit its own market (depending on the number of efficient competitors, and the extent of tacit collusion, within that market).

Such a cartel might not be very powerful because it would not eliminate all risks of potential competition. However, if there were relatively few other potential partners for a competing buying group—which was at least possibly the case, given the high level of participation in Topco of chains in the relevant size range—then the impact of the limitation on potential competition would be more significant. Further, if the agreement to limit competition had a relatively low cost of administration, then even small gains might well exceed those costs, making it sensible to form and run the cartel.

Prima facie, the Topco territorial agreement was low cost. It was part of an on-going joint venture to engage in joint buying and to create a private label; adding territorial decisions to other normal business would not likely increase administrative costs by much. The agreements were easily enforced. Entry in violation of the rules would be visible and expulsion would be costly to a member in light of the substantial cost savings from participating in Topco. Moreover, there were means for orderly entry into and exit from the agreement to allocate markets.

In the litigation, Topco argued that the free-rider hypothesis explained the territorial exclusivity. As we will see, the government never engaged with that claim nor did it fully develop the cartel hypothesis, although the trial staff had uncovered some evidence that suggested its potential validity. The extrinsic contemporary evidence, however, favors the cartel hypothesis over the free-rider hypothesis. For one, there appears to have been little advertising of house brands, with such advertising generally being done as a complement to national-brand advertising to demonstrate the existence of lower-priced in-store alternatives.[27] Indeed, studies indicate that advertising of house brands has little effect on a retailer's market share and that factors such as convenience play a much greater role in consumer store choice than any specific element of the product line or prices.[28] Although Topco members would likely have preferred to gain whatever advantage they could from consumer recognition of the various Topco brands—Topco actually had twenty different brands for the consumer to recognize—it is questionable whether a Topco member would be more likely to enter a new market

---

[27] An examination of the Sheboygan Press for various months in 1960, 1962, 1964, 1966, 1973, 1974, and 1975 found that Topco-member Sav–O–Foods' advertisements sometimes included two of Topco's house brands, Food Club and Top Frost, but always as a component of an advertisement that featured a number of traditional brand names. *See also* Joint Appendix, *supra* note 6, at 244–45 ("We often advertise it [our Topco merchandise] in tandem with the nationally advertised merchandise. We will have the nationally advertised product and right underneath it we put the Topco product to show the variation in price. We will not do that always. We will do that on occasion.") (Topco member Penn Fruit). *See generally* FRANK J. CHARVAT, SUPERMARKETING 84–87, 184–185 (1961) (very little money spent on advertising of private labels).

[28] *See* Robert East et al., *Loyalty to Supermarkets*, 5 INTERNAT. REV. RETAIL, DISTRIB. & CONSUMER RES. 99 (1995) (ease of access is important factor in choice of grocery store and retaining repeat business); Rej Sethuraman, *The Effect of Marketplace Factors on Private Label Penetration in Grocery Products*, MARKET SCIENCE INSTITUTE, Rep. #92–128 (1992) (advertising of house brands does not increase the retailer's market share); Arch G. Woodside & Randolph J. Trappey, III, *Finding Out Why Customers Shop Your Store and Buy Your Brand: Automatic Cognitive Processing Models of Primary Choice*, 32 J. ADV. RES. 59 (1992) (speed of checkout and location were the most important factors in choosing a store).

because the new entrant could "save" whatever investment in brand recognition the incumbent had made. Other entry costs would likely loom much larger (*e.g.*, retail site acquisition and construction, warehousing facilities) and play a far greater role in the entry decision. In any event, the new entrant would still need to promote the Topco brands to take advantage of this alleged brand recognition, thereby sharing the benefits of such advertising with its Topco-member rival that carried the same brands. On the other hand, not having a house brand at all could be a substantial deterrent to entry. Without a private label the retailer would have no lower-priced alternative to the national brands to offer to consumers and there did not appear to have been any good alternatives to Topco for providing such brands. Indeed, if there was any point that Topco itself stressed it was that having a house brand was essential for effective competition in the retail supermarket business.

The Litigation

Initiating the Law Suit

On January 27, 1966, the owner of a regional grocery chain complained to the Antitrust Division that Topco had refused to let his business join the organization. The initial investigation treated this primarily as a boycott case.[29] The staff lawyers collected information about Topco's organization, sales, and the restraints it imposed on competition.

On June 12, 1967, the Supreme Court announced its decision in *United States v. Sealy, Inc.*[30] A group of mattress manufacturers had established Sealy to develop and collectively market mattresses under a single, nationally advertised trademark. Sealy licensed all its manufacturer/shareholders to make and sell its mattresses, but the agreements limited both the territory within which the participants could offer such mattresses and the prices at which they could sell them. The trial court allowed the territorial assignments but held the price restraints unlawful. The government appealed the decision allowing the territorial divisions (Sealy did not appeal the price fixing decision) and the Supreme Court reversed. Characterizing the territorial allocations "as the creature of horizontal action by the licensees," the Court then addressed Sealy's argument on the application of the per se rule:

---

[29] *See* Memorandum to the Files, from Charles D. Mahaffie, Jr., Acting Chief, Litigation Section, Subject: Grocery Buying; Complaint Against Topco (Jan. 27, 1966) (reporting complainant's argument that under *Associated Press*, a boycott case, Topco was not allowed to exclude him because of his "competitive situation") (authors' files). A preliminary investigation was authorized on March 1, 1966. *See* Memorandum from Charles D. Mahaffie to Willard R. Memler at 1 (April 28, 1966) (authors' files).

[30] 388 U.S. 350 (1967). *See generally* Willard F. Mueller, *The Sealy Restraints: Restrictions on Free Riding or Output?*, 1989 Wis. L. Rev. 1255.

It is urged upon us that we should condone this territorial limitation ... because of the absence of any showing that it is unreasonable. It is argued, for example, that a number of small grocers might allocate territory among themselves on an exclusive basis as incident to the use of a common name and common advertisements, and that this sort of venture should be welcomed in the interests of competition, and should not be condemned as *per se* unlawful. But condemnation of appellee's territorial arrangements certainly does not require us to go so far as to condemn that *quite different situation*, whatever might be the result if it were presented to us for decision. For here, the arrangements for territorial limitations are part of "an aggregation of trade restraints" including unlawful price-fixing and policing. Within settled doctrine, they are unlawful under § 1 of the Sherman Act without the necessity for an inquiry in each particular case as to their business or economic justification, their impact in the marketplace, or their reasonableness.[31]

On January 15, 1968, seven months after the decision in *Sealy*, the United States Justice Department filed *Topco*, an action that arguably involved that "quite different situation." By that time the case had moved from a focus on the refusal to deal with an applicant for membership to a concern over the validity of the territorial agreement among Topco members not to compete with each other. Donald Turner, the Assistant Attorney General in charge of the Antitrust Division and a highly regarded scholar in the field, recommended suit because he thought the price fixing distinction suggested in *Sealy* was "inexplicable," leaving defendants room to argue a possible justification for territorial restraints not accompanied by price fixing.[32] "Territorial agreements have always been deemed as plainly unlawful as price-fixing," Turner wrote. *Topco* should be brought as a per se case "to clarify this important aspect of horizontal restraints arising out of the *Sealy*-type corporate structure."[33]

Turner personally chose the lead trial attorney for the case, Hugh Morrison, and instructed the trial staff that they were to focus on the market allocation restraints without any additional information. This limitation frustrated the staff to some extent because they believed that

---

[31] 388 U.S. at 357–58 (emphasis added) (internal citations omitted).

[32] Turner headed the Antitrust Division while on leave from Harvard Law School. In addition to his legal training, Turner had received an economics Ph.D. and had co-authored an influential book arguing for the application of economics to antitrust decision-making. *See* CARL KAYSEN & DONALD F. TURNER, ANTITRUST POLICY: AN ECONOMIC AND LEGAL ANALYSIS (1959). For further biographical information, see Stephen G. Breyer, *Donald F. Turner*, 41 ANTITRUST BULL. 725 (1996).

[33] Attorney General Memorandum, *supra* note 2, at 4.

there was evidence that the market allocation was used to support price fixing and other restraints on competition. The result was a trial staff with very limited ability to add factual detail to its offensive case or to probe very deeply into the factual arguments made by the defense.

In retrospect, it is notable that the Topco facts did not fit one key element of the Supreme Court's hypothetical in *Sealy*: Topco members did not engage in "common" (*i.e.*, joint) advertising of their brands. Indeed, individually Topco members spent little to promote those brands. The primary means of promoting sales was to place the house brand products next to the national brand with posted prices for each. But this distinction was not fully developed at trial and was lost in later proceedings. The *Topco* case was to be a vehicle for getting judicial review of the application of the per se rule to a horizontal non-price agreement to allocate territories and markets.

A Settlement?

On June 20, 1968, five months after the complaint was filed, counsel for Topco proposed a settlement.[34] The offer was to create a single "alternate brand" for Topco's principal products (about 400–500 of the 1200 private label items Topco then supplied). The alternate brand would be "available to any member for sale anywhere," that is, on a non-exclusive basis. These 400–500 principal products would also continue to be available to Topco members under the existing Topco brand names on the current exclusive territorial basis (Topco used five different brand names for this group of products). The offer also proposed to make the remaining 700–800 Topco-branded products available to members on a non-exclusive basis (Topco used fifteen different brand names for these products).

Although the offer stressed cost as a reason for not covering all Topco products with an alternative label, the offer did implicitly concede that it was practically feasible to create at least a limited competing brand. And the offer recognized that exclusivity was not necessary across the board. Apparently there were key items for which Topco members wanted exclusivity; others were not as important.

The major question presented by the settlement proposal was whether creating the alternate brand would make it practical for Topco members to enter each other's territories. One critical point was that the alternate brand would not be exclusive. In the letter presenting the settlement offer, counsel for Topco argued that private label merchandizing "is a fact of life," adding that if a "competitor has the same brands,

---

[34] *See* Letter from John T. Loughlin to Hugh P. Morrison, Jr., June 20, 1968 (authors' files).

the brands are not private and the retailer has no interest in them."[35] But if that were the case, why would anyone be interested in the second label that Topco proposed to create, a label which any competing member could also use? Indeed, if Topco really was not concerned about preventing competition between its members, and was willing and able to create a second brand, why didn't it offer to provide *that* brand on an exclusive basis so that a member with the new brand could enter another Topco member's territory and have a true private label to compete effectively against the member with the Topco brands? Either brand exclusivity was not so important, which undercut its argument for the territorial allocations, or exclusivity was important, which meant that the settlement would not encourage entry.

There was a second critical problem with the idea of an alternate brand. Suppose that a Topco member were looking to expand into a new territory with just a few stores. Would it be economically feasible to expand with a completely different brand of private label products, even on just the 400 "principal products," or would the costs of inventorying and warehousing that separate line of products make such expansion unlikely? The government had earlier concluded that Topco's territorial restrictions on Topco-branded products effectively—and intentionally— precluded any expansion at all into a competitor's territory, because even if the new entrant could obtain its private label elsewhere, the costs of separate distribution would be too high.[36] Having the alternate label provided by Topco, rather than by some other cooperative, would not change the economics of that expansion.

It was on the second ground that Hugh Morrison, the lead trial attorney, quickly rejected Topco's settlement proposal.[37] He did so rely- ing in part on internal Topco documents which had justified the decision

---

[35] *Id.* at 6.

[36] Government trial counsel, after reviewing the problems of carrying non-Topco brand products along with Topco brand products, had earlier concluded:

> [I]t is . . . obvious that the real effects of the territorial restrictions are not limited to the Topco branded items, for it is impossible to avoid the conclusion that the conspirators, by imposing such severe restrictions with respect to the Topco items, fully intended and expected a complete and orderly allocation of all grocery products.

Memorandum from Hugh P. Morrison, Jr. and Theodore M. Jones, Jr., to Charles D. Mahaffie, Jr., Chief, General Litigation Section; Subject—Grocery Chain Stores: Topco Associates, Inc.,—Fact Memorandum Supporting Proposed Complaint at 8 (Sept. 22, 1967) (authors' files).

[37] *See* Memorandum from Hugh P. Morrison, Jr. and Theodore M. Jones, Jr., to Gerald A. Connell, Assistant Chief, General Litigation Section, July 3, 1968 (authors' files). Morrison's recommendation to reject the settlement was agreed to by his supervisors in the Antitrust Division on the same day. See Department of Justice Routing Slip from Connell to Hummell, 7/3/68 (authors' files).

not to create a second family of labels on the ground that Topco members would not want to operate in two different territories with two different sets of brands. But there was no probing of the real economics of such expansion, either in the Topco document or by the government, nor was there any focus on whether an exclusive second label might actually be attractive to some of the Topco members either for entry into a new market or for a member's entire operations.[38] The theory of the case rested on the assumption that there was no reason for the territorial restrictions on Topco-branded goods other than to block expansion and that only by ending the restriction would there be territorial invasions. Neither the actual economics of expansion, nor the economics of creating a second brand, really mattered. That is, the economics of alternatives to Topco's single-brand approach didn't matter until the Supreme Court brought up the issue in oral argument—and Howard Shapiro remarked that Topco could "do wonders" with a smaller second line of labels.

The Trial

With the rejection of Topco's settlement offer, the parties prepared for trial. Preparations were not extensive. Neither side engaged in much discovery. The government employed no expert witnesses and took no depositions, not even of the two expert witnesses the defense called at trial. Key facts on sales figures and individual market shares were agreed to by stipulation or provided in interrogatories.

Even abbreviated discovery, though, turned up intriguing documents. Some documents showed treaties reached among Topco members: The president of one chain writes to another, thanking him for "the time you spent with me recently at the American Hotel in Miami Beach," and sets out their agreement: He won't open a store in Madison, Wisconsin, where the other firm operates; he will just operate in a small town 14 miles away and promise not to advertise in the Madison papers.[39] The president of Penn Fruit, a major Topco licensee in Philadelphia, reports on the "territorial conflict" between his chain, with an exclusive license in Baltimore, and Giant, then operating in Baltimore and applying for full membership in Topco. The Penn Fruit representative indicates his willingness to "give up" his license in Baltimore "if he could be given

---

[38] There was some testimony at trial relating to the willingness of Topco members to use an alternate brand. *See* Joint Appendix, *supra* note 6, at 297 ("We talked to Topco about creating a second label, and we even offered to abandon our position with the first label, with the present Topco labels even thought we had a big investment with it, thinking of a longer road.") (testimony of Topco member).

[39] *See* Letter from William A. Grassar, Executive Vice President–General Manager, Scultz Sav–O Stores, Inc., to Mr. Richard Waxenberg, Eagle Food Center, Inc., reproduced in Joint Appendix, *supra* note 6, at 420 (GX 53).

assurance that other members would do the same in territories licensed to them on an exclusive basis but which were not part of their 'prime' or 'home base' territory." Others at the meeting at which this was proposed thought it was a swell idea—cede territory to new members in outlying areas so long as "nothing should be done to impair a member's exclusive license in its 'prime' territory."[40] The "Territory Committee" subsequently reports on other similar treaties. Big Bear, located in Columbus, Ohio, but holding an exclusive far to the north in Toledo, allows a limited incursion by ACF–Wrigley into Toledo; Hart's, located in Rochester N.Y., agrees to let P & C Foods from Syracuse open outside Rochester; Furr's, operating in South Texas, agrees to share its rights in North Texas with ACF–Wrigley.[41]

Other documents simply showed the extent to which Topco members were kept informed of the plans their fellow members had for expansion. A list created in 1964 shows requests for new territories around the country, along with a "notice of intent to open stores in new territory," pointing to where there are areas of territorial overlap. The list begins by referencing an earlier Topco resolution requiring all members to be informed of such plans "so that each Member will have reasonable opportunity to raise objections to any change."[42]

The government was preparing for a per se trial, however, so it never explored the implications of these documents. The case was viewed more as one involving a structural matter—how was Topco put together formally, from which one could infer how Topco members would act—rather than as a case focusing on the actual conduct of the parties involved. Indeed, missing from the evidence were direct documents from any of the Topco members clearly showing that a Topco member had decided not to enter a particular market because another member already had an exclusive. But also missing were any defense documents giving examples of a Topco member, using a different private label, making a significant entry into a market in which another Topco member had an exclusive license.

The result of the government's per se approach was a trial which was a model of economy. The trial began on February 25, 1969. Hugh Morrison waived opening statement, introduced into evidence documents obtained from Topco plus several newspaper advertisements showing

---

[40] *See* Excerpt From Minutes of Special Topco Membership Meeting, January 13, 1961, reproduced *id*. at 412–13 (GX 52).

[41] *See* Excerpt From Minutes of Special Topco Board of Directors Meeting, March 20, 1961, Report of Territory Committee, reproduced *id*. at 414 (GX 52).

[42] *See* Board of Directors Dec. 12, 1957, reproduced *id*. at 428 (GX 71); Topco Associates Inc. Memorandum, To Principals of Topco Member Companies, Re Territory Requests and Notices of Intent (June 3, 1964), reproduced *id*. at 429 (GX 72).

two different chains advertising Topco-branded products in the same newspaper, and then rested. Morrison called no live witnesses and took only a few minutes to present the government's case.[43]

This left the defense free to make the record for its justification. Taking seven trial days, the defense presented Topco's chief operating officer, six executives of supermarket chains that were Topco members, and two expert witnesses (one marketing expert, one economist). Their testimony was presented to show that private labels were necessary to allow Topco members to compete more effectively, but that individual Topco members were too small to create a private label themselves; that private labels were good for consumers because they provided more choice of products at lower cost (but with higher margins for retailers!); and, critically, that private labels could be "private" only if members had exclusive territorial rights.

Of course, the defendant had no obligation—or desire—to explore the question whether there were "less restrictive means" than exclusive territories for providing Topco members with the competitive tool of a private label, as Shapiro would later argue in the Supreme Court that there were and as Topco's proposed settlement had shown that there could be. Whatever holes there were in Topco's justifications for territorial exclusivity had to come out on cross-examination. But cross-examination was a strategically limited tool. The effort to pursue fully the "many paths of reasonableness" suggested by the defense might very well have ended up undercutting the government's premise that Topco's purported reasons were legally irrelevant in any event.[44]

The case was tried without a jury, with the trial judge, Hubert Will, taking a very active role in questioning the witnesses, almost more active than the lawyers. Will had been unhappy with the government's case from the beginning, a position that he made sufficiently clear in pretrial proceedings that Morrison chose not to move for summary judgment even though the documentary evidence on which the government relied was undisputed. The trial testimony did not alter Will's view. Sometimes he seemed to feed questions to the defense (asking a Topco executive whether territorial exclusivity is "essential to the survival of Topco," to which the executive replied, "yes"). Sometimes he seemed skeptical of the defense (arguing with the defense economist that price competition would be greater if private labels were available at more than one store, so that consumers could more readily compare price). Sometimes he inadvertently brought out testimony that strengthened the government's

---

[43] See *Topco,* 319 F. Supp. at 1040; Minute Order, United States District Court, Northern District of Illinois, Eastern Division, Honorable Hubert L. Will, Feb. 25, 1969 (authors' files).

[44] The phrase is Joseph Tate's, who second-chaired the trial with Morrison. Telephone Interview with Authors, July 7, 2006.

case (asking a Topco executive rhetorically whether Topco really had a problem with members expanding into each other's territory, to which the executive pointed out that "the country is getting smaller" and there is "more jumping around" into new areas where other members could be). And sometimes he simply related his own experience, for example, in his father's drug store where they bought unlabeled cough syrup and made their own "private label" to attract customers ("Head Off Your Cough or Cough Off Your Head. Use Will's White Pine Tar and Cough Syrup").

Judge Will handed down his opinion six months after the parties filed their post-trial briefs.[45] As was apparent through the trial, he viewed Topco as a vehicle that allowed its members to do exactly what the national chains could do without incurring antitrust liability, that is, create a private label and decide where it should be sold. He did not believe that Topco was a "restrictive organization" whose members were "primarily interested" in keeping new members out and "protecting their exclusivity."[46] Rather, territorial exclusivity was required if members were to invest the time and money to promote the Topco brand. Will found it difficult to determine whether the territorial restriction resulted in a "substantial diminution" in competition in Topco-branded products.[47] But even if it did, that loss was "far outweighed" by the increased ability of Topco members to compete with the national chains and other supermarkets operating in their territories.[48] His conclusion was direct: "[T]he relief which the government here seeks would not increase competition in Topco private label brands but would substantially diminish competition in the supermarket field.... Only the national chains and the other supermarkets who compete with Topco members would be benefitted. The consuming public obviously would not."[49]

The Supreme Court's Decision

The Supreme Court that decided *Topco* was a court in transition. Only four Justices remained from the Court in 1967 when *Sealy* and *Schwinn* were decided, the last time the Court had applied the per se rule to territorial allocations.[50] Justice Fortas, who authored both opin-

---

[45] *See* 319 F. Supp. 1031 (N.D. Ill. 1970).

[46] *See id.* at 1042.

[47] *See id.*

[48] *Id.* at 1043.

[49] *Id.*

[50] Justice White, who joined the majority in *Topco*, was on the Court for *Sealy* and *Schwinn* but had not participated in either. *Schwinn* held that vertical non-price restraints were illegal "without more" and is discussed *supra* chapter five.

ions, resigned in 1969, the same year that Warren Burger replaced Earl Warren as Chief Justice. Justices Black and Harlan had resigned from the Court two months before *Topco* was argued, but their replacements, Justices Powell and Rehnquist, did not participate in the *Topco* argument or decision. Just five years after *Topco* was decided, Justice Powell would direct a "new antitrust majority" to overrule *Schwinn* and hold vertical non-price restraints subject to a rule of reason.[51]

Topco was assigned to Justice Marshall, who had been Solicitor General when *Sealy* and *Schwinn* were argued. Although Marshall had not argued either case, he certainly would have been familiar with the arguments favoring the application of the per se rule and would have understood the litigation costs associated with trying antitrust cases under a rule of reason. Marshall wrote his draft in less than two weeks and by December 7, 1971, three weeks after oral argument, he had a majority.[52] The opinion did not issue until March 29, 1972, however, delayed apparently to allow time for Chief Justice Burger to prepare and circulate a dissent.[53]

Marshall's opinion stresses the importance of per se rules. It gives little hint of the factual questions that troubled the Court during oral argument.[54] Relying on past cases, the Court reiterated its view that

---

[51] *See* Continental T.V., Inc. v. GTE Sylvania Inc., 433 U.S. 36 (1977).

[52] Chief Justice Burger asked Justice Douglas to assign the *Topco* opinion. *See* William O. Douglas, Letter to The Chief Justice (Nov. 19, 1971) (unpublished document on file as part of the Papers of William O. Douglas, Library of Congress, Manuscript Div., Box 1527, Case File O.T. 1971 Argued Cases, 70–82–70–86). On November 19, 1971, Douglas informed Burger that he was "inclined to assign it to Thurgood" and that he would consult with him to "see what his wishes are." *Id.* Justice Marshall's first draft was circulated on December 2, 1971. *See* First Draft, United States v. Topco Assocs., Inc., No. 70–82 (stamped, From: Marshall, J.; Circulated: Dec. 2, 1971) (unpublished document on file as part of the Papers of William O. Douglas, *id.*).

For letters joining the opinion, *see* William J. Brennan, Jr., Letter to Thurgood Marshall Re: No. 70–82—United States v. Topco Associates (Dec. 3, 1971) (unpublished document on file as part of the Papers of Thurgood Marshall in Library of Congress, Manuscript Div., Box 84, Folder 10); William O. Douglas, Letter to Thurgood Marshall (Dec. 3, 1971) (unpublished document on file *id.*); Byron R. White, Letter to Thurgood Marshall Re: No. 70–82—United States v. Topco Associates (Dec. 3, 1971) (unpublished document on file *id.*); Potter Stewart, Letter to Thurgood Marshall Re: No. 70–82—United States v. Topco Associates (Dec. 7, 1971) (unpublished document on file *id.*).

[53] Chief Justice Burger circulated his dissent on February 23, 1972. *See* United States v. Topco Associates, Inc., No. 70–82, Dissenting Opinion of Chief Justice Burger (Feb. 23, 1972) (unpublished document on file as part of the Papers of Thurgood Marshall in Library of Congress, Manuscript Div., Box 84, Folder 10).

[54] Justice Blackmun's one page of notes of the Court's conference discussion makes no mention of the factual issues, reporting debate about the meaning of *Sealy* (Stewart and White) and the importance of per se rules (Brennan—"administratively essential to viability of § 1"). The Chief Justice was skeptical: "This per se rule is one you have to have

"horizontal territorial limitations ... are naked restraints of trade with
no purpose except stifling of competition."[55] The Court did note the
"recent commentary on the wisdom of *per se* rules,"[56] but came down
strongly on the side of not getting into the business of weighing "destruction of competition" in one area against an alleged increase in
competition elsewhere. Instead, the Court sided with free entry into
markets, analogizing the economic right to enter markets and compete
to the personal freedoms provided by the Bill of Rights. "Antitrust laws
... are the Magna Carta of free enterprise," the Court wrote.[57] Entry
should not be governed by a group of private competitors who had "no
authority" to do so.[58]

But little hint about factual concerns is not no hint. Embedded in
the Court's opinion are echoes of some of the factual points stressed by
Shapiro in his oral argument, indicating that a rough rule of reason
balancing may have been going on just below the opinion's surface.

In terms of anticompetitive effect, Shapiro argued that the government had demonstrated that the agreement inhibited expansion by
members into each other's territories. The Court agreed, finding proble-
matic the district court's contrary finding that Topco's denials of requests for member expansion into competing territories had no "appreci-

---

when you can't prove your case." *See* Notes titled "70–82" (undated) (handwritten)
(unpublished document on file as part of the Papers of Harry A. Blackmun in Library of
Congress, Manuscript Div., Box 139, Folder 11). There is no mention in Justice Blackmun's
notes of Justice Marshall's views, *see id.* Justice Douglas' notes of the Conference
discussion, which provide brief descriptions of each Justice's views, simply state for
Marshall: "reverses." *See* Notes titled "Conference, November 19, 1971, No. 70–82 – U.S.
v. Topco Asso." (handwritten) (unpublished document on file as part of the Papers of
William O. Douglas, *supra* note 52). Justice Blackmun, in his notes of the oral argument,
however, did not take down the arguments regarding the need for per se rules, but
concentrated on factual points. He noted Shapiro's arguments that Topco "could achieve a
private brand for each" and that Topco members "can compete with each other sans
adverse results" and he made note of GX 102 to which both Shapiro and Grimm referred.
See Notes titled "No. 70–82-ADX—United States v. Topco Associates, Inc., Argued:
November 16, 1971" (handwritten) (unpublished document on file as part of the Papers of
Harry A. Blackmun, *supra*).

[55] 405 U.S. 596, 608 (1972) (internal quotation marks omitted).

[56] *Id.* at 609 n.10.

[57] *Id.* at 610. For earlier use of this term to describe the antitrust laws, *see* ALBERT H.
WALKER, HISTORY OF THE SHERMAN LAW iv (1910) ("The Sherman Law is the Magna Charta
among the statutes of the United States."); Woods Exploration & Producing Co. v.
Aluminum Co. of America, 438 F.2d 1286, 1302 (5th Cir. 1971) ("Our antitrust laws
constitute our economic magna carta, designed to protect against predatory oppression.
Conceived as such a writ they must not be facilely negated.").

[58] 405 U.S. at 610.

able influence" on members' actual expansion decisions.[59] Pointing out that the district court had accepted Topco's argument that "territorial divisions are crucial" to Topco's existence, it was "difficult to understand" how Topco could "simultaneously urge that territorial restrictions are an unimportant factor in the decision of a member on whether to expand its business."[60] The agreement to allocate territories must have had some anticompetitive bite.

What about the procompetitive justification that was the heart of Topco's defense? Shapiro had warned the Court away from weighing because of the complexity of the economic analysis that would be required. But Shapiro had also emphasized a case where two supermarkets carrying Topco-branded products had competed against each other "all over the place," showing that private label exclusivity was not a requirement for success, and had raised questions about the plausibility of Topco's justification in light of the "second label" option. Shapiro's example of successful Topco-member competition makes less abstract the Court's view that the Sherman Act guarantees "to each and every business" the "freedom to compete—to assert with vigor, imagination, devotion, and ingenuity whatever economic muscle it can muster." This is exactly what the Plum and Meijer chains had done in Michigan. And Shapiro's questioning of the plausibility of Topco's justification helps us understand how the Court could write that horizontal restraints are not to be tolerated because they are "allegedly" developed to increase competition.[61] Judge Will, of course, had found that the Topco restraints *were* developed to increase competition. Shapiro provided the doubt, perhaps enough doubt to make it easier for the Court to be confident that Topco's rebuttal argument might be flawed and a per se approach justifiable.

Chief Justice Burger wrote a dissent which argued that a rule of reason was the appropriate approach to the case, stressing the economic justification for a group of "small chains" (as he characterized Topco) to join together in a "cooperative endeavor."[62] Relying on Judge Will's findings of fact and opinion, Burger accepted the defendant's justifica-

---

[59] *See* 405 U.S. at 606 n.8.

[60] *Id.*

[61] *See id.* at 610.

[62] *See id.* at 613. Justice Blackmun, in a concurring opinion, wrote that the decision "will tend to stultify Topco members' competition with the great and larger chains" but that he believed the per se rule was to "so firmly established by the Court that, at this late date, I could not oppose it." *Id.* at 611. Blackmun's notes before oral argument indicate that, as a general matter, he disliked per se rules and preferred a rule of reason approach. See Memorandum, No. 70–82—United States v. Topco Associates, Inc. at 4 (signed "H.A.B.") (Nov. 15, 1971) (unpublished document on file as part of the Papers of Harry A. Blackmun in Library of Congress, Manuscript Div., Box 139, Folder 11).

tion for exclusivity, seeing this as a case where the restraints were adopted to increase competition.[63] Without territorial exclusivity Topco's members "will have no more reason to promote Topco products through local advertising and merchandising efforts than they will have such reason to promote any other generally available brands."[64] This would mean the end of Topco's private label and a lessening of competition— "grocery staples marketed under private-label brands with their lower consumer prices will soon be available only to those who patronize the large national chains."[65] Perhaps trade-offs are difficult to weigh, Burger argued, but judicial convenience and predictability are not reason enough to avoid the examination of "difficult economic problems."[66]

Marshall's opinion never responded to any of Burger's arguments, however, and the draft that Marshall had circulated prior to Burger's dissent was handed down without change. This failure to engage is unfortunate, but perhaps understandable. The then-current state of the law presented the Court with polar choices—either a strict per se rule or a full rule of reason. A little more than four years before, the Court in *Schwinn* had rejected the government's effort to switch from a per se rule to a rule of presumptive illegality, subject to rebuttal.[67] No one even sought such an approach in *Topco*, however, and the record itself was so devoid of factual development that the Court had little ability to reference directly any of the factual issues that had been of concern at oral argument.

Topco's rhetoric thus reflects "per se" mode. Indeed, the only change that Marshall made in his first draft related to *Sealy* and the per se rule. Marshall wrote in his first draft, in footnote 9, that *Sealy*'s discussion of price fixing was "collateral" to the holding that territorial allocations were per se unlawful.[68] The second draft treated *Sealy* more

---

[63] Burger noted at the outset of his dissent that for a grocery chain to produce a private label it must have at least $250 million in annual sales, but probably $500 million for "optimum efficiency." 405 U.S. at 614 n.1 (citing findings of fact). Given that Topco members collectively had $2.5 billion in annual sales, this meant that Topco's size was five times greater than necessary for "optimum efficiency" in creating a private label program. When combined with the data on geographic proximity of Topco members, *see supra* note 21 and accompanying text, this may be further indication that Topco increased its membership not to achieve efficiencies in creating a private label, but to provide some additional protection from competition.

[64] *Id.* at 624.

[65] *Id.*

[66] *See id.*

[67] *See Schwinn*, 388 U.S. at 374 n.5.

[68] *See* First Draft, United States v. Topco Assocs., Inc., No. 70–82 at 12 n.9 (Dec. 1971) (unpublished document on file as part of the Papers of Thurgood Marshall in Library of Congress, Manuscript Div., Box 84, Folder 10).

cleanly. Marshall re-wrote the text so that one paragraph now began: "*United States v. Sealy, supra*, is, in fact, on all fours with this case." He also rewrote footnote 9: "It is true that in *Sealy* the Court dealt with price-fixing as well as territorial restraints. To the extent that *Sealy* casts doubt on whether horizontal territorial limitations, unaccompanied by price-fixing, are *per se* violations of the Sherman Act, we remove that doubt today."[69]

With the language in footnote 9, and the Court's per se rhetoric, Donald Turner's decision to bring the case and frame it as he had was fully vindicated. Gone was *Sealy*'s "inexplicable" distinction between horizontal territorial allocations with price fixing and those without. The per se rule was now clearly applicable to non-price horizontal territorial allocations. Turner's risky litigation strategy had succeeded.

But not so fast.

Topco's Aftermath

Judge Will's Order

Following the Supreme Court's decision the government prepared a decree to enjoin Topco from limiting or restricting "in any way" the territories within which "any member firm may sell products procured from or through Topco." Topco, however, wanted permission to designate "areas of primary responsibility" for its members, with the right to terminate members that did not adequately promote Topco brands in those territories. Topco also wanted to require profit pass-over arrangements which would require a member selling in another member's designated territory to compensate that member for the sales made in that territory.[70]

Morrison flatly rejected Topco's proposals as non-negotiable, and defense counsel then sought a meeting with the newly-appointed head of the Antitrust Division, Thomas Kauper. Kauper, the fourth head of the Antitrust Division to deal with *Topco*, saw "no reason" to meet. Kauper felt that allowing areas of exclusive responsibility and profit pass-overs treated the case "as a vertical territorial restraint case," where distribution restraints are imposed by a manufacturer interested solely in the efficient distribution of its products. "While I do not in fact agree with the analysis used by the Court in Topco," Kauper wrote, "it is certainly

---

[69] *See* Second Draft, United States v. Topco Assocs., Inc., No. 70–82, at 13 n.9 (Dec. 1971) (unpublished document on file as part of the Papers of Thurgood Marshall in Library of Congress, Manuscript Div., Box 84, Folder 10). Justice Douglas wrote to Marshall that "I am glad you added footnote 9 to Topco. I am still with you." William O. Douglas, Letter to Thurgood Marshall (Dec. 9, 1971) (unpublished document on file *id.*).

[70] *See* Memorandum from Hugh P. Morrison, Jr. to Gerald A. Connell, Chief, General Litigation Section, Aug. 30, 1972, at 1, 3 (authors' files).

clear that this is not a vertical case and that the Court, at least, viewed it as a simple horizontal division case." Given that decision, "I do not see how we can agree to the provisos proposed."[71]

Judge Will saw the matter differently. At a hearing on September 19, 1972, six months after the Supreme Court's decision, Will accepted Topco's proposals and entered a final judgment adding Topco's proposals to the decree that the government had drafted. Morrison quickly filed a motion to alter the judgment, arguing that the combination of areas of primary responsibility and profit pass-overs would "unquestionably" result in continuing the offense about which the government had complained. The new provisions, Morrison argued, were more restrictive than the ones struck down by the Supreme Court, for they would prevent the limited competition that had earlier occurred when members with non-exclusive territories found themselves competing against each other—competition to which Shapiro had pointed in his Supreme Court argument. Topco had never seen a need for pass-over payments before. Why should it be able to adopt them now, after its regime of exclusive territories had been "condemned by the Supreme Court"?[72]

The government was unable to get Will to alter his final decree, however, other than to add that the pass-over clause should not be used "to achieve or maintain territorial exclusivity for any member firm."[73] Will still saw the case as one where protection of the Topco brand was necessary and the Supreme Court's decision had not persuaded him otherwise.

Will's decision necessitated another trip to the Supreme Court, now to complain that the remedy entered would permit the "continuation or renewal of the collective allocation of territories among competing sellers of Topco branded products which this Court held to be illegal *per se*

---

[71] Routing Slip from Thomas E. Kauper to Mr. Rashid, Mr. Morrison, Mr. Connell, Re: U.S. v. Topco Associates, Inc., Aug. 30, 1972 (authors' files).

[72] *See* Plaintiff's Memorandum in Support of Motion to Alter or Amend Judgment, United States v. Topco Associates, Inc., Civ. Action No. 68–C–76, at 3, 4, 8–9 (Oct. 3, 1972) (authors' files).

[73] In *Sealy*, the district court's decree enjoined the defendants from agreeing to any restrictions on "sales of Sealy products within a prescribed territory." *See* United States v. Sealy, Inc., 1967 Trade Cas. ¶ 72,327 (N.D. Ill. 1967) (§ IV). When the *Sealy* decree was entered, however, the government had told the district court, at the defendant's request, that "[w]e do not interpret this language as prohibiting per se ... areas of primary responsibility clauses, or pass-over provisions." The government added that it was not "implying any view as to the legality of such clauses" nor was it suggesting that such clauses "would not violate the decree" if they had the effects prescribed in the decree. The defendant in *Topco* relied on the record colloquy in *Sealy* to support its requested relief and it reproduced the colloquy in its brief to Judge Will. *See* Memorandum of Defendant in Opposition to Plaintiff's Motion to Alter or Amend Final Judgment, United States v. Topco Associates, Inc., Civ. Action No. 68–C–76 at 4, App. B (Oct. 16, 1972) (authors' files).

under Section 1 of the Sherman Act."[74] This time, however, the government was unable to convince the Court to consider the case on its merits. Instead, in October 1973, a year and a half after the first *Topco* decision, the Court affirmed Judge Will's order in a memorandum decision, without opinion.[75] The only member of the original *Topco* majority to disagree was Justice Douglas, who would have set the case for oral argument. None of the others—including Justice Marshall—apparently believed that Will's order merited full Supreme Court consideration.

It is hard to know what to make of the Court's decision. Perhaps it confirms the view that the Court had really been doing a "quick" rule of reason balance all along: Pure horizontal territorial exclusivity agreements prevented all possible horizontal competition and were presumed unlawful, a presumption not adequately rebutted by the weak free-rider argument. Areas of primary responsibility and profit pass-over provisions, on the other hand, overcame the presumption of illegality that attaches to horizontal agreements because the provisions were consistent with economic efficiency in distributing Topco-branded products and dealt with whatever free-rider problems might exist. Or perhaps the affirmance just means that the Court felt it unwise to use its time to decide whether the district court's remedial decree was an abuse of discretion.[76] The Court's memorandum affirmance, unfortunately, gives us no sure way to know.

Topco's Reception By Commentators and Courts

The government's litigation approach in *Topco*, along with the Court's unwillingness to engage with Burger's dissent or to acknowledge any skepticism about the factual validity of Topco's justification, has left the case vulnerable to subsequent criticism. Professor Robert Pitofsky is one of the few commentators who has written that *Topco's* result was correct, arguing that "it is impossible to see why those [joint purchasing] efficiencies could not have been achieved without the territorial restriction."[77] Other commentators have been less kind. Professor Alan Meese

---

[74] Jurisdictional Statement, United States v. Topco Associates, Inc., No. 72–1477, at 4–5 (draft, April 1973) (authors' files).

[75] *See* United States v. Topco Assocs., Inc., 414 U.S. 801 (1973). The Court now included Justices Powell and Rehnquist, who had not participated in the earlier decision.

[76] *But cf.* United States v. Glaxo Group Ltd., 410 U.S. 52, 64 (1973) (although district courts have "large discretion" in framing their decrees, the Court "has recognized 'an obligation to intervene in this most significant phase of the case' when necessary to assure that the relief will be effective") (reversing district court's refusal to order compulsory patent licensing and compulsory sales of patented product). *Glaxo* was decided after the first *Topco* decision and before the second.

[77] *See* Robert Pitofsky, *A Framework for Antitrust Analysis of Joint Ventures*, 74 GEO. L.J. 1605, 1620–1621 (1986). Pitofsky argued both that there could have been separate

has branded *Topco* as "one of the most telling exemplars of Populist era jurisprudence" (contrasting Populism with "the modern—and sounder— approach to antitrust exemplified by *Sylvania* and *BMI*").[78] Professor Timothy Muris called *Topco* "one of the most infamous antitrust cases ever," a case "founded on judicial expediency, not economics" and one now appropriately viewed as "outside the antitrust mainstream."[79] Even Donald Turner, who brought the case to establish firmly the per se rule for all horizontal territorial restraints, appears to have backed away from the *Topco* decision. Turner later wrote: "However, as the Supreme Court indicated in *Broadcast Music* and *NCAA* (impliedly reversing its reasoning in *Topco*), the *per se* rule plainly should not apply to agreements that may be reasonably ancillary to legitimate horizontal forms of economic cooperation such as lawful joint ventures."[80]

Although one court has written that *Topco* and *Sealy* must be regarded as "effectively overruled,"[81] the announcement of *Topco*'s death has proven premature. In 1991 the Supreme Court decided *Palmer v. BRG of Georgia, Inc.*,[82] involving an agreement between two bar review providers that had been competitors in Georgia. Under the agreement

---

labels ("a Brown's Topco line and a Black's Topco line") and that the less restrictive alternative of areas of primary responsibility and profit pass-overs chosen by Judge Will were all that were necessary to solve a free rider problem. Others have pointed out (correctly, we believe) that grocery store private label territorial exclusivity does not involve a free rider problem but is simply done to provide competitive advantage over rivals. *See* Thomas C. Arthur, *A Workable Rule of Reason: A Less Ambitious Antitrust Role for the Federal Courts*, 68 ANTITRUST L.J. 337, 365 n.183 (2000).

[78] Alan J. Meese, *Farewell to the Quick Look: Redefining the Scope and Content of the Rule of Reason,* 68 ANTITRUST L.J. 461, 469, 478 (2000).

[79] *See* Timothy J. Muris, *The Federal Trade Commission and the Rule of Reason: In Defense of Massachusetts Board*, 66 ANTITRUST L.J. 773, 789 n. 71, 795, 796 (1998). Muris correctly observes that "[t]he opinion . . . ignored the procompetitive aspects of the private label program and never determined whether the territorial restrictions were reasonably designed to contribute to that program." *Id.* at 794.

[80] *See* Donald F. Turner, *The Durability, Relevance, and Future of American Antitrust Policy*, 75 CALIF. L. REV. 797, 802 (1987).

[81] *See* Rothery Storage & Van Co. v. Atlas Van Lines, Inc., 792 F.2d 210, 225–26 (D.C. Cir. 1986) (Bork, J.). *Compare* General Leaseways, Inc. v. National Truck Leasing Ass'n, 744 F.2d 588 (7th Cir. 1984) (although recognizing a "tension" between *Topco* and *Sylvania*, no need to resolve the tension at the preliminary injunction stage because defendant had not yet made a "plausible" free-rider argument; on a "quick look," "the division of markets among National Truck Leasing Association's members is a per se violation of section 1") (Posner, J.).

[82] 498 U.S. 46 (1991).

one firm left the Georgia market, promising never to return; the remaining firm promised never to compete with the departing firm outside of Georgia. After the departure, the remaining firm substantially raised its price. The Supreme Court granted certiorari and, without hearing oral argument, reversed per curiam the district court's grant of summary judgment for the defendants. The Court quoted *Topco* for the proposition that agreements between competitors "to allocate territories to minimize competition" are illegal: " '[H]orizontal territorial limitations . . . are naked restraints of trade with no purpose except stifling of competition' " and are therefore per se unlawful. The parties in *Topco* "had simply agreed to allocate markets." So, too, in *BRG*. The agreement in question was therefore "unlawful on its face."[83]

What Happened to Topco Associates?

Topco Associates has survived and prospered. After entry of the decree Topco never once made use of the right to employ primary responsibility limits or profit pass-overs,[84] even though Topco members began to enter each others' territories and today many of its members compete with each other.[85] This suggests that there were no sunk costs on which new entrants could take an effective free-ride. The end of the territorial limits simply opened the door to more robust competition among efficient regional competitors. Today, Topco has more than 50 members with combined sales second only to those of Wal–Mart.[86] It has expanded the number of products it provides to its members and in 2001 combined with Shurfine International, a major food wholesaler with its

---

[83] *See id.* at 49–50. Although the facts in *BRG* were stronger than in *Topco*, in that the plaintiff alleged a substantial price effect and the defendant did not assert any procompetitive justification, *see* Palmer v. BRG of Ga., Inc., 874 F. 2d 1417, 1435 (11th Cir. 1989) (dissenting opinion), the Supreme Court did not mention either point when discussing *Topco* or the territorial allocation. *See* 498 U.S. at 49–50. Justice Marshall dissented from summary disposition on the ground that such dispositions deprive litigants of a fair opportunity to be heard. He agreed that the limited information before the Court indicated that the lower courts had erred. *See id.* at 50.

[84] Telephone interview with Victor Grimm, August 1, 2006. Topco's first compliance report stated that there had been no "agreements related to passovers" and that in response to member queries, Topco had confirmed that "members may sell Topco brands in areas served by other Topco members." Letter from Victor E. Grimm to Elliot H. Moyer, Dep't of Justice, March 6, 1974, at 2 (authors' files). In subsequent annual reports Topco never made reference to any use of the passover right. Copies of the reports are on file with the authors.

[85] For example, Topco members Giant Eagle and Miejer compete in Toledo, Ohio, *see* http://www.gianteagle.com/main/store_locator.jsp and http://www.meijer.com/storelocator/default.aspx., and Wegman's and Weis compete in Northeastern Pennsylvania, *see* http://www.wegmans.com/about/storeLocator/results.asp?region=6 and http://www.weis.com/storelocator.php?order_id=&session=. A list of Topco's current members can be found at http://www.topco.com/membr_ownr.htm (last visited Jan. 18, 2007).

[86] *See Topco Tackles a Changing Environment*, PLBuyer, November 2003 (sales for 2003), available at http://www.topco.com/PLBuyerArticle1103.pdf.

own house brands, to create an even larger enterprise.[87] Chief Justice Burger's fears have not been realized.

After entry of the decree, and recognizing that its members were now much more likely to compete with each other, Topco increased the number of labels it used so that its members could have unique private brands.[88] As noted earlier the costs of developing a label were quite modest and, with the development of computer based graphics in the 1980s and 1990s, those costs likely declined even further.

This subsequent history confirms that the cartel hypothesis better explains the role of Topco's territorial allocations. The restrictions had helped reduce and regulate potential competition among efficient regional grocery chains but had little to do with promotional investments and free riding. Topco has continued to perform its joint purchasing and private labeling functions without the territorial restrictions and without using the pass-over and primary responsibility clauses that its counsel had secured from Judge Will. Had Topco used the primary responsibility and pass-over clauses to regulate inter-member competition, as the government feared, it would have run the risk of being held in violation of the decree.

With today's warehouse stores and Wal–Mart's entry into food retailing, the relative efficiencies of the differing categories of retailers may have changed. The warehouse stores and Wal–Mart now seem to have the edge in efficiency and each has great capacity to bargain for good prices from suppliers. National chains other than Wal–Mart appear to be less efficient while the surviving small stores increasingly rely on location and hour advantages to offset their relative inefficiency in operations.

Conclusion: *Topco*'s Closer Look

A closer look at *Topco* indicates that the conventional caricature of *Topco* misses the mark. Even though the Court in *Topco* still wrote in flat per se language, it was not indifferent to the factual issues the case presented. The Court saw the anticompetitive effects of the territorial allocations and was likely skeptical of Topco's purported justifications. The Court's decision to protect free market entry against private cartel control, which had kept likely potential entrants from each other's markets, was thus not made on a completely doctrinal basis. The Court's below-the-surface consideration of the facts was at least a "closer look," even if it was not the "deliberate" one today's Supreme Court would

---

[87] *See* Ellen Almer, *Topco, Shurefine Approve Merger*, Chicago Business, Oct. 30, 2001 available at http://chicagobusiness.com/cgi-bin/news.pl?id=3683&bt=Topco+Associates+LLC&arc.

[88] Telephone interview with Victor Grimm, August 1, 2006.

require.[89] Viewed this way, *Topco* sits Janus-like, its rhetoric looking backward to the rigid "per se" and "rule of reason" dichotomy the Court had been using but its underlying decisional-apparatus looking forward to the more flexible approach used today, where courts give clearer consideration to proffered procompetitive justifications.

How would *Topco* be decided today? Certainly there would be greater analysis of the procompetitive justification Topco advanced. But that analysis might very well have strengthened the government's case. There is sufficient indication in the under-developed record that Topco's territorial exclusivity was a cartel effort to suppress potential competition rather than a legitimate effort to deal with a free-rider problem. Fuller development of those facts would have freed the government to do what its trial strategy at that time prevented—tell a counter-story about private labels, develop the evidence relating to the economics of expansion and second labels, and explore the question whether Topco members had any viable alternative private labels available for equivalent entry. As the case was presented, however, rebuttal of Topco's justification was relegated to conclusory paragraphs in briefs and, ultimately, to Supreme Court oral argument. This was a successful strategy in 1972, but in the long run it has turned out to be an unsatisfactory one.

Antitrust courts today continue to struggle with achieving the proper balance between predictability, administrability, and accuracy. That struggle is increasingly being played out at the full rule of reason end of the spectrum. Indeed, the Court and the Justice Department today seem as committed to pushing antitrust cases in that direction as the Court and the Justice Department in 1972 were committed to pushing antitrust cases toward the per se end of the spectrum.

There is wisdom to moving away from the old per se approach, but before we decide that we are today at the perfect "equilibrium" point, it would be well to remember that there are costs to maintaining, in Justice Marshall's words, a "flexible approach." Fuller inquiries may turn out to make litigation needlessly complex if extensive litigation is needed to justify obvious results.[90] Open-ended rules can encourage anticompetitive behavior in core cartel areas—price, customers, and territories—where we would do better to encourage parties to seek more competitive solutions, as Topco Associates eventually did.

Clear rules have their rewards. Donald Turner was right to bring *Topco* and the Court was right to favor free entry over territorial treaties among competitors. There are complicated areas in antitrust, but the Topco agreement, on closer look, turns out not to be one of them.

---

[89] California Dental Association v. FTC, 526 U.S. 756, 779, 781 (1999).

[90] *See, e.g.*, Polygram Holdings v. FTC, 416 F.3d 29 (D.C. Cir. 2005) (opinion makes evident the massive investment of prosecutorial resources to challenge a restraint that had little or no justification and minimal economic impact).

*

7

By Stephen Calkins*

Broadcast Music, Inc. v. Columbia Broadcasting System, Inc., 441 U.S. 1 (1979).

What a great story! Tin pan alley, media from radio to the internet, client lists that included Aaron Copland and John Philip Sousa, lawyering by three luminary law firms and at least three future courts of appeal judges—and a Supreme Court opinion that managed to be simultaneously a landmark and a mere episode in a saga stretching almost a hundred years and featuring almost that many judicial opinions! Read narrowly, the Supreme Court's opinion in *Broadcast Music, Inc. v. Columbia Broadcasting System, Inc.*[1] merely held that the Second Circuit erred when it condemned as per se illegal the blanket music licenses employed by American Society of Composers, Authors and Publishers ("ASCAP") and Broadcast Music, Inc. ("BMI"). (A "blanket" ASCAP license conveys rights to all of ASCAP's works; a "per-program" license is of identical effect but for a single program; the "per-use" license that CBS had sought would have resulted in payment of a fee for each performance of an ASCAP composition.[2]) Perhaps thanks in part to some

---

* Professor of Law and Director of Graduate Studies, Wayne State University Law School. The author thanks Richard B. Dwyer for his extensive research assistance and Kristin Pell for helping finalize the chapter.

[1] 441 U.S. 1 (1979).

[2] *Id.* at 5 ("blanket licenses ... give the licensees the right to perform any and all of the compositions owned by the members or affiliates as often as the licensees desire for a stated term," with fees that "are ordinarily a percentage of total revenues or a flat dollar amount"); *id.* at 11 (per-program); *id.* at 27 n.8 (Stevens, J., dissenting) (per-program license is "simply a miniblanket license"); CBS v. ASCAP, 400 F. Supp. 737, 747 n.7

noteworthy contributions by amici, however, the opinion is also a broadly-applicable explication of issues of fundamental importance to antitrust.[3]

With this grand a story, the toughest question is where to begin. "At the beginning" might seem a safe bet—but the beginning was in 1913 and quite disconnected from a 1979 opinion. "At the end" is another common choice—but the story has not yet ended. Instead, let us begin with Frank Easterbrook.

Frank Easterbrook is currently a distinguished judge on the United States Court of Appeals for the Seventh Circuit and a Senior Lecturer at the University of Chicago Law School, his alma mater.[4] He is a prolific author and frequent public speaker, equally well known for his insight and his irreverence. Before going on the bench in 1985, he had served on the Chicago faculty (teaching, among other things, antitrust), beginning in 1979. He was (and is) an enthusiastic proponent of the Chicago School of antitrust. But at the key moment in our story—January 15, 1979—he was serving in the Carter Administration as Deputy Solicitor General.

That January morning found Easterbrook at the Supreme Court where he was representing the United States, amicus curiae in support of defendants/respondents ASCAP and BMI.[5] ASCAP was represented by Jay H. Topkis of Paul, Weiss, Rifkind, Wharton & Garrison, an accomplished lawyer whose clients have included Vice President Spiro Agnew, the baseball star Curt Flood, and LADY CHATTERLY'S LOVER.[6] BMI was represented by Amalya L. Kearse of Hughes Hubbard & Reed, apparently the first African–American elected to the partnership of a major Wall Street law firm and the first woman elected a fellow of the American College of Trial Lawyers.[7] Five months after the *Broadcast Music* argu-

---

("Under the 'per-use' system proposed by CBS, it would continue to license its music through ASCAP and BMI, but in a substantially different way than it does under the blanket license. CBS would pay ASCAP or BMI a specified fee for each performance of a composition . . . plus an administrative fee.").

[3] For a review and commentary on the role of amici in antitrust cases more generally, see Stephen Calkins, *The Antitrust Conversation*, 68 ANTITRUST L.J. 625 (2001).

[4] For background on Judge Easterbrook, see his University of Chicago biography, at http://www.law.uchicago.edu/faculty/easterbrook (last visited Dec. 16, 2006).

[5] In his antitrust casebook, Easterbrook cutely observes as follows: "Indeed, the United States appeared as *amicus curiae* and argued against the application of a per se rule. The Court found this significant. Why?" RICHARD A. POSNER & FRANK H. EASTERBROOK, ANTITRUST 142 n.5 (2d ed. 1981).

[6] *See* Jay Topkis biography, http://www.paulweiss.com/lawyers/detail.aspx?attorney= 248 (last visited Dec. 16, 2006).

[7] *See* Biographical information, http://www.ca2.uscourts.gov/ (last visited Dec. 16, 2006); *One Summer, Two Friends,* http://www.giving.umich.edu/leadersbest/winter2005/

ment Ms. Kearse was sworn in as the first woman and the second African–American judge on the United States Court of Appeals for the Second Circuit.[8] (Perhaps appropriately for a role in a case about entertainment, Judge Kearse is known both for being a five-time national bridge player and for her musical creativity.[9]) Columbia Broadcasting System, Inc. ("CBS") was represented by Alan J. Hruska of Cravath, Swaine & Moore, like Topkis a Yale Law School graduate and a leading appellate lawyer.[10]

Topkis, Kearse, and Easterbrook, all urging reversal, each took 15 minutes, with Topkis reserving a little time for rebuttal. The first 25 minutes of argument were intensely fact-specific and, frankly, quite dull, save only when Justice Stevens observed of Topkis, "You studiously avoid answering the question."[11] (Topkis replied, "Not deliberately, I

---

twofriends.html (last visited Dec. 16, 2006). *But cf.* Tom Goldstein, *Amalya Lyle Kearse,* N.Y. Times, June 25, 1979, at B2 (she was the "first female black partner in a major Wall Street firm").

[8] *See One Summer, Two Friends, supra* note 7; 2d cir. judges, http://www.ca2.uscourts.gov/ (last visited Dec. 16, 2006).

[9] U Michigan Law School Professor (and former Wayne State Dean) John Reed

especially recalls her creativity and initiative. On one occasion, he was preparing some songs for entertainment at an Association of American Law Schools meeting that involved parodies based on music from Broadway musicals of the day. "I was stuck for a song to make a particular point. She [Kearse] heard me about this and, without prior announcement, simply placed on my desk one morning a set of words to be sung to the music from 'The Music Man' that filled the bill perfectly."

Michigan Greats, at http://www.research.umich.edu/news/michigangreats/kearse.html (last visited Dec. 16, 2006). When confirmed for the court of appeals, the New York Times described her as having spent the past two years in "almost nonstop work." " 'You work a lot, almost all the time, every weekend and evening,' she said. 'Working days are 12 to 15 hours long. Literally, there is no time for anything else.' " N.Y. Times, *supra* note 7. The story also quoted Jay Topkis: " 'She has a slightly glacial exterior, but she is a delightful person,' said Jay Topkis. . . . 'I don't know of an appointment that I have been so enthusiastic about in quite some time.' " *Id.*

[10] A year after the argument, Business Week quoted Hruska, then co-chairman of a Commission on the Reduction of Burdens and Costs in Civil Litigation, as follows:

"The document production process in large litigations is very costly, bizarre, and most often consists of avoidable steps," says New York attorney Alan J. Hruska. . . . If a company could be made to comply with a request that said "just please give me all the documents that you wish weren't written," Hruska quips, discovery would be relatively simple and cheap. Instead, the system places a premium on evasiveness.

The Costly Paper Chase Clogging the Courts, Business Week, June 23, 1980, at 134.

[11] Transcript of Oral Argument at 12, Broadcast Music, Inc. v. Columbia Broadcasting System, Inc., 441 U.S. 1 (No. 77–1528). The transcript does not indicate the name of the Justice asking a question, so all references to particular Justices are based either on the oralist's reference to a name or to *Supreme Court Hears Argument on Legality of 'Blanket'*

assure you, Your Honor.''[12]) As Kearse's argument came to a close, the Court was focusing narrowly on one specific dispute between ASCAP and Warner Brothers.[13]

Easterbrook walked to the lectern and shifted the focus from facts to theory:

> MR. EASTERBROOK: Mr. Chief Justice, and may it please the Court:

> The United States believes that three considerations govern the proper disposition of this case. First, under what circumstances should agreements among competitors be held unlawful per se; second, are the blanket licenses of ASCAP and BMI so likely to be anti-competitive that they come within this class; and, third, if blanket licenses are not always unlawful, should a per se rule nonetheless be employed because of the particular circumstances of one user or class of users in music. I will address those question in turn.

> My first proposition is that per se rules should be employed only when a particular species of conduct is so likely to be anti-competitive that a particular trial of particular circumstances would not be worth the time and effort because there are so few justified examples of that species. In those circumstances, there is no reason to go through a full trial.

> Per se rules are attractive precisely because they are understandable and certain.... But if certainty alone were enough to call for per se treatment, all of antitrust law would quickly be reduced to a series of homilies. There must be some reason for each rule.[14]

With that bold opening, the whole tenor of the argument changed. Now the Court was engaged in the big picture, and it remained there throughout Easterbrook's argument. CBS's Hruska had not gotten far into *his* argument about how thoroughly ASCAP[15] was controlling price

---

Licensing of Copyrighted Music, Antitrust & Trade Reg. Rep. (BNA) No. 897, at A–7 (Jan. 18, 1979).

[12] *Id.* Justice Stevens had asked whether "there [was] anything in the arrangements between ASCAP and its members which would preclude ASCAP from licensing a portion of its portfolio." *Id.* at 10. Topkis explained, "It is not a question that has ever been raised in ASCAP's history and all I can say is that I think it would startle ASCAP's members to be told that some of their works were being licensed and not others." *Id.* at 12.

[13] Transcript, *supra* note 11, at 22–24.

[14] Transcript, *supra* note 11, at 24–25.

[15] As was done during the litigation, this account will generally refer to ASCAP rather than separately to ASCAP and BMI, since the Court considered there to be few significant

when Justice Rehnquist stopped him and demanded a response to the argument that an appropriate analogy was to two firms forming a partnership, which should not be condemned as per se illegal.[16] Although Rehnquist credited the contention to petitioners, it was actually made only by amici: the Solicitor General[17] and an extraordinary collection of composers—Aaron Copland, Eubie Blake, Ira Gershwin, Virgil Thomson, and the estates of Bela Bartok, Duke Ellington and Igor Stravinsky, among others—represented by Yale Law Professor and future federal court of appeals judge Robert Bork.[18] Bork, who credited the insight to Judge Taft in *Addyston Pipe*,[19] had made the same point in academic writing.[20]

After initially avoiding the question, Hruska unfortunately responded that two firms that formed a partnership were engaged in price fixing.[21] This prompted Justice Rehnquist to demand of Hruska whether he agreed with Judge Taft in *Addyston Pipe*.[22] Further perceived evasion

---

differences between them. *See* 441 U.S. at 6 n.5 ("Unless the context indicates otherwise, references to ASCAP alone in this opinion usually apply to BMI as well.").

[16] Transcript, *supra* note 11, at 39.

[17] Brief for the United States as Amicus Curiae at 19.

[18] Brief for Aaron Copland, et al., as Amici Curiae, at 13.

[19] United States v. Addyston Pipe & Steel Co., 85 F. 271, 280 (6th Cir. 1898), *aff'd*, 175 U.S. 211 (1989), *cited, Copland Amicus Brief*, at 13.

[20] Bork is best known for popularizing the point in his landmark book published the year before the argument, ROBERT H. BORK, THE ANTITRUST PARADOX 265 (1978), which was included in a string cite by ASCAP, Brief for Petitioners, *BMI v. CBS*, at 28. That work's treatment borrowed from Robert H. Bork, *The Rule of Reason and the Per Se Concept: Price Fixing and Market Division (Part II)*, 75 YALE L.J. 373, 377 (1966), on which famous former FTC Commissioner Philip Elman relied to make the partnership point briefly in the amicus brief he filed, Brief for the Performing Right Society Ltd. and Societe Des Auteurs, Compositeurs Et Editeurs De Musique as Amicus Curiae at 9.

[21] Transcript. *supra* note 11, at 40.

[22] Transcript, *supra* note 11, at 39–40 (emphasis added):

QUESTION: Mr. Hruska, what is your answer to the petitioner's contention that if you have two individual general contractors that go into a partnership, they cease competing, too, and bid as a unit rather than formally (sic) as they did supplying two separate prices....

    . . . .

QUESTION [by Justice Rehnquist]: And what is your answer to the question about the two general contractors who form a partnership and from then on bid singly rather than separately?

MR. HRUSKA: *Well, I think under existing law that is price fixing.* However I should make this point: I think that it is entirely a more difficult question when you get to two individual entities, otherwise competing entities which if they were to merge would clearly not violate section 2 and nevertheless are fixing prices. Now, the—

prompted an exasperated Rehnquist to demand, "do you or do you not agree with Judge Taft's observation in the *Addyston Pipe* case?"[23] Hruska responded that the logic of his position would suggest that the formation and operation of a partnership was illegal but the law did not have to go that far—to which an unnamed Justice (perhaps Rehnquist again) observed, "If I understand it, you would like to stay on both sides of this question."[24]

CBS had lost. But although amici in the Supreme Court surely encouraged the Court to think broadly in crafting its opinion, CBS probably lost the case far earlier.

I. INTRODUCTION: THE PER SE RULE
AND THE RULE OF REASON

For the reader new to antitrust, a bit of doctrinal background might help. Antitrust's origins lie in the common law. More particularly, although the Sherman Act declares unlawful every contract "in restraint of trade," the Supreme Court early observed that "the legality of an agreement ... cannot be determined by so simple a test, as whether it restrains competition. Every agreement concerning trade, every regulation of trade, restrains."[25] Legality was to be determined by a rule of reason, or so the Court held in 1911.[26]

But did this mean that the reasonableness of fixed prices was a defense? Not at all, declared the Court in the important 1927 opinion, *United States v. Trenton Potteries Co.*: "The aim and result of every price-fixing agreement, if effective, is in the elimination of one form of competition.... Agreements which create such potential power may well be held to be in themselves unreasonable or unlawful restraints, without the necessity of minute inquiry whether a particular price is reasonable or unreasonable...."[27] Later, in *Socony–Vacuum*, the Court wrote that "this Court has consistently and without deviation adhered to the principle that price-fixing agreements are unlawful per se under the Sherman Act and that no showing of so-called competitive abuses or evils ... may be interposed as a defense."[28] Thus was the "per se rule" christened.

QUESTION: Do you think Judge Taft was wrong in his expression of views in the Addyston case?

[23] Transcript at 41.

[24] Transcript at 43.

[25] Chicago Bd. of Trade v. United States, 246 U.S. 231, 238 (1918).

[26] Standard Oil of N.J. v. United States, 221 U.S. 1 (1911).

[27] 273 U.S. 392, 397 (1927).

[28] United States v. Socony–Vacuum Oil Co., 310 U.S. 150, 218 (1940).

In the decades that followed *Socony*, much of antitrust consisted of the gradual extension of the per se rule to cover additional conduct. The per se blanket was extended to cover tying,[29] price-fixing of maximum prices,[30] resale price maintenance,[31] group boycotts,[32] post-sale territorial restraints imposed by a manufacturer on a distributor,[33] vertically-imposed maximum prices,[34] and horizontal division of territories.[35] Changes seemed always in favor of increased liability, prompting now-Professor Easterbrook to ask, "Is There A Ratchet in Antitrust Law?"[36]

Professor Easterbrook answered his own question in the negative, and he was able to do so because the Burger Court, with four Nixon appointees, had called a halt to the constant expansion of the per se rule. Two cases set the stage for *BMI*. In *Continental T.V., Inc. v. GTE Sylvania, Inc.*,[37] the Court deliberately overruled its 1967 *Schwinn* opinion and held that non-price vertical restraints should be judged under a rule of reason. The Court made clear "that departure from the rule-of-reason standard must be based upon demonstrable economic effect rather than—as in Schwinn—upon formalistic line drawing."[38] Then, in *Professional Engineers*, the Court reviewed a court of appeals decision that had condemned a concerted bidding-process restriction as per se illegal, and, rather than simply affirming it, enigmatically wrote that the defendant's proffered justification "rests on a fundamental misunderstanding of the Rule of Reason."[39] The Court affirmed the court of appeals's condemnation of a restraint that "[o]n its face ... restrains trade,"[40] seemingly applying a per se rule while nonetheless sketching the contours of the rule of reason[41] and weighing the defendant's

---

[29] International Salt Co. v. United States, 332 U.S. 392 (1947).

[30] Kiefer–Stewart Co. v. Joseph E. Seagram & Sons, 340 U.S. 211 (1951).

[31] United States v. Parke, Davis & Co., 362 U.S. 29 (1960); *see also* Dr. Miles Medical Co. v. Park & Sons Co., 220 U.S. 373 (1911) (same concept without the phraseology).

[32] United States v. General Motors Corp., 384 U.S. 127 (1966).

[33] United States v. Arnold, Schwinn & Co., 388 U.S. 365 (1967).

[34] Albrecht v. Herald Co., 390 U.S. 145 (1968).

[35] United States v. Topco Associates, 405 U.S. 596 (1972).

[36] Frank H. Easterbrook, *Is There a Ratchet in Antitrust Law?*, 60 TEX. L. REV. 705 (1982).

[37] 433 U.S. 36 (1977).

[38] 433 U.S. at 58.

[39] United States v. Nat'l Soc'y of Prof'l Eng'rs, 435 U.S. 679, 681 (1978).

[40] *Id.* at 693.

[41] For the classic distinction between the per se rule and the rule of reason, see *id.* at 692:

justification (and finding it wanting). To this day, courts and scholars disagree about whether *Professional Engineers* is a per se or a rule of reason case.[42] Any doubt that remained after *Professional Engineers* about whether the heyday of the per se rule was over was removed by *BMI*.

II. THE ORIGINS OF *BMI*: ENDLESS LITIGATION

The *BMI* case had its origins in harmony that quickly devolved into ugly disputes. In 1913, Victor Herbert composer of, among other things, 43 operettas (including "Babes in Toyland"),[43] visited Shanley's Restaurant near Times Square and heard the band playing his song, "Sweethearts," from his current Broadway show of the same name.[44] The restauranteur was not paying royalties, reasoning that he was not charging admission. Herbert, aided by other composers and publishers, filed a test case, and, when an association of hotel and restaurant owners came to Shanley's defense, Herbert, John Philip Sousa, and seven others formed ASCAP. Herbert and Sousa (who sued over the wrongful playing of his march, "From Maine to Oregon"[45]) won their lawsuits in an opinion written by Justice Holmes.[46] ASCAP promptly filed scores of lawsuits and started issuing licenses, eventually licensing much of the music industry.[47]

There are, thus, two complementary categories of antitrust analysis. In the first category are agreements whose nature and necessary effect are so plainly anticompetitive that no elaborate study of the industry is needed to establish their illegality—they are "illegal per se." In the second category are agreements whose competitive effect can only be evaluated by analyzing the facts peculiar to the business, the history of the restraint, and the reasons why it was imposed. In either event, the purpose of the analysis is to form a judgment about the competitive significance of the restraint; it is not to decide whether a policy favoring competition is in the public interest, or in the interest of the members of an industry.

[42] Stephen Calkins, California Dental Association: *Not a Quick Look but Not the Full Monty*, 67 ANTITRUST L.J. 495, 523 n.139 (2000) (citing different views).

[43] *See* http://en.wikipedia.org/wiki/Victor_Herbert (last visited Dec. 20, 2006).

[44] Leonard Allen, *The Battle of Tin Pan Alley*, 181 HARPERS 514, 516 (Oct. 1940); *see also* Herbert v. Shanley, 242 U.S. 591 (1917). Recordings of the operetta continue to be offered for sale. The triggering song can be heard by visiting http://www.amazon.com/Sweethearts–Rudolf–Friml/dp/B00001R3MB (last visited Dec. 20, 2006).

[45] This work, too, remains available and can be sampled on-line. *See* http://www.amazon.com/Great–American–Marches–II–Philip/dp/B000002SNV (last visited Dec. 20, 2006).

[46] Herbert v. Shanley, 242 U.S. 591 (1917).

[47] Comment, *Music Copyright Associations and the Antitrust Laws*, 25 IND. L.J. 168, 169 (1950); Robert P. Merges, *Contracting into Liability Rules: Intellectual Property Rights and Collective Rights Organizations*, 84 CALIF. L. REV. 1293, 1330–33 (1996).

Change came with the advent of radio, which created a substantial revenue stream and ASCAP's chief antagonists.[48] Encouraged by industry complaints, in 1934 the Department of Justice filed a lawsuit seeking to dissolve ASCAP, but after four days moved to adjourn the suit.[49] When ASCAP's licensing demands kept escalating, broadcasters eventually responded in 1939 by forming a rival organization, BMI.[50] The government also responded by filing new civil and even criminal proceedings, which soon resulted in the entry of the critically important 1941 consent decrees.[51] Among other provisions, the 1941 ASCAP decree prevented ASCAP from receiving exclusive rights to compositions, prevented discrimination, and required ASCAP to offer a "per-program" license (in addition to its customary blanket license which conveyed rights to all of ASCAP's music for all programs).[52]

The coming of motion pictures provided a new source of ASCAP revenue, and soaring royalty demands prompted a lawsuit that resulted in an opinion sweepingly condemning ASCAP's behavior with respect to that industry.[53] Prompted by that decision, industry complaints, and recognition of the importance of accommodating television, DOJ renegotiated the 1941 decree.[54] The 1950 decree, among other things, prohibit-

---

[48] Marcus Cohn, *Music, Radio Broadcasters and the Sherman Act*, 29 Geo. L.J. 407, 426 n.98 (1941).

[49] Comment, *supra* note 47, at 177–78; Cohn, *supra* note 48, at 424.

[50] 441 U.S. at 5; *see* Cohn, supra note 48, at 420; Comment, *supra* note 47, at 171–72. Although founded to challenge ASCAP, BMI soon came to function very similarly.

[51] United States v. ASCAP, 1940–43 Trade Cas. (CCH) ¶ 56,104 (S.D.N.Y. 1941) (with the legendary Thurman Arnold as Assistant Attorney General); *see* Comment, *supra* note 47, at 178. A very similar decree was entered against BMI, United States v. BMI, 1940–43 Trade Cas. (CCH) ¶ 56,096 (E.D. Wis. 1941).

[52] *See* Memorandum of the United States in Support of the Joint Motion to Enter Second Amended Final Judgment, United States v. ASCAP, Civ. No. 41–1395 (WCC) (S.D.N.Y. Sept. 4, 2000), at 10–11, *available at* http://www.usdoj.gov/atr/cases/f6300/6395. htm:

> The most significant provisions of the initial 1941 consent decree prohibited ASCAP from obtaining exclusive rights to license its members' compositions; prohibited ASCAP from discriminating in price or terms among similarly situated licensees; required ASCAP to offer licenses other than a blanket license, including, in particular, . . . a 'per-program' license . . . ; [and] required that radio network licenses also cover the local radio stations' broadcast of the networks' programs (a 'through-to-the-audience' license) . . . . ;

see also Comment, *supra* note 47, at 178 ("Under the compromise ASCAP and B.M.I. were no longer to be the exclusive agents for their members if any member preferred to deal individually with music users.").

[53] Alden–Rochelle v. ASCAP, 80 F. Supp. 888 (S.D.N.Y.), *remedy modified*, 80 F. Supp. 900 (S.D.N.Y. 1948).

[54] United States v. ASCAP, 1950–51 Trade Cas. (CCH) ¶ 62,595 (S.D.N.Y. 1950); *see* Sigmund Timberg, *The Antitrust Aspects of Merchandising Modern Music: The ASCAP*

ed licensing movie theaters and extended the decree to television. AS-CAP was required to grant a non-exclusive blanket license to anyone requesting one; it was ordered "to use its best efforts to avoid any discrimination among the respective fees fixed for the various types of licenses which would deprive the licensees or prospective licensees of a genuine choice from among such various types of licenses;" and what came to be known as a "rate court" was created: if ASCAP and any applicant could not agree on a reasonable fee, "the applicant therefore may apply to this Court for the determination of a reasonable fee."[55]

It is hard to exaggerate the extent to which ASCAP has lived in courtrooms. If one checks Shepard's citations for the subsequent history of the original 1941 consent decree, one finds 55 subsequent court orders in this or related proceedings, some as recent as 2004.[56] (BMI's consent decree has stimulated a more modest number of proceedings, the most recent of which was in 2005.[57])

Aside from the government consent decrees and amendments there-of, the most important predecessor litigation to the *BMI* case was *K–91, Inc. v. Gershwin Publishing Corp.*,[58] a case in which two Assistant Attorneys General for Antitrust ("AAG's") played important roles—but in which ASCAP was not even a party. An attractive group of plaintiffs, including Irving Berlin, Richard Rogers, and Cole Porter, sued three radio broadcasting companies that had been knowingly and deliberately operating without paying royalties.[59] The only defense was a claimed

---

Consent Judgment of 1950, 19 LAW & CONTEMP. PROBS. 294, 301 (1954) ("This earlier Decree had done little more than assuage the radio-broadcasting industry's antitrust grievances against ASCAP; it needed to be accommodated to the impact of television and other new developments within the mass entertainment field. Furthermore, it was proving a most fertile source of complaints to the Department of Justice, both from the users of ASCAP's music and from the membership of ASCAP itself.").

[55] Amended 1950 ASCAP decree Sections VI, VII & IX(A). The decree was further amended in 1960. United States v. ASCAP, 1960 TRADE CAS. (CCH) ¶ 69.612 (S.D.N.Y. 1960).

[56] United States v. ASCAP, 333 F. Supp. 2d 215 (S.D.N.Y. 2004) (refusing to certify an appeal and leaving the current dispute headed for trial); *see, e.g.,* United States v. ASCAP (*In re* Application of Shenandoah Broadcasting, Inc.), 331 F.2d 117 (2d Cir. 1964) (declining to interpret decree to require ASCAP to issue a new category of license).

[57] United States v. BMI, 426 F.3d 91 (2d Cir. 2005) (vacating decision of district court and remanding for further proceedings). The 1966 version of the decree, United States v. BMI, 1966 TRADE CAS. (CCH) ¶ 71,941 (S.D.N.Y. 1966), *as amended,* 1996–1 TRADE CAS. (CCH) ¶ 71,378 (S.D.N.Y. 1994) (establishing a rate court procedure), has been addressed in seven judicial entries.

[58] 372 F.2d 1 (9th Cir. 1967).

[59] Tempo Music, Inc. v. International Good Music, Inc., 143 U.S.P.Q. 67 (W.D. Wash. 1964) (consolidated case names included Berlin et al. v. International Good Music and

antitrust violation and copyright misuse. District Judge Murphy, pleading illness and comforted by the presence of "competent counsel" for both sides "who will present adequately their arguments to the Court of Appeals," held without giving any reasoning therefore that plaintiffs had not violated the antitrust laws, ordered payment of $1,000 in damages and $15,000 in attorneys fees, and enjoined future copyright infringement.[60]

On appeal, the Ninth Circuit affirmed, in an opinion by former AAG Stanley Barnes.[61] The court stressed three aspects of the amended ASCAP decree: all rights "must be nonexclusive," all fees "must be reasonable" (set by the court in the event of a dispute), and all licenses must be on the same terms and conditions.[62] To the court, per Judge Barnes, the second point was critical:

> ASCAP cannot be accused of fixing prices because every applicant to ASCAP has a right under the consent decree to invoke the authority of the United States District Court for the Southern District of New York to fix a reasonable fee whenever the applicant believes that the price proposed by ASCAP is unreasonable.... In short, we think that as a potential combination in restraint of trade, ASCAP has been 'disinfected' by the decree.[63]

The court also noted, as "an additional reason," the non-exclusive nature of the license grant.[64]

Over the dissent of Justice Black, the Supreme Court denied certiorari.[65] One has to guess that the amicus brief that the Court invited from the Solicitor General, which Assistant Attorney General (and Harvard Law Professor) Donald Turner co-authored[66] (and which counseled against granting certiorari), could have made a difference. The brief placed great weight on the parties' stipulation that licenses from individual composers could not possibly be granted:

Porter et al. v. Jones et al.; defendants attempt to have ASCAP joined as a party had been unsuccessful).

[60] *Tempo Music*, 143 U.S.P.Q. at 68–69. Plaintiffs were represented by the Paul, Weiss firm and Seattle counsel.

[61] Barnes had been AAG from May 1, 1953, to July 3, 1956. See http://www.usdoj.gov/atr/timeline.htm (last visited Dec. 17, 2006).

[62] 372 F.2d at 3.

[63] 372 F.2d at 4.

[64] 372 F.2d at 4.

[65] 389 U.S. 1045 (1968).

[66] 389 U.S. 1045, 1045 (1968) (Memorandum of United States by Solicitor General Griswold, Assistant Attorney General Turner, and Howard E. Shapiro). Turner was AAG from June 1, 1965 to June 1, 1968. *See* http://www.usdoj.gov/atr/timeline.htm.

If this market is to function at all, there must be ... some kind of central licensing agency by which copyright holders may offer their works in a common pool to all who wish to use them.... And because users' requirements for separate pieces are continuous, the volume of demand enormous, and the value of each single performance small, separate negotiations on a per piece basis are not practicable. There is simply no escaping, as a practical matter, the licensing of the works in bulk.[67]

The brief also wrote more generally about the Sherman Act:

The Sherman Act has always been discriminatingly applied in the light of economic realities. There are situations in which competitors have been permitted to form joint selling agencies or other pooled activities, subject to strict limitations under the antitrust laws to guarantee against abuse of the collective power thus created. *Associated Press v. United States*, 326 U.S. 1; *United States v. St. Louis Terminal*, 224 U.S. 393; *Appalachian Coals, Inc. v. United States*, 288 U.S. 344; *Chicago Board of Trade v. United States*, 246 U.S. 231. This case appears to us to involve such a situation.[68]

The brief cautioned that the 1950 consent decree did not automatically immunize ASCAP's behavior, warned that ASCAP "requires the closest scrutiny under the antitrust laws," and noted that the Government may have to seek modification of the consent decree "[a]s conditions change"—such as if "developments in computer technology" solves "the difficult problem of accounting for millions of separate performances each year," which "might warrant a completely new approach."[69] For the present, and in light of the stipulation of impracticability, "petitioner should at least have come forward with evidence demonstrating a reasonable possibility that alternative methods are feasible."[70]

Petitioner having failed to do so, the court ruled against it in an opinion that would prove important a decade later.

III.   THE *BMI v. CBS* LITIGATION

A.   District Court

District Judge Morris E. Lasker was unimpressed with the way the *BMI v. CBS* lawsuit came about. CBS had "lived quite happily" with blanket licenses, never exploring any alternatives, until a fee dispute

---

[67] Memorandum for the United States as Amicus Curiae, K–91, Inc. v. Gershwin Publishing Corp. (filed Dec. 1967), at 9–10, included as appendix to Brief for the United States as Amicus Curiae, *BMI*.

[68] Memorandum at 8–9.

[69] Memorandum at 12–13 & n.10.

[70] *Id.* at 12.

prompted BMI to notify CBS on October 29, 1969, that it was terminating CBS's license effective January 1, 1970. After failed negotiations between BMI and CBS (which was represented by Donald Sipes, a new vice president who "was almost completely unacquainted with the intricacies of music licensing" and who consulted only three persons, none business persons with relevant expertise[71]), on December 19 CBS sent a written demand to ASCAP and BMI for a license with " 'payments measured by the actual use of your music.' " Before that date, "CBS thought very little about revising its licensing practices;" indeed, the evidence "suggests that CBS did not even view music licensing as a business problem until immediately prior to suit." ASCAP and BMI replied that they were willing to negotiate, but CBS filed its lawsuit on December 31.[72]

CBS also got off on the wrong foot by refusing to pay royalties on the BMI compositions it was using and then, when BMI counterclaimed for a preliminary injunction requiring payment of fair value, by arguing that it should pay only on a "per use" basis, i.e., the way it would pay were it to win its case in chief. District Judge Lasker quickly ruled in BMI's favor, noting, in the process, that "CBS is a substantially larger and stronger organization than BMI."[73]

Perhaps inspired by BMI's success, ASCAP moved for summary judgment on the grounds that the issue before the court had been definitively resolved in the *K–91* case discussed above. ASCAP lost the battle but may have won the war. *K–91* was "an entirely different ball game than the one we are attending," Judge Lasker ruled, because the parties had stipulated that there were no "practical alternatives" to the kinds of licenses ASCAP was offering.[74] This was "the antithesis of CBS' position," which demanded a " 'per-use' license (payment measured by the actual use of copyrighted music)."[75] In this connection Judge Lasker gave great weight to the SG's brief in *K–91* and its argument that " '[i]f the market is to *function at all* there *must* be ... some kind of central licensing system,' " but that if " 'the record here furnished any substantial basis for concluding that practical alternatives exist to bulk licensing

---

[71] 400 F. Supp. at 754. Mr. Sipes was a lawyer who originally worked for talent agencies, then NBC and CBS. In 1975 (the year of Judge Lasker's major opinion) he moved to MCA Inc. where he later became president of Universal Television. Leonard Sloane, *Business People*, N.Y. Times, Nov. 13, 1981, at D2.

[72] 400 F. Supp. at 754.

[73] CBS v. ASCAP, 320 F. Supp. 389, 393 (S.D.N.Y. 1970) (requiring an annual fee of $1,607,000, which was the pre-litigation year fee and the largest ever paid by CBS to BMI, subject to the right of either party to show changed circumstances).

[74] 337 F. Supp. at 400.

[75] 337 F. Supp. at 397 & 400 (footnote omitted).

of recorded music, a different case would be presented...' "[76] Accordingly, Judge Lasker reasoned, genuine issues of fact existed. (Judge Lasker was unimpressed with ASCAP's suggestion, found persuasive by the *K–91* court, that any problems were solved by the nominal right of individual composers and licensees to make their own arrangements, a right that was probably " 'more apparent than real.' "[77])

Although Judge Lasker thus denied ASCAP's motion, in the process of doing so he "agree[d] with the Ninth circuit that a rule of reason test and not a *per se* test should be applied to ASCAP's activities."[78] Rather than cite the Ninth Circuit, however, Judge Lasker quoted from the SG's *K–91* amicus brief about the essentiality of a "centralized licensing system," and wrote, in words obviously inspired by the SG's brief, that "[w]hen economic realities of the market place dictate such treatment the Supreme Court has often applied the rule of reason test to activities which would otherwise call for the *per se* test"—citing the same four Supreme Court cases cited by the SG.[79]

After an eight-week trial on liability[80] at which three distinguished economists testified,[81] Judge Lasker dismissed CBS's complaint. Again building on the *K–91* case, he focused on the practicability of CBS's securing direct licenses from individual composers as "the key factual issue in the case"[82]—an issue he resolved decisively against CBS. In reaching this conclusion, he found it "highly relevant" that "CBS has made no effort to obtain the kinds of licenses it now complains defendants are unwilling to grant."[83] There was no "evidence that any ASCAP member or BMI affiliate has ever refused or even threatened to refuse to grant CBS direct performance rights.... To the contrary, there is

---

[76] 337 F. Supp. at 400 (emphasis supplied by court).

[77] 337 F. Supp. at 401 (quoting Schwartz v. BMI, 180 F. Supp. 322, 333 (S.D.N.Y. 1959)).

[78] 337 F. Supp. at 398.

[79] 337 F. Supp. at 398.

[80] In oral argument before the Court, Kearse quipped, "When the trial started, there were I believe six or seven variety programs [for which blanket licenses are particularly important] on CBS. By the time trial was over, there was only one." Transcript, *supra* note 11, at 19.

[81] 562 F.2d at 134 n.12 ("Judge Lasker had the benefit of the expert testimony of three distinguished economists, Franklin M. Fisher for CBS, Robert Nathan for ASCAP and Peter O. Steiner for BMI."). Dr. Fisher, for instance, was a full professor of economics at MIT and had won the John Bates Clark Medal, often thought of as the Nobel Prize for economists under 40. He was later to testify against the government in the *IBM* monopolization case and then for the government in the *Microsoft* case.

[82] 400 F. Supp. at 747.

[83] 400 F. Supp. at 752–53.

impressive proof that copyright proprietors would wait at CBS' door if it announced plans to drop its blanket license."[84] In reaching this conclusion, Judge Lasker dismissed the views of CBS's star economist witness, Franklin Fisher, disparagingly noting that Dr. Fisher "has never spoken to a writer or publisher."[85] This conclusion about the availability of individual licenses was at the heart of Judge Lasker's ruling, supporting his conclusion that ASCAP and its members and BMI had not agreed not to compete, nor boycotted, nor engaged in tying, nor monopolized any market. Prices were not "fixed," he ruled, for this reason and because "CBS has always negotiated the price for its licenses with ASCAP and BMI."[86]

B. Second Circuit

On appeal, the Second Circuit reversed, with an August 8, 1977, opinion authored by Murray I. Gurfein. Judge Gurfein had achieved fame when, during his first week as a U.S. District Judge nominated by President Nixon, he had been assigned the Pentagon Papers case and refused to enjoin their publication.[87] In spite of that President Nixon nominated him for promotion to the Second Circuit, where he had served since August 1974. Also on the panel were Robert P. Anderson and Leonard P. Moore, Johnson and Eisenhower nominees who had both assumed senior status in 1971.[88] All three were to be deceased within four years of the Supreme Court's decision.[89]

Although ASCAP and BMI lost, in that the court reversed Judge Lasker, the way they lost paved the way for future victory. For one thing, the court, although expressing doubts about the viability of individual licensing, found that this "essential finding" of Judge Lasker was not clearly erroneous.[90] It accordingly affirmed the dismissal of the tying, block-booking, and monopoly claims. The court also helped the defendants when it turned to remedy, as noted below.

With respect to price fixing, however, it found a violation. This court, too, quoted extensively from the SG's *K–91* amicus brief, which it

---

[84] 400 F. Supp. at 766 & 779.

[85] 400 F. Supp. at 766.

[86] 400 F. Supp. at 781.

[87] *See* Murray Gurfein, http://en.wikipedia.org/wiki/Murray_Gurfein (last visited Dec. 22, 2006).

[88] *See* Robert Palmer Anderson, http://en.wikipedia.org/wiki/Robert_Palmer_Anderson; Leonard Page Moore, http://en.wikipedia.org/wiki/Leonard_Page_Moore (last visited Dec. 21, 2006).

[89] Judge Anderson died May 2, 1978, Judge Gurfein December 16, 1979, and Judge Moore December 7, 1982.

[90] 562 F.2d at 135.

interpreted as adopting a sensible " 'market necessity' concept as a very limited and narrow exception to the per se rule against price-fixing."[91] But it reasoned that if direct-licensing is an alternative—which, paradoxically, ASCAP and BMI had sought to establish at trial, against the protests of CBS—then any necessity defense falls away. Nor has the possible reasonableness of a price ever been a defense to price-fixing. Here, the blanket license "involves the fixing of a collective price" and inevitably "dulls his [the copyright owner's] incentive to compete," so, given that this price-fixing is not saved by market necessity, it is unlawful.[92] Judge Moore strangely concurred while objecting to the court's conclusion, which he characterized as only a minor disagreement.

Having held the blanket license to television networks per se illegal, the court then substantially qualified this conclusion, in two ways. First, the court dropped a footnote observing that "in no way" was it intimating that the blanket license generally was illegal—to the contrary, *K–91* was a correct application of the "market necessity" defense and "CBS concedes that market necessity would probably justify ASCAP blanket licenses for restaurants, night clubs, skating rinks and even radio stations."[93] Second, the court offered wholly unnecessary observations about remedy, a subject that Judge Lasker had not addressed at all. It would be a sufficient remedy, the court wrote, "if ASCAP itself is required to provide some form of per use licensing which will ensure competition among the individual members."[94] This would be sufficient, the court wrote in an odd conclusion to an opinion finding per se illegal price fixing, because "[t]he blanket license is not simply a 'naked restraint' ineluctably doomed to extinction," but rather serves a "market need."[95]

In short order the decision was vigorously criticized in case comments in the Harvard and Yale law reviews, the former because the wrong-headed "market necessity" defense should have persuaded the court not to apply the per se rule, the latter because the wrong-headed "market necessity" defense would eviscerate the per rule that the court *should* have been applied (with a legislative fix offering the ultimate solution).[96] ASCAP and BMI (but not CBS, which had lost on its tying

---

[91] 562 F.2d at 137.

[92] 562 F.2d at 139–40.

[93] 562 F.2d at 140 n.26.

[94] 562 F.2d at 140.

[95] 562 F.2d at 140.

[96] Case comment, *The Middleman as Price Fixer:* Columbia Broadcasting System, Inc. v. American Society of Composers, Authors & Publishers, 91 HARV. L. REV. 488, 497 (1977);

and monopolization claims), successfully sought review in the Supreme Court.

C. Supreme Court

At the Supreme Court, ASCAP's brief highlighted those two case comments and attacked the "market necessity defense," which it said would destroy the per se rule. Its principal arguments were that joint sales agencies are not per se illegal, and ASCAP should not be, in part because it is the user (CBS) who chooses whether to take a package license, as recognized by the *K–91* opinion.[97] BMI criticized the Second Circuit for applying the per se rule "even though it found blanket licensing not inherently bad." It, too, argued that joint sales agencies have been tested under the rule of reason; it stressed the benefits of blanket licenses—as noted by *K–91*.[98]

The Solicitor General's brief took a different, much more theoretical approach, asking when per se rules were appropriate. A heading answered: "An Arrangement is Unlawful Per Se Only If It Is Part Of A Class Of Arrangements That Is Demonstrably Anticompetitive." The contrasting example, the SG suggested, was the partnership agreement that Judge Taft in *Addyston Pipe* explained should be judged by the rule of reason. (As noted above, Robert Bork's brief for Aaron Copland et al. also emphasized the partnership analogy.) The brief's analysis is captured by a heading and its two subheadings:

> B. Performing Rights Societies Are Not "naked Restrains," and So A Detailed Inquiry Into Their Competitive Consequences Is Necessary....
>
> 1. The blanket license is a unique product....
>
> 2. Blanket copyright licensing saves the costs of transacting for individual copyrights and of enforcing the owner's rights.[99]

The brief sought to reconcile the government's *K–91* brief, which it interpreted as calling for rule of reason treatment (not a "market necessity" exception).[100] Finally, it cautioned that ASCAP and BMI might

---

Note, CBS v. ASCAP: *Performing Rights Societies and the Per Se Rule*, 87 YALE L.J. 783, 797 (1978). Among the member of the Harvard Law Review for volume 91 was future Chief Justice John G. Roberts, Jr. 91 HARV. L. REV. 69 (1977).

[97] Brief for Petitioners (ASCAP), *CBS v. ASCAP*.

[98] Brief for Petitioners Broadcast Music, Inc., et al., *BMI v. CBS*. The BMI brief also criticized the Second Circuit for glossing over the differences between ASCAP and BMI.

[99] Brief for the United States as Amicus Curiae, *CBS v. ASCAP*, at 16–20. AAG Shenefield has said that the brief "was one of the things that happened during my time of which I was proudest." E-mail from John Shenefield, formerly Assistant Attorney General, to Stephen Calkins (Dec. 12, 2006) (on file with author).

[100] Brief for the United States as Amicus Curiae, *CBS v. ASCAP*, at 21 n.18.

well flunk review under the rule of reason, which deserved attention if the issue had not been waived.

CBS filed much too long of a brief—nine separate headings spread over 176 pages. As one Justice griped during the argument, "I hate to continue the intermission, but sometimes the theory has trouble filtering through a very, very long brief."[101] CBS lead by arguing that ASCAP and BMI were fixing prices, and the consent decrees did not change this, nor did CBS's failure ever to ask for individual licenses. CBS's second heading addressed the arguments of the SG and Aaron Copland, largely by arguing that the claimed benefits of blanket licenses were overstated. CBS interpreted the famous *K–91* brief as endorsing a per se rule with a "market necessity" exception, rather than full rule of reason treatment.[102] For competitive harm, CBS pointed to the likelihood that a blanket music will result in excessive use of copyrighted music (because there is no incremental cost), both absolutely and in preference to the commissioning of new compositions. The brief ended by defending the court of appeals's per-use license even though it was "not our preferred alternative."[103]

At least some Justices were baffled by the court of appeals's position, the oral argument revealed. Mr. Hruska was asked for his understanding of "the theory of the Court of Appeals . . . in indicating that the only thing that is wrong with this arrangement is that licensing is not on a per-use basis?"[104] When Hruska responded to further questions by stating that he endorsed and supported the Second Circuit's call for per-use licensing while still preferring broader relief, Justice White (the

---

[101] Transcript, *supra* note 11, at 45.

[102] CBS pointed to a DOJ amicus brief filed subsequent to *K–91*, in which the government supported NBC's demand that ASCAP offer it a license of only part of ASCAP's repertory. Brief for Respondent at 16–17 (quoting from Brief for Plaintiff, United States v. ASCAP, Dkt. 71–1487 (2d Cir. brief filed July 1971)). The 1971 DOJ amicus was attached as an appendix to Brief of NBC, Amicus Curiae, *CBS v. ASCAP*, at 4 (complaining that the 1978 DOJ brief before the Supreme Court "is in sharp conflict with the position it took in 1971"). The 1971 brief explained that *K–91* was supportable only on grounds of practical necessity, and since NBC wanted to start licensing directly that justification was gone and ASCAP's refusal to cooperate was "a per se antitrust violation." 1971 Brief at 15. (NBC took a new ASCAP license and withdrew its appeal, and the case was never judicially resolved.) The AAG on the 1971 brief was the very pro-enforcement Richard W. McLaren.

Although the point was never developed at oral argument, CBS, foreshadowing discussions of the "quick look" and truncated analysis, suggested that antitrust could adopt a variety of formulations for this kind of situation: absolute per se illegality; per se illegality unless the defendant pleads and proves market-functioning necessity; rule of reason limited to a defendant-pled claim of necessity; full rule-of-reason triggered by a plea of market necessity, etc. Brief for Respondent, *CBS v. ASCAP*, at 105–06.

[103] Brief for Respondents, *BMI v. ASCAP*, at 171.

[104] Transcript, *supra* note 11, at 58.

author of the Court's subsequent opinion) responded sharply: "I don't know how you can have it both ways. Right now there is a remand to the District Court under which a per-use licensing . . . would be tried out, and under your theory it shouldn't be tried at all."[105]

Earlier in the argument Hruska was pressed on another key issue: "But in this case the government particularly stresses the point that ASCAP sells a product that no one composer could sell, namely the blanket license, and that the blanket license has independent economic utility. How do you respond to that?"[106] Hruska argued that the benefits were neither "appreciable" nor "significant"[107]—but the Court was not persuaded. Nor did the Court seem persuaded to disagree with the assertions of Kearse and Easterbrook that copyright holders would "line up at CBS' door" if CBS but asked for individual licenses.[108]

IV. THE OPINION

No one listening to the oral argument could have been surprised that CBS lost; and, indeed, the odds were heavily against it once certiorari was granted and the SG decided to side with petitioners, given that CBS had lost so sweepingly at trial and the court of appeals had approved of the fact-finding and exhibited its uneasiness in that odd discussion of remedy. And lose CBS did: the Court unanimously agreed that the Second Circuit was wrong to condemn the blanket license as per se illegal. Justice White's opinion for the Court was joined by Chief Justice Burger and Justices Brennan, Steward, Marshall, Blackmun, Powell, and Rehnquist.[109]

Although the outcome may have been foreordained, the extraordinary role played by amici might well have stimulated the Court to write a different kind of opinion. That opinion commences its analysis by announcing that "easy labels do not always supply ready answers."[110] CBS argued that ASCAP was literally engaged in price fixing, but "[l]iteralness is overly simplistic and often overbroad. When two partners set the price of their goods or services they are literally 'price

---

[105] Transcript, *supra* note 11, at 60.

[106] Transcript, *supra* note 11, at 53.

[107] Transcript, *supra* note 11, at 54.

[108] Transcript, *supra* note 11, at 20 (Kearse); *see also id.* at 32 (Easterbrook).

[109] Justice Stevens dissented, arguing that the Court should have applied the rule of reason and found a violation because the blanket license reflected an agreement that limited price competition when there is no reason why, absent that license, a competitive market would not develop.

[110] 441 U.S. at 8.

fixing,' but they are not per se *in violation of the Sherman Act.*"[111] Citing *Addyston Pipe*—a case that been cited only by amici—for this, the Court concluded its opening by announcing that "it is necessary to characterize the challenged conduct as falling within or without that category of behavior to which we apply the label *'per se* price fixing.'"[112] In short, "price fixing" is a label to be applied after some analysis, rather than a label that avoids the necessity of analysis.

The test for whether to apply the per se rule, Justice White wrote for the Court, is "whether the practice facially appears to be one that would always or almost always tend to restrict competition and decrease output, and in what portion of the market, or instead one designed to 'increase economic efficiency and render markets more, rather than less, competitive.'"[113] Apparently no brief suggested this formulation, which has come to be quoted in case after subsequent antitrust case.[114] In applying the test, the Court reviewed the two factors highlighted by the SG (the "substantial lowering of costs" and the fact that "the whole is truly greater than the sum of its parts: it is, to some extent, a different product"[115]). The Court also wrote that "the substantial restraints placed on ASCAP and its members by the consent decree must not be ignored," and, because there was no impediment to individual licenses, CBS "had a real choice."[116] The Court reversed the finding of per se illegality and remanded for application of the rule of reason, assuming that issue had been preserved.

V. AFTERWARD

On remand, ASCAP and BMI promptly moved for summary judgment on grounds that CBS had not argued for illegality under the rule of reason. A panel consisting of Judges Moore, Gurfein, and Lumbard (replacing Judge Anderson, deceased), denied the request, issued a scheduling order, and asked the United States to remain active in the case.[117] Oral argument was held four and a half months later, and five

---

[111] 441 U.S. at 9.

[112] 441 U.S. at 9.

[113] 441 U.S. at 19–20 (quoting United States v. United States Gypsum Co., 438 U.S. 422, 441 n.16 (1978), where the sentence begins, "The exchange of price data and other information among competitors does not invariably have anticompetitive effects; indeed such practices can in certain circumstances increase economic efficiency....").

[114] No version of these words can be found in the score of briefs in the WESTLAW database.

[115] 441 U.S. at 21–22.

[116] 441 U.S. at 24.

[117] CBS v. ASCAP, 607 F.2d 543 (2d Cir.1979).

months thereafter a panel consisting of Judges Moore, Lumbard, and Newman (replacing Judge Gurfein, who died after the oral argument), affirmed Judge Lasker's decision and ordered the complaint dismissed.[118] The court, in an opinion by Judge Newman, found that there was no restraint of trade because Judge Lasker had properly found "that CBS can feasibly obtain individual licenses from competing copyright owners and that it incurs no risk in endeavoring to do so" because were it to seek individual licenses and fail, the DOJ consent decree would permit it instantly to have resorted to the blanket license with the fee being determined retroactively, if necessary, by the court.[119]

Perhaps unfortunately, that is not the end of the story. Subsequent courts have issued 53 opinions applying, enforcing, or modifying the ASCAP consent decree, and litigation is continuing.[120] Most important, DOJ and ASCAP agreed to a second amended final judgment, which was entered in 2001.[121] In connection therewith, DOJ filed lengthy memoranda in support of the judgment and in response to public comments.[122]

One senses from those documents government frustration that the market is not functioning better after more than 60 years of government regulation. For instance, DOJ complains that "notwithstanding the AFJ's [1950 amended final judgment's] requirement that ASCAP offer broadcasters a genuine economic choice between the per-program and blanket license, ASCAP has resisted offering a reasonable per-program license, forcing users desiring such a license to engage in protracted litigation, and often successfully dissuading users from attempting to take advantage of competitive alternatives to the blanket license."[123] Although DOJ appears to take comfort in the decline of ASCAP to a 45–55% market share (BMI has a comparable share, and SESAC, Inc., the third performing rights organization ("PRO"), founded in 1930, has less than 5%),[124] there is no suggestion that the long-promised individual

---

[118] CBS v. ASCAP, 620 F.2d 930 (2d Cir.1980).

[119] 620 F.2d at 938; *see also* Buffalo Broadcasting Co. v. ASCAP, 744 F.2d 917 (2d Cir. 1984) (upholding blanket license to local television stations).

[120] LEXIS shepardizing, December 19, 2006.

[121] United States v. ASCAP, 2001–2 TRADE CAS. (CCH) ¶ 73,474 (S.D.N.Y. 2001).

[122] Memorandum of the United States in Support of the Joint Motion to Enter Second Amended Final Judgment, United States v. ASCAP, Civ. No. 41–1395 (S.D.N.Y. filed Sept. 4, 2000); Memorandum of the United States in Response to Public Comments on the Joint Motion to Enter Second Amended Final Judgment, United States v. ASCAP, Civ. No. 41–1395 (S.D.N.Y. Mar. 16, 2001).

[123] Memorandum in Support, *supra* note 122, at 28.

[124] Memorandum in Support, *supra* note 122, at 6–7; *see About Us,* at http://www.sesac.com/aboutsesac/about.aspx (last visited December 20, 2006).

licenses have started to be issued in meaningful numbers. Instead, the newly-amended order seeks to increase competition by making per-program and per-segment licenses viable alternatives to the blanket license—by ensuring "that a substantial number of users within a similarly situated group will have an opportunity to substitute enough of their music licensing needs away from ASCAP to provide some competitive constraint on ASCAP's ability to exercise market power with respect to that group's license fees."[125]

The constraints under which DOJ was operating are evidenced by its confession, in the response to public comments, that DOJ and ASCAP "could not reach agreement" either on requiring "alternative licensing arrangements" or on "the scope of the Court's discretion to order" such arrangements.[126] Somewhat poignantly, DOJ repeats the hope it first expressed in 1960,[127] later to be echoed by the Supreme Court,[128] that technology may solve the ASCAP problem: "Eventually, as it becomes less and less costly to identify and report performances of compositions and to obtain licenses for individual works or collections of works, these technologies may erode many of the justifications for collective licensing of performance rights by PROs."[129]

VI. AN APPRECIATION

BMI came at an important time in the Court's antitrust history. The Warren Court had been replaced by the Burger Court: Between 1969 and 1975, Chief Justice Warren and Justices Black, Douglas, Fortas, and Harlan had been replaced by Chief Justice Burger and Justices Powell, Stevens, Blackmun and Rehnquist. *General Dynamics* had proven that the Government now *could* lose a merger case,[130] and *GTE Sylvania* had

---

[125] Memorandum in Support, *supra* note 122, at 32.

[126] Memorandum in Response, *supra* note 122, at 22 & n.20 (noting disagreement about a pending appeal later lost by ASCAP-supported BMI, United States v. BMI, 275 F.3d 168 (2d Cir. 2001) (listing John Shenefield, formerly the AAG who co-authored the SG amicus in *BMI v. CBS*, as counsel for ASCAP)).

[127] *See supra* text at note 69.

[128] *BMI*, 441 U.S. at 21 n.34 ("And of course changes brought about by new technology or new marketing techniques might also undercut the justification for the practice.").

[129] Memorandum in Support, *supra* note 122, at 9 n.10 ("The Department is continuing to investigate the extent to which the growth of these technologies warrants additional changes to the antitrust decrees against ASCAP and BMI, including the possibility that the PROs should be prohibited from collectively licensing certain types of users or performances."). For an argument that even today, the legitimate efficiencies could be achieved by less restrictive means, see Ariel Katz, *The Potential Demise of Another Natural Monopoly: Rethinking the Collective Administration of Performing Rights*, 1 J. Comp. L. & Econ. 541 (2005).

[130] United States v. General Dynamics Corp., 415 U.S. 486 (1974).

brought a new emphasis on economics to antitrust jurisprudence[131] and
Justice Stevens's opinion for the Court in *Professional Engineers* had
focused courts' attention on the limited kinds of procompetitive justifications that would be countenanced.[132] The *BMI* opinion commanded lower
courts to think before applying per se rules, and that directive has been
critically important to modern antitrust.

BMI's influence can be seen partly in the frequency with which it is
invoked. More than 550 cases, 15 by the Supreme Court, have cited it.
More than 125 cases have quoted the famous "facially appears to be one
that would always or almost always tend to restrict competition" wording.

More important, the opinion has been at the center of one of
antitrust's great debates, on the role and place of per se rules and the
rule of reason.[133] A year after the opinion was issued, the Court in
Catalano, Inc. v. Target Sales, Inc.[134] reminded the antitrust world that
per se rules still had a role to play. Two years later, *BMI* was at the
center of the dispute within a badly divided court in *Arizona v. Maricopa
Medical Soc'y*.[135] Thereafter, the *BMI* touchstone language was quoted
and applied in the pivotal *NCAA* case[136] and the important *Northwest
Wholesale* decision.[137] The District of Columbia Circuit devoted extensive
attention to it—explaining that *BMI* along with *NCAA* and *Northwest
Wholesale* had "reformed the law of horizontal restraints"—in its important opinion declining to apply the per se rule in *Rothery Storage*.[138] (The
author of the opinion was the former advocate Robert Bork.) *BMI* was
also at the center of the Seventh Circuit's important opinions in *Polk
Brothers*[139]—by Judge and former advocate Frank Easterbrook—and
General Leaseways.[140]

---

[131] Continental T.V., Inc. v. GTE Sylvania, Inc., 433 U.S. 36 (1977).

[132] National Society of Professional Engineers v. United States, 435 U.S. 679 (1978).

[133] *See* Stephen Calkins, *Perspectives on State and Federal Antitrust Enforcement*, 53
Duke L.J. 673, 703–25 (2003) (setting out the "story of the search for a middle category of
antitrust analysis," in which *BMI* is the "most important decision").

[134] 446 U.S. 643 (1980) (per curiam).

[135] 457 U.S. 332 (1982).

[136] NCAA v. Board of Regents, 468 U.S. 85, 100 & 103 (1984).

[137] Northwest Wholesale Stationers, Inc. v. Pacific Stationery & Printing Co., 472 U.S.
284, 290 (1985).

[138] Rothery Storage and Van Co. v. Atlas Van Lines, Inc., 792 F.2d 210, 225 (D.C. Cir.
1986) (restraints ancillary to joint venture judged under rule of reason).

[139] Polk Bros. v. Forest City Enters., Inc., 776 F.2d 185 (7th Cir. 1985) (covenant not to
compete between two parties to a new venture judged by rule of reason).

[140] Gen. Leaseways, Inc. v. Nat'l Truck Leasing Ass'n, 744 F.2d 588 (7th Cir. 1984)
(Posner, J.) (market division per se where not ancillary to efficiency-creating integration);

Of course, *BMI* can serve as a cornerstone of a great debate only because it failed to resolve the issue, itself. The Court set out what has become the classic test for choosing between the per se rule and the rule of reason, but in choosing the latter it pointed to two factors, cost-savings and the reality that the blanket license "is, to some extent, a different product,"[141] without making clear whether both were essential to the decision. The Court muddied the waters further five years later when, in *NCAA v. Board of Regents*,[142] it wrote that "there is often no bright line separating per se from Rule of Reason analysis."[143] It reprised this theme again in *California Dental Association v. FTC* when it quoted Professor Areeda's observation that " '[t]here is always something of a sliding scale in appraising reasonableness....' "[144] Lower courts have struggled to identify some middle category of analysis most commonly referred to as a "quick look," while the FTC has refined this notion by attempting to identify "inherently suspect" activity.[145] It is critical that antitrust be able, in appropriate cases, to condemn behavior without proof of the full-blown rule of reason (what I have termed "the Full Monty"[146]), while also giving appropriate attention to legitimate justifications, but accomplishing this remains a work in progress. So long as per se rules remain important to antitrust, i.e., unless some kind of "sliding scale" becomes accepted and fully operational, courts are likely to pay continued attention to *BMI,* a case that may have begun precipitously (as Judge Lasker thought), but that has made a lasting impact, thanks in part to the noteworthy roles played by participating amici both in *BMI* and earlier in *K–91, Inc. v. Gershwin Publishing Corp.*

---

see also Wallace v. IBM, 467 F.3d 1104, 1107 (7th Cir. 2006) (Easterbrook, J.) (The Free Software Foundation's GNU General Public License "does not restraint trade. It is a cooperative agreement that facilitates production of new derivative works, and agreements that yield new products that would not arise through unilateral action are lawful. See, e.g., Broadcast Music, Inc.....").

[141] 441 U.S. at 21–22.

[142] 468 U.S. 85 (1984).

[143] 468 U.S. at 104 n.26.

[144] 526 U.S. at 780.

[145] *See, e.g.,* Polygram Holding, Inc. v. FTC, 416 F.3d 29 (D.C. Cir. 2005).

[146] Calkins *Full Monty, supra* note 42.

8

George L. Priest and Jonathan Lewinsohn[*]

Aspen Skiing: Product Differentiation and Thwarting Free Riding as Monopolization

The Supreme Court's 1985 *Aspen Skiing* case,[1] with perhaps *Alcoa* as an exception, represents the high-water mark of Supreme Court Sherman Act Section 2 jurisprudence. In *Aspen Skiing*, the Court transformed *Alcoa's* principle of general antagonism to monopolization into antagonism to specific practices: *Aspen Skiing* held that a legitimate monopolist[2] may not engage in practices that harm competitors—more precisely, may not change practices in ways that harm competitors, thus endorsing a form of status quo legitimization of practices—unless the monopolist can present good efficiency reasons for doing so.

[*] John M. Olin Professor of Law and Economics, Yale Law School; Law Clerk to the Honorable Richard A. Posner, 7th Circuit Court of Appeals; respectively. The authors wish to thank many who agreed to be interviewed for this paper: D.R.C. "Darcy" Brown, former President, Aspen Skiing; Dave Danforth, Owner, Publisher, Reporter, Aspen Daily News; Arthur Boots Ferguson, Jr., Holland & Hart, Denver (attorney for Ski Co.); Steve Marolt, former business associate of Whip Jones, founder of Aspen Highlands; William Maywhort, Holland & Hart, Denver (attorney for Ski Co.); Sue Smestad, former Secretary, Ski. Co.; Bill Stirling, former Mayor, Aspen; Tucker Trautman, Dorsey & Whitney, LLP, (attorney for Highlands); Anonymous Family Member of Whip Jones; Anonymous former Highlands lift operator. The authors are also grateful to the Program for Studies in Capitalism, Yale Law School, for support.

[1] *Aspen Skiing Co. v. Aspen Highlands Skiing Corp.*, 472 U.S. 585, 105 S.Ct. 2847, 86 L.Ed.2d 467 (1985) (hereinafter *"Aspen Skiing"*). The Court of Appeals' opinion in the case will be separately referenced.

[2] Whether the Aspen Skiing Co. actually possessed a monopoly and, if so, its legitimacy will be discussed, *infra* TAN n. 38.

More precisely, the Court held in *Aspen Skiing* that a monopolist—the Aspen Skiing Company ("Ski Company"[3]) which owned three of the four mountain ski areas in Aspen—violated Section 2 of the Sherman Act when it refused to continue offering a joint four-mountain ski ticket with its smaller rival, Aspen Highlands. The decision implicates the obligation of monopolists to deal with competitors including in the context of so-called "essential facilities". One ground of the Court of Appeals' affirmation of the jury's verdict against the Ski Company was based upon the "essential facilities doctrine." The Supreme Court, however, avoided ruling on the issue, and the jurisprudence concerning "essential facilities" remains undetermined today. In *Aspen Skiing*, the Court, on purported economic efficiency grounds, found a case where a monopolist's refusal to deal with a competitor could generate antitrust liability.

As shall be explained, the case is important historically: It stands at the mid-point of the Supreme Court's shift from the populist interpretation of the antitrust laws of the 1950s and 1960s[4] to the economic efficiency—consumer welfare—interpretation that has dominated since. *GTE–Sylvania* and *Pueblo Bowl–O–Mat* were decided in 1977; *BMI*, *NCAA* and *Monsanto v. Spray–Rite* in 1984; *Aspen Skiing* in 1985; *Matsushita* in 1986; and *Sharp Electronics* in 1988. *Aspen Skiing* should be viewed as a transition case. Though not generally appreciated, the case represents an attempt by the Court to redefine the standards for the analysis of monopolistic practices under Section 2 along the lines of the new economic approach to antitrust jurisprudence where the dominant value is effect on consumer welfare.

The Court's fledgling application of economics, however, was not well worked out and cannot generally be defended, in part because of the peculiar factual context that faced the Court given the legal strategy that the Ski Company pursued; in part because the Court misinterpreted sections of Robert H. Bork's The Antitrust Paradox on which it relied as support for its analysis. During its next term, the Court would apply economic analysis again in a Section 2 action, in *Matsushita*, with far greater success, vastly constraining the availability of complaints claiming predatory pricing. And the economic analysis of the Court has

---

[3] At the time of the underlying lawsuit, the Aspen Skiing Corporation owned Ajax and two wholly-owned subsidiaries, Buttermilk Mountain Skiing Corporation and Snowmass Skiing Corporation. While the case was pending before the Circuit Court of Appeals, the three mountains were reorganized into a partnership, the Aspen Skiing Company. The reason for the reorganization is not clear; perhaps to avoid the appearance of conspiracy among three competitors against a fourth, though this was never an issue in the litigation. For convenience, we treat the Ski Company as having existed throughout.

[4] To be generous: the Court's antitrust interpretations during those years were not entirely consistent with a coherent populist theory.

continued to advance in succeeding years. *Aspen Skiing* is the weakest of the Supreme Court's opinions since *GTE–Sylvania* in which the Court has adopted and applied the consumer welfare standard.

Because the case dealt with alleged monopolistic refusals to deal, and not with predatory pricing eclipsed by *Matsushita* and *Brooke Group, Aspen Skiing* survives as a precedent, though survives thinly. In the Court's most recent Section 2 practice case, *Verizon v. Trinko,* Justice Scalia, writing for the Court (how enthusiastically the Court shares his views is another question), pronounced that *Aspen Skiing* stood "at or near the outer boundary of § 2 liability."[5] As we shall see, it is an unusual boundary; more so when the underlying facts of the case are understood.

Skiing in Aspen: The History

Aspen, Colorado today (2007) is one of the swishiest of destination skiing locations[6] in the world. Each year, millions of skiers fly in, ski, and partake of wonderful restaurants and cultural events. Of Aspen residents, some—the extremely wealthy—have homes in town or nearby. Others—including the staff, most of whom are also skiers—live as closely as they can; most in somewhat adjacent rural areas. The trial in *Aspen Skiing* was affected by these class differences.

Apparently, the first (Anglo) settlers of what would become Aspen arrived in 1879, thirty years after the California gold rush; twenty years after the first (much smaller) Colorado gold rush; but equally intent on mining.[7] Aspen was founded next to the Roaring Fork River which facilitates mining by washing away mining detritus and gives life to the town by access to water. Silver was discovered nearby and by 1892, Aspen had become the third largest city in the State, claiming the nation's richest silver mine, producing in 2005 dollars, $185 million per year. To give a picture of the town at the time, it had ten churches, two railroads (according to the historical record, but difficult to believe for a city in a mountain valley), street cars, an opera house and electric street lights (again, abnormally early). Residents described Aspen as "the most wonderful silver mining camp in the world."[8]

---

[5] *Verizon Commun. v. Law Off. of Curtis Trinko,* 540 U.S. 398, 409 (2004).

[6] A "destination skiing location" is one at which the predominant set of skiers lives elsewhere: in the case of Aspen and other Colorado ski areas, flying in from around the country and the world to ski at the destination for a constrained period of time. This fact was—or, as will be explained, should have been—important for the market definition issues in the case.

[7] Diane Tegmeyer, *The Aspen Book: A Complete Guide* at 7 (1992).

[8] *Id.* at p. 10.

Aspen's economy was based on silver but after the 1893 repeal of the Sherman Silver Purchase Act,[9] silver prices plummeted, and Aspen's economy was devastated. By 1929, Aspen's population had dwindled to 350.[10] Aspen was nearly a ghost town.

The modern history of Aspen begins in World War II, when the Army's 10th Mountain Division trained there in preparation for ski-warfare to reoccupy Scandinavia. One of these soldiers was an Austrian, Friedl Pfeiffer, who saw the skiing potential of the area. Pfeiffer later met a Chicago industrialist, Walter Paepcke, who had also identified the unique characteristics of Aspen, but was more interested in cultural events. Paepcke, along with his brother-in-law Paul Nitze,[11] provided Pfeiffer with funds to start the Aspen Skiing Corporation which inaugurated the first chair-lift on Aspen Mountain, later called Ajax, in 1946. From the start, Pfeiffer saw the market for Aspen skiing as beyond local. To attract attention to Aspen as a ski location, Pfeiffer convinced the U.S. World Alpine Championships to be held there in 1949. To develop a cultural reputation, Pfeiffer arranged for the University of Chicago to hold a Goethe Bicentennial in Aspen in 1950.[12]

Pfeiffer, Paepcke and Nitze formulated the concept of Aspen as a destination-area ski resort. An important early partner, however, was D.R.C. "Darcy" Brown, a local rancher, whose family owned mining leases at the base of the mountain, an obstacle to development. Brown traded the leases for shares of the Ski Company and a position on the board of directors. Brown was a considerable person; he later served in the Colorado Senate and on the Federal Reserve Board. As the only Ski Company board member living in the area, he accepted a position as executive vice president and shortly after became president in 1957 or 1958,[13] a position he held for 25 years.

---

[9] The Sherman Silver Purchase Act, enacted in 1890 (the same year as the Sherman Anti-trust Act), required the U.S. government to purchase 4.5 million ounces of silver per month to support the national currency. This was a populist act, seeking to increase the money supply to reduce the effective costs of fixed debt. The Act, however, provided that government notes to purchase the silver could be redeemed in either silver or gold. Because of the disparity between gold and silver prices—and because of differential volatility in those commodities—many converted silver holdings into gold, depleting the government's gold reserves—an illustration of Say's law. After the financial panic of 1893, the Purchase Act was repealed to prevent depletion of the nation's gold reserves.

[10] Tegmeyer, *supra* n. 7, at 9.

[11] Nitze was an important Cold War diplomat.

[12] The Goethe Bicentennial sought to attract to Aspen "[t]he leading scholars, humanitarians and musicians of the world". *See* Henrietta W. Hay, To Meet Albert Schweitzer . . . , Grand Junction (CO) Daily Sent., Feb. 4, 1991.

[13] There is some confusion as to whether Brown became President in 1957 or 1958. *See* Scott Condon, DRC Brown: More Than a Company Man, Aspen Times, Aug. 26, 2004, at

During his tenure, Brown expanded the Company by acquiring and developing other mountains in Aspen as well as other destination ski resorts: in Colorado—Breckenridge, in nearby Summit County; in British Columbia—Blackcomb, near Whistler; in Alberta—Fortress Mountain; and in Spain—Bacquiera–Beret.[14] Under Brown, skiing in Aspen increased dramatically, "going from 259,000 skier visits during winter 1964–65 to 1.23 million in 1978–79."[15] Brown was the driving force behind the Ski Company's actions in the case.

Brown is described by former associates as having run the Ski Company with the same hard-nosed, no-nonsense attitude that he had developed as a rancher.[16] As he saw it, ski areas were in the "uphill transportation business"[17]—by which he meant that his focus was ski lift efficiency—leaving no place for "public relations measures like snow hostesses, base area picnics, [or] a childrens' ski school."[18] Brown saw his market as national and international and had little patience for nurturing relationships with the community. Brown believed that the Ski Company needed to market Aspen as a vacation alternative to Sun Valley, Utah, Switzerland and, later, Vail and Steamboat Springs in Colorado. Thus, he catered services to visiting tourists, often at the expense of the locals. For example, under Brown, the Ski Company's season passes—of interest only to locals, not to one-week visitors—were priced considerably higher than those of its local competitor, Highlands, and included limits on the days that locals could ski.[19] There were serious tensions between the Ski Company and the townspeople,[20] and in

A11(hereafter Condon) and John Sabella, The Mountain Moguls, Aspen Times, Dec. 8, 1977 at 1–B, 2–B (hereafter Sabella). Brown, at the time of our interview, age 93, cannot remember. Interview Jonathan Lewinsohn with D.R.C. Brown, Jan. 20, 2004 (hereafter Brown Interview).

[14] Sabella, *supra* n. 13, at 1–B.

[15] Condon, *supra* n. 13. Other evidence shows 1.4 million skiers in 1978–79, Joint Appendix, *Aspen Skiing Co. v. Aspen Highlands Skiing Co.*, 472 U.S. 585 (1985) (hereafter JA) (Plaintiff's Ex. 97).

[16] Interview Lewinsohn with Sue Smedstad, Former Secretary, Aspen Ski Co., Jan. 20, 2004 (hereafter Smedstad Interview).

[17] Interview Lewinsohn with Bill Stirling, former Mayor of Aspen, Jan. 21, 2005 (hereafter Stirling Interview).

[18] Smedstad Interview, *supra* n. 16. As we shall see, these are aspersions on the Highlands business model.

[19] In a 1977 interview, Brown explained, "The only thing that keeps this town going is the visitors, and we had a great number of complaints about the way visitors were being treated on Aspen Mountain. The Mountain was being overused by a relatively small segment of the public that was paying a very cheap price for it." Sabella, *supra* n. 13.

[20] In 1972, a group of young activists led by Michael Kinsley (now a prominent journalist, former Editor of the New Republic and, currently, American editor of Guardian

1972 a Colorado U.S. Senator held hearings over the Ski Company's pricing practices.[21]

The second ski area to be developed in Aspen, Aspen Highlands, the plaintiff in the underlying antitrust action against the Ski Company, was founded in 1957. The U.S. Forest Service[22] had concluded that Ajax "was getting crowded, and ... that a ski area ought to be started at Highlands."[23] The owner of a local Aspen lodge, Whipple "Whip" Van Ness Jones, Jr., took the lead. In 1956, he approached the Ski Company with a proposal for joint development, but was turned down. At trial, he testified that the Ski Company president (Darcy Brown's predecessor) had told him, "We've got plenty of problems at Aspen now, and we don't think we want to expand skiing at Aspen."[24]

Jones had started his career as an investment banker in St. Louis and later was a member of the New York Stock Exchange. He first visited Aspen for the 1950 Goethe Bicentennial, and dropped out of investing the same year, returning to Aspen, in his words, as a "ski bum". Prior to Highlands, he had built and managed the popular local Smugglers Lodge.[25] Jones used money received in the settlement of his first divorce to build Highlands.[26]

Jones had a different vision for Highlands than the Ski Company had for Ajax. Jones wanted Highlands to be Aspen's "affordable, laid back" alternative.[27] Jones hired Norwegian Olympic champion Stein Erickson to design the mountain and to run its ski school. Erickson built a jump at the base of the mountain which he used to delight crowds with skiing acrobatics. Highlands emphasized low prices over capital improvements and became a favorite of the locals. Erickson left for Utah in the mid–1960s. To replace him, Jones hired a Swiss instructor, Fred Iselin, who introduced the then-controversial Gradual Length Method (GLM)

Unlimited), Stacy Standley and Herb Klein, organized protests over the Ski Company's price discrimination against locals. *See* Condon, *supra* n. 13; Stirling Interview, *supra* n. 17; *see generally*, "Host Discount Pass Available at Ski Corp.," Aspen Times, Nov. 2, 1978 at 22–C.

[21] *See* Defendant's Answer to Amended Complaint, Aspen Highlands Skiing Corp. v. Aspen Skiing Corp. (D. CO. 1981).

[22] All of Aspen's ski areas include Forest Service land. Thus, a Forest Service permit is a prerequisite to building, and requires annual renewal.

[23] *Aspen Skiing* at p. 2850, n.3.

[24] *Id.*; JA, *supra* n. 15, at 19.

[25] Sabella, *supra* n. 13.

[26] Interview, Lewinsohn with family member of Whip Jones, Jan. 21, 2005 (individual asked to remain anonymous) (hereafter Family Interview).

[27] "Whip Jones. Builder of Aspen Highlands Dies," Aspen Daily News, June 30, 2001.

for teaching skiing in which beginners start on short skis before gradually moving up to standard equipment. Over the years, GLM became the preferred teaching method, and the Highlands Ski School became a regional draw. Jones used the Ski School along with acrobatic exhibitions and events such as wine and cheese parties to attract skiers to Highlands.[28]

The third ski area in Aspen, Buttermilk, was opened in 1958 by one of the original Ski Company founders, Friedl Pfeiffer, and another Ski Company director, Art Pfister. As directors, they had attempted to convince the Ski Company to open a ski school for beginning and intermediate skiers because Ajax Mountain is notoriously steep, even at the bottom. Pfister testified that, "our President at the time [Darcy Brown's predecessor] wasn't very enthusiastic about skiing, and we weren't making any money. So Friedl and I went ahead with the project", building the area on adjacent ranches that they owned. They operated the area modestly for three years and in the fourth, "finally got a Forest Service permit to go all the way up to the top." The two disagreed about the location of the upper lift—Pfister testified that it was a violent disagreement—and Pfister ultimately sold out to Pfeiffer.[29] A year later, and after Darcy Brown had become President, the Ski Company bought out Buttermilk and invested heavily in capital improvements, moving lifts and adding new ones over the succeeding years.[30] Not surprisingly given Buttermilk's modest position in 1964, there is no record of any antitrust concern—not a complaint by Highlands nor government inquiry—over the Ski Company's acquisition of Buttermilk.

The fourth ski area in Aspen, Snowmass, was developed in 1967. A former ski racer, William Janss with associates, had acquired ranches in the Snowmass Valley and had obtained ski area permits from the Forest Service. The Janss group, however, was interested in developing real estate at the base of the mountain; they sold the company holding the permits to the Ski Company, which developed the mountain on its own.[31] Snowmass, with its wide mix of beginner and intermediate trails, ultimately became the dominant mountain, capturing over 50 percent of the Aspen ski market.

Thus, by the late–1960s, the Ski Company owned three of the four skiing mountains in Aspen. The Company had acquired these properties by legitimate means: First, it developed Ajax. Second, it acquired Buttermilk, a modest beginners' hill, which it later developed, through substan-

---

[28] Id.

[29] JA, *supra* n. 15, at 139–41.

[30] Id.

[31] *Aspen Skiing* at 2850 n. 5.

tial capital investments, into a serious skiing area. Third, it acquired the Forest Service permit rights to Snowmass and invested heavily to develop it, to great commercial success. The definition of monopolization in *Grinnell* is the "willful acquisition or maintenance of [monopoly] power as distinguished from growth or development as a consequence of a superior product, business acumen, or historic accident."[32] If possession of three of the four mountains in Aspen constituted a monopoly, the Ski Company had obtained it by legitimate means: through growth and development, business acumen, internal investment. There was no merger of competitors to form monopoly here.[33] Indeed, prior to the management of Darcy Brown, the Ski Company had turned down the opportunity to develop Highlands—which could have been developed without antitrust concern and would have consolidated the Ski Company's control over skiing at Aspen. As it happened, a much different character, Whip Jones, developed Highlands according to a radically different business plan.

Marketing Skiing in Aspen

The antitrust issue in the *Aspen Skiing* case derived from the firms' sales distribution practices directed towards destination-area skiers. According to trial testimony, in 1958 Friedl Pfeiffer, one of the founders of the Ski Company and, at the time, co-owner of Buttermilk, arranged a lunch with Brown, recently appointed President of the Ski Company, and Jones, who had founded Highlands the year before, to propose the development of an all-Aspen ski pass.[34] For reasons that are unclear, the concept was not introduced until the 1962–63 skiing season and not as an interchangeable pass, but rather in the form of the sale of a six-day coupon booklet where individual coupons could be redeemed for a day pass at any of the three mountains, with revenues from booklet sales distributed according to the proportion of coupons redeemed at each mountain. This joint marketing arrangement was continued when the Ski Company acquired Buttermilk in 1964, and extended to include Snowmass after its development by the Ski Company in 1968. The

---

[32] *United States v. Grinnell Corp.*, 384 U.S. 563, 570–71, 86 S.Ct. 1698, 1703–04, 16 L.Ed.2d 778 (1966), quoted in *Aspen Skiing*, 108 S.Ct. 2854 n. 19.

[33] By all accounts, at the time of the Ski Company's acquisition in 1964, Buttermilk was not a serious competitor of Ajax; Buttermilk had only one fledgling lift for use by the beginners ski school. As mentioned, the Ski Company invested heavily after the acquisition to develop and expand Buttermilk.

[34] JA, *supra* n. 15, at p. 20 (testimony of Whip Jones). Brown, who still lives in Aspen, has no memory of this lunch. Brown interview, *supra* n. 13. As will be discussed, the Supreme Court took particular note that Pfeiffer got the idea from an all-area ski pass he knew about in his native St. Anton, Austria. *Aspen Skiing* at 2850 n. 7.

booklet sold at a slight discount over the price of daily passes, at least at the Ski Company mountains.[35]

As a booklet of six one-day coupons, the arrangement was obviously designed to be attractive to out-of-town skiers coming to Aspen for a week. The six-day, three-mountain coupon booklet, however, was only one of many pricing devices adopted over the years to promote skiing in the area. The Ski Company, separately, offered two-mountain (Ajax and Buttermilk) and later three-mountain (Ajax, Buttermilk and Snowmass) passes in six-day and three-day packages, sometimes experimenting with four-day and seven-day sets.[36] Indeed, until 1968 with the opening of Snowmass, the Ski Company's own six-day two-mountain (Ajax and Buttermilk) pass outsold the all-Aspen three-mountain pass (that included access to Highlands) two-to-one.[37] Following expansion to include Snowmass, however, the all-Aspen four-mountain booklet began to dramatically outsell the Ski Company's own three-mountain passes, a fact to which the Supreme Court ultimately attributed substantial importance.[38] Throughout this period, the Ski Company also experimented with a variety of multiple-day passes exclusively for its own three mountains: It offered three-day, three-mountain passes for the seven seasons between 1971 and 1978, but not for the three seasons from 1968 through 1971; it offered six-day three-mountain passes in 1968–69, 1969–70, 1972–73 and 1977–78, but not in 1970–71 and 1970–72 or during the four ski seasons from 1973 through 1977.[39] As we shall see, although the Supreme Court was aware of the history of these pricing experiments,[40] it disregarded them in its analysis of the purported efficiency of the all-Aspen pass.

Prior to the 1971–72 season, the Ski Company and Highlands collaborated to form Aspen Reservations, Inc. (ARI) a central advertising and reservation system designed to expand destination-area marketing.[41] With the formation of ARI, the concept of the all-Aspen pass was shifted from the sale of a six-day booklet of interchangeable coupons to the sale of a six-day "around the neck pass" giving access to any of the four

---

[35] *See, infra* TAN 63.

[36] JA, *supra* n. 15, at 154–55.

[37] *Id.* at 24.

[38] *Aspen Skiing* at 2850–51, 2859. Interviews with a number of industry participants have failed to uncover a cogent reason for this phenomenon, although increased marketing by ARI, discussed *infra*, may account for it.

[39] JA, *supra* n. 15 at 154–55 (testimony of Kay Taylor, Ski Company ticketing executive); *see also id.* at 83 (testimony of Peter Sullivan, Ski Company marketing executive).

[40] *Aspen Skiing* at 2850–51.

[41] JA, *supra* n. 15 at 24.

Aspen mountains. The motivation for the around-the-neck pass over the interchangeable coupon was skier convenience. The coupon booklet required a skier to redeem each coupon daily for a pass at a single mountain, often requiring waiting in a substantial line; the around-the-neck pass, in contrast, allowed the skier to go directly to the slopes without the need to stop at the ticket hut, and even to switch mountains during the day if desired. The around-the-neck pass, however, complicated the distribution of revenues as between the Ski Company and Highlands. With the coupon booklet, Highlands received its share of revenues based upon the number of coupons it had redeemed. With the around-the-neck pass, some other method of determining comparative usage had to be derived. The firms agreed to have statistical surveys conducted on specific days.[42] As shall be discussed, this change in practice was only one—but an important one—of the sources of increasing friction between the Ski Company's President, Darcy Brown, and Highlands' owner, Whip Jones, over the period.

As mentioned, Brown pursued a substantially different business model for the Ski Company and its mountains than did Jones for Highlands. Under Brown, the Ski Company was a highly conservative operation, intent on improving skiing quality for the purpose of attracting destination-area skiers. The Ski Company paid no dividends to its shareholders; Brown plowed all earnings into new equipment and maintenance.[43] Brown invested in the latest skiing technology, installing the first high-speed four-seat lift in Colorado and state-of-the-art snowmaking.[44]

Quite to the contrary, Jones minimized capital investments in Highlands. Business associates and family members describe Jones as viewing Highlands as a "cash machine".[45] The then-Mayor of Aspen described Highlands at the time as a "beaten down resort".[46] The owner of the *Aspen Daily News* caricatured Highlands' aging lift equipment as constituting "the only operating ski museum in the world."[47] Highlands'

---

[42] *Id.*

[43] Condon, *supra* n. 13; Brown Interview, *supra* n. 13; Smedstad Interview, *supra* n. 16.

[44] As Brown explained in a 1977 Aspen Times interview: "We have always had a consistent policy of reinvesting all of our cash flow in improvements and expansion . . . and until the board of directors decides otherwise, that policy will continue." Sabella, *supra* n. 13 at 2–B.

[45] Family Interview, *supra* n. 26; Smedstad Interview, *supra* n. 16; Interview, Lewinsohn with Steve Marolt, former business associate of Whip Jones, Jan. 23, 2005 (hereafter Marolt Interview).

[46] Stirling Interview, *supra* n. 17.

[47] Interview, Lewinsohn with Dave Danforth, founder and owner, *Aspen Daily News*, Jan. 20–21, 2004.

employees were given minimal training, and its lifts had no derailment mechanisms even after they had become standard in the late–1970s. When the *Aspen Daily News* ran a story about a chair derailment at Highlands and its subsequent effort to cover-up the incident, the paper was expelled from the mountain; Highlands repaired the specific problem, but did not install new equipment.[48] Buildings at the base of the mountain were literally crumbling, and trails went weeks between groomings.

The Ski Company and Highlands focused on a different base clientele. The Ski Company was almost entirely designed to be attractive to destination-area skiers. Brown developed the Ski Company as a "staid and somber bastion of 'quality' skiing",[49] as mentioned, often at the expense of the interests of locals. Highlands, in contrast, charged lower prices to make itself attractive to locals. With a ski jump at the bottom of the hill, Highlands staged weekly skiing acrobatics, offered mid-summit

[48] Seven chairs derailed. The lift was finally stopped just as the eighth chair—the first with passengers—was crossing the derailment spot. John Sabella, "Lift Problems are Alleged at Highlands", Aspen Times, Aug. 24, 1978 at 3–A; E-mail from Dave Danforth, *supra* n. 47, to Lewinsohn, 9/24/2004 (on file with authors).

[49] John Sabella, "Ski Corp. Adds Coney Island Touch at Area," *Aspen Times*, Aug. 10, 1978 at 26–B.

picnics,[50] NASTAR,[51] and other events, which Ski Company personnel regarded as "gimmicks" and "public relation stunts."[52]

Typically, a firm, like the Ski Company, that invests heavily in capital improvements to enhance the quality of the skiing experience for consumers benefits when its major local competitor, Highlands, fails to match those investments. The joint-ticket, all-Aspen pass, however, complicated that dynamic. Jones saw that Highlands would benefit from the custom of destination-area skiers. There was no need to rely entirely on local business. Thus, he readily joined the ARI national marketing plan, the funding of which was based on relative Ski Company–Highlands' market shares.[53] But for Jones and Highlands, that was largely the end of it. Jones did not invest in national advertising.[54] Jones' advertising expenditures were concentrated in local print and radio, obviously, of no value to enhancing the destination-area market.[55] Indeed, even though Jones participated in the joint ARI venture, years later, Brown continued to complain that it was a struggle to get Jones to pay his portion of the ARI budget.[56] Jones declined to join the National Ski Area Association, explaining to a local ski consultant that "Aspen Skiing Corporation belongs, [so] I don't need to. They take care of the big things, and I take care of my operation."[57]

There were other administrative complications of operating the joint-pass that Jones avoided, shifting costs to the Ski Company. There was testimony at the trial strongly suggesting that, when customers sought refunds relating to the joint-pass, Highlands sent them to the Ski Company, rather than processing them at Highlands. Though at trial Highlands denied having such a policy,[58] records showed that during the 1977–78 season, the final season of the joint-pass prior to the lawsuit, Highlands had processed less than one percent of total refunds for the year: Highlands, $800 (0.72 percent); the Ski Company, $110,000.[59] The

---

[50] JA, *supra* n. 15, at 25 (testimony of Whip Jones).

[51] *Id.* at 26. NASTAR is a popular nationwide program that establishes races and handicaps for amateurs.

[52] Smedstad Interview, *supra* n. 16.

[53] JA, *supra* n. 15 at 35 (testimony of William Comstock, Highlands executive).

[54] Jones admitted that he never advertised nationally. JA, *supra* n. 15 at 32.

[55] *Id.*, at 36–37 (testimony of William Comstock) (When asked, Where does Highlands advertise, he answered, "[O]n the radio, the Aspen Times, and there is a free handout newspaper [in Aspen] called the Aspen Flyer ... [the purpose] is to improve the guest attendance at the Aspen Highlands, and I would refer to it as improve market share.")

[56] Brown interview, *supra* n. 13.

[57] JA, *supra* n. 15, at 177 (testimony of Stacey Standley (one of the 1972 protesters against the Ski Company's price discrimination against locals; *supra* n. 20), at the time broker between Twentieth–Century–Fox and Highlands over a possible acquisition; see n. 107 *infra*).

[58] JA, *supra* n. 15 at 86 (testimony of Valorie Britt, Highlands ticket agent).

[59] *Id.* at 160 (testimony of Kay Taylor, Ski Co. ticketing executive).

all-Aspen four-mountain pass also led some skiers to believe that all four areas were jointly owned, and Ski Company officials often received complaints about the conditions at Highlands. Years later, in a newspaper interview recounting the litigation, Brown described Highlands as a "schlocky operation, with bad food, and poor maintenance", believing that it harmed Aspen's reputation in competition with other destination ski areas.[60]

The relations between the Ski Company—whose President was Darcy Brown—and Highlands—whose owner was Whip Jones—was probably also affected by Jones' personality. Jones' attorneys presented him as a loveable underdog at trial, but in our interviews, both business associates and family members regard Jones, who died in 2001 at age 91, in quite different terms. One former business associate, who claimed to have fond feelings for Jones, also described him as "one of the ugliest human beings possible" and "a horrible person who cared only about the buck."[61] A family member stated that Jones had made his first fortune "by selling custody of his children to their mother" after the children had testified in favor of him at the divorce proceeding.[62]

The most fractious subject of dispute between the firms, however—and the subject that would ultimately lead to the antitrust litigation between them—was the division of revenues from the joint-pass. As mentioned, with the shift from the coupon booklet to the around-the-neck pass, it was necessary to shift the method of determining relative shares of joint-ticket revenues. Jones insisted on distribution based on usage: according to relative percentage of skiers at Highlands versus at the Ski Company mountains. This method initially sounded fair, and the Ski Company agreed to it. Nevertheless, because of the discount included in the six-day pass and the difference in daily ski pass prices as between Highlands and the Ski Company, division by usage benefited Highlands at Ski Company expense. As an illustration, during the 1977–78 season (the final season of the joint pass prior to the lawsuit), the six-day, four-mountain pass sold for $77 which equals upon distribution, $12.83 per day. The Ski Company's single-day price was $13; Highlands' was $12.[63] Thus, at $12.83 per skier, Highlands received more, and the Ski Company, less, than what it would have received by selling single-day passes.

---

[60] Condon, *supra* n. 13.

[61] Marolt Interview, *supra* n. 45. In 1977, Highlands received the maximum fine for threatening not to rehire seasonal employees if they filed for unemployment. "Highlands Fined $4,000 in District Court," Aspen Times, Oct. 27, 1977 at 25–B.

[62] Family Interview, *supra* n. 26.

[63] *See* Brief for the Petitioner/Plaintiff, Aspen Skiing Co. v. Aspen Highlands Skiing Corp., 472 U.S. 585 (1985) at p. 25.

Not only did the Ski Company absorb all of the discount of the six-day pass, a part of what it absorbed went to Highlands.

In Brown's mind, for the Ski Company, this problem was exacerbated by the method of determining relative usage through statistical surveys. Brown complained that the surveys were "highly unreliable", conducted by "scruffy college students",[64] with poor "appearance, deportment, [and] attitude".[65] And there were reasons to believe that Jones cheated on the survey process. Apparently, the surveys were only able to count total skiers, not skiers who had purchased four-mountain, six-day passes. A former Highlands lift operator told us that Jones paid locals to "pack the lines" on days when joint-ticket surveys were being taken.[66] At trial, a Highlands' expert witness admitted that, throughout the early 1970s, the skier visit counts submitted by Highlands in its annual reports to the Forest Service were inconsistent with Highlands' own internal ticket audits.[67] Brown told us that he always believed that the Ski Company lost money on the four-mountain pass.[68]

The two firms continued the four-mountain joint-pass arrangement during the three ski seasons between 1973 and 1976. Two unrelated events, however, would upset the delicate agreement between them. First, in 1975, the Attorney General of Colorado brought a lawsuit against both the Ski Company and Highlands, claiming price-fixing and restraint of trade with respect to their collaboration over the marketing entity, ARI.[69] The two firms entered a consent agreement promising to price individual day-pass tickets prior to meeting to discuss the four-mountain, six-day pass, and agreeing to sell ARI to an independent buyer. The settlement agreement did not prohibit the joint four-mountain pass.

In retrospect, the Colorado Attorney General's action can be seen as largely ineffectual. The two firms' agreement on the price and allocation of revenues of the four-mountain, six-day pass—aimed at destination-area skiers—was inevitable if there was to be a joint-ticket. That agreement implicated the prices the two firms set for single-day passes

---

[64] Brown Interview, *supra* n. 13.

[65] *Aspen Skiing*, 472 U.S. at p. 591.

[66] Interview Lewinsohn with former Highlands lift operator (who requested anonymity), Jan. 21, 2005; *see also*, Bill Rollins, "Highlands Gambles on Four–Area Pass," Aspen Times, Oct. 15, 1981 at 13–B.

[67] JA, *supra* n. 15, at 128 (testimony of Ted Farwell).

[68] Brown interview, *supra* n. 13.

[69] JA, *supra* n. 15 at 27 (testimony of Whip Jones: "The Attorney General felt that because we owned [the four-mountain pass] jointly there was a chance that we might be discussing the pricing of tickets and so forth ...").

to a generally local clientele because of arbitrage. Furthermore, if the Attorney General accepted the utility of the Ski Company–Highlands joint four-mountain, six-day pass aimed at destination-area skiers, insisting on separate ownership of the marketing entity selling such passes provides no economic benefit.

The principal impact of the Attorney General's lawsuit, however, appears to be that it raised the awareness of the Ski Company that it had legal grounds for operating independently of Highlands. Thereafter, the Ski Company appears to have adopted as a working justification for separating itself from Highlands the doctrine set out decades earlier in *Colgate*:

> In the absence of any purpose to create or maintain a monopoly, the [Sherman] act does not restrict the long recognized right of trader or manufacturer engaged in an entirely private business, freely to exercise his own independent discretion as to parties with whom he will deal. And, of course, he may announce in advance the circumstances under which he will refuse to sell.[70]

As we shall see, while the Ski Company focused principally on the second portion of the doctrine—"own independent discretion . . . to announce in advance the circumstances under which he will refuse to sell"—the courts would read the *Colgate* doctrine in its entirety.

The second event that triggered the ultimate dispute was a record low snowfall in Aspen during the 1976–77 ski season. Because of the poor snow conditions, skier visits to Aspen that season fell by almost 60 percent, from 1.24 million in 1975–76 to 529,000 in 1976–77.[71] The decline put substantial financial pressure on the Ski Company's commitment to continued capital investment on its mountains. The lack of snowfall, however, was even more devastating to Highlands because of the way Jones managed the mountain. At trial, Jones explained:

> [W]e have always made a point of opening Aspen Highlands on Thanksgiving Day; and that year our snow was very light, but we opened and we didn't get the snow that we expected to have. We sort of skied out our snow.

> Aspen Mountain didn't open until January 8th that year, and they had a pretty good storm right about that time, and the storm helped them and didn't help us very much; so our percentage went down because of the fact that we opened prior to the time that they did.[72]

---

[70] *United States v. Colgate & Co.*, 250 U.S. 300, 307 (1919).

[71] JA, *supra* n. 15 at 183 (Plaintiff's Exhibit 97).

[72] *Id.* at 27.

As Jones indicates, Highlands' percentage share of skiers plummeted in 1976–77. Between 1973 and 1976, Highlands' share had remained in the 17 percent to 18 percent range;[73] during the 1976–77 season, its share fell to 13.2 percent.[74]

Having suffered a substantial decline in revenues in 1976–77, but still with plans for additional capital improvements both at the Ski Company's three mountains in Aspen and at its other three ski areas, Brown decided for the 1978–79 season to take a tougher position in his negotiations with Jones over the four-mountain pass.[75] First, he insisted on changing the basis for allocating joint revenues, abandoning the surveys that he regarded as unreliable and negotiating a fixed share for Highlands. He initially offered Highlands no more than 13.2 percent of the joint-ticket revenue, its survey share during the "no snow" season of 1976–77. The parties ultimately settled at 15 percent,[76] still lower than Highlands' average share in the preceding years.

For the next year, 1978–79, Brown was even more determined to end the four-mountain pass.[77] After consulting with counsel who advised him based upon *Colgate* that the matter was purely a contract issue— that is, that Brown could set any terms he wanted[78]—Brown offered Highlands no more than a 12.5 percent share of joint revenues. Jones responded variously: he proposed reinstating the coupon booklet which allocated shares based on actual usage; he proposed installing a form of electronic counting; he proposed hiring a disinterested firm "such as Price Waterhouse" to conduct the surveys.[79] Brown rejected all of Jones' counter-offers; not surprisingly, the coupon booklet was inconvenient for skiers; electronic counting was technologically infeasible;[80] and a firm like Price Waterhouse—however independent—could still not deal with

---

[73] Highlands' shares were 17.5% in 1973–74; 18.5% in 1974–75; and 16.8% in 1975–76. *Id*. (testimony of Whip Jones); *Aspen Skiing* at p. 2851.

[74] *Id*.

[75] Brown Interview, *supra* n. 13. Again, Brown believed that the Ski Company lost money on the four-mountain ticket. *See* TAN 68, *supra*. Brown and the Ski Company directors had decided to sell the Ski Company to Twentieth–Century–Fox in 1977. Brown remained as President; there is no indication that Twentieth–Century–Fox executives had any influence over the Ski Company's relationship with Highlands prior to the lawsuit.

[76] *Aspen Skiing* at p. 2852.

[77] Brown Interview, *supra* n. 13.

[78] Interview Lewinsohn with Arthur Boots Ferguson, Holland & Hart, Attorney for Ski Company, Jan. 21, 2005.

[79] JA, *supra* n. 15 at 29.

[80] Jones testified at trial, "we were never able to get IBM or NCR interested in" developing such a system. *Id*.

Jones' packing of Highlands' lift lines on survey days. Brown refused to budge from his 12.5 percent offer. In a recent interview, the former Ski Company Secretary told us that the 12.5 percent offer was defensible because it equaled the "cheating-adjusted reality."[81] At the time, however, a Ski Company Director, Art Pfister, injudiciously quipped to a Highlands executive that Brown knew that the 12.5 percent share was "an offer that Mr. Jones could not accept"[82], a statement that was to prove of substantial significance in the courts.

For the 1978–79 season, therefore, there was no all-Aspen, four-mountain pass. The Ski Company reinstituted the six-day, three-mountain pass for its own mountains alone, which it had not offered since 1974.[83] Jones for Highlands tried another marketing ploy. He developed what he called the "Highlands Adventure Pack" that contained one three-day pass for Highlands and coupons that could be redeemed for cash, including for three days of skiing at Ski Company mountains.[84] The coupons were backed by deposits at local Aspen banks and, apparently, were accepted as tender by local merchants.[85] The Ski Company, however, refused to accept them. Although the courts, including the Supreme Court, viewed the Ski Company's refusal to redeem these coupons as evidence of anti-competitive intent because it seemed against the Company's economic self interest, the Adventure Pack was a clever ploy to increase Highlands' share of sales. The Adventure Pack comprised one *three-day* pass for Highlands and coupons equal to the price of three days of skiing at Ski Company mountains though, of course, they could also be redeemed for further skiing at Highlands. Upon buying the Highlands Adventure Pack, therefore, skiers were committed to spending, at the minimum, 50 percent of their time skiing at Highlands, a far greater share than had been the historical practice under the four-mountain ticket. At trial, the Ski Company's marketing director testified that the Company had turned down the coupons because it decided that it would "not support [its] competition."[86] Art Pfister, the Ski Company director

---

[81] Smedstad Interview, *supra* n. 16.

[82] JA, *supra* n. 15 at 53 (testimony of William Comstock). In his own testimony, Pfister defended the statement explaining that "I remember riding in with [Comstock], and I probably—I have heard what he said, and I probably did say that because I figured that Whip would not take a deal unless he had the best end of it." *Id*. at 142. A family member told us that Jones had a reputation in town as a savvy businessman who rarely came out on the wrong side of a deal. Family Interview, *supra* n. 26.

[83] JA, *supra* n. 15 at 80.

[84] *Id*. at 43. Jones had attempted to buy Ski Company daily passes in bulk, but the Ski Company refused to sell them. *Id*. at 34 (testimony of James Wentzel, Highlands Executive). Regrettably, we were unable to determine whether Highlands offered full price.

[85] *Id*. at 44 (testimony of William Comstock).

[86] *Id*. at 85 (testimony of Peter Sullivan).

who had made the "offer he cannot accept" comment, testified that the Ski Company's attitude about Jones was "[we] don't want to kill him, but [we] don't want to help him."[87]

During subsequent years, and after the lawsuit had been filed, Highlands tried other methods to market its Adventure Pack, which still included the three-day pass to Highlands. During the 1979–80 season, instead of the coupons, the Pack included American Express Travelers' Cheques in an amount equal to three days of access to Ski Company mountains; during the 1980–81 season, it included equivalent money orders,[88] both of which, as legal tender, the Ski Company would have to accept. The Adventure Pack, however, did not prove successful. During the 1978–79 season, ARI sold over $1 million of Ski Company's six-day, three-mountain passes; only $33,000 in Adventure Packs.[89] For this or other reasons, Highlands' market share of skiers continued to decline: during the 1978–79 season to 13.1 percent; during 1979–80 to 12.5 percent; during 1980–81 to 11.0 percent.[90] The courts, including the Supreme Court, would attribute all of this decline to the elimination of the four-mountain joint-pass;[91] of course, there are many other possible explanations, including Jones' reluctance to make capital investments at Highlands.

Following the 1978–79 season with the elimination of the joint-pass, the Ski Company acted to distance itself more significantly from Highlands, taking actions that would further turn the courts against it. As one prominent example, prior to the dispute and while the four-mountain pass was still available, ARI had placed a large photograph in the Aspen Airways waiting room at the Denver airport, labeled "There's Only One Aspen", showing the four mountains and explaining the availability of the six-day, four-mountain ticket. In 1979, after discontinuing the four-mountain pass, the Ski Company, citing a need to change a telephone number, replaced it with an identical photograph of the Aspen mountains, but with only the Ski Company's three mountains identified.[92] The Supreme Court, emphasizing the anti-competitive character of

---

[87] *Id*. at 141.

[88] For the 1979–80 season, the second without the four-mountain pass, the Ski Company raised its daily rate from $15 to $16. Since American Express did not have Travelers Cheques in $48 denominations, Highlands needed to use $50 checks and increase the cost of the Adventure Pack by $2. *See, id*. at 62 (testimony of Bernard McMahon, Jr., Highlands marketing executive). For the 1980–81 season, Highlands solved this problem by replacing the Travelers Cheques with money orders. *Id*. at 67.

[89] "Highlands Sues Aspen Skiing Corp.," Aspen Times, Aug. 2, 1979 at 5–A.

[90] *Aspen Skiing* at 2853.

[91] *Id*.

[92] E-mail, Tucker Trautman (Highlands' Attorney) to Lewinsohn, Feb. 4, 2005 (on file with authors). We have not been able to determine exactly how the Ski Company obtained control over the ARI photograph.

the act, took particular note that the Ski Company had placed the name of its Buttermilk Mountain directly above the actual Highlands Mountain in the photograph.[93] The Ski Company made other adjustments to national advertising, changing text to delete reference to Highlands— some of them hilariously amateurish.[94]

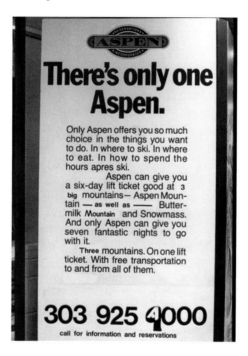

Again, the courts gave substantial attention to these marketing efforts as evidence of anti-competitive intent and effect. Highlands attorneys got Ski Company officials to concede at trial that 33 to 40 percent of first-time visitors to Aspen connected through Aspen Airways in Denver and, thus, were exposed to the altered photograph.[95] But the effect of these actions was surely overemphasized. The only skiers

---

[93] *Aspen Skiing* at 2852 n. 12. This characterization is not quite accurate. Highlands and Buttermilk are neighboring mountains, one minute apart by car. In the revised photograph, the Buttermilk label does begin over Highlands, but extends over the point on the photo where Buttermilk is located. (Altered photo available from authors.)

[94] Brown recalls the changes in the photograph and advertising as "stupid, unauthorized ideas." Brown Interview, *supra* n. 13, attributable to the then-marketing director. Sue Smedstad, former Ski Company Secretary, remembers Brown's angry reaction at the time when he was informed about the signs. Smedstad Interview, *supra* n. 16.

[95] JA, *supra* n. 15 at 105 (testimony of George Madsen, Ski Company marketing executive).

traveling to Aspen via Aspen Airways were destination-area skiers, a group to which Highlands never aimed advertising.

Highlands filed suit against the Ski Company on August 1, 1979.

The Litigation

Jones began planning his lawsuit against the Ski Company as soon as it became clear that the four-mountain pass would be discontinued.[96] The complaint alleged both monopolization by the Ski Company and conspiracy between the Ski Company and ARI to reduce sales of Highlands' Adventure Packs.[97] The trial ran for 18 days and was held before a Denver federal jury, not an Aspen one. Highlands, nevertheless, brought scores of local residents as witnesses, all hostile to the Ski Company. It had not helped that the Ski Company had announced that it was raising the daily pass price by $6 per day shortly before the trial.[98]

At the trial, the Ski Company largely relied on the expert testimony of a professor from the University of Colorado, Charles Goeldner, whose professed field was "ski economics." Jones family members told us that, years later, whenever Jones would reflect on the case, he would "thank God for Professor Goeldner," because the professor's aloof, arrogant, and combative demeanor helped reinforce the jury's unfavorable opinion of the Ski Company.[99] Goeldner presented industry statistics seeking to establish that the destination-area market was international, but also testified as to the Ski Company's superior product and to alleged free-riding by Highlands.

Highlands' case sought to establish that, destination-area aside, Aspen was a distinct sub-market and that the multi-area ticket was a distinct product. Highlands also emphasized that where the Ski Company owned ski areas outside Aspen, the Company was happy to participate in all-area ticketing. Thus, for Breckinridge in Summit County, Colorado, it readily continued a joint-area ticket—"Ski the Summit"—with other Summit County ski areas, Copper Mountain, Arapahoe, and Keystone.[100] Similarly, at its British Columbia ski area, Blackcomb, it had been the driving force in favor of a joint-pass with the nearby Whistler.[101]

---

[96] Interview, Lewinsohn with Tucker Trautman (Highlands attorney), Jan. 31, 2005 (hereafter Trautman Interview).

[97] Plaintiff's Complaint, Aspen Highlands Skiing Corp. v. Aspen Skiing Corp. (D. Colo. 1979) at ¶ ¶ 26, 27 (a)–(c), 30.

[98] "Aspen Will Suffer from High Lift Price," Aspen Times, June 4, 1981 at 2–A.

[99] Family Interview, *supra* n. 26.

[100] JA, *supra* n. 15 at 29.

[101] Trautman Interview, *supra* n. 96.

Highlands also emphasized the success of its beginners Ski School: both showing that several Ski Company executives had sent their children to the Highlands' school[102] and showing that Ski School attendance had dropped substantially after discontinuance of the four-mountain ticket.[103]

The final and apparently most effective part of Highlands' case, however, consisted of its demonstration of the Ski Company's "dirty tricks": the offer that Jones could not accept, the altering of the Denver airport photograph, its changing of the advertising materials, and the like. In a recent interview, the Ski Company's trial attorney told us that he had not expected testimony of this nature.[104]

The jury decided almost entirely in favor of Highlands. Most importantly, it decided as a matter of fact that Aspen constituted a distinct sub-market and the multi-area ticket constituted a distinct product, and that the Ski Company had acted to monopolize that product in that market.[105]

Damagingly, the Ski Company's lawyers did not object properly to the jury instructions to preserve the market definition issue for appeal. This would prove fatal to the Ski Company, and unnecessarily. The antitrust claim related to the Ski Company's actions with respect to the six-day, four-mountain pass, which was almost entirely of attraction to destination-area skiers, not to the local Aspen market. Given that that was the subject of dispute, there should have been no legal grounds for the definition of a distinct Aspen sub-market and, thus, no showing of monopolization. The Ski Company's attorneys' failure to preserve that issue predestined the outcome of the litigation.

The jury found that Highlands had suffered damages equal to $2.5 million, trebled under the Sherman Act to equal $7.5 million. The trial court Judge ordered reinstatement of the four-mountain ticket for a three-year period. The Ski Company did not request a stay pending appeal, according to its attorney because it did not want to risk accruing additional damages during the time required to complete the appeal.[106]

The Ski Company, of course, appealed the verdict to the 10th Circuit.[107] On appeal, the Ski Company argued that the trial court had

---

[102] Apparently because their children were too young for the Buttermilk School. JA, *supra* n. 15 at 143.

[103] *Id*. at 70, 170.

[104] Interview, Lewinsohn with William Maywhort, Holland & Hart, Attorney for Ski Company, Jan. 26, 2005 (hereafter Maywhort Interview).

[105] The jury rejected the Ski Company–ARI conspiracy claim.

[106] Maywhort Interview, *supra* n. 104.

[107] For the appeal, the Ski Company changed attorneys. At trial, the Ski Company had been represented by the venerable Denver firm, Holland & Hart. By the time of the appeal,

improperly allowed the jury to define a sub-market consisting of Aspen skiing areas alone. As mentioned, however, the trial attorneys had not challenged the jury instructions on the definition of sub-market directly, though they had raised the point in their motion for a directed verdict.[108] The Court of Appeals held that this was insufficient to "apprise[] the district court of the grounds on which [the Ski Company] now challenges the instructions given."[109] With this, the Aspen-only market definition and the multi-area product definition stood, and the Ski Company had been found liable for monopolizing them.

The Court of Appeals affirmed the jury's monopolization verdict on two separate grounds. First, the Ski Company had violated Section 2 by withholding from Highlands an "essential facility"—analogizing the joint-ticket to the jointly-owned railroad terminal in *Terminal Railroad*.[110] Second, although the Appeals Court acknowledged that *Colgate* afforded discretion to a private "trader or manufacturer . . . to announce . . . the circumstances under which he will refuse to sell"—the Ski Company's principal substantive legal defense—the Court emphasized the initial clause of the doctrine that constrained that discretion to "the absence of any purpose to create or maintain a monopoly." The Court found in the record plenty of evidence of Ski Company intent to monopolize in its insistence on a 12.5 percent Highlands' share, its refusal to accept Highlands' Adventure Pack coupons, in the advertising changes, indeed, in its behavior toward Highlands in its entirety.[111]

The Supreme Court in an opinion by Justice Stevens affirmed the verdict unanimously.[112] Prior to the Supreme Court's consideration, Highlands had cleverly tailored the issues to improve its position. First, it announced that it would not seek extension of the trial court's injunction mandating the offering of the four-mountain ticket;[113] second,

---

the corporate owner of the Ski Company, Twentieth–Century–Fox, had been acquired by the oil magnate, Marvin Davis, who turned the case over to his own attorneys, Williams & Connolly, of Washington, D.C.

[108] *See, Aspen Highlands Skiing Corp. v. Aspen Skiing Co.*, 738 F.2d 1509, 1514 (10th Cir. 1984).

[109] *Id.* at 1515.

[110] *Id.* at 1520–21.

[111] *Id.* at 1522, & n. 18.

[112] Justice White, formerly a famous Colorado athlete, recused himself. Although no official grounds are given for recusal, years later White told Highland's attorney that he had simply known too many people on both sides. E-mail, Tucker Trautman to Lewinsohn, 4/5/2005 (on file with authors).

[113] *Aspen Skiing* at n. 23. Highlands wanted to defuse the question of the appropriateness of a "court-ordered scheme of mandatory joint marketing" which the Ski Company had emphasized in its briefs. *See* Brief of Plaintiff/Respondent, *Aspen Skiing*, at p. 1.

it abandoned reliance on the Court of Appeals' essential facilities ruling, limiting the Supreme Court's review to the intent to monopolize count.[114] These tactics substantially simplified the Court's analysis.

The Supreme Court found that the Ski Company had violated Section 2 because its actions were contrary to the central ambition of the antitrust laws: to benefit consumer welfare. *Aspen Skiing* is not typically viewed as one of the Court's Chicago-school opinions but, at heart, that is the only way to explain it. First, the Court emphasizes that the Ski Company's refusal to offer the joint-pass constitutes "an important change in a pattern of distribution that had originated in a competitive market and had persisted for several years."[115] Second, according to the Court, there were strong reasons to believe that the four-mountain ticket was efficient and satisfied consumer demand. The Court emphasized that all-area tickets were common in many other ski locations, and that the Ski Company had participated in them itself at some of its other areas. The Court also referred to extensive testimony from the record indicating consumer disappointment over the unavailability of the four-mountain pass. Finally, the Court stressed that the Ski Company had offered no efficiency justifications for its refusal to offer the joint-pass. Why would it turn down the Highlands' Adventure Pack vouchers which were as good as cash? Why would it reject surveys by Price Waterhouse? If the Ski Company monitored skier volume at each of its three mountains, why could volume not be monitored at Highlands?[116] The alteration of the photograph and the national advertisements surely could not represent gains to efficiency.

The Court's opinion relies heavily on passages from Robert H. Bork's *The Antitrust Paradox*, citing it both in the text and in four separate footnotes. Bork is cited for the propositions that patterns of distribution that develop over time, if they persist, should be regarded as efficient;[117] that the antitrust laws must distinguish forms of exclusion that are efficient from those that are merely exclusionary;[118] and that

---

[114] *Id.* at 2862 n. 44; 2856. Highlands' attorney told us that he abandoned the essential facilities holding because the Justice Department had informed him that it was planning to file an amicus brief challenging the 10th Circuit's ruling on this issue. E-mail from Tucker Trautman to Lewinsohn, 1/31/2005 (on file with authors).

[115] *Id.* at 2858.

[116] Not addressed—probably not presented to the Court—was the reason that the Ski Company monitored usage according to each of its mountains: it was required to do so by the Forest Service for its annual permit renewal. The Ski Company, of course, did not have to worry about padding the skier population on survey days at its own mountains.

[117] *Id.* at n. 31, citing Robert H. Bork, *The Antitrust Paradox* (1979) at p. 156 (hereafter Bork).

[118] *Id.* at n. 33, citing Bork at p. 138 and n. 39, citing Bork at p. 157.

showing anti-competitive intent is not difficult because improper exclusion is always deliberately intended.[119]

In this light, *Aspen Skiing* can be understood as a continuation of the Court's adoption of the consumer welfare standard enunciated in preceding cases *GTE–Sylvania, Pueblo Bowl–O–Mat, BMI, NCAA* and *Monsanto v. Spray–Rite* and in many cases thereafter including *Matsushita, Brooke Group, Kahn,* and *Trinko.* The Court sought in *Aspen Skiing* to apply the consumer welfare standard to Section 2 refusal to deal claims. According to the analysis, where a distribution practice is identified as efficient—which is to say, beneficial to consumers—and a monopolist changes the practice without providing efficiency justifications, a Section 2 violation is proved.

Aspen Skiing Reconsidered

Unlike the Court's other Chicago-school, consumer welfare-based opinions, however, *Aspen Skiing* subsequently has had modest influence. Since 1985, the Supreme Court itself has cited the opinion only four times and never as the controlling basis for decision.

Why has its influence been so limited? Perhaps because the Court has recognized that it is seldom evident how to identify a truly efficient distribution practice that unambiguously enhances consumer welfare.[120] In this regard, there are two reasons that the foundation of the Court's analysis is weak. First, the Court gave exaggerated and, perhaps, misplaced influence to a conceptual rumination of Robert Bork. The principal passage of Bork's *The Antitrust Paradox* on which the Court relies is a hypothetical discussion by Bork of potential methods of predation:

> *Disruption of Distribution Patterns.* In any business, patterns of distribution develop over time; these may be reasonably thought to be more efficient than alternative patterns of distribution that do not develop. The patterns that do develop and persist we may call the optimal patterns. By disturbing optimal distribution patterns

---

[119] *Id.* at p. 2857 & n. 29, citing Bork at p. 160.

[120] The Court's opinion was immediately attacked by members of the Chicago-school. *See,* Thomas J. Campbell, The Antitrust Record of the First Reagan Administration, 64 Tex. L. Rev. 353 at 360–61 (1985); and in a highly perceptive article by Frank H. Easterbrook, On Identifying Exclusionary Conduct, 61 Notre Dame L.Rev. 972 (1986). *See also* efforts to constrain the opinion's effect. *Olympia Equipment Leasing Co. v. Western Union Telegraph Co.,* 797 F.2d 370, 379 (7th Cir. 1986) (Posner, J.) ("The Aspen Highlands decision . . . is narrowly written. If it stands for any principle that goes beyond its unusual facts, it is that a monopolist may be guilty of monopolization if it refuses to cooperate with a competitor in circumstances where some cooperation is indispensable to effective competition.")

one rival can impose costs upon another, that is, force the other to accept higher costs.[121]

To this point, the passage would seem to track the facts of the Ski Company–Highlands' relationship, though with two exceptions. First, as discussed earlier, there were many pricing changes over the years in Aspen. The Ski Company experimented with three-day; four-day; six-day; seven-day; three-mountain tickets sold simultaneously with four-mountain tickets in some years, but not others. Moreover, Highlands' Adventure Pack did not represent the continuation of the all-Aspen four-mountain ticket: by including a three-day ticket to Highlands, it sought aggressively to increase Highlands' market share. At a very high level of abstraction, the all-Aspen ticket may appear persistent, in the economic evolution mode suggested by Bork, but that characterization ignores the crucial subsidiary issues of the appropriate division of revenues and of free riding that, in fact, doomed the relationship. The question of the appropriateness of a mandatory, court-defined joint-ticket—an issue that Highlands successfully finessed—is central here.

Second, Bork's discussion refers to the disruption of distribution as imposing "higher costs" on the monopolist's rival. It is not immediately evident that discontinuance of the six-day, four-mountain ticket or the advertising changes imposed higher costs on Highlands, since Highlands did not generally advertise for destination-area skiers.[122] Perhaps the Court considered Highlands' failure with its Adventure Pack as demonstrating some higher cost. As the passage continues, however, it is evident that Bork is referring to a form of theoretical predatory practice in which the monopolist inflicts the same costs on itself by changing the method of distribution as it imposes costs on its competitor, as in prototypical predatory pricing:

> This may or may not be a serious cost increase, but if it is (and the matter can only be determined empirically), the imposition of costs may conceivably be a means of predation. The predator will suffer cost increases, too, and that sets limits to the types of cases in which this tactic will be used for predation. There is a further complication, moreover, in that the behavior involved will often be capable of creating efficiencies. Thus, the law cannot properly see predatory behavior in all unilaterally enforced changes in patterns of distribution.

---

[121] Bork at p. 156, cited in *Aspen Skiing* at n. 31.

[122] Highlands' total advertising budget increased from $125,847 for the 1977–78 season—the last season with the joint-ticket—to $139,844 for the 1978–79 season: the first season without the joint ticket, not obviously the consequence of predatory behavior. Brief for Petitioner/Plaintiff, Aspen Skiing Corp. v. Aspen Highlands Skiing Corp., 472 U.S. 585 (1985) at 25.

This is not *Aspen Skiing*. As mentioned, Brown thought that the Ski Company lost money on the four-mountain ticket, though this fact was surely not brought home sufficiently in the litigation. The final two sentences of this passage are more telling: Changes in distribution practices might create efficiencies; the law should be cautious in this regard. Following this discussion, Bork goes on in the section to state the more typical Chicago-school view: "The real danger for the law is less that predation will be missed than that normal competitive behavior will be wrongly classified as predatory and suppressed."[123] And Bork has difficulty presenting any real-world examples of the practice he is discussing. He suggests that *Chicago Board of Trade* may provide an illustration—where the Board limited after-hour sales of "to arrive" grain to the closing "call period" price.[124] But he does not appear entirely convinced himself. Instead, the purpose of this section of the book on disrupting distribution practices appears to provide a signal—that otherwise might be missed by the reader—that Bork accepts the potential plausibility of *some* theories of predatory behavior. As Bork states in the section, "I want to merely note that the possibility of predation, however slim it may be, cannot be entirely excluded on theoretical grounds."[125] This is faint support for the Court's theory in *Aspen Skiing*.

The second reason that the Court's analysis in the case has proven weak is the peculiar and unrepresentative factual basis of the case that resulted from the failure of the Ski Company's trial attorneys to adequately address either at trial or, as a consequence, on appeal the question of market definition. In hindsight, it appears obvious that the market for the six-day, four-mountain ticket should be defined as national or international destination-area ski locations. Given that market definition, all issues change. First, the Aspen Ski Company surely did not monopolize that market. Second, in that market, Highlands was not a competitor, so that even if the Ski Company is viewed as harming Highlands, it was not a harm to competition. Third, when the relevant market is seen as destination-area ski resorts, the efforts of the Ski Company to differentiate its product from Highlands become more salient. Viewing the relevant market as Aspen alone, the Court saw the Ski Company's efforts to marginalize Highlands as reducing consumer choice. Where the relevant market is national and international destination ski resorts, the Ski Company's substantial and continuous capital investments—in contrast to Highlands'—represent Ski Company actions to differentiate its product to enhance the skiing experience for destination-area skiers. These points were lost when the trial court approved

---

[123] *Id.* at 157.

[124] *Id.* at 158–59.

[125] *Id.*

the jury's definition of the market as Aspen-alone and the Ski Company's trial attorneys failed to preserve the issue for appeal.

Aftermath

As a general proposition, misguided antitrust opinions have only temporary effect. Unless a misguided doctrine is deeply embedded and vigorously enforced,[126] markets will prevail. And the market prevailed in Aspen. Jones took his gain from the verdict—by the time of judgment plus interest, $11.4 million—and deposited it in his bank; no capital investments to improve skiing at Highlands.[127] Despite the continuation of the four-mountain pass, Highlands fortunes continued to decline. It was reported that, by the late–1980s, Highlands was losing $500,000 per year on gross revenue of $2 to $3 million. The Ski Company, in contrast, thanks to Brown's different business model, generated annual revenues at that time of $40 million.[128] As mentioned, the Ski Company had been acquired by Twentieth–Century–Fox in 1977 which, subsequently, was purchased by the investor, Marvin Davis. Davis later sold it to the Crown family of Chicago.

In 1992, Jones attempted to stanch Highlands' continued losses by placing the firm into a charitable trust and donating it to his alma mater, Harvard University. It was reported—this is a fact we cannot verify—that the donation netted Jones $20 million in tax savings.[129] Shortly after, Harvard's Trustees sold Highlands to a Texas real estate magnate, Gerald Hines. In 1993, eight years after the Supreme Court's ruling, Hines merged Highlands with the Ski Company. By this point, the Justice Department agreed that the relevant market was not Aspen, but national destination-area skiing. There was no antitrust challenge to the merger, nor to the consolidation of other Colorado ski areas in subsequent years.[130]

Today, most North American ski areas are owned by one of four skiing conglomerates: American Skiing Corp.; Booth Creek Ski Holdings; Intrawest; or Vail Corp.[131] Owning just four mountains—however spectacular the conditions and the locale—the Aspen Skiing Company is a minor player in the national skiing market.

---

[126] Perhaps a good example is *Dr. Miles*.

[127] Bill Rollins, "Highlands Gambles on Four–Area Pass," Aspen Times, Oct. 15, 1981 at 13–B.

[128] "Ski Merger May Perk Up Aspen," N.Y. Times, Nov. 19, 1993 at 37A.

[129] Family Interview, *supra* n. 26.

[130] Penny Parker, "King of the Mountains Merger of Vail, Railcorp Holdings Seen as a Sign of Things to Come," Denver Post, Jul. 28, 1996 at G–01.

[131] John Briley, "Need a Lift? Our Annual Report on the Ski Season Ahead," Wash. Post, Nov. 8, 1998 at E–01.

*

9

Donald I. Baker

The *Superior Court Trial Lawyers Case*—A Battle on the Frontier Between Politics and Antitrust

If ever there were a high-visibility antitrust case that was much more about political principles than immediate practical consequences, *Superior Court Trial Lawyers* was it. On one side was a group of emotional and ideological lawyers who believed that indigent criminal defendants were not getting the quality of representation to which they were entitled under the Bill of Rights because their lawyers were poorly paid for doing an often less-than-sufficient job of defending such indigent defendants in the District of Columbia Superior Court. On the other side were some ultra free market Federal Trade Commission officials who welcomed the chance to bring a high-visibility price-fixing case against lawyers and probably had little sympathy for the respondents' Sixth Amendment concerns. In the middle was the "victim"—a generally liberal city government which tacitly accepted the respondents' "boycott" as an acceptable "political" endeavor on behalf of a downtrodden political constituency.

Out of this very interesting but very local dispute came a hard-fought six-year battle over when and how to apply the per se prohibitions of the Sherman Act to an agreement among market participants who had both broader political motives and personal economic stakes. Should such an agreement be struck down as a "per se boycott" without any inquiry into the rationale or circumstances behind the activity? Or should it be entirely exempt as political speech? Or should the participants at least be offered some chance to justify their conduct under the fact-based Sherman Act "rule of reason"?

The FTC leadership had picked an unlikely prosecution and then pursued it with unwavering vigor—arguing that the integrity of the per se rule for cartel activities was at stake. The respondents passionately believed that they were exercising constitutional rights on behalf of a deprived community and that FTC officials were a collection of right wing zealots with no concern for the plight of indigent criminal defendants. The lawyers who energetically defended the respondents on a pro bono basis believed that the respondents were the unfortunate victims of a politically-motivated case and that their "boycott" was essentially a "political" endeavor that deserved no prosecution or at least rule of reason treatment. (I was one of those lawyers and had no difficulty supporting my clients' cause.)

Interestingly, the antitrust bar seemed to have been rather divided on the case as it went forward. Many saw the case as a potential example of the "hard cases make bad law" principle—with the defense opening the door to economically-powerful bullies disrupting governments and markets. A good many others saw the "boycott" as a political tactic and wondered why the FTC felt impelled to inject itself into such a highly local dispute that had produced an apparently politically-satisfactory result for the local leaders. Still others just wished the case would just disappear without a trace.

The FTC may have expected to get a nice "we won't do it again" consent order rather than an all-out legal battle with well-armed opponents. But the willingness of some very experienced antitrust lawyers to energetically represent the ideologically-committed respondents on a pro bono basis seems to have been critical to this local battle becoming a national landmark. (Pro bono cases for antitrust defendants are rare indeed!)

A.   *The Road to War (1975–1983)*

When the Supreme Court determines that the Constitution requires a democratically-elected government to do something affirmative and costly on behalf of a politically unpopular group, such as prisoners or criminal defendants, politicians often have difficulty responding effectively. The *Superior Court Trial Lawyers* case arose out of such a political reality—the lack of public support for a criminal defendant's Sixth Amendment right to effective defense counsel. Why should a politician vote to spend public money to help criminal suspects avoid jail after they have been arrested by the police?

In larger jurisdictions, the government will generally establish a "public defender office," staffed by government-employed lawyers, to handle the government's Sixth Amendment obligations to provide effective defense for the indigent criminal. In addition, at both federal and local levels, courts often appoint individual private lawyers to defend indigent criminals at rates set by statute.

This dual system was used in the District of Columbia—a center of both crime and national media—where the Superior Court was only two blocks from the FTC headquarters. However, the DC Public Defender Service (PDS), a prestigious organization, represented only 8–10% of DC defendants. Meanwhile, private lawyers appointed by the courts under the DC Criminal Justice Act ("CJA lawyers") represented 85% of the defendants. The FTC Administrative Law Judge who tried the *Superior Court Trial Lawyers* case found that, "[t]he District is unique among major urban jurisdictions in its reliance on assigned private lawyers to handle[] such a large percentage of its huge indigency caseload."[1] "[B]ecause of the sharp increase in cases and delays, the amount the city spends to provide lawyers for indigent defendants [] increased nearly 50 percent since 1978 to $5 million last year and [was] projected to reach $6 million [the] next year, an increase of 20 percent."[2]

The political dispute that erupted in 1983 arose because the statutory pay for the CJA lawyers had not been increased in 16 years, despite the serious inflation that had taken place during the 1970s.[3] Meanwhile, the PDS was receiving almost 40% of DC's expenditures for indigent defense, even though they were handling less than 10% of the caseload.[4] The contrast between the prestigious PDS, which handled many of the most serious cases and was a much sought-after employer of young criminal lawyers, and the lowly "5th Street lawyers," who handled most of the cases, was striking.[5] The latter were limited by the 1967 Criminal Justice Act to $30 per hour for court time, $20 per hour for other time. Moreover, the overall per case limitations of $400 for misdemeanors, $1000 for felonies, and $1000 for appeals meant that a CJA lawyer's effective hourly rate was often below the $30/20 per hour ceilings. The

---

[1] *Superior Court Trial Lawyers Assn.*, Dkt. 9171, 107 F.T.C. 510, 1984 FTC LEXIS 16, ALJ Findings ¶ 19 (hereinafter "ALJ Findings").

[2] "Rights Question Surfaces Amid DC Legal Crunch," Ed Bruske and Al Kamen, The Washington Post, July 24, 1983, A1.

[3] "According to association president Ralph Perrotta, association members became particularly upset about the pay issue recently after the Senate approved some $25 million for improvements in the city's corrections system and to hire seven additional judges for Superior Court [after corrections officials and judges complained of case loads]." "Lawyers' Group Votes to Strike," Ed Bruske, The Washington Post, Aug. 12, 1983, B1.

[4] ALJ Findings ¶ 51.

[5] "The very virtues of PDS, however, tend to instill an elistist attitude among its lawyers that is not conducive to a close, mutually supportive relationship with the CJA lawyers who more often than not come from more humble backgrounds." ALJ Findings ¶ 51 n.160.

average CJA lawyer worked out of home or in an unstaffed office and made about $20,000 in the 1980s.[6] "That's not a lot of money for somebody who's had seven years of higher education ... It's just terribly low," said the DC Bar president who was a partner in a prominent DC law firm.[7] Indeed, one judge, who had asked not to be identified, said "It's amazing that they can even find people who can read and write to come down here and take cases at those rates."[8] But the broader implications were recognized by many, including the local ACLU director, who said, "Not only is it unfair to the lawyers, but it's unfair to the defendants who get short shrift from their lawyers."[9]

The impact of these very low rates of compensation on the quality of representation being provided to indigent criminals had been a source of concern to the organized bar in DC for a long time—but the situation did not become a matter of media attention and more general public dialogue until a strike was threatened in 1983.[10] And, almost certainly, the local media attention and public dialogue helped attract the FTC in the summer of 1983.

Back in 1975, a joint committee of the Judicial Conference of the DC Circuit and the DC Bar had generated a report, the Austern–Reznick Report, that recommended that the CJA lawyers' statutory rate be increased to $40. The committee found that court-assigned

> "criminal lawyers continue to be treated as appendages to the system. They are desperately needed, but they are inadequately compensated and frequently abused.... [A] system which is heavily weighed against the indigent defendant in terms of the compensation that his attorney will receive raises serious questions of equal

---

[6] ALJ Findings ¶ 29 n.102. The statute also imposed a $42,000 annual limit on a lawyer's annual income from CJA work (which was raised to $50,000 after the Strike). ALJ 29 n.102. But because few CJA lawyers had come close to the annual limit, this was not a major element in the dispute that led to the strike.

[7] "Lawyers' Group Votes to Strike," Ed Bruske, The Washington Post, Aug. 12, 1983, B1 (quoting David Isbell of Covington & Burling).

[8] Ibid.

[9] Ibid., (quoting Arthur Spitzer, director of National Capital Area chapter of the ACLU).

[10] "Judge Henry H. Kennedy Jr., articulating a view shared by some judges, said he 'doubts whether every aspect of each case is fully considered' and wonders if an attorney didn't have another moment or two more to make his case, whether he wouldn't tip the balance the other way." "Rights Question Surfaces Amid DC Legal Crunch," Ed Bruske and Al Kamen, The Washington Post, July 24, 1983, A1 "In February 1980, CJA lawyers went on strike when some Superior Court judges questioned the quality of certain defense lawyers and refused to authorize total payment for their services." "Attorneys strike for higher fees," David Sellers, The Washington Times, Sept. 6, 1983, 6A.

protection. The indigent's rights under the Constitution are no less than the rights of the well-to-do".[11]

Seven years later the DC Bar issued a new report, "Horsky Report," reemphasizing the conclusions of the 1975 report, saying that the situation had been aggravated by the intervening inflation; and the DC Bar passed a resolution in favor of increasing the CJA lawyers' rates to at least the levels that had been recommended in 1975. The FTC ALJ found that, "The support of the uptown bar for the cause of the CJA lawyers has been unwavering."[12] But support from others was generally lacking. As the ALJ found,

"[I]ndigent criminals and their lawyers are not a politically significant constituency. . . . The inability of lawyers for the indigent to command political support (on both the national and local levels) may also reflect the spillover effect from the public's image of the criminal lawyers. In general, this image is not favorable."[13]

Low pay and low esteem for "5th Street Lawyers" tended to limit the group to (i) ideologically committed, and/or (ii) otherwise unemployed lawyers. They were mostly young and, more often than not, relatively inexperienced, as the more experienced tended to move on.[14]

In any event, there were continuous lobbying efforts during 1983 to get the 1967 hourly rates and per case fee ceilings increased. SCTLA's efforts drew sympathy but not action from DC political establishment (ostensibly for lack of funds). The Mayor had a critical say on expenditures under the DC home rule government, and one City Councilman's assistant was quoted as telling the SCTLA leaders, "if the Mayor wants you to have it, he can get it."[15] Meanwhile the Mayor's counsel told the same people that the Council would have to act first.[16]

---

[11] ALJ Findings ¶ 31.

[12] ALJ Findings ¶ 35.

[13] ALJ Findings ¶ 52–53.

[14] "For years, lawyers who represent the poor in Washington have had a mixed reputation. The CJA system traditionally has attracted not only ambitious young lawyers at the start of their careers, but older hands known as the 'Fifth Streeters,' because many of them have offices around the courthouse on Fifth Street NW. Some were considered vultures, eager to make a fast buck at the expense of defendants rights, who wouldn't recognize their clients if they saw them and who spent much of their time playing poker or drinking whiskey inside the courthouse. 'Some of them would come up so drunk you couldn't talk to them straight,' said one veteran official in the U.S. attorney's office. Most of those lawyers have been chased away by a more vigilant DC Bar, and courthouse observers, including many judges, say the quality of CJA lawyers has improved dramatically in recent years." "Lawyers' Strike: Wages v. Ideals a Big Issue," Ed Bruske, The Washington Post, Sept. 9, 1983, B1.

[15] CA App 252.

[16] Ibid. 208–9.

Dean Wiley Branton of Howard University Law School offered the CJA lawyers some practical political advice. There was no active constituency or compelling reason for the DC Government to generate the necessary funds. "In a nutshell I told them . . . that they were going to have to do something dramatic to attract attention to get any relief. . . . And I probably used an expression, you will have to raise hell about this to attract somebody's attention."[17]

B. The "Strike" (September, 1983)

The "strike" vote was taken on August 11 by a large and enthusiastic meeting of SCTLA members—calling for collective refusal to accept new case assignments beginning on September 6. A substantial number of members signed a petition that said: "We the undersigned private criminal lawyers in DC Superior Court agree that unless we are granted a substantial increase in our hourly rate, we will cease accepting appointments under the Criminal Justice Act."[18]

This effort received a knowing political wink from the Mayor in a friendly meeting on August 29. "You do what you have to do, and I will do what I have to do."[19] A genuine crisis in the courthouse, he explained, would justify "emergency" mayoral action. " 'I'm very sympathetic to the problem. Twelve years is a long time to go with a pay rate that hasn't been changed," Barry said. But he added, "As mayor, I don't have any responsibility. My action has nothing to do with what the [CJA lawyers] may or may not do in September." [20]

During the interim period, the SCTLA generated many messages to the community; it courted the press and generated quite a lot of press coverage.[21] Thus, The Washington Post was reporting that,

> "The problem with this strike is not that lawyers are underpaid, but that underpaying them makes a mockery of the right to counsel, by leading the lawyers who handle these cases to take on overwhelming loads. . . . This strike has highlighted the fact that the lawyers have not been properly paid because nobody cares about their clients. And that's a strike against the city fathers."[22]

---

[17] Ibid. 410 ALJ ¶ 40.

[18] FTC Complaint ¶ 6, ALJ Findings ¶ 40.

[19] ALJ Findings ¶ 50.

[20] "Strike Seen By Lawyers for Indigent," The Washington Post, Aug. 30, 1983, C1.

[21] ALJ Findings ¶ 58; see also *FTC* v. *Superior Court Trial Lawyers Association*, 493 U.S. 411, 450 n.8 (Brennan J dissenting).

[22] "The Defense," Dorothy Gilliam, The Washington Post, Sept. 17, 1983, B1. Even the indigent defendants were not particularly helpful to their counsels' cause. One was quoted as saying, "You guys are on easy street compared to us." Ibid.

The Chief Judge of the U.S. District Court, Harold Greene, also wrote a strong op-ed piece in favor of the strikers:

> "Lawyers contend the rates discourage skilled attorneys from taking court cases.... Anyone who believes that criminal defendants in the District of Columbia will, on a continuing basis, receive adequate representation from lawyers who make so little money that they will be able to survive only by engaging in desperate maneuvers is living in a fool's paradise."[23]

Bar sympathy and low rates prevented qualified substitutes from emerging. As the ALJ found,

> "The overall response of the uptown lawyers to the PDS call for help was feeble, reflecting their universal distaste for criminal law, their special aversion to compelled indigency representation, their near epidemic siege of self-doubt about their ability to handle cases in this field, and their underlying support for the demands of the CJA lawyers."[24]

Nobody in the Superior Court or the DC Government seemed to have seriously contemplated trying to use their powers to force the 14,000 members of the DC Bar, in private practice in Washington, to take up the cases foregone by the less than 200 CJA regulars.[25] Rather, the DC Government seemed to have regarded the "strike" as a political gambit to which they had some sympathy.

In any event, the strike led to a political compromise based on interim rates. The ALJ found that, "The strike succeed[ed] when key figures in the District's criminal justice system—[the director] of PDS and the Chief Judge of the Superior Court—became convinced that the system was on the brink of collapse because of the refusal of the CJA lawyers to take on new cases."[26] Upon receiving a communication to this

---

[23] "Be Fair to Lawyers—and Defendants," Federal District Court Chief Judge Harold H. Greene, The Washington Post, Sept. 12, 1983, A13. This is, of course, the same Judge Greene who was so well known to antitrust lawyers because of his central role in administering the Modified Final Judgment in *U.S. v. AT & T, 552 F.Supp. 131 (D.D.C 1982)* aff'd sub nom. *U.S. v. Maryland,* 460 U.S. 1001 (1983).

[24] ALJ Findings ¶ 60.

[25] The day before the strike, the Washington Post reported: "The battleground shifted to phone lines last week as strikers and PDS officials fought for the hearts and minds of attorneys at the city's biggest law firms, seeking commitments to stay away or step in. Some firms reported serious dissension among partners on what to do, but most echoed the sentiments of Wilmer, Cutler & Pickerings's Michael Helfer: 'I think we're going to do it [accept cases from the court if required to do so]. There is a lot of sympathy here, everyone thinks the rates [to CJA lawyers] are ridiculous. But when the court calls, you've got to go." "Lawyers," The Washington Post, Al Kamen and Ed Bruske, Sept. 5, 1983, B2.

[26] ALJ Findings ¶ 61.

effect, the Mayor invited the SCTLA leaders to a "friendly" meeting at a downtown restaurant. "The Mayor shook hands all around and congratulated the SCTLA leadership on the success of the boycott. The Mayor then stated that since an emergency now existed, [the rate increase bill] could be taken up as emergency."[27] As one of the individual respondents testified at the FTC hearing: "[I]t is almost like theatre. [The Mayor] has to be able to come in as the rescuer, the man on the white horse and say, well, I am going to solve this huge crisis in the court system."[28]

The emergency legislation, unanimously enacted by the DC City Council on September 20, 1983[29], would increase the DC Government's CJA expenditures by $4–5million per year.[30] Thus a very small group of underpaid lawyers was able to shut down the DC criminal justice system and secure a political victory. Clearly the SCTLA lawyers had mixed motives; they wanted both more income for themselves, and the ability to be more effective in vindicating their clients' Sixth Amendment rights.

At the courthouse, the "victory" proved a less than total one for the CJA regulars. The ALJ found that, "[t]he immediate impact ... has been a sharp increase in the number of lawyers willing to take on CJA cases because of the higher fee schedule."[31] This new competition apparently did what economists predicted—improved the quantity and quality of representation received by the indigent clients. But within two months, the Washington Post reported: "Original members of the association now remember the old rates with fondness as they try to compete with a flood of new lawyers attracted by the higher pay."[32] It added, "the declining case volume for individual lawyers has forced many to look for new ways of earning more on each case they are assigned ... [including] filing more defense motions on legal points, thus expanding the work they do for individual clients."[33]

C. *Battle Lines Joined (Late 1983)*

   1. Federal Trade Commission

The FTC responded to all this local political activity by opening an antitrust investigation before the strike even took place. The Washing-

---

[27] ALJ Findings ¶ 63.

[28] Perotta, CA App. 495–6.

[29] ALJ Findings ¶ 68.

[30] ALJ Findings ¶ 71.

[31] ALJ Findings ¶ 72.

[32] "Superior Court Lawyers Find Raise Cuts their Pay," Ed Bruske, The Washington Post, Nov. 24, 1983, B1.

[33] Ibid.

ton Post reported that this investigation "concerns how collective actions that lawyers might take could affect prices at the court."[34] The article noted some similarities to an FTC case against Michigan physicians (where the Commission had decided that a doctors' boycott designed to prevent legislative reduction of Medicaid payments was illegal).[35] Meanwhile, also in August, 1983, the delegates at the annual American Bar Association convention had just voted "to seek an exemption from [sic] FTC antitrust enforcement jurisdiction."[36]

The staff decision to open an investigation of the threatened CJA "strike" in DC occurred in a broader bureaucratic context within the Commission in mid–1983. The Chairman was a highly-regarded but conservative economist (James C. Miller III), who favored more vigorous antitrust enforcement against restraints in the professions. He particularly liked the idea of bringing some cases against lawyers. Meanwhile, the new (and also well regarded lawyer-economist) Chief of the Bureau of Competition, Tim Muris, assigned a separate section the responsibility of developing non-medical cases involving professionals. Muris and the staff liked the *Michigan Medical* effort and wanted to expand the "politically motivated boycott" frontier to coercive efforts by other professionals.[37]

Then along came the SCTLA's "strike" meeting and public announcement *three blocks away from the Commission headquarters*. At the same time, the FTC staff recognized that this was an odd event and that the SCTLA was not a well-entrenched professional organization as in *Michigan Medical* and some of the other professional organizations it was investigating. Apparently, Commission staff informally warned some of the leaders that the "strike agreement" violated the antitrust laws. One staff member was even sent to a public SCTLA meeting to give this warning in person, but was not allowed to speak. The CJA lawyers clearly regarded themselves as "employees" of the Superior Court—and thus entitled to strike—while the FTC regarded them as "independent contractors" who were barred from making price-related agreements with each other.

---

[34] "FTC Said to Be Probing Legality of Trial Lawyers' Planned Strike," Ed Bruske, The Washington Post, Aug. 27, 1983, B8.

[35] Michigan State Medical Society, 101 FTC 191 (1983).

[36] FTC: Watch, No. 173, 6 (Sept. 23, 1983). Some had expressed concern that the FTC had suffered from "professional courtesy" in not having pursued lawyers, but the FTC Watch thought this argument was without significant merit. Ibid. I concur.

[37] The new head of the group assigned the non-medical investigations, Ken Starling, was thoroughly familiar with *Michigan Medical*—having, as Commissioner David Clanton's attorney-advisor, been much involved in research and writing Commissioner Clanton's opinion for the Commission in that case.

Once the DC Council enacted the emergency legislation, the Commission no longer had an antitrust remedy against the price increase itself.[38] All it could do was seek a "sin no more" order. Such a remedy was regarded as worthless vis-à-vis an amorphous and easily-disbanded association. Thus the staff's goal in proposing the case was to attain cease and desist orders against the four SCTLA ringleaders who were ultimately charged—Ralph Perotta, Karen Koskoff, Reginald Addison and Joanne Slaight. The staff recognized that the Superior Court had the legal power to order the CJA regulars and the other active members of the DC Bar to serve as counsel for indigent defendants.[39] Thus the FTC complaint had to be "a per se or nothing" claim (as one former staff member explained it), because this legal duty on DC Bar members would help make it highly unlikely that the staff would ever be able to prove that the CJA regulars had "market power" in an antitrust sense.

The staff recommendation generated a considerable amount of internal discussion about the interesting issues presented by the unusual mixture of political and legal agendas. Internally, many staff members probably agreed with the FTC: Watch comment: "The staff recommendation for an administrative complaint puts the Commissioners and their agency in a delicate political situation. While economists and antitrust practitioners may tend to see the SCTLA action as a classical antitrust violation, the public at large is more likely to view the matter as a 'poor person's' issue."[40]

When the complaint was ultimately issued on December 16th, Commissioner Michael Pertschuk, the former Carter-appointed Chairman, publicly dissented because of his view that the action "represents a poor exercise of prosecutorial discretion." He noted the "local and limited nature of the lawyer's [sic] effort . . . and the fact that they were underpaid."[41] Also, "[t]he theoretical 'victim,' the District of Columbia,

---

[38] Apparently there had been some staff discussions with the Department of Justice about whether the Department might seek an injunction prior to the increase going into effect. But the Department decided against this course—perhaps because enjoining the DC Government would not make sense and any other injunction would be very hard to supervise.

[39] Such a system of involuntary appointments had been used during a prior "strike" of CJA lawyers in 1974; and apparently maintained the system for several months, until additional funds were appropriated. Lefstein, CA App. 422–434.

[40] FTC: Watch, No. 173, 6 (Sept. 23, 1983). FTC: Watch is a newsletter produced by two former members of the FTC public relations staff. It is widely read by those who practice before the commission and is well known for its reasonable access to internal gossip and its sometimes spicy comments on the agency's activities.

[41] 107 FTC 510, 513 (1984).

never asked for our intervention nor asserted its own antitrust prohibitions."[42]

2. Superior Court Trial Lawyers Association ("SCTLA")

This was a loose knit group that the ALJ found "nevertheless functions as a viable entity around which the CJA lawyers are organized."[43] It was a DC non-profit corporation whose certificate of incorporation had been revoked in 1981, was unable to locate its bylaws, and had "no reliable membership list."[44]

The SCTLA held open meetings and debates at the Superior Court lawyers' lounge (events that were open to any member of the DC Bar); and at the time of the strike some of these meetings were televised. The meetings were lively, sometimes tumultuous affairs, in connection with the strike and the subsequent litigation with the FTC. The rank and file strongly supported the long legal battle with the FTC. This was not surprising given the fact that they tended to be ideologically committed and were not having to pay any legal costs to defend their ideals!

3. The Individual Respondents

The FTC investigation focused heavily on four SCTLA leaders—Ralph Perotta, Karen Koskoff, Reginald Addison and Joanne Slaight. The first three were SCTLA President, Vice President and Secretary respectively. Ms. Slaight was chair of the so-called "Strike Committee". Mr. Perotta had had a long career in public interest law and had run an unsuccessful campaign for the Democratic nomination to the US Senate in Rhode Island. The other three were younger lawyers with 2–4 years experience. All four depended on CJA work for about 90% of their income, and thus had significant personal economic stakes in the rates for which they were energetically seeking reform. They were clearly strong and effective leaders and spokesmen. The FTC staff was probably correct in concluding that the "strike" would not have succeeded politically without them—and hence they were the key to the case.

When the Commission's complaint had been approved but not yet issued, these four individuals were apparently offered a consent decree settlement that would have enjoined them from future "boycott" or disruptive activity. However, they declined to negotiate anything along these lines with the FTC staff because they saw such an order as a serious interference with their First Amendment rights to advocate political change and more effective government funding for the defense of indigent criminal suspects' rights.

---

[42] Ibid.

[43] ALJ Findings ¶ 4.

[44] ALJ Findings ¶ 2, 3.

4. Sutherland Asbill & Brennan

I had joined the firm in September 1983, just a week before the CJA "strike." Sutherland was an Atlanta-and-Washington firm with a distinguished practice in the tax area, but also a history of concern about civil rights issues, particularly in the South. It had recently become a more significant antitrust firm, led by long-time litigator, Willis Snell. By September 1983, the firm had at least seven full-time antitrust lawyers. The four partners included two former Justice Department leaders (Douglas Rosenthal and myself) and a younger litigator who would go on to become Chairman of the ABA Antitrust Section, Mike Denger. The four partners all worked extensively on the SCTLA case, along with associate Will Tom, who eventually argued the case in the Supreme Court.

How and why the firm got so involved in the SCTLA battle is both interesting and, I think, a bit uncertain. Doug Rosenthal was clearly the catalyst. But the rest of us, like most of the so-called "uptown bar," saw the obvious inequity being imposed on the CJA lawyers by the political realities. Going after poor peoples' lawyers seem to us a perverse use of the antitrust law—and, the more we got into it, the more it seemed like an attempt to suppress political speech.

The Sutherland Asbill management, led by Mac Asbill Jr., was willing to pursue what the firm regarded as "good causes" and this, I suspect, was a major factor in allowing the antitrust group to go ahead with this project. As in Europe in 1914, nobody expected the long and expensive war that was to ensue—but never, for the next five years, did I hear anyone in the Sutherland firm question the mounting commitment of resources that we were making to the case.[45] Even if the firm became involved initially, why did it make such a sustained commitment of resources over the next five years? The answer, I think, is that the antitrust group was so enthusiastic about the case and willing to work so hard that no one thought paying client work was being sacrificed. In any event, it is striking that 50% of the time expended was by partners (whose time accounted for 69% of the nominal value of Sutherland Asbill's efforts).[46]

---

[45] It may have helped that the *paying* antitrust practice at Sutherland was successful and growing, while the SCTLA team was willing to work extra hours to make the case successful.

[46] As shown on Figure 1, the firm's records show that it devoted 5788 hours of professionals' time to the case, with a nominal value of $754,320. The case was mostly about legal principles rather than contested facts, with the result that the proportion of paralegal time (18%) was considerably lower than one would have expected in normal antitrust litigation. There was no other pro bono effort of comparable size going on in the firm during the time of this case.

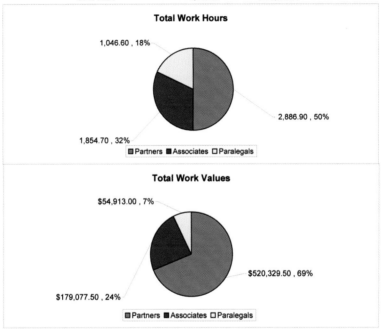

Figure 1

Sutherland, Asbill & Brennan

Superior Court Trial Lawyers Case

Work Hours/Values

	Total Work Hours	Total Work Values
Partners	2,886.90	$520,329.50
Associates	1,854.70	$179,077.50
Paralegals	1,046.60	$54,913.00
Sum Total	5,788.20	$754,320.00

Total Work Hours

1,046.60 , 18%

2,886.90 , 50%

1,854.70 , 32%

☐ Partners ■ Associates ☐ Paralegals

Total Work Values

$54,913.00 , 7%

$520,329.50 , 69%

$179,077.50 , 24%

☐ Partners ■ Associates ☐ Paralegals

5. District of Columbia Government

As Commissioner Pertschuk mentioned in his dissent, the DC Government was conspicuously quiet, sitting on the sidelines, even though it was the "victim" of the alleged antitrust violation.[47] Rather, it accepted the "strike" as an understandable political exercise under the circumstances, instead of an illegal antitrust boycott. If the political leadership thought an antitrust violation was involved, the DC Corporation Counsel could have used the DC Antitrust Act to stop the boycott. In any event,

---

[47] This fact was a critical part of the ALJ's "no harm no foul" decision discussed in the next section.

it appears that DC Government neither encouraged nor opposed the FTC's effort.

Thus, the SCTLA case was a symbolic battle from the outset. The DC Government was not complaining and the FTC could not to seek to undo the increase granted by Government. Meanwhile, the individual respondents and most SCTLA members were outraged at the case, did not face serious adverse consequences if they lost, and were not paying legal fees as long as Sutherland Asbill was willing to defend their principles for them.

D.   The Limited Battle Over Evidence (1984)

The filing of the FTC's complaint led almost immediately to a prompt and efficient trial before an experienced Administrative Law Judge (Morton Needleman) in the late Spring of 1984. There was no doubt about the existence of an "agreement"—only sharp dispute about the justifications for it, and the market implications. Thus complaint counsel's case-in-chief took only a week (starting May 7), while the defense's case ran for less than two weeks (May 13–25). Rebuttal evidence was offered by the FTC on June 8 and the record closed on July 20. Judge Needleman issued an exhaustive opinion three months later.

The complaint counsel argued that this was just a plain old-fashioned price fixing case, requiring nothing more than proof of an "agreement" that had some "price" effect. The ALJ rejected this simplistic approach:

> "[G]iven the Commission's total lack of institutional experience in dealing with the constitutional, political and social pressures permeating the criminal justice field, I was persuaded in the trial of this matter to allow respondents to make a full record so that both the trier of the facts and reviewing authorities might have before them any special circumstances surrounding a boycott in this unfamiliar area."[48]

The complaint counsel continued with it as an "old fashioned price fixing case"—just calling as witnesses the Director of the PDS, the PDS Chief of Staff, and two CJA lawyers to establish that the strike had occurred and was disruptive.

In response, the SCTLA counsel called five SCTLA leaders, two DC Bar Presidents, three "uptown lawyers," and the former Dean of the Howard University Law School, who had advised the SCTLA leaders that "they were going to have to do something dramatic to attract

---

[48] 107 F.T.C. 510, at p. 91 (1986). In support of this conclusion, the ALJ cited the Supreme Courts recent decisions *Broadcast Music Inc. v. CBS*, 441 U.S. 1 (1979) and *NCAA v. Board of Regents*, 468 U.S. 85 (1984) as justifying a fuller inquiry into what plaintiffs had alleged were per se Sherman Act violations.

attention in order to get any relief."[49] In addition, SCTLA called three professors as expert witnesses on legal ethics and political speech. Interestingly, neither side called the Mayor or members of the DC Council, which had approved the "emergency" legislation in 1983.

Interestingly, the "uptown lawyer" witnesses included two antitrust leaders—Jim Rill (who would become Assistant Attorney General for Antitrust in 1989) and Jim Loftis (who would become Chairman of the ABA Antitrust Section in 1996). Both testified, as did other bar witnesses, that the existing statutory pay levels in 1983 were inadequate to assure reasonable quality of representation for indigent criminal defendants. They and the other lawyer witnesses also testified that, if they had been required by the Superior Court to serve as counsel for indigent defendants during the strike, they would have complied. The then current DC Bar President, David Isbell, described the SCTLA strike as "an effort toward bringing effective public attention to the problem of inadequate compensation" for the CJA lawyers.[50] His predecessor, John Pickering, testified that the success of the strike "simply indicates that eventually everybody understood that there was a legitimate grievance here . . . and it was time to do something about it."[51]

The respondents' experts supported the conclusion of the earlier bar studies that the existing levels of compensation were entirely inadequate—leading the ALJ to find that "every expert who had studied the problem had concluded that the pre-boycott rates, which had not been adjusted for over 10 years, were woefully inadequate."[52] The respondents experts also testified that the Superior Court had the power to compel the CJA regulars and other active members of the DC Bar to serve as counsel for indigent defendants; and that such system of involuntary appointments had been successfully used during a prior "strike" of CJA lawyers in 1974 maintained for several months, until additional funds were appropriated by the DC Government.[53]

Judge Needelman's long decision ultimately dismissed the Complaint, but in doing so made several findings that were important to his decision and the subsequent history of the case.

> 1. "While the hoopla organized by SCTL did attract media attention and editorial support, there is no credible evidence that the District's eventual capitulation to the demands of the CJA lawyers

---

[49] Quoted in ALJ Findings ¶ 40.

[50] CA App. 385.

[51] CA App. 309–310.

[52] 107 F.T.C. 510, at p. 92.

[53] Lefstein, CA App. 422–434.

was made in response to public pressure, or, for that matter, that this publicity campaign actually engendered any significant measure of public pressure."[54]

2.   "The best proof of the power of the CJA lawyers lies in the fact that the boycott succeeded."[55]

3.   The boycott "was a singularly curious form of coercion. For the record also shows that the boycott was not vigorously opposed by the Mayor who believed that an increase was fully merited but could not be brought about unless the city was confronted with an actual emergency demonstrating the importance of the CJA lawyers to the administration of the criminal justice system. (The Mayor was hardly alone in his view that an increase was justified.)"[56]

4.   "[T]he record here lends itself to more than just a colorable claim of strong political motivations even though the immediate effect was a fee increase.... [T]he CJA lawyers sincerely believed the protection of the constitutional rights of their clients was directly related to reduce caseloads, which, in turn, was a function of the rate change."[57]

5.   "But even more important is the evidence indicating that city officials (and practically everyone else concerned with the criminal justice system) were convinced in 1983 that (a) the optimum economic price was inadequate to satisfy the 'political' (i.e., constitutional) requirement of effective representation, and (b) the CJA lawyers were unlikely to achieve higher fees if they continued to rely on communicative political petitioning alone."[58]

The full record was what Judge Needelman used in crafting a novel decision dismissing the complaint. He rejected the respondents' defense that their activity was entirely protected from antitrust by the so-called *Noerr–Pennington* doctrine that immunizes collective petitions to government to take anticompetitive action. However, he then dismissed the complaint on some case-specific "political" grounds (reflected in points 3–5 above):

"I see no point in striving resolutely for an antitrust triumph in this sensitive area when this particular case can be disposed of on a more pragmatic basis—there was no harm done.... [T] evidence strongly indicates that in this instance the boycott was viewed by city

---

[54] ALJ Findings ¶ 58.

[55] ALJ Findings ¶ 70.

[56] 107 F.T.C. 510, p. 92.

[57] Id. at pp. 93–94.

[58] Id. at p. 94.

officials as the only feasible way of getting a rate increase, which was unpopular with the general public but supported by virtually all elements of the community concerned with implementing the public policy behind the Sixth Amendment."[59]

The familiar (and sometimes spicy) antitrust newsletter, *FTC: Watch* offered some practical commentary in support of Judge Needelman's "no harm no foul" decision.

> "[W]e think there's a lot more at stake here than one normally finds in the antitrust cases. This case constitutes an assault on poor people's lawyers. If the FTC should win, the record ... indicate[s] that poor people charged with crimes will receive lower quality representation. That representation, taken as a whole, is already pretty poor.

> "Needelman, in our opinion, has attempted to tell the FTC what just about everyone outside the Reagan Administration already knows: this was a stupid case—stupid politically because it involves beating up on poor people's lawyers and stupid legally because, at the end, it could force the Supreme Court to choose between the rights of people charged with criminal acts and the reach of the antitrust laws. The antitrust laws are not likely to win that test."[60]

Of course, the Editor's prediction that, "The antitrust laws are not likely to win that test" proved to be wrong—but only at the end a long game with many twists and surprising turns.

E.   The Heart of the Conflict (1985–88)

Now that the case had been tried and decided by the ALJ, a somewhat repetitive appeals process ensued—with each side refining the arguments that it had made during the trial. Commission counsel continued to argue the "plain old-fashioned price-fixing boycott" theory, first before the full Commission and then the DC Circuit. The SCTLA counsel responded by stressing the "political" dimensions that had been so persuasive before Judge Needelman. In addition, they repeated their unsuccessful argument that the respondents were entitled to a *Noerr–Pennington* exemption, i.e., flat exemption from antitrust liability, because the "strike" was a form of politically lobbying. (As we shall see, this broad argument would fail to persuade the Commission, the Court of Appeals, or any Supreme Court Justice.)

Thus the crucial battle turned out to be whether the per se rule had to be applied because the "strike" was labeled a "price fixing boycott" or whether the rule of reason applied because the strike contained an

---

[59] Id. at p. 96.

[60] *FTC: Watch*, No. 198, 18 (October 26, 1984).

important element of "political speech" by economically interested speakers. The choice was crucial for both sides, because the FTC surely knew that, if the rule of reason applied, it would have to prove "market power." Proving that a small group had "market power" in a city in which the courts could have called on 14,000 practicing lawyers surely seemed fanciful![61] To the extent that it ever faced the issue, the Commission mixed political and economic factors to argue in favor of the ALJ's conclusion that "[t]he best proof of the power of the CJA lawyers lies in the fact that the boycott succeeded."[62]

1. The Commission Reverses the ALJ and Takes the Per Se Road (1985–86)

It took almost two years for the Commission to take up the case. When they did, SCTLA counsel argued not only the legal merits of their *Noerr–Pennington* and "rule of reason" arguments, but that the case was an unwise exercise in prosecutorial discretion and should be dropped for that reason. At the end of my oral argument, I said that,

> "There are two quotes that say it all. One is from Anatole France about 'the evenhanded majesty of French justice that denies both rich and poor alike the right to sleep under the bridges of Paris.' The other is from Kenny Rogers' song, 'The Gambler'—'You've gotta know when to hold 'em. You've gotta know when to fold 'em. You've gotta know when to run.' "

But all to no avail. Commissioner Mary Azcuenaga's extensive opinion (on behalf of the three Commissioners still there when it was issued) was an extended choral work with several often-repeated themes:

- The DC Government was getting the quality of CJA services that was satisfactory to it. "The city's purchase of CJA legal services is based on competition.... [T]he city's offering price before the boycott apparently was sufficient to obtain the amount and quality of legal services that it needed."[63]

- Political disagreements over the adequacy of those services were irrelevant to the antitrust analysis. "We see no reason to suppose ... that the District would ever purchase services inadequate to meet its obligations under the law."[64]

- Self-interest predominated. "Although we do not question the respondents' genuine concern for their clients, we find ... that

---

[61] To the extent that the SCTLA regulars had leverage, it was apparently because they were the only lawyers that were willing to work voluntarily on a regular basis for the very low CJA wages (which one might label a "reverse Cellophane Trap").

[62] ALJ Findings ¶ 70.

[63] LEXSTAT TRADE REG, REP (CCH) Commission Op. at 5.

[64] Ibid. Commission Op. at 10.

the respondents' purpose in conducting boycott was [to] improve their own economic well-being."[65]

- Social choices. "What the respondents are really suggesting is that they should be allowed to force their collective judgment of the appropriate price-quality mix for legal services on the city."[66]

- Political petitioning. "There are many different ways to communicate, ranging along a broad spectrum from pure speech to violent actions.... The First Amendment right to petition the government does not include the right to be effective."[67]

- Economically-interested petitioning. "Permitting a price-fixing boycott directed at the government as buyer does not foster the *Noerr* goal of free exchange of information between the people and the government. At the same time, prohibiting such conduct does not interfere with anyone's ability to choose to sell his services to the government or to make his views on the appropriate price known to the government."[68]

All this added up to a finding that the SCTLA "strike" was a "price fixing boycott" and the political dimensions were irrelevant. "We conclude ... that the SCTLA lawyers' boycott was a per se violation.... Our conclusion would be the same under a rule of reason analysis."[69] However, no evaluation was undertaken of the "market power" dimension normally required in a rule of reason case. Thus the stage was set for an interesting trip to the Court of Appeals.

2.   The DC Circuit Reverses the Commission and Takes the Rule of Reason Road (1987–88)

On appeal, the SCTLA case was assigned to an eminent and conservative panel consisting of Robert Bork, Douglas Ginsburg and Lawrence Silberman. All three had served in the Department of Justice—Bork as Solicitor General, Ginsburg as Assistant Attorney General for Antitrust, and Silberman as Deputy Attorney General. Robert Bork was, of course, a celebrated antitrust scholar with a serious interest in First Amendment issues, but in the midst of the briefing schedule he was nominated for the Supreme Court and dropped off the panel.[70] He was replaced by

---

[65] Ibid. Commission Op. at 12.

[66] Ibid. Commission Op. at 13.

[67] Ibid. Commission Op. at 15–16.

[68] Ibid. Commission Op. at 18.

[69] Ibid. Commission Op. at 2.

[70] After the Bork nomination had failed in highly contentious confirmation fight in the Senate, President Reagan nominated Douglas Ginsburg—but his nomination was soon

Spottiswood Robinson, a long-serving Circuit Court Judge with a strong civil rights background.

In the course of this appeal, the SCTLA team refined their arguments about "supply disrupting speech" as an acceptable form of political expression. The SCTLA reply brief even explained how the FTC's narrow approach to political speech by economically-interested actors would have led the Commission to attack the Boston Tea Party—because some of the nefarious "Indians" were local tea merchants outraged by the monopoly that Parliament had given to the East India Company. During the oral argument, the court explored this "supply disrupting speech" issue in some detail—with Judges Silberman and Ginsburg being particularly active.

When the decision came out 11 months after the oral argument, the "political speech" argument produced a narrow, but probably decisive, victory for the SCTLA appellants.[71] The decision was written by Judge Ginsburg, with a strong concurring opinion by Judge Silberman. Like the ALJ and the Commission, the Court rejected the SCTLA *Noerr–Pennington* defense.[72] But it accepted their argument that the political dimensions of the SCTLA "strike" mandate a rule of reason "market power" inquiry rather than per se liability,

> "We agree with the petitioners in one important regard: the Commission must apply the antitrust laws to the facts of this case with a special solicitude for the First Amendment rights of these petitioners and others, who like them, engage in concerted action to advance both their political agenda and their own economic welfare at the expense of government."[73]

Judge Ginsburg's opinion went on to explain that antitrust laws "should be applied prudently and with sensitivity. In this instance, such prudence and sensitivity require that the FTC prove that the petitioners had economic power in the relevant market [because] otherwise there is simply too much risk that the antitrust laws will be used to penalize those who are able, through collective action to wield political power in a way that serves their own interests."[74]

---

dropped because he was reported to have smoke marijuana while teaching at Harvard Law School. In any event, this brief diversion did not prevent Judge Ginsburg from writing the DC Circuit's decision in the SCTLA case.

[71] Superior Court Trial Lawyers Assn. v. Federal Trade Commission, 856 F.2d 226 (D.C. Cir.1986).

[72] Ibid. at 241–247.

[73] Ibid. at 233.

[74] Ibid. at 234.

The court found the use of "rule of reason" rather than per se prohibition justified by a 1968 Supreme Court decision, *United States v. O'Brien,* which had held that "a government regulation is sufficiently justified ... if the incidental restriction on alleged First Amendment Freedoms is no greater than essential to the furtherance of that interest."[75] Using the per se rule (which is "only a rule of 'administrative convenience and necessity'") in this case "ignores the command of *O'Brien* that restrictions activity protected by the First Amendment be *'no greater than essential'* to preserve competition from the sclerotic effects of combination."[76] Thus, "[w]e hold only that the evidentiary shortcut to antitrust condemnation without proof of market power is inappropriate as applied to a boycott that served, in part, to make a statement on a matter in public debate."[77] Rather the FTC is required to be able to "reject the possibility that the effects [of the boycott] were the product simply of the rough and tumble of municipal politics."[78]

Judge Silberman concurred in a short, forceful opinion. "The difficulty in this case," he explained, "is determining whether [the SCTLA] prevailed because of political appeal or commercial might."[79] He then spelled out his thinking which was so appropriate for someone who had spent considerable time in the political arena:

> "Motivation then, in the sense of the absence of desire for personal enrichment, cannot be the determinate of what speech is protected as political..... [T]he proper distinction between political and commercial activity must ... turn on the *means employed* in eliciting a governmental response. [I]f one gets one's way from the government *qua* legislator because of political persuasiveness, there is no liability. But using market power to coerce the government *qua* economic actor creates a distortion of the market and the political process. Since a boycott has the potential either to persuade or coerce, however, the only proxy we have ... is the degree of market power that they enjoy."[80]

Thus ended an imaginative effort by three experienced jurists to accommodate the Sherman Act and the First Amendment in the context of what Judge Ginsburg appropriately described as "commercial activity

---

[75] 391 U.S. 367, 377.

[76] 856 F.2d 226, 249 (emphasis in original).

[77] Ibid. at 250.

[78] Ibid.

[79] Ibid. at 253.

[80] Ibid. at 254 (emphasis in the original).

with a political impact."[81] The only problem was that the FTC knew that they would lose under a "market power" standard and therefore the Commission had to take the next step.

F. The Curious Trip to the Supreme Court (1988)

The FTC, undaunted by its defeat before a distinguished DC Circuit panel, petitioned the Supreme Court for certiorari on its own without the support of the Solicitor General (as it had been entitled to do under a 1974 statute). It treated the Court of Appeals decision as a broad challenge to what it called "the oldest and clearest of antitrust doctrines"[82] The FTC argued that the SCTLA strike was a "naked price fixing boycott" and that

> "The opinion accords favored treatment to price-fixing boycotts in which (1) competitors first make 'active efforts to appeal to the public for support of their demand' (2) suggest a governmental target and (3) style their subsequent boycott as a continuation of this effort ... The court's new rule ... opens the door wide to a multitude of actual or threatened price-fixing boycotts ... that begin with an entirely lawful public effort by the conspirators to persuade the government to confer the benefit they seek."[83]

The absence of the Solicitor General from the FTC's cert. petition was a clear indication that the Justice Department did not see the Ginsburg decision as having such devastating consequences for antitrust enforcement.[84]

The FTC told the Court that the case presented these two questions:

> "1. Whether the Sherman Act's *per se* prohibition against naked horizontal price-fixing agreements is unconstitutional (in violation of the First Amendment) as applied to price-fixing boycotts that are part of a larger public campaign by economic competitors to obtain for themselves and economic benefit from the government.
>
> 2. Whether this Court's repeated holding that '[a]s a matter of law, the absence of proof of market power does not justify a naked restriction on price or output' is inapplicable to a naked price fixing boycott that leads to demonstrated anticompetitive effects but that

---

[81] Ibid. at 247.

[82] *Petition for a Writ of Certiorari to the United States Court of Appeals for the District of Columbia Circuit* at 11 (quoting Bork).

[83] *Petition for a Writ of Certiorari to the United States Court of Appeals for the District of Columbia Circuit* at 17–18.

[84] The Solicitor General normally feels that he is a guardian of the Supreme Court's docket and therefore will not support a petition for certiorari even if the Justice Department disagrees with the decision below.

is part of a larger public campaign by economic competitors to obtain for themselves an economic benefit from the government." (Emphasis added)[85]

The SCTLA responded that the "The FTC's approach to this factually unusual case is constitutionally blind, [and] its error was carefully dealt with by the court of appeals."[86] It argued that,

"By characterizing the Respondents' conduct as a 'price-fixing boycott', and a 'naked restraint on price or output,' the FTC seeks to avoid *any* inquiry into its political context ... The FTC attempts to resolve both the First Amendment and antitrust issues by labels rather than analysis."[87]

SCTLA said that the case did not merit review by the Supreme Court. Consistent with that position, it stated the "Question Presented" by the case in this case-specific way:

"Where a group of individuals have engaged in 'a boycott [which] served, in part, to make a statement on a matter of public debate,' concerning interests besides their own, and where the boycotters were a small proportion of those legally qualified to offer the affected service, does use of the *per se* antitrust rule—'the evidentiary shortcut to antitrust condemnation without proof of market power'—constitute a restraint on political expression that is 'greater than is essential to the furtherance of [the government's] interest' in preserving market competition?"[88]

But there was another complexity that suddenly surfaced at the certiorari stage—a split among the Respondents. Douglas Rosenthal, who had been a leader in getting Sutherland Asbill to take the case back in 1983, had left to join another firm in 1988. He was as close as anybody to the four individual respondents (Perrotta, Addison, Koscoff and Slaight) and he began representing them as parties distinct from the SCTLA, which was still represented by Sutherland Asbill. The Individual Respondents decided that the Court of Appeals victory was not good enough—and that the four individuals ought to be entirely exempt under the First Amendment and the *Noerr* Doctrine. Accordingly, they wanted to file a cert. petition challenging the lower court decision as being too narrow—which we at Sutherland thought was a dreadful idea at this stage of the proceedings. After arguing, we ultimately compromised and

---

[85] *Petition for a Writ of Certiorari to the United States Court of Appeals for the District of Columbia Circuit* at I.

[86] *Respondents' Brief in Opposition* at 2.

[87] *Respondents' Brief in Opposition* at 12–13.

[88] Ibid. at i.

collaborated in filing a somewhat unusual pleading—a *conditional cross petition*—which in essence told the Supreme Court, "if you decide to accept the FTC's petition, then you should review the following question:"

> "Whether a boycott directed at both furthering the constitutional rights of indigent criminal defendants and the economic benefit of their 'striking' lawyers is beyond the scope of the antitrust laws."[89]

As a participant in this drama, I was very unhappy about having to file this cross-petition. It is rare indeed for any party to affirmatively seek Supreme Court review of its own *victory* in the Court of Appeals. Yet this was being advocated here by the Individual Respondents and their counsel. Filing a cross petition seriously undercuts the normal arguments that a respondent wants to make when opposing a request for Supreme Court review (e.g., very unusual facts, limited applicability in other circumstances, and lack of conflict with other Courts of Appeal). In filing the cross-petition, we had to assert the Noerr issue was important and the SCTLA case was a good opportunity to resolve it.[90] As someone who thought we had been lucky to draw the panel we had in the Court of Appeals, I was very anxious that the Supreme Court not be tempted into trying to review a very imaginative decision by Judge Ginsburg echoing points we had made in our briefs. . . . But Rosenthal's clients persisted, so we filed the cross-petition.

Meanwhile, another illuminating incident occurred. Ernie Isenstadt, the FTC Assistant General Counsel and its very capable advocate in the Court of Appeals,[91] approached some of the Sutherland Asbill lawyers with a settlement feeler from the FTC. Would our clients agree to a settlement that would have (a) the FTC drop its case against the association and the individual respondents, in return for (b) the Respondents joining an FTC motion to the DC Circuit requesting that its opinion be entirely vacated, thus depriving it of any precedential value?

There was apparently a meeting of SCTLA members in the Lawyers Lounge at the Superior Court, where this tentative idea was debated and rejected. The SCTLA lawyers were emotionally committed to the case

---

[89] *Cross–Petition for a Writ of Certiorari to the United States Court of Appeals for the District of Columbia Circuit* at i.

[90] We had made this broad *Noerr* argument all the way up the line, but without success. I had thought it was a likely loser because the respondents both (a) had clearly engaged in a coercive boycott and (b) had serious economic stake in the legislative action that they were seeking. The *Noerr* argument essentially was that such circumstances were entirely outside the antitrust laws so long as the boycott activity also had a significant "political" dimension.

[91] He would also represent the FTC very capably in the Supreme Court oral argument.

and were unwilling to leave the Commission decision as the final word in the case. Thus this decision is hardly surprising.

The Cross Petition to the Supreme Court and the SCTLA members' rejection of a settlement feeler underscored that the litigation was more about principles than practical consequences. The worst that could happen to the association and four Individual Respondents was a "never do it again" order. It was costing the SCTLA nothing to pursue the case and the four Individual Respondents were probably more hawkish than the rank-and-file membership.

As we know, the Supreme Court granted certiorari on both sides' "Questions Presented" and thus took us to the final chapter of this splendid little drama.

G.   *The Arguments Before the Supreme Court (1989)*

The parties essentially offered expanded versions of what they had asserted in their cert. petitions. Now, however, the Solicitor General and the Justice Department Antitrust Division participated in the FTC briefing of its case, while the four Individual Respondents were represented by Rosenthal and not Sutherland Asbill. Thus there were two long merits briefs for the Respondents—Sutherland's for the SCTLA and Rosenthal's new firm, Coudert Brothers, for the four Individual Respondents.

In its main brief, the FTC argued that, "There is no more reason to permit *vigilante price fixing* than to permit any other form of unlawful action undertaken by those purporting to further some higher purpose."[92] The Commission expanded its Armageddon argument about the broad impact of the lower court decision:

> "There is, in short, no way to confer the right of 'expressive boycott' upon competing lawyers without also conferring it upon insurers, doctors, pharmacies, accountants, engineers, and a multitude of other competitors who seek every day to promote both their parochial economic interests and their vision of the public good in the public arena."[93]

It also added one new "Question Presented" to the two that it had included in its cert. petition:

> "Whether, assuming that the *per se* rule of illegality does not apply, an antitrust plaintiff must satisfy any required showing of market power by offering proof apart from the boycotters' successful efforts

---

[92] *Brief for the Federal Trade Commission* at 24 (emphasis added).

[93] *Brief for the Federal Trade Commission* at 35.

to restrict the output of, and increase the price for, the service they offer."[94]

On the other side, the SCTLA offered a more extensive set of questions than it had in opposing the FTC's petition. The key difference was to introduce the First Amendment-flavored idea of a "legislative petitioning boycott." This is well illustrated in the second of the four questions that SCTLA presented:

> "Whether the antitrust laws should be construed to condemn a legislative petitioning boycott *per se*, without any inquiry into whether the boycott participants did or even could exercise economic coercion."[95]

The four Individual Respondents also used the "legislative petitioning boycott" as the centerpiece of their argument—as illustrated by the second of their three "Questions Presented:"

> "Whether a legislative petitioning boycott, in which the primary motive of the boycotters is to engage in political expression, is beyond the scope of the antitrust laws, even if such conduct causes incidental commercial effects."[96]

Looking at the dispute from a slightly higher elevation, one can see that the key difference between the two sides is that (a) the FTC sought to disaggregate the Respondents' lobbying/strike conduct but aggregate its market effects, while (b) the Respondents sought to aggregate their conduct but disaggregate its effects. This is how it worked.

(a) Conduct. The FTC argued that, "The *per se* rule prohibited respondents' boycott—their concerted refusal to deal—not their speech, their lobbying, or their press relations."[97] Meanwhile, Respondents argued that the boycott was an integral part of their lobbying campaign. "There was also expert testimony that 'direct action' is often the only way of attracting media attention for groups lacking status and prestige, and that boycott-like actions are often far better ways of obtaining continuing attention than other actions such as demonstrations."[98]

(b) Effects. The FTC's brief assumed that it was the "strike" alone that brought about the successful result and therefore the CJA lawyers must have market power ("the boycotting lawyers fully

---

[94] *Brief for the Federal Trade Commission* at I.

[95] *Brief for the Respondents* at i.

[96] *Brief of the Individual Respondents* at i.

[97] *Brief for the Federal Trade Commission* at 12.

[98] *Brief for the Respondents* at 19.

realized their expectation").[99] Meanwhile, SCTLA emphasized the importance of its political lobbying efforts as a factor in the outcome ("There are reasons to pause before inferring market power from detrimental effects when political power may be the more explanatory variable").[100]

Each side had a point. The FTC was no doubt right that the SCTLA effort would not have succeeded without the "strike"—the work stoppage that dramatized the main issue to the public. The SCTLA was right that the "strike" would not have succeeded had it not been part of a broader publicity and media campaign that featured Sixth Amendment issues and generated broader political support.[101] Thus the Court of Appeals appears to have gotten it just right when it described the "strike" as "commercial activity with a political impact."

By contrast, the Supreme Court was offered two polar views. The FTC's was that, because the challenged conduct involved a "commercial" dimension, it was subject to normal "naked restraint" treatment. At the other extreme, the Individual Respondents argued that because of the "political" dimension, "It is irrelevant whether the CJA lawyers pressured the legislature, whether the legislature was also a buyer, or whether the strikers were economically self-interested."[102]

H.   The Supreme Court Reverses (1990)

The FTC's effort persuaded six Justices that the Commission had it just right.[103] The Court also held unanimously that there was no general *Noerr* exemption just because the Respondents sought legislation.

The six-Justice majority emphasized that the "strike" was "not only a boycott but also a horizontal price fixing arrangement"[104] and, thus, deserved per se prohibition. Writing for majority, Justice John Paul Stevens bought the FTC's core argument that (a) the "strike" should be separately evaluated from of the Respondents' political and media activities; and (b) "the per se rules ... have the same force and effect as any other statutory commands."[105]

---

[99] *Brief for the Federal Trade Commission* at 13, 42.

[100] Ibid., quoting the Court of Appeals decision.

[101] *Brief for the Federal Trade Commission* at 47. This was the uncontested testimony at the hearing before the FTC ALJ.

[102] *Brief for the Federal Trade Commission* at 19.

[103] *Federal Trade Comm. v. Superior Court Trial Lawyers Assn.*, 493 U.S. 411 (1990).

[104] Ibid. at 436 n.19.

[105] Ibid. at 433.

Justices Brennan, Marshall and Blackmun dissented. They argued that, "The Court's concern for the vitality of the *per se* rule, moreover, is misplaced in the light of the fact that we have been willing to apply rule-of-reason analysis in a growing number of group—boycott cases. . . . The plainly expressive nature of the Trial Lawyers' campaign distinguishes it from boycotts that are the intended subjects of antitrust laws."[106]

The split on the Court seemed unusual and illuminating. Justice John Paul Stevens, a liberal and a generally pro-antitrust jurist, wrote a stirring majority opinion in favor of the per se rule on behalf of himself and several generally conservative Justices who had frequently expressed concern about per se antitrust rules (Scalia, O'Connor, and Rehnquist). They were joined by Justices White and Kennedy, who had less pronounced histories. Meanwhile, three liberal Justices—who had authored some of the most important government victories in antitrust cases—dissented on First Amendment grounds. Justices Brennan, Marshall, and Blackmun clearly saw the First Amendment rights and values as being predominant.

The whole picture seems even more ironic when one realizes that the opinion writers in the DC Circuit, Judges Ginsburg and Silberman, were conservative jurists who usually had more in common with the Chief Justice and Justice Scalia than they had with the three Supreme Court dissenters.

There is an explanation which is consistent with my recollection of the oral arguments in both courts: Judges Ginsburg and Silberman, seeing the case as interesting and unusual, were willing to give more sustained attention and hard thought than the Supreme Court Justices seemed willing to do. Thus the lower court was willing to look at and weigh the political context with a fairly sensitive eye, while the Supreme Court majority seemed content to dispose of the case by sticking it somewhat awkwardly into a jurisprudential box with a "per se" label on it. The high water mark of analytical inanity came when Justice Stevens sought to compare the per se antitrust rule to the prohibitions on stunt flying and automobile speeding. Here is what he wrote, presumably with a straight face:

> "The *per se* rules in antitrust law serve purposes analogous to *per se* restrictions upon, for example, stunt flying in congested areas or speeding. Laws prohibiting stunt flying or setting speed limits are justified by the State's interest in protecting human life and property. Perhaps most violations of such rules actually cause no harm. No doubt many experienced drivers and pilots can operate much more safely, even at prohibited speeds, than the average citizen.

---

[106] Ibid. at 453 (Brennan, J., dissenting).

"If the especially skilled drivers and pilots were to paint messages on their cars, or attach streamers to their planes, their conduct would have an expressive component. High speeds and unusual maneuvers would help to draw attention to their messages. Yet the laws may nonetheless be enforced against these skilled persons without proof that their conduct was especially harmful or dangerous.

"In part, the justification for these *per se* rules is rooted in administrative convenience. They are also supported, however, by the observation that every speeder and every stunt pilot poses some threat to the community. An unpredictable event may overwhelm the skills of the best driver or pilot, even if the proposed course of action was entirely prudent when initiated. A bad driver going slowly may be more dangerous than a good driver going quickly, but a good driver who obeys the laws is safer still.

"So it is with boycotts and price fixing. Every such horizontal arrangement among competitors poses some threat to the free market."[107]

Justice Brennan's dissent took on "this non-sequitur" directly:

"I cannot countenance this reasoning, which upon examination reduces to the Court's assertion that since the government may prohibit airplane stunt flying and reckless automobile driving as categorically harmful ... [I]t may also subject expressive political boycotts to a presumption of illegality without even inquiring as to whether they actually cause any of the harms of the antitrust laws are designed to prevent. This non-sequitur cannot justify the significant restriction on First Amendment freedoms that the majority's rule entails."[108]

Given Justice Stevens' normal First Amendment instincts,[109] Justice Brennan was not the only one who was unhappy with the inapt stunt flying and speed limits justifications given for applying a per se prohibition to conduct where a "political speech" element was clearly present.

I. Is There Message for the Future or Just a Wonderfully Unusual Legal Saga? Or Both?

Per se rules have—often appropriately—been on retreat in the last half century; but the *SCTLA* decision probably pumped a little extra juice into the per se tank by insisting on per se resolution of a borderline

---

[107] Ibid. 433–434.

[108] Ibid. at 437.

[109] See, e.g., Wallace v. Jaffee, 472 U.S. 38 (1985).

case. Each case that reaches the Supreme Court tends to have some highly specific dimensions. One doubts that Justices Scalia and Kennedy are likely to be much moved in the future by the fact that they had joined Justice Stevens in beating the drum for per se liability in the *SCTLA* case.

Supply disrupting protests for political goals have long been a way of life in the U.S. and other democratic countries, and the *SCTLA* decision may make these a little more precarious in the future when some clear economic benefit would be likely to flow to the politically-motivated supply disrupters if they are successful.

In the end, the *SCTLA* case was a battle over basic legal principles in circumstances where neither side had much incentive to settle—and thus it made its way all the way to the Supreme Court with its unusual facts, while offering some illuminating insights into judicial thinking when faced with a highly unusual set of politically-flavored facts and their legal consequences.

Ultimately, the sad thing about the case was that the Supreme Court did not think it worth trying to accommodate the Sherman Act and First Amendment as the Court of Appeals had struggled to do. Thus Douglas Ginsburg's imaginative opinion ended up getting trumped by much less reflective effort, for reasons criticized by the Supreme Court dissenters. Was Justice Stevens—a bright and often imaginative jurist— just too busy to think hard about the issues as Judges Ginsburg and Silberman had done? Or did he really find the "stunt flying/speed limit" simplicity persuasive?

The write-up of the Commission's Supreme Court victory in the familiar antitrust newsletter, *FTC: Watch,* provided a wonderfully irreverent epitaph on the case: "We think congratulations are in order to the entire Commission for succeeding where all others have failed: prosecuting antitrust charges against a respondent with so few financial resources that it qualified for *pro bono* representation. A true Reagan Administration landmark."[110]

---

[110] *FTC: Watch*, No. 314, 11 (Jan. 29, 1990).

10

A. Douglas Melamed and Daniel L. Rubinfeld[*]

U.S. v. Microsoft: Lessons Learned and Issues Raised

I. INTRODUCTION

Overview of the Case

On May 18, 1998, the U.S. Department of Justice, 20 individual states, and the District of Columbia filed suit against the Microsoft Corporation claiming that Microsoft had monopolized the market for personal computer ("PC") operating systems ("OS"s) and had used its monopoly to engage in a wide range of antitrust violations.[1] The case was tried in Federal District Court from October 19, 1998, through June 24, 1999. The court reached its findings regarding the facts of the case on November 5, 1999, and its legal conclusions on April 3, 2000. Microsoft's appeal to the Circuit Court of Appeals for the District of Columbia was decided on June 28, 2001. The appellate court affirmed the monopolization claim, reversed other conclusions by the District Court, and remanded the case to the District Court to find an appropriate remedy. Following extensive settlement discussions among the various parties, the Department of Justice (DOJ) and Microsoft reached a settlement agreement. Nine states opted not to join the settlement and proposed a different remedy. A 32–day remedy trial was held, and on November 1,

---

[*] Rubinfeld served initially as Deputy Assistant Attorney General for Economics, and later as a consultant during the course of the investigation and trial. Melamed served initially as Principal Deputy Assistant Attorney General and later as Acting Assistant Attorney General until shortly after the government filed its brief in the Court of Appeals in January 2001.

[1] *United States v. Microsoft*, Civil Action No. 98–1232. One state settled with Microsoft before the case went to trial.

2002, the District Court issued a remedy ruling, which was ultimately upheld by the Court of Appeals.

Microsoft's antitrust problems did not end with the Government's case. Microsoft was sued privately by multiple parties and in most cases settled for substantial sums. After its own investigation, the European Commission (EC) concluded that Microsoft's bundling of its operating system with its "player" (which allows a user to stream audio or video content from the web) violated Article 82 of the European Commission Treaty. The EC ordered Microsoft to pay a substantial fine and to put onto the market a second version of its current operating system, Windows XP, without a player. Microsoft has appealed the EC's ruling to the Court of First Instance, and (absent a settlement) could take that appeal further to the European Court of Justice.

There is no doubt that, from the public's perspective, *U.S. v. Microsoft* was the antitrust case of the 1990s and perhaps for decades before that. The investigation, the trial, and its aftermath received wide press coverage throughout. A number of the major actors in the drama became household names, as much a result of the public relations battle among the parties as of the litigation itself. There remains however, substantial debate as to the ultimate legal import of the case. In this essay, we will explain why we believe the case was indeed a significant antitrust case that has important implications for antitrust enforcement in the 21st Century. *U.S. v. Microsoft* not only proved that the Government could litigate a complex case in a dynamic, high technology industry in a timely fashion, but also reinvigorated Section 2 of the Sherman Act. The case provided a foundation for antitrust enforcement in the "new economy."

Industry Background

The Microsoft Corporation is a relatively young corporation. It was founded in 1975 as a software programming company by Bill Gates and Paul Allen in the Gates' family garage. IBM, the leader at the time in mainframe computing, had decided to enter and to develop the personal computer business. IBM had the necessary hardware technology but needed a software operating system. After IBM approached Microsoft, which did not have its own operating system at the time, Microsoft bought an OS, which it then licensed to IBM. Bill Gates and his colleague Steve Ballmer had the foresight to realize that PCs themselves would be cloned and therefore have limited value, but that the OS owned by Microsoft would provide a unique, highly valuable asset.

From its inception, Microsoft enjoyed exceptional success that paralleled the incredible growth of the PC desktop business. In the process, thousands of Microsoft employees have become millionaires. Many attribute this success to Microsoft's skill and foresight in realizing the value associated with control over a key PC asset, while others add the element of luck; all would agree, however, that Microsoft has shown an uncanny ability to adapt its business plans and to market innovative technology successfully.

Microsoft had initially faced stiff competition from competing operating systems, including in particular the operating system of the Apple McIntosh and IBM's OS/2 system. Apple was a significant threat because it was the first to popularize a color graphical user interface ("GUI"). It is now believed by many that Apple made strategic business errors in opting not to license its operating system or its key components to others in the 1980s and in charging a relatively high price for its computers. As will be seen, however, Apple's "closed architecture" strategy, which was strongly opposed by Microsoft at the time, became the heart of Microsoft's strategy a decade later. What is not widely understood is that Apple made (with hindsight) a second strategic error: It provided a royalty-free license of its GUI to Microsoft for use in Windows 1.0, which was Microsoft's first GUI-based operating system. In return, Microsoft produced a version of Microsoft Excel for the MacIntosh and agreed not to sell a version of Excel for other operating systems for one year. This license was an important element in Microsoft's successful defense of Apple's subsequent claim that the Windows' GUI violated Apple's claimed copyright of the "look and feel" of the Apple GUI.

Although Windows 1.0 and 2.0 were not commercial hits, Windows 3.1 and its desktop successors (Windows 2000 and Windows XP) were enormous successes. Not surprisingly, with its rapid growth in an increasingly important industry, its economic achievements, and its aggressive competitive style, Microsoft came under antitrust scrutiny. Various government agencies and private plaintiffs questioned whether Microsoft had used a range of anticompetitive practices to restrain competition, to exclude competitors, and to expand its market power beyond the operating system market. With hindsight, it appears that the very practices that raised antitrust issues in the late 1990s may have originated in the Gates' family garage.

II.   LEGAL CLAIMS AND CHALLENGES

The Microsoft Investigations[2]

The Federal Trade Commission (FTC) undertook the first government investigation of Microsoft. The FTC examined Microsoft's software

---

[2] For a more complete overview of the issues raised in the case, see Daniel Rubinfeld, "Maintenance of Monopoly: *U.S. v. Microsoft, The Antitrust Revolution*," 4th Edition, (John E. Kwoka, Jr. and Lawrence J. White, eds., New York: Oxford University Press) 476 (2004).

licensing practices with PC original equipment manufacturers (OEMs). Although two Commissioners wanted to bring an antitrust case against Microsoft at the end of the three-year investigation, they did not constitute the majority needed for an FTC complaint.[3]

This victory for Microsoft was short-lived because DOJ undertook its own investigation almost immediately thereafter. A year later, on July 15, 1994, DOJ filed a complaint claiming that Microsoft's contracts with OEMs were exclusionary and anticompetitive and that their purpose was to allow Microsoft to maintain its monopoly in the market for PC operating systems. Microsoft and DOJ immediately settled, with Microsoft signing a consent decree pursuant to which it agreed to restrict its licensing activities in a number of ways.[4] An important aspect of the consent decree was the agreement that Microsoft would not tie software products together by conditioning its operating system license on the license of other software products. But the agreement explicitly permitted Microsoft to continue to develop "integrated" products. The distinction between an anticompetitive tie and pro-competitive product integration became a central issue in the litigation that followed.

At about this time, the PC business itself was approaching what Microsoft CEO Bill Gates later called an "inflection point." The rapid development of the Internet created a need for software that would allow PC users to move beyond the desktop and to be able easily and efficiently to access the Internet. The first highly successful version of such software—which came to be known as a web browser—came from Netscape. In a very short period, Netscape's "Navigator" browser became the market leader; it accounted for approximately 70% of browser usage in 1996.

Microsoft was initially slow to realize the potential significance of the Internet, but it redirected its efforts aggressively towards Internet browser software beginning in 1996. It developed its browser—known as Internet Explorer or IE—and, in order to promote its acceptance in the marketplace, required OEMs to license and install Internet Explorer on all new PCs offered with the Windows 95 operating system.

In what one might view as the precursor to the Section 2 case that would follow, DOJ returned to court in late 1997, this time alleging that Microsoft had tied IE and the OS in violation of the 1995 consent decree. Microsoft argued that IE and the OS together constituted the kind of integrated product that was expressly permitted by the decree. DOJ was initially successful: On December 11, 1997, Judge Thomas Penfield Jackson issued a preliminary injunction ordering Microsoft to separate

---

[3] The Commission vote was 2–2. One Commissioner did not participate.

[4] *United States v. Microsoft Corporation*, 1995–2 Trade Cas. ¶ 71,096 (D.D.C. 1995).

its Windows 95 OS and IE. But, on appeal the U.S. Court of Appeals for the District of Columbia sided with Microsoft, ruling that Microsoft had offered evidence that the combination of IE and the OS provided functionality that was not available without product "integration."[5] The appellate court made clear, however, that its decision was based on its reading of the consent decree and not on broader antitrust principles.

The "Microsoft Case"

What became known as the "Microsoft case" began on May 18, 1998, when the DOJ, led by Assistant Attorney General Joel Klein, 20 states, and the District of Columbia brought suit against Microsoft, led by its general counsel William Neukom and, of course, Bill Gates. In its complaint, DOJ alleged that Microsoft had engaged in a range of practices involving agreements with OEMs, Internet service providers ("ISPs"), and others that had the purpose and effect, not of enhancing efficiency or benefiting consumers, but rather of protecting Microsoft's OS monopoly and excluding Netscape and other rivals. The heart of DOJ's case was the claim that Microsoft's conduct constituted unlawful maintenance of Microsoft's OS monopoly in violation of Section 2 of the Sherman Act.[6] DOJ also alleged that Microsoft had attempted to monopolize the market for Internet browsers in violation of Section 2 of the Sherman Act and that tying its IE browser to the Windows operating system violated Section 1 of the Sherman Act.[7] The Section 2 monopolization claim was a rare historical event; DOJ's last major Section 2 case, against AT&T, had been filed more than 20 years earlier and led to the breakup of AT&T into a long-distance company and a number of regional Bell Operating Companies.

The Theory of the Case

In the years prior to the filing of the Government's case, it became apparent to Microsoft that the Netscape Navigator browser could serve as the foundation for a software "platform" that had the potential to compete with Microsoft's Windows 95 (and later Windows 98) operating system. Operating systems provide application programming interfaces ("APIs") through which applications interact with the operating system and, thus, with the computer hardware. Applications developers must write their programs to interact with a particular operating system's APIs. The time and expense of then "porting" the application to a different operating system can be substantial.

---

[5] *United States v. Microsoft Corp.*, 147 F. 3d 935 (D.C. Cir. 1998).

[6] 15 U.S.C. § 2.

[7] 15 U.S.C. § 1.

The Windows OS accounted for the vast majority of PC operating system sales and the vast majority of the installed base of PC users. In large part because of the large number of Windows OS users, a huge number of applications, including the highly successful Office suite, had been written for Windows. The array of applications available for the Windows OS enhanced the value of that OS, both because it enabled the operating system to be useful to users with a wider range of application needs and because, when selecting an OS, users value confidence that they will be able to use other, unanticipated applications if their application needs change. It would be very difficult for a firm successfully to offer a competing operating system unless users of that OS would be able also to use a very substantial number of applications. Because much of the costs of developing and marketing applications are sunk (i.e., cannot easily be of value elsewhere) and costs of revising applications so that they can run on different operating systems are substantial, an application initially written for the Windows OS cannot easily be ported to another operating system. Applications developers are, moreover, less likely to write applications for other OSs that have far fewer users. There is, in other words, a "chicken-and-egg" problem, in which one cannot sell a new OS without an abundance of applications, and applications will not be written for a new OS until it has lots of users.

In antitrust parlance, this chicken-and-egg problem meant that Microsoft's OS monopoly was protected by a formidable entry barrier: the need for a huge body of applications available to users of competing OSs. This entry barrier, which came to be known as the "applications barrier to entry" (ABE), was central to the Microsoft case.

Netscape Navigator threatened to reduce that entry barrier. Navigator (and other browsers) relied on Java, a "cross-platform" programming language that was developed and marketed by Sun Microsystems. Java and Navigator, which could themselves run on both the Windows OS and other operating systems, gave applications programmers the ability to write programs that, without additional porting expense, would run on all operating systems. Java and Navigator functioned in effect as a form of "middleware," software that sits on top of an operating system and serves as the foundation for other applications. According to the DOJ, Netscape threatened Microsoft because its browser had the potential to distribute cross-platform Java to independent software developers. If those developers chose to write applications for other operating systems (such as IBM's OS/2 or Linux) or if they wrote directly to Navigator APIs (in which case the applications could be accessed by any operating system capable of using Navigator), the ABE would be reduced, and the Windows monopoly would be at risk.

Brief Overview of the Antitrust Issues

At the heart of the *Microsoft* case was DOJ's claim that Microsoft had engaged in a range of anticompetitive acts whose purpose and effect were to severely limit the commercial viability of the Netscape browser and thus to deflect the threat that the Netscape and Java middleware posed for Microsoft's OS monopoly. DOJ did not question the lawfulness of Microsoft's historical success that had led to its OS monopoly, but rather alleged that Microsoft was using its monopoly to thwart new competition and thereby threatened consumers with higher prices and diminished innovation in the future.

In response, Microsoft argued that it was not a monopoly, because it faced significant competitive threats in a highly dynamic industry, and that its conduct was pro-competitive because it brought innovations (such as the integration of IE with the Windows OS) to consumers and aided the distribution of those innovations. Microsoft argued that imposition of antitrust penalties for its conduct would diminish incentives for aggressive competition and would lead to less, rather than more, innovation.

The Outcome

In its April 3, 2000, opinion, the district court found in favor of DOJ on almost all of its claims. The Court ruled for the Government with respect to its Section 2 claims, including both its core maintenance-of-monopoly claim regarding the PC OS market and the separate attempted monopolization claim regarding the browser market, and on the claim that Microsoft had tied the IE browser to the OS in violation of Section 1. Although the Court rejected DOJ's claim that certain of Microsoft's agreements with third parties constituted exclusive dealing in violation of Section 1, it effectively prohibited those agreements because they were a part of the Section 2 violations.

Judge Jackson then accepted the Government's proposed remedies, which included conduct remedies that would limit Microsoft's use of exclusive contracts and its control over the PC "desktop." He also supported the Government's proposal that Microsoft be divided into two smaller companies—an operating system company and an applications company. The latter would maintain control over the browser business, although the OS company would retain property rights with respect to the current version of the browser. Judge Jackson agreed to stay his remedies until after the appeals court heard the case.

In an *en banc* hearing, the entire Court of Appeals for the District of Columbia Circuit heard Microsoft's appeal of the case. The unanimous appellate decision contained positive elements for both sides. From Microsoft's perspective, the appeal was partially successful because the appeals court (i) reversed Judge Jackson's decision that Microsoft had attempted to monopolize the browser market and (ii) remanded (sent back) the case to the lower court for a rehearing on the remedy issue and on DOJ's tying claim. But the decision was generally regarded as a victory for the Government because the court (i) upheld the maintenance of monopoly claim; (ii) in so doing, found almost every aspect of the conduct challenged by DOJ to be illegal; and (iii) generally accepted DOJ's economic theories, factual allegations, and legal framework. The Court of Appeals' rejection of DOJ's attempt-to-monopolize claim and remand of the tying claim had little practical consequence because the conduct on which those claims were based was found to be unlawful as part of the maintenance of monopoly claim.

In the initial remedy proceedings before Judge Jackson, DOJ (under Assistant Attorney General Joel Klein) recommended a structural remedy—a breakup of Microsoft into an operating system company and an applications company. DOJ believed that behavioral remedies were likely to be either ineffective or so intrusive and cumbersome as to be inefficient. DOJ argued that a breakup of Microsoft would likely encourage competition and lead to greater innovation. Despite DOJ's arguments, the Court of Appeals expressed skepticism about a structural remedy when it remanded the case to the District Court.

A different District Court judge, Judge Colleen Kollar–Kotelly, presided over the case on remand. DOJ (now in a new Administration, and led by Assistant Attorney General Charles James) chose not to pursue either the Section 1 tying claims or a structural remedy. Instead, after extensive negotiations, DOJ (and nine of the plaintiff states) agreed with Microsoft on the terms of a conduct remedy that included three basic components. First, the remedy sought to prevent Microsoft from excluding rivals from the OEM channel of distribution by prohibiting restrictive licensing agreements and outlawing retaliatory measures against OEMs by Microsoft. Second, it attempted to keep open the ISP distribution channel by placing limits on Microsoft's ability to discourage others from developing, promoting, or distributing non-Microsoft middleware products. Third, the settlement included a series of compliance measures whose goal is to facilitate enforcement of the other terms of the settlement agreement.

A number of states opposed the proposed settlement and argued that it would be ineffective. Their primary concern was that the proposed settlement did not prohibit Microsoft from bundling Microsoft non-browser middleware into the Windows operating system. Absent such prohibition, they argued, Microsoft would be free to tie other kinds of middleware software to the OS in order to exclude similar software offered by others that threatened the Windows monopoly. The opposing states also argued that the proposed consent decree would not effectively prohibit retaliatory conduct and restrictive licensing practices, would not effectively open the ISP channel of distribution, and would allow Microsoft to withhold needed technical information from developers of rival middleware. Finally, they argued that the proposed enforcement mechanism would be ineffective.

Judge Kollar–Kotelly's ruling was generally supportive of the settlement agreement reached between DOJ (and the settling states) and Microsoft. While the court rejected most of the more aggressive remedies proposed by the nine litigating states, the Court did order more stringent compliance procedures that were sympathetic to issues raised by the litigating states. The Court of Appeals affirmed Judge Kollar–Kotelly's order.

III. THE TRIAL

The Players

In a somewhat unusual move, DOJ hired New York attorney David Boies as Special Trial Counsel to lead its trial team. Boies joined the team near the end of DOJ's multi-year investigation and shortly before the complaint was filed. He was supported at the trial by the talented group of government staff attorneys and economists that had handled the investigation.[8]

Microsoft's trial team was lead by John Warden of Sullivan & Cromwell in New York. He was aided by a first-rate group of attorneys from his and other firms and from Microsoft itself. William Neukom, Microsoft's General Counsel, appeared throughout the trial.

While antitrust had seemed like a dry subject to the public and the press, let alone to a generation of law students, this trial marked a sea change. The courtroom was packed every day of the trial, with the press claiming a substantial share of the seating capacity. It is often thought that there are few surprises at trial, because both sides are well informed by the discovery process; but there were surprises at this trial. One of the first resulted from Microsoft's decision not to call CEO Bill Gates as a witness to tell Microsoft's story. That decision was not surprising. Gates had been subjected to three days of videotaped deposition by the Government. His answers to numerous questions appeared nonresponsive and evasive, and he failed to recall a number of significant e-mails concerning browser competition. But, in a surprising turnaround, the Government chose to introduce Gates' testimony, in the form of excerpts from his videotaped deposition, as part of *its* case.

---

[8] The states were represented most actively by Steven Houck of the New York State Antitrust Bureau.

Another peculiarity of this high-tech trial was that none of the three principal players in the trial—David Boies, John Warden, and Judge Jackson—was known to be an extensive PC user. David Boies, for one, while knowledgeable about the computer industry, relied heavily on the use of yellow legal pads.

Because the legal issues in the case involved substantial, complex issues of economics, each of the parties put forward its own economic expect. Franklin Fisher of MIT was the U.S. Government's economic expert, and his former Ph.D. student Richard Schmalensee, also of MIT, was Microsoft's expert. Rick Warren–Boulton was the States' economic expert.

The Parties' Strategies

There was a sharp divergence between the litigation strategies of the two parties. DOJ's strategy was to build up the elements of each of the legal claims in a detailed, traditional manner, first developing its view of market definition (an Intel-based PC OS market), then explaining why Microsoft had monopoly power in that market, and finally moving on to develop a foundation for each of the alleged anticompetitive practices. As part of its evidence, DOJ introduced email and other documentary materials that supported its view that Microsoft had intended the conduct complained of to harm Netscape and Java, rather than to benefit consumers.

By contrast, Microsoft not only attacked the evidentiary basis of DOJ's case, but also tried to win a broad, perhaps ideological victory by attacking the economic and legal premises of the Government's case. Thus, Microsoft countered DOJ's case by arguing that as a competitor in a dynamic, high technology market it should be protected from the application of classic, static competition principles, which it said could undermine its ability to innovate and to compete for the next generation of PC customers. While the Government focused on the specific details of Microsoft's conduct—for example, that Microsoft had excluded IE from the Add/Remove utility in Windows 98—Microsoft addressed the facts at a higher level of generality—for example, that bundling IE and Windows offered benefits to consumers. Along the way, Microsoft argued that there is no valid PC OS market, that there were no significant barriers to entry, that Microsoft did not have monopoly power, and that none of Microsoft's practices injured competition.

As noted, DOJ began its case by attempting to prove the existence of a PC OS market in which Microsoft had monopoly power. As to market definition, DOJ introduced evidence that the functionality and uses of products with Intel-based operating systems were substantially different from the functionality and uses of mobile, hand-held computers, workstations, mainframe computers, and other alternatives that Microsoft argued should be included in the market. DOJ then undertook to prove monopoly power through evidence of Microsoft's stable, high market shares and the presence of high barriers to entry (the applications barrier to entry). The Government's first exhibit was a simple, yet effective black and white table, listing the market shares of each of the PC OS competitors over a period of years.

By conventional antitrust standards, DOJ's evidence on market definition and market power was compelling. Microsoft faced a strategic decision. Should it take on a difficult fight about market definition and monopoly power, or should it admit to having a lawful monopoly gained through its "skill, foresight, and industry." The former would give Microsoft multiple ways to win the case and offered the possibility of a victory that, because it concerned market structure, would be valuable in future cases; but it risked squandering Microsoft's credibility by making arguments that were very unlikely to succeed and that seemed on their face to be almost untenable. The latter alternative would enable Microsoft to focus on issues about its conduct on which it was more likely to prevail.

Microsoft chose the former strategy. Its decision to concede nothing had a major impact on the trial. The Government's aggressive case on market definition and market power undermined Microsoft's credibility and made some of the Microsoft's witnesses appear unreliable. Ultimately, DOJ was successful not only on the ultimate market definition and market power issues, but also in persuading Judge Jackson about the applications barrier to entry (a term coined during the case itself), which was critical to DOJ's allegations about Microsoft's conduct.

The difficulties Microsoft faced on the market definition and monopoly power issues were exemplified by one of Microsoft's early trial exhibits, an elaborate, colorful exhibit (Figure 1) entitled, "Microsoft Faces Long–Run Competition from Many Known and Unknown Sources." The exhibit and associated testimony left the impression that, while current competitors (OS/2, Linux, the BE operating system) may not provide much competitive restraint, the prospect of future competition was sufficient to limit Windows' ability to raise price or restrict output. Ultimately, the exhibit (and associated testimony) did not succeed; having to depend on "unknown" competition to argue against monopoly power was asking for too much, at least absent proof that there were no entry barriers.

With respect to Microsoft's exclusionary conduct, a central issue in both the Section 1 and Section 2 claims was whether Microsoft had effectively foreclosed important channels of distribution from Netscape's browser (Navigator). Microsoft's first exhibit on the issue, entitled "There are Many Channels Used to Distribute Software," was simple,

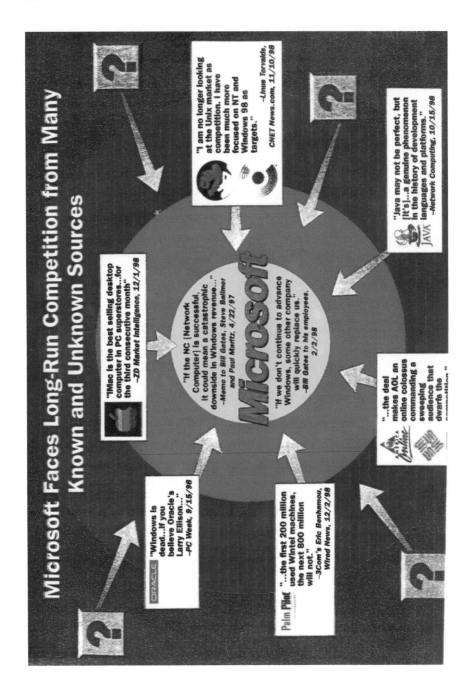

There Are Many Channels Used to Distribute Software

	Channel	Netscape	Microsoft
1	Retail sales through computer "superstores", electronics stores, department stores, and small, specialized retailers	✓	✓
2	Mail order sales	✓	✓
3	Bundling with other software	✓	✓
4	Bundling with hardware other than computer systems	✓	✓
5	Pre-loading via Windows desktop	✓	✓
6	Packaging of disks or a CD with new computer systems	✓	✓
7	Direct sales through telemarketing	✓	✓
8	Direct sales to corporate accounts	✓	✓
9	Direct mail	✓	✓
10	Distribution with magazines and newspapers	✓	✓
11	Internet sign-up with downloading or mailing of software	✓	✓
12	Free Internet downloads	✓	✓
13	Promotional agreements with other Web-sites	✓	✓
14	Use of copies of free software from friends or work	✓	✓

yet effective (see Figure 2). Its listing of fourteen channels of distribution, with check marks for Netscape and Microsoft in each channel, delivered the clear message that Netscape's access to customers was not restricted. It was left to DOJ in rebuttal to point out that, while Netscape had access to all those channels, its access to most of them, including the most important channels, was significantly restricted.

A second, elaborate graphical illustration of the same point was likely less effective, at least with respect to Judge Jackson (although it did entertain the reporters sitting in the courtroom). The colorful, artistic exhibit (see Figure 3) was entitled "Pre-loading Software on Windows is One of Many Ways to Distribute Software to Consumers." In the exhibit, a group of consumers is situated on an island. Software is distributed to those consumers through parachuting individuals (Internet download), a blimp (promotional agreements), a sailboat (retail sales), a man on a high wire (direct sales), a gondola (bundling with hardware/software), a man on a motorcycle crossing a bridge (distribution through magazines and newspapers), a man on a horse (direct mail), a motor boat (mail order sales), and a rail line (Windows desktop).

Figure 3

Ultimately, Microsoft was able to convince Judge Jackson that there was not sufficient evidence of foreclosure (i.e., evidence that 40 percent of the distribution channels were foreclosed) for a finding of exclusive dealing in violation of Section 1. But both Judge Jackson and the unanimous Court of Appeals found the evidence of foreclosure sufficient for DOJ's maintenance of monopoly claim under Section 2.

One can imagine an even more colorful graphical rebuttal exhibit illustrating DOJ's allegations about Microsoft's aggressive conduct. But DOJ in fact used few demonstrative exhibits and focused instead on Microsoft's emails, documents, and deposition testimony. The contrast in approach may have had the effect of making DOJ's case appear grounded in the evidence, and Microsoft's based on metaphor.

IV. WHAT THE CASE DECIDED

On one level, the legacy of the case is straightforward. The government prevailed on its maintenance of monopoly claim but not on its other claims. Both Judge Jackson and the Court of Appeals found almost every aspect of Microsoft's conduct challenged by DOJ to be illegal because of its effect on the OS market. The unlawful conduct included restrictive terms in Microsoft's license agreements with OEMs; commingling of browser and non-browser files in Windows; removing IE from the Add/Remove utility; restrictive agreements with Internet Access Providers, Internet Content Providers, and independent software vendors; dealings with Apple Computer and Intel; and various agreements and deception regarding Java. The Court of Appeals rejected DOJ's attempted monopolization and tying claims for legal reasons having to do with DOJ's failure to prove the requisite effects of the same conduct in the separate browser market.

The conduct remedy ordered after the remand from the Court of Appeals no doubt constrained Microsoft's behavior in some ways, but Microsoft's monopoly of the PC OS market appears unabated. The potential threats to Microsoft's market power that are discussed today—from companies like Google—were not anticipated when the case was brought. Some believe that the remedy actually did lower entry barriers to the market and promoted competition from rival suppliers of middleware, but whether they are correct is a difficult question whose answer will become clear only over time.

Although the impact of the case on Microsoft's PC OS monopoly is uncertain, the case appears to have had a larger impact on Microsoft overall. The government case spurred numerous private lawsuits that Microsoft settled at substantial cost, and the case likely encouraged government actions in the EU, Korea and elsewhere that have been, at the very least, burdensome and costly for Microsoft. The clear message would seem to be that being found to have violated the antitrust laws in a government enforcement action can be very costly—and is therefore something to be avoided—quite apart from any injunctive remedy obtained by the government.

The most important legacy of the case is thus likely to be, not its impact on Microsoft's OS monopoly, but rather its impact on antitrust enforcement. The Government had brought a Section 2 case against IBM in the late 1960s; the case lasted for over a decade before it was finally dropped. The IBM case is now widely viewed as a failure of Government enforcement; while the Government's allegations may have had force when the investigation of IBM first began, those allegations were no longer valid by the time the case was ready for trial. *U.S. v. Microsoft* is easily contrasted. The time period between the investigation and the trial on the merits was about three years, and the issues at trial were clearly salient at that time.

The issue of timing was crucial because the computer industry was and is highly dynamic and technology intensive. The computer industry represented the protypical "new economy" industry. *U.S. v. Microsoft* was the first government case to deal directly with the so-called "new economy" and, as noted, the first government Section 2 case of any kind in nearly 20 years. Partly because of Microsoft's strategic choices, a wide range of both basic and arcane issues were fully litigated and ultimately resolved by a unanimous Court of Appeals.[9] The government prevailed on most of these issues, including its Section 2 claim. Some might point to the lack of resolution with respect to the tying claims and the ineffectiveness of the ultimate remedy as failures. But the ability to put forward an effective case and to reach a timely resolution on the merits of a new economy case is significant; and the judicial resolution of those issues that were decided is likely to inform antitrust law for a generation.

The resolution of important antitrust issue in a dynamic, high technology industry is the most important legacy of the Microsoft case. Some of these issues concerned the economics of the new economy; others concerned antitrust law itself.

Economic Issues—Thinking About the Information Economy[10]

History is written by the winners and rewritten by the losers, often so much so that one forgets what it was like before the battle. The Microsoft case affected how we think about the information economy in several ways.

---

[9] The final disposition of the case was substantially delayed, however. Following a change in presidential administrations, the Court of Appeals' remand with respect to remedy and related settlement discussions and administrative proceedings extended the case for several years.

[10] *See generally* Franklin M. Fisher and Daniel L. Rubinfeld, "U.S. v. Microsoft: An Economic Analysis," *The Antitrust Bulletin* 1 (Spring 2001).

Network Effects. Central to the government's theory was the concept of "network effects," the idea that some products become more valuable as they become more widely used and that widely used products are to some extent insulated from competition from other products, even if those other products were superior in some sense. The concept is easy to understand with respect to what are called "direct network effects," such as the benefit to a telephone user from being able to reach lots of other telephone users that are connected to the network. In the Microsoft case, however, the government built its barrier to entry argument on "indirect network effects"—the idea that OS users benefit indirectly from a large base of users of the same OS because that base attracts applications which in turn make the OS more valuable, much the way VHS defeated Betamax in the VCR standard war largely because more motion pictures were released in the VHS format.

The idea behind the ABE was that an OS entrant would face a daunting "chicken-and-egg" problem in that it could not find customers for its OS unless it could assure them that they would be able to use thousands of applications with the OS and it could not get application writers to write applications for the OS until it had millions of customers. The ABE was central to the government's case because it provided the motivation both for the development of middleware, such as Navigator, and cross-platform languages, such as Java, and for Microsoft's efforts to exclude them. ABE was a new concept.

Microsoft and its allies vigorously opposed the idea and importance of network effects, both in general and with respect to the operating system, and argued that there were no significant barriers to entry. In articles, speeches and briefs, they disputed the historical examples used by early proponents to explain the idea of network effects, and they disputed the logic and legal significance of network effects. Further, they attacked a straw man by arguing that firms do not retain their dominance forever, even in markets characterized by network effects. This argument was especially infelicitous because the government's case was premised on the proposition that, while network effects enabled Microsoft to exercise monopoly power, they did not so insulate Microsoft from competition as to make application of the antitrust laws meaningless.

In the end, Judge Jackson and the Court of Appeals agreed completely with the government's analysis. The idea of network effects is now an important staple of antitrust law and economics that defendants and plaintiffs alike take for granted. That was not so before the Microsoft case. Had Microsoft's attack been successful, antitrust enforcement in dynamic, high technology industries would have suffered a serious setback.

Non–Leverage Tying. The core of the government's case was the allegation that Microsoft wanted to exclude the Navigator browser from the browser market in order to protect its OS monopoly. The idea was that, if Navigator achieved nearly ubiquitous distribution in the browser market, it might become a form of cross-platform middleware that would attract applications and thereby undermine the ABE because users of any OS would be able to access and use those applications through Navigator.

The principal means used by Microsoft to exclude Navigator, according to the government, were the various steps Microsoft took to bundle IE with Windows—commingling files, changing the Add/Remove utility, preventing OEMs from removing the IE icon from the desktop, and so on. It was, to our knowledge, the first time that tying of separate products had been challenged principally on the ground that it protected an existing monopoly in the dominant or tying product (here, the OS), rather than as a scheme to leverage that monopoly into market power in an adjacent market (here, in the browser market). Microsoft disputed the theory, arguing among other things that it was inconsistent both to allege that the browser posed a competitive threat to Windows and to define the relevant market to include only the OS and not the browser.

Both Judge Jackson and the Court of Appeals agreed with the government's theory. The idea that tying can be used to protect a monopoly in the tying product market is now an accepted part of antitrust analysis.[11]

Market Definition and Market Power. The government alleged that the market consisted of PC OSs, on the ground that there are no good substitutes for their particular set of functions, and that Microsoft had monopoly power in that market. For the latter point, the government relied on Microsoft's large and stable market share and the fact that Microsoft was able to impose onerous conditions on OEMs and others who wanted access to the Windows OS.

Microsoft disputed these allegations, largely by means of an argument that traditional antitrust concepts are not applicable to the "new economy." According to Microsoft, it held only a precarious position in a high-tech industry characterized by Schumpeterian or winner-take-all competition in which one firm would have a large share for a short while, only to be displaced when another firm developed a better product. Thus, Microsoft argued, despite its large share of OS sales, it was not able to exercise market power because it had to strive diligently to anticipate and compete against future rivals.

---

[11] *See, e.g.*, Dennis Carlton and Michael Waldman, "The Strategic Use of Tying to Preserve and Create Market Power in Evolving Industries." 33 *Rand Journal of Economics* 193 (Summer 2002).

In the end, both Judge Jackson and the Court of Appeals agreed with the government that, as long as there are barriers to entry to the relevant market, the kind of Schumpeterian competition described by Microsoft is not inconsistent with the existence of monopoly power. Indeed, the government's case was at bottom an effort to establish antitrust restrictions on conduct that might undermine such competition. By agreeing with the government on these matters, the courts ensured that antitrust would remain relevant and applicable to the new economy.

Legal Issues—How to Think about Antitrust

The Microsoft case resolved, sometimes explicitly and sometimes implicitly, a wide range of legal issues. Some involved matters of legal doctrine; others involved more subtle questions of antitrust methodology.

Dynamic, High Technology Industries. Microsoft's allies argued that antitrust principles were either inapplicable—because based on outmoded, static modes of analysis—or should be relaxed—in order not to interfere with rapidly changing markets—in dynamic, high tech industries. But Judge Jackson and the Court of Appeals essentially agreed with the government that the same antitrust principles apply to all industries, although they of course need to be applied with sensitivity to the particular facts. It is now well-accepted, as Judge Posner put it, that "antitrust doctrine is supple enough, and its commitment to economic rationality strong enough, to take in stride the competitive issues presented by the new economy."[12]

Intellectual Property. In something of a precursor to the current controversies at the intersection of antitrust and intellectual property law, Microsoft made sweeping arguments about the implications of its copyright and other intellectual property. "The company claims," the Court of Appeals said, "an absolute and unfettered right to use its intellectual property as it wishes."[13] Such a right, Microsoft seemed to reason, was necessary in order for Microsoft and others to gain from their intellectual property the rewards intended for the creative or innovative effort that created the intellectual property.

The courts rejected Microsoft's argument. The Court of Appeals said that it "borders on the frivolous."[14] The courts thus made clear in effect, as DOJ and FTC had stated in their Guidelines for the Licensing of

---

[12] Richard A. Posner, "Antitrust in the New Economy," 68 *Antitrust L. J.* 925 at 925 (2001).

[13] *United States v. Microsoft,* 253 F.3d 34, 63 (D.C. Cir. 2001) (en banc) (per curiam).

[14] *Id.*

Intellectual Property, that "intellectual property is essentially comparable to any other form of property."[15] The Guidelines state that the agencies "apply the same general antitrust principles to conduct involving intellectual property that they apply to conduct involving any other form" of property:

> An intellectual property owner's rights to exclude are similar to the rights enjoyed by owners of other forms of private property. As with other forms of private property, certain types of conduct with respect to intellectual property may have anticompetitive effects against which the antitrust laws can and do protect. Intellectual property is thus neither particularly free from scrutiny under the antitrust laws, nor particularly suspect under them.[16]

Product Design. In the 1997 proceeding, in which DOJ alleged that Microsoft had tied IE to its Windows OS in violation of the 1995 consent decree, Microsoft had argued that product design should be a safe harbor under the antitrust laws on the ground that judicial oversight is more likely to interfere with desirable innovation than to prevent anticompetitive conduct. The three-judge Court of Appeals panel in that proceeding was sympathetic to the argument. It held that review of product design should be "narrow and deferential," that a court should not "embark on product design assessment," and that the issue is not whether the combination of functionalities into a single product is a *"net* plus but merely whether there is a plausible claim that it brings some advantage."[17]

That proceeding concerned the meaning of the earlier consent decree. In the subsequent antitrust case, the unanimous en banc Court of Appeals took a very different approach. Where particular aspects of Microsoft's product design excluded rivals, the court required Microsoft to establish a pro-competitive justification for the design. The court held that both the commingling of browsing and other code in the same file and excluding IE from the Add/Remove Programs utility were unlawful because they tended to exclude Navigator and Microsoft offered no justification for them. The Court of Appeals upheld other aspects of Microsoft's product design that were shown to serve legitimate purposes.

The Court of Appeals noted that courts are as a general rule "properly very skeptical about claims that competition has been harmed by a dominant firm's product design changes."[18] But it plainly rejected

---

[15] Department of Justice, Antitrust Division, and Federal Trade Commission, "Antitrust Guidelines for the Licensing of Intellectual Property" (April 6, 1995), § 2.0.

[16] *Id.* at § 2.1.

[17] *United States v. Microsoft,* 147 F.3d at 949–950 (emphasis in original).

[18] *United States v. Microsoft Corp.*, 253 F.3d at 65.

any notion of a safe harbor or an unwillingness to undertake a "design assessment." Indeed, the en banc court said, "[t]o the extent that the [1998] decision completely disclaimed judicial capacity to evaluate 'high-tech product design,' it cannot be said to conform to prevailing antitrust doctrine."[19]

Broad Brush or Fine Tooth Comb. Resolution of any legal dispute requires determining implicitly or explicitly the level of generality at which the conduct at issue will be assessed. The parties in the Microsoft case disagreed profoundly about this issue.

DOJ examined Microsoft's conduct in detail. According to DOJ, it was permissible for Microsoft to bundle IE with Windows at no additional change, but it was not permissible for Microsoft to prevent OEMs from deleting means of accessing the browser or to deny users that ability by excluding IE from the Add/Remove utility; Microsoft was permitted to offer IE to Internet Access Providers free of charge but not to offer them promotional inducements in exchange for their commitment not to distribute Navigator; Microsoft could design and offer its own version of a Java Virtual Machine, but it could not design its Java development tools so that program developers would unwittingly design programs that would run only on Windows; and so on.

Microsoft almost uniformly approached the case at a higher level of generality. It treated the Add/Remove issue as one of product design, the IAP agreements as efforts to promote its platform, the Java development tools as part of its Java product improvement, and so on.

Judge Jackson and the Court of Appeals consistently took the government's approach and assessed Microsoft's conduct in detail. In this respect, the Microsoft case clearly stands for the proposition that any discrete aspect of a monopolist's conduct that tends to exclude rivals may be illegal unless there is a legitimate, pro-competitive justification for that particular aspect of the conduct.

Cumulative Effects and Course of Conduct. Microsoft argued throughout the case that each of the various acts complained of was too insignificant to exclude Navigator from the market. The Government, by contrast, argued that anticompetitive acts whose effects are too insignificant to be unlawful by themselves can become unlawful if their cumulative effect is significant enough.

The Court of Appeals did not explicitly resolve this dispute, explaining that it "need not pass on" the government's argument because Judge Jackson had not pointed "to any series of acts, each of which harms competition only slightly but the cumulative effect of which is

---

[19] *Id.* at 92 (citation omitted).

significant enough" to be unlawful.[20] But the Court appeared implicitly to agree with the government when it held that certain agreements with independent software vendors were unlawful on the ground that, although they affected only a "small channel for browser distribution," they had a "greater significance" because Microsoft had also largely foreclosed other channels.[21]

The Role of Rules. Both parties tried to rely on antitrust rules when they thought the rules favored them. Microsoft, as noted, argued that product design and use of intellectual property were beyond the reach of the antitrust laws. In addition, having persuaded Judge Jackson that its various exclusive dealing agreements did not violate Section 1 because they tied up less than 40 percent of the market, Microsoft argued that the same 40 percent rule should apply to the Section 2 claims. For its part, the government argued that, because there appeared to be separate demand for IE and Windows, they constituted separate products the bundling of which was illegal under the per se rule applicable to tying.

The Court of Appeals rejected such a rule-based approach. "Even assuming" that Judge Jackson was correct about exclusive dealing agreements under Section 1, the Court said, a monopolist can violate Section 2 by using exclusive contracts "in certain circumstances."[22] And the Court held that the automatic or per se rule against tying did not apply to this case because of the particular attributes of "platform software."[23] The Court of Appeals was relentless in eschewing formalistic rule-based analysis in favor of careful attention to the facts.

Causation. Except for the few types of conduct that are unlawful per se under the antitrust laws, conduct, no matter how offensive, can violate the antitrust laws only if it injures competition in the market as a whole. Microsoft argued that no such effect had been proven. It reasoned that the idea that Navigator and Java, if unimpeded by Microsoft, would have spurred OS competition and eroded Microsoft's dominance was sheer conjecture unsupported by proof.

The Court of Appeals rejected Microsoft's argument. While it cautioned that "Microsoft's concerns over causation have more purchase in connection with the appropriate remedy issue,"[24] it held that causation can be inferred "when exclusionary conduct is aimed at producers of

---

[20] *Id.* at 78.

[21] *Id.* at 72.

[22] *Id.* at 70.

[23] *Id.* at 89–95.

[24] *Id.* at 80.

nascent competitive technologies" as well as when it is aimed at producers of established substitutes.[25] In such a case, the question is not whether the nascent technologies "would actually have developed into viable" substitutes but whether they "reasonably constituted nascent threats."[26]

Tying. In addition to the non-leverage tying theory under Section 2, described above, the government also pursued a more traditional per se tying claim under Section 1. The theory behind this claim was that Microsoft had injured competition in the browser, or "tied product," market by tying the browser to the OS. The government argued, among other things, that the OS and the browser should be regarded as separate products for this purpose because there was separate demand for them. The district court agreed.

The court of appeals reversed, holding that the per se ban on tying is inapplicable to platform software. The court reasoned that the separate demand test is not suitable for rapidly changing products such as platform software because evidence of separate demand in the past would not reflect possible benefits from integration into a single product of software functionalities that had previously been sold as separate products. Although the court's decision purported to be narrowly focused on platform software, its reasoning could be applied more broadly and might signal a deeper judicial skepticism about the per se tying rule.

Anticompetitive Conduct Under Section 2. One of the major unresolved issues in antitrust is the standard for determining when conduct is "anticompetitive" for purposes of Section 2. The government argued, as it has argued since, that conduct is anticompetitive when it would not make business sense for the defendant but for its tendency to exclude rivals and thus create or maintain market power for the defendant. Microsoft did not articulate a specific standard but generally argued that firms should be given wide berth lest antitrust enforcement inhibit innovation.

The Court of Appeals did not explicitly agree with either party. Instead, it articulated its own test: Conduct is anticompetitive if (i) it harms the competitive process and (ii) either (a) is not shown to further efficiency or to have some other pro-competitive justification or (b) the anticompetitive harm outweighs its pro-competitive benefit.[27]

It is not clear precisely what this test means. The DOJ test and the Court of Appeals test are in substance identical with respect to points (i) and (ii) (a) of the Court's test. Where they appear to diverge is with respect to conduct that both harms competition and furthers a legitimate

[25] *Id.* at 79.

[26] *Id.*

[27] *Id.* at 58–59.

purpose. DOJ proposed to decide those cases by inquiring whether the conduct would have made sense for the defendant—whether it would have been profitable—even if it had not harmed competition. The Court of Appeals proposed instead "weighing" the two competing effects, but it did not articulate any metric or algorithm for the weighing.

The Court of Appeals had little occasion to undertake any such "weighing" because it found that almost all of Microsoft's exclusionary conduct served no legitimate purpose at all. In the two or three instances in which the court concluded that the conduct did offer a pro-competitive benefit, the court upheld the conduct without elaborate balancing. Its opinion might be read to mean that any procompetitive benefit is enough to outweigh harm to competition. If so read, it would in this respect stand for the unremarkable proposition that conduct by a monopolist that injures competition and serves no legitimate purpose is illegal. But the balancing test articulated by the Court appeared to go further, and the Court's facile treatment of the balancing exercise might simply have reflected the Court's belief that those few aspects of Microsoft's conduct that did offer a procompetitive benefit posed only an insubstantial threat to competition. The legacy of the case with respect to the standard for anticompetitive conduct is unclear.

V. SUMMING UP

The Microsoft case was a contest between two fundamentally different approaches to antitrust law. The government built its case from the facts, with meticulous attention to the details. It did not broadly attack Microsoft's right to compete aggressively, to innovate and to bring its products to markets. It attacked instead specific aspects of Microsoft's conduct that it believed went too far—conduct that both interfered with rivals' ability to gain widespread market acceptance for their products and did not advance any meaningful, legitimate, pro-competitive interest.

Microsoft, by contrast, advanced broad, sometimes ideological arguments. Its defense emphasized the dynamic nature of the industry, the importance of innovation, reasons why courts should not interfere with product design or the use of intellectual property, and the quality of its products. It often ignored entirely allegations that specific aspects of its conduct harmed rivals without serving any legitimate purpose. It sought a sweeping victory that would largely free it from antitrust scrutiny.

As to this difference in approach, the government was the clear winner. The Court of Appeals' unanimous en banc opinion was remarkable for its lack of ideology and sweeping rhetoric, its careful attention to detail and its unwillingness to rely on formalistic legal rules. Perhaps the most important lesson of the case is that—in spite of all the press attention and editorial ferment that the case provoked—it was ultimately the details that mattered.

11

Jonathan B. Baker and Robert Pitofsky*

A Turning Point in Merger Enforcement: *Federal Trade Commission v. Staples*

1. Opening Day

The first day of merger trials is usually a staid and dry affair. Not so with Staples–Office Depot. At the rear of the courtroom, counsel advocating the merger hung a large banner with the emphatic message "Save Even More." Defense counsel's opening statement was illustrated with a large number of exhibits and charts and with audio interludes. And every seat in the courtroom was taken—by lawyers, journalists, and stock market speculators (arbitrageurs) betting on who would win and who would lose the case.

The court proceeding was not an effort by the government to block the merger permanently. Rather its goal was to obtain a preliminary injunction preventing the merger from being consummated pending a full trial. Without that kind of injunction, the parties can often scramble the assets of the two firms with the result that a remedy is close to impossible. On the other hand, mergers are time sensitive: a long pending transaction held up by government review in a full trial can have an adverse effect on the morale of executives and staff, adversely affect stock market prices, and harm firm reputations (particularly of the acquired firm) in the marketplace. As a result, the award of a preliminary injunction usually means the end of the deal in practical terms.

* Jonathan Baker is Professor of Law, Washington College of Law, American University; Robert Pitofsky is Joseph and Madeline Sheehy Professor of Antitrust Law, Georgetown University Law Center. We are grateful to Bill Baer and George Cary for helpful discussions, and to Farrell Malone of Georgetown University Law Center and Ian Hoffman of William and Mary Law School, for their excellent assistance in preparing this paper; errors of course are ours.

The lead attorneys for the government and for the merging firms—George Cary for the government, and Donald Kempf for the merging parties—laid out the essentials of their case in opening statements to Judge Thomas Hogan. As is common in merger cases, there was no jury. Cary explained that the merger would have an effect on a market that he described as consumable office supplies—that is, pencils, pens, post-it notes, paper, even staples—the sort of product that people return again and again to purchase. It would not include furniture, business machines and computers. He described how the office supply superstore concept had only been initiated a dozen years earlier, with Staples in the lead, and at its maximum had more than twenty participants. By the time of the hearing, the industry had grown fantastically—Staples and Office Depot together accounted for more than $10 billion in annual sales—but there were only three office supply superstore chains left: the merging parties, Office Depot and Staples, and OfficeMax. He explained that the government case would be primarily a matter of documents and that the government intended to prove that in geographic areas where three office supply superstores were present and competed, prices were at their lowest; when two were present prices increased; and prices were at their highest when there was only one. He said the government would demonstrate that Office Depot generally had lower prices than Staples and was cutting into its profitability. Staples faced a stark decision: either meet Office Depot's lower prices in the marketplace and reduce its own profits or acquire Office Depot by merger. It chose the latter. He then stated what he thought was the heart of the government's case:

> "What will be the effect on prices? The key fact of this case, Your Honor, is that where Office Depot and Staples compete, their prices are five to ten to fifteen percent lower than where they don't compete. ... All of the evidence directly answers the ultimate question ... Will prices likely be higher after the merger than they would have been without the merger?"[1]

Don Kempf responded for the defendants in a variety of ways. He argued first that the government's description of the marketplace was wildly wrong. Rather than carve out the three office supply superstores as a separate competitive arena, he argued that mass merchandisers like Wal–Mart and KMart, traditional small store retailers, direct mail and internet sales compete with superstores in the sale of office supplies and, therefore, those sellers should be included in the market. In a "properly defined" product market, the combined market share of Staples and Office Depot would be somewhere between and five and six percent, well below any sensible line where a merger should be challenged. He then noted that the whole history of the office supply superstore segment had

---

[1] Transcript (May 19, 1997) at 13–14.

been one of reducing prices to consumers, referring time and again to the "productivity loop." Under that theory, the large scale superstores can extract lower prices from stationery and other suppliers and then pass those lower prices along to consumers, as they had consistently done in the past, in order to increase market share. With larger market shares, the superstores could return to their suppliers and achieve even lower prices.

Kempf used the productivity loop to support his argument that high levels of concentration in this particular industry would not lead to higher prices. He emphasized that experience showed the opposite: as the industry consolidated, and the number of superstore chains declined over the previous decade from twenty to three, prices had continued to decline. The government's pricing evidence was simply "cherry picking" of unrepresentative examples and "nonsense correlations," according to Kempf. Finally, he said he was prepared to demonstrate that somewhere between $5 and $6 billion in savings could be achieved through improved efficiencies, and again that history showed that the office supply superstores passed along large portions of those efficiencies to consumers. He sidestepped the point that the government would constantly press: even conceding that prices had declined in the office supply superstore segment of the economy, the government contended they would have declined even more in the presence of vigorous competition.

2. The Players.

The government's challenge to the proposed merger of Staples and Office Depot was no small deal. Staples was the second largest office supply superstore chain in the United States with 550 stores and revenues of about $4 billion; Office Depot was the largest office supply superstore chain with more than 500 stores and revenues of a little over $6 billion. The only other substantial office supply superstore chain was OfficeMax, also with more than 500 stores.[2] All three chains were growing rapidly, each adding roughly one hundred stores per year nationwide and expanding into regions historically served by other chains.

As emphasized in the opening statements, one central question was whether office supply superstores were a separate product market in which adverse effects on competition could be measured. If the superstores were a market unto themselves, then the result of the merger would be to reduce the number of players from two to one in 15 cities and from three to two in 27 more cities—more than enough concentration to attract the most serious government attention.[3] Also, if the companies remained separate, it was predictable that each would invade

---

[2] *FTC v. Staples, Inc.*, 970 F. Supp. 1066, 1069 (D.D.C. 1997).

[3] *Id.* at 1081.

the turf of the other over time, whereas the merger would eliminate that kind of future competition.[4]

In the late 1990s the United States witnessed one of the most intense merger waves in the history of the country.[5] Robert Pitofsky, one of the authors of this chapter, took office as Chairman of the Federal Trade Commission (FTC) in 1995 pledging an activist antitrust agenda. One of his first moves was to appoint Jonathan Baker (the other author of this chapter) as head of the agency's Bureau of Economics. The Commission voted to challenge a few mergers in 1995 and 1996.[6] But the 1997 challenge to the Staples–Office Depot was far more important and controversial.

The effort to obtain a preliminary injunction, beginning May 19, 1997, lasted only five days but it was exceptionally spirited.[7] Each side was given only fifteen total hours of trial time, including cross-examination of witnesses, and a chess clock was used to keep track. Before the trial, the Commission had reviewed hundreds of boxes of documents and had taken 18 depositions; at trial, the defendants called eight live witnesses and introduced some 6,000 exhibits. After the trial, nine states filed amicus briefs supporting the Federal Trade Commission's case. On

---

[4] *Id.* at 1082.

[5] In 2000, the Federal Trade Commission (FTC) received a record high 4,926 merger filings, representing a 222.1% increase over the number of filings in 1991. FTC Bureau of Competition & DOJ Antitrust Division, Annual Report to Congress Fiscal Year 2000, 1, *available at* http://www.ftc.gov/os/2001/04/annualreport2000.pdf (last visited June 20, 2006).

[6] Rite Aid's proposed acquisition of Revco, a merger of two large pharmacy chains, was abandoned by the parties shortly after the FTC announced its intention to block the deal in court, in April 1996. Press Release, Federal Trade Commission, *Rite Aid Abandons Proposed Acquisition of Revco After FTC Sought To Block Transaction* (April 24, 1996), *available at* http://www.ftc.gov/opa/1996/04/ritenogo.htm (last visited June 21, 2006). A natural gas pipeline acquisition that the FTC concluded would raise prices to industrial customers around Salt Lake City was also abandoned after the FTC announced its challenge, in late 1995. Press Release, Federal Trade Commission, *FTC To Challenge Questar Acquisition of Kern River, Alleging Monopoly Over Natural Gas Transmission Into Salt Lake City Area* (Dec. 27, 1995), *available at* http://www.ftc.gov/opa/1995/12/questr.htm (last visited June 21, 2006). In early 1996, the FTC went to court to challenge a Grand Rapids, Michigan hospital merger. The district court concluded that certain conditions it placed on the merger would solve the competitive problem the FTC had identified without need to enjoin the transaction; that decision was on appeal during the *Staples* litigation. *FTC v. Butterworth Health Corp.*, 946 F. Supp. 1285 (W.D. Mich. 1996), aff'd 121 F.3d 708, 1997 WL 420543 (6th Cir. 1997) (unpublished table opinion). As is usual in merger enforcement, the FTC resolved its competitive concerns in a number of other cases—such as Time Warner's acquisition of Turner Broadcasting in late 1996—through consent settlement, without need to go to court. *See In the Matter of Time Warner, Inc.*, 123 F.T.C. 171 (1997) (consent order).

[7] The hearing concluded with four hours of oral argument about two weeks later.

the other hand, stock market speculators and the national press were overwhelmingly of the view that the companies would prevail and the government would lose its first big merger case of the 1990s.

3.   Merger Enforcement in the United States.

Merger policy issues have been central in the development of American antitrust policy since the enactment of a federal antitrust law in 1890. Difficult policy questions arise because the consequences of mergers can be good or bad or a little of both. Mergers can eliminate rivals and then the combined firm can raise prices to consumers. Mergers can also be a problem by reducing the number of firms in a market with the result that the remaining firms can coordinate sales policies and act like monopolists by coordinating their marketing efforts. There is also a general policy view that high levels of concentration undermine incentives to achieve efficiency and to innovate.[8] On the other hand, in most markets, mergers among relatively small companies pose no threat of monopoly or coordinated behavior and can lead to efficiencies. The combined firm may produce at a lower cost, engage in more aggressive research and development, or allow superior management to take over additional resources.

Merger enforcement in the United States has been remarkably inconsistent over the years. For example, in the 1960s, the United States had a very aggressive merger policy—most people would now say overly aggressive—and successfully struck down mergers among very small firms in unconcentrated markets.[9] In the 1980s, during the second term of the Reagan administration, merger enforcement came close to disappearing.[10] The challenge in the 1990s, during the first Bush Administra-

---

[8] The most eloquent statement of that perspective—now a little out of date—was by Judge Learned Hand in 1945:

> Many people believe that possession of unchallenged economic power deadens initiative, discourages thrift, and depresses energy; that immunity from competition is a narcotic, and rivalry is a stimulant, to industrial progress; that the spur of constant stress is necessary to counteract an inevitable disposition to let well enough alone.

United States v. *Aluminum Co.*, 148 F.2d 416, 427 (2d Cir. 1945).

[9] There are many cases that illustrate the point, but the most indefensible under current standards is *United States* v. *Von's Grocery Co.*, 384 U.S. 270, 281 (1966) where a merger combining grocery firms in Los Angeles of 4.7% and 4.2%, respectively, was struck down even though the number of chains in Los Angeles was on the increase and there were few barriers to new firms entering the market. *See also United States* v. *Pabst Brewing Co.*, 384 U.S. 546 (1966) (combined market shares of 4.5% in one market where violation was found); *Brown Shoe Co.* v. *United States*, 370 U.S. 294, 347–48 (1962) (horizontal merger violations found in some markets with combined market shares of 5% and low entry barriers; violation in the vertical line—between a shoe manufacturer and shoe store outlets—in the 1% to 2% category).

[10] The rate of federal enforcement actions (challenges as a fraction of proposed mergers) during the second term of the Reagan administration was roughly half the typical

tion and then the Clinton years, was to find a middle of the road merger policy that was active in protecting the welfare of consumers from merger-induced higher prices or reductions in quality, while at the same time being sensitive to protect incentives to improve efficiency and productivity and to achieve innovation. The FTC's challenge to the Staples–Office Depot proposed merger was regarded as a major test of its ability to restore effective and sensible merger enforcement—avoiding the undue activism of the 1960s and the extreme under-enforcement of the 1980s—while at the same time indicating the agency's willingness to litigate when the situation called for direct confrontation.

4. The FTC Decides to Challenge

The "first blush or initial gut reaction of many people," Judge Hogan later wrote, is that with so many different types of retailers competing to sell office supplies, a merger of two office supply superstore chains would be unlikely to permit the merged firm to exercise market power.[11] If post-merger Staples "raised prices after the merger, or at least did not lower them as much as they would have as separate companies, . . . consumers, with such a plethora of options, would shop elsewhere."[12] Although every merger reported to the federal enforcement agencies receives some review, the FTC staff cannot practically give each a hard look, and indeed the vast majority are given early termination—that is, they are allowed to proceed without a "second request" for additional information. Why did this transaction, seemingly unlikely on its face to raise an antitrust problem, receive close scrutiny from the FTC's merger enforcers?

Shortly after the merger was announced in September 1996, the FTC staff obtained a report from Prudential Securities, which followed the office superstores market for investors. Prudential Securities surveyed prices for a market basket of office supplies in Paramus, New Jersey, a town in which Staples and OfficeMax competed but not Office Depot, and compared them with the prices for the same market basket purchased in Totowa, New Jersey, twenty-five minutes away, where all three superstore chains competed. According to Prudential Securities, the additional competition from Office Depot led to five percent lower prices.[13] This report suggested to the FTC staff that the loss of competi-

---

rate before and after. Thomas B. Leary, The Essential Stability of Merger Policy in the United States, 70 Antitrust L.J. 105, 139 (2002); *see* Thomas G. Krattenmaker and Robert Pitofsky, Antitrust Merger Policy in the Reagan Administration, 33 Antitrust Bull. 211, 213 (1988).

[11] *Staples*, 970 F. Supp. at 1075.

[12] *Id.*

[13] Discussed and cited in Serdar Dalkir & Frederick R. Warren–Boulton, Prices, Market Definition, and the Effects of Merger: Staples–Office Depot, in The Antitrust

tion among office superstore chains could affect prices, and was one reason the FTC decided to give the proposed merger a close look.

During a typical merger investigation, the FTC staff reviews documents, testimony and data from the merging firms and their executives, and collects similar information from both rivals and customers. Many company documents treated the office supply superstore market as separate and distinct. Also, some unusual information came from consumers. For example, in March 1997, the FTC received a complaint from Thomas Russ of Leesburg, Florida, a "cost-conscious consumer" who owned a small real estate agency and shopped for office supplies "on a continuous basis."[14] The customer sent in two advertising circulars, one from a newspaper in Leesburg, Florida, where he lived and the other from a newspaper in nearby Orlando. (See Figure 1, p. 317.) Office

Figure 1

Comparison of Office Depot's Prices in Two Florida Cities

Revolution: Economics, Competition, and Policy 143, 153 (John E. Kwoka, Jr. & Lawrence J. White eds., 3d ed. 1999).

[14] Transcript (May 23, 1997) at 137. The FTC has published a study showing that strongly credible customer complaints and "hot" internal firm documents clearly predicting merger-related anticompetitive effects make an agency challenge more likely. Federal Trade Commission, Horizontal Merger Investigation Data, Fiscal Years 1996–2003 (available at <http://www.ftc.gov/opa/2004/02/horizmerger.htm>).

Depot was the only superstore chain in Leesburg, but all three major chains competed in Orlando. The ads were identical except for the prices, which were systematically lower in Orlando. "I believe that the lack of competition in Leesburg explains the higher prices compared to the Office Depot stores in Orlando," the consumer later wrote in a declaration. "As a result of these price differences, I am very worried that Staples and Office Depot will be able to raise prices in markets where they directly compete, such as Orlando, Florida."[15]

5. Litigation Context

In April 1997, seven months after Staples' acquisition of Office Depot was announced, the FTC voted to seek a preliminary injunction in the Washington, D.C. federal district court.[16] The FTC had jurisdiction to review mergers since the agency was established in 1914. The "glory days" of the Warren Court extended roughly from 1962, when the first merger was challenged under revised Section 7 of the Clayton Act, until 1974 when the Supreme Court, in a five-four opinion, upheld a merger in the face of a government challenge. During that 12–year stretch, the government never lost a merger case in the Supreme Court.

During the following two decades, the Antitrust Division of the Department of Justice and the FTC brought few cases, in part because of the advent of pre-merger notification in 1976, requiring that mergers above a certain size be notified to the government, which permitted the enforcement agencies to resolve most competitive problems by negotiating a consent settlement. When the agencies did go to court, moreover, they no longer could count on winning. Accompanying the mediocre won-loss record were two common perceptions about the FTC in particular: first, that it would almost always settle with "half a loaf" in terms of remedy because it was afraid to go to court, and, second, in the rare instances when the agency did litigate it was out-lawyered both in numbers of opposing lawyers and their superior skill.[17] The common

---

[15] Transcript (May 23, 1997) at 166. The FTC staff also was able to compare an ad for Staples stores in Charlottesville, Virginia, where Staples competes with Office Depot, and Fredericksburg Virginia, where it faces no superstore competition. The ads ran on the same day and involved the identical products and pictures; the only difference was that prices were lower in the city in which Staples and Office Depot competed head-to-head. Both sets of advertisements were included in the evidence the FTC later presented in the preliminary injunction hearing.

[16] The merging firms had negotiated a possible settlement with the FTC staff that would have permitted the merger to go forward after sale of 63 stores to OfficeMax. Chairman Pitofsky and two other commissioners, a majority of the Commission, voted to reject the settlement and challenge the proposed merger in court; one voted instead to accept the proposed settlement as a solution to the competitive problem; and one did not believe the proposed merger would harm competition and thus that it needed no settlement. Press Release, FTC Rejects Proposed Settlement in Staples/Office Depot Merger (April 4, 1997) (available at <http://www.ftc.gov/opa/1997/04/stapdep.htm>).

[17] The *Staples* case was no exception in terms of numbers of legal staff. The FTC assigned perhaps five full-time lawyers to litigate the case, another ten back-ups. The FTC

perception was that the Staples/Office Depot challenge would be David versus Goliath and that David, seeking a market limited to office supply superstores, was pursuing an implausible theory. The press and most stock-market speculators thought the court would not enjoin the merger.

6. CEO Testimony

The compressed hearing schedule heightened the importance of every witness. One of the highlights was the testimony of Thomas Stemberg, the Chairman and CEO of Staples. Stemberg was called to the witness stand on the fourth day of the hearing. Through his testimony, which lasted more than four hours, both the merging firms and the FTC emphasized their main themes.

On direct, Stemberg explained how he had pioneered the office superstore business, opening the first Staples store in May 1986. From the start, Staples planned to attract customers by selling office supplies at a thirty to fifty percent discount compared to the prices charged by retail stationary stores. By 1992, he said, he had come to "embrace the productivity loop" strategy.[18] "The overwhelming reason people come to us is price," Stemberg stated. "[I]f we were ever to lose our low-price edge, . . . we would be in a lot of trouble."[19]

Stemberg further explained how the various other retailing channels for office supplies responded to Staples' growth and success: some traditional dealers formed buying cooperatives, mail order stationers lowered prices and reduced delivery times, and discount stores expanded assortments and cut prices. As a result, prices in office product retailing generally have been declining. "[E]verybody started pointing their guns at us" and became price competitive with the superstores, leading Stemberg to look for new ways to push the productivity loop. "I believe this merger will allow us to ratchet down our prices to a whole new level," he declared.[20]

Cross-examination centered on one of Staples' marketing documents, the firm's 1996 pricing strategy, which stated "Over time our

---

also assigned eight economists full-time to the investigation and litigation and made what is likely the most extensive commitment of resources to econometric analysis in any government antitrust case, before or since. By contrast, the merging firms reportedly fielded a team of 70, including 40 lawyers, and spent $13 million in legal fees and related costs. Amy Singer, Staple Removers, American Lawyer 45 (Oct. 1997).

[18] Transcript (May 22, 1997) at 209. That strategy was described by an earlier defendant witness, a Wall Street retailing expert who helped invent the term, as a "virtuous circle" where lower costs are passed on to consumers in the form of lower prices or better service, and the resulting increase in sales leads to lower costs as a fraction of sales, allowing the firm to reduce costs and prices further.

[19] Transcript (May 22, 1997) at 209, 213–14.

[20] Transcript (May 22, 1997) at 229–31.

goal is to be competitively priced on a market-by-market basis with other office superstores on all items." Stemberg acknowledged that the pricing document referred to office superstores as "primary competitors," and that it described markets as "non-competitive" if Staples had no superstore rivals, regardless of the presence of other types of retailers.[21] In response to questioning, Stemberg agreed that Office Depot and Office-Max had more impact on Staples' prices and margins than other retailers; that Staples created new price zones with lower prices in response to entry by rival office superstore chains but not in response to entry by mass merchandisers like K–Mart and Wal–Mart; and that the price index Staples developed shows that its prices in every Office Depot pricing zone were lower than its prices in the non-competitive zone and its prices in Staples' warehouse club zones. (A Staples document showing how its price index varied by zone is reprinted as Figure 2, p. 320.)[22]

Figure 2

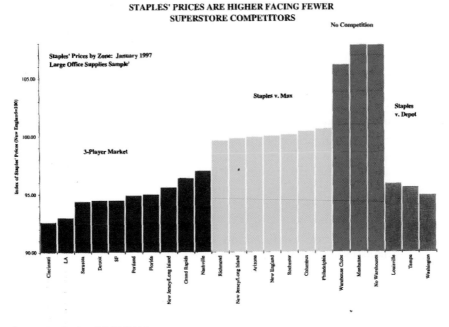

STAPLES' PRICES ARE HIGHER FACING FEWER
SUPERSTORE COMPETITORS

' Based on an office supply sample accounting for 90% of Staples' sales.
Data source attached.

---

[21] On redirect, Stemberg noted that the company's pricing manual also states, "Computer superstores, consumer electronics stores, and warehouse clubs are considered to be secondary competition. Although the office superstores are our primary competition, we will conduct price-checks at secondary competitor locations so that we can be sensitive to their pricing."

[22] On efficiencies, Stemberg acknowledged in cross-examination that if Staples had less competition in a market, it was not as necessary to pass on cost reductions as quickly as when it had competition, and that competition with Office Depot led Staples to reduce its costs.

7. Expert Testimony on Pricing

The pricing evidence, around which the entire case pivoted, was the main subject of expert economic testimony on both sides. The experts had undertaken an extensive analysis of the pricing data using statistical tools. Although Judge Hogan later said he decided the case based on company documents rather than the econometrics,[23] the econometric back and forth shaped how the two sides framed the pricing evidence in examining all the witnesses.

The argument among experts was about why Staples prices are lower in markets where it faced superstore competition, as shown in the pricing documents emphasized by the government. The merging firms argued that the data were misleading. Prices were high in non-competitive markets, they contended, for the same reason that other superstores had not entered those markets: costs of doing business—for example, real estate rents—were high. If so, the loss of superstore competition would not lead to higher prices. Prices would stay low, near costs, in the merging firms' view because they were kept honest by competition from non-superstore retailers. To tell whether the merging firms were right when they contended that cross-city pricing comparisons were misleading, the economic experts for both sides looked at whether prices fell when Office Depot entered a market served by Staples, or vice versa.[24] But the experts did not agree on how the data on the price response to entry should be interpreted.[25]

The econometric battle over how to interpret Staples' pricing data shaped the examination of fact witnesses. On direct examination, Thomas Stemberg cited cross-city differences in costs to explain why Staples prices were higher in a large metropolitan area served by multiple

---

[23] Ken Auletta, World War 3.0: Microsoft and Its Enemies 221–22 (2001).

[24] The experts agreed that by focusing on price changes within metropolitan areas, where costs change slowly over time, they could largely avoid the possibility that price changes simply reflected cost changes.

[25] The debate is described from an FTC perspective in Jonathan B. Baker, Econometric Analysis in *FTC v. Staples*, 18 J. Pub. Pol'y & Marketing (1999). For further discussion of the economic evidence by the various experts who testified in the case, see generally Serdar Dalkir and Frederick R. Warren–Boulton, Prices, Market Definition and the Effects of Merger: Staples–Office Depot (1997) *in* John E. Kwoka & Lawrence J. White, eds., The Antitrust Revolution 143 (3d ed. 1999) (co-authored by the FTC's primary economic expert); Orley Ashenfelter, David Ashmore, Jonathan B. Baker, Suzanne Gleason, Daniel S. Hosken, Empirical Methods in Merger Analysis: Econometric Analysis of Pricing in *FTC v. Staples*, 13 Int'l J. Econ. Bus. 265 (2006) (co-authored by the FTC's primary econometric expert); Jerry A. Hausman and Gregory K. Leonard, Documents vs. Econometrics in *Staples* (Sept. 1, 1997) (available at http://www.nera.com/Publication.asp?p_ID=2744) (co-authored by the merging firms' economic expert).

superstore chains, like Washington, D.C., than in a smaller city then served only by Staples, like Bangor, Maine. On cross-examination, the FTC responded by focusing on the price response to superstore entry. It sought to establish that a Staples store in Sumpter, South Carolina had been moved from a higher priced to a lower priced zone, reducing its prices, when it became evident that the store was in competition with Office Depot stores in Columbia and Florence, South Carolina.

Although Judge Hogan did not base his decision on the econometric testimony, he interpreted the documentary evidence on pricing using the approach the experts had suggested for the data: by analyzing how Staples altered its prices when Office Depot came into town, and not simply relying on price differences across cities in reaching his conclusions.

8. Efficiencies Witnesses

Just before Thomas Stemberg testified, Staples called to the stand the company's Senior Vice President of Integration to testify about the cost savings anticipated from the merger. She described her blue chip credentials: a college degree from Princeton, an M.B.A from MIT, a law degree from Harvard, work experience at Bain, a leading management consulting firm, and five years at Staples. The integration process she managed, from which the company's cost savings projections were developed, involved fifteen task forces staffed by more than 200 executives from the two companies and supported by a host of highly-regarded management consulting firms, including the Boston Consulting Group, A. T. Kearney and Ernst & Young. After months of work, the witness testified, she and her team concluded that the acquisition would generate $5 billion or more in cost savings.[26]

The FTC's first rebuttal witness was David Painter, the Assistant Director for Accounting in the agency's Bureau of Competition. After thirty years at the agency, working his way up through the ranks, he was about to retire. Painter testified that in the three months before the hearing, he spent one thousand hours—averaging roughly seventy hours a week—reviewing the merging firms' efficiency analyses and preparing his report.

Painter testified that he was "astounded" to discover that the efficiency claims asserted by the companies were five times what the board of directors was told to expect when asked to approve the transaction. According to Painter, a substantial portion of the cost savings

---

[26] Cross examination focused on the extent to which the projected savings could have been obtained by Staples or Office Depot as stand alone firms, without need for merger. Other problems with the projections were described by the FTC's accounting expert. As will be discussed in section 9.b below, Judge Hogan had a number of reservations about the efficiency claims.

Staples claimed should not count because they could have been achieved by the merging firms on their own; in other cases the projected cost savings were based on assumptions inconsistent with the facts; and in still other instances, the estimation methodology employed by the Staples integration team was not documented adequately to permit him to evaluate their reliability. After detailed, painstaking analysis, Painter concluded that roughly 40% of the estimated cost savings were improperly attributed to the merger and another third were unsubstantiated.

With time on the chess clock running short, the Staples side elected to respond to Painter's methodological arguments in their brief, and to focus the cross-examination on Painter's credibility. The Staples lawyer highlighted the resources and credentials of the Staples efficiency team. He asked about the large number of senior executives and top-flight management consulting firms involved in Staples' task forces. These consulting firms "all sound very impressive to me," Painter agreed. The cross-examination continued: "They get a lot of MBAs coming right out of the best schools, don't they, those firms?" Answer: "I think so."[27]

The cross-examining attorney drew the contrast with Painter's credentials: an accounting degree from a state university, three months in a management training program at a local department store, then three decades at the FTC. Painter had no prior experience in the office products business, was not a CPA, had not completed any post-graduate work, and had not published in a professional journal.

This cross-examination backfired. Judge Hogan did not question Painter's credibility. Instead, his opinion appears to go out of the way to affirm it. Judge Hogan described Painter's testimony as "compelling" and said he reached his conclusions as to efficiencies "based primarily on Mr. Painter's testimony."

9. Opinion of the Court

At an early point in his decision, Judge Hogan made remarks that would have given some degree of satisfaction to the defendants. As we noted earlier, the key introductory legal issue was to describe the area of competition where the proposed merger would have a competitive effect. In that connection, the Judge said the following:

"The Court recognizes that it is difficult to overcome the first blush or initial gut reaction of many people to the definition of relevant product market as the sale of consumable office supplies through office supply superstores. The products in question are undeniably the same no matter who sells them and no one denies that many different types of retailers sell these products. After all, a combined

---

[27] Transcript (May 23, 1997) at 268.

Staples–Office Depot would only have a 5.5% share of the overall market in consumable office supplies."[28]

Then in the conclusion of his opinion, Judge Hogan praised Thomas Stemberg and his colleagues as pioneers in introducing the office supply superstore concept that revolutionized the office supply business, not just by introducing their own steep discounts, but by forcing many others in a broadly defined description of the industry to focus on cutting their prices, leading to a general decrease in price of office products across the board. As a result, manufacturers and suppliers were forced to implement efficiencies in their own businesses in order to compete in the sale of their products.[29]

But between those two instances of encouraging words for Staples, the FTC won just about every point.

a.   Pricing Evidence and Market Definition. The heart of the FTC's case was the assertion that prices were higher in metropolitan areas where there was only one superstore and that the merger would exacerbate that situation. With only a little hyperbole, George Cary, the lead attorney for the FTC, has termed *Staples* a "one fact case."[30] Judge Hogan carefully examined the documents and the expert testimony on the pricing issue and concluded with respect to both Office Depot and Staples that their prices on average were more than 5% higher in cities where they faced no competition.[31] The court noted that the anticompetitive effect of the merger was not necessarily that prices would rise from present levels, but only that they would be higher after the merger than they would have been had there been no merger.[32]

The pricing evidence was ultimately the reason the FTC succeeded in court. There were two routes by which it could have been employed to

---

[28] *Staples*, 970 F. Supp. at 1075.

[29] *Id.* at 1093.

[30] The one fact about prices was also the FTC's answer to Staples claim that easy entry would solve the competitive problem. If entry were so easy, the FTC asked rhetorically, why hadn't new superstore competition undermined the price premium in cities lacking superstore competition? In his opinion, Judge Hogan quickly disposed of defendants' ease of entry argument. He observed that the number of office supply superstores had dropped from 20 to 3 over the past several years, and that failed superstore entrants included large, well-known retail establishments such as K–Mart, Montgomery Ward, Ames and Zayres. Unless the new entrant could open a large number of stores to achieve economies of scale equivalent to the three existing superstores, it could not be an effective competitor. The court concluded that even if some large chain stores *could* enter the market, there was simply no evidence in the record before him that they *would* in fact do so in the event of a post-merger price increase.

[31] *Staples*, 970 F. Supp. at 1076.

[32] *Id.* at 1092.

decide the case for the government. The FTC, in litigating the case, and the court, in deciding it, framed the pricing evidence as a basis for defining a narrow product market, of consumable office supplies sold through superstores. The court noted that if the merger were to go through the combined firm would have a 100% market share in 15 metropolitan areas and a dominant market share in 42 other metropolitan areas across the country.[33] If a merger creates a monopoly, it is generally easy to conclude that competition will be harmed, with little need for detailed analysis of competitive effects.[34]

The court was encouraged to see the product market as narrow, confined to the superstore distribution channel, through a litigation tactic employed by the FTC lawyers. In a motion to the court, they suggested that Judge Hogan get in his car and drive to Rockville, a northern suburb of Washington, DC, where he would find office supply superstores and all the other retail outlets defendants' claimed were in the market. It would have been awkward for defense counsel to resist the idea that the Judge should take a look at the stores for himself, and they did not oppose the suggestion. Judge Hogan accepted the invitation, and one weekend drove around visiting the various outlets, including Staples, Office Depot, CompUSA, Best Buy, CVS, K–Mart, Giant Food and Wal–Mart. Based on his observations he found in the superstores a unique combination of size, selection, depth, breadth of inventory and the type of customers they target and attract. His conclusion:

> "No one entering a Wal–Mart would mistake it for an office super-store. No one entering Staples or Office Depot would mistakenly think he or she was in Best Buy or CompUSA. You certainly know an office superstore when you see one."[35]

Judge Hogan noted that the products involved were the same no matter where they were purchased and therefore, in a sense, all sources could be regarded as a market. But he quickly added that there could be "well-defined submarkets" in which sellers could raise price without losing an unacceptable portion of their business, and noted that the submarket concept had been recognized by the Supreme Court and lower court cases many times in the past.[36]

---

[33] *Id.* at 1081. Geographic market definition was not contested. Judge Hogan pointed out that just about the only thing the parties in the case did not disagree about was that metropolitan areas are the appropriate geographic markets. *Id.* at 1073.

[34] The government's Horizontal Merger Guidelines indicate that efficiencies are unlikely to carry the day in a merger to monopoly or near-monopoly.

[35] *Staples*, 970 F. Supp. at 1079.

[36] *See id.* at 1075 (citing *Brown Shoe Co. v. United States*, 370 U.S. 294 (1962); *Rothery Storage & Van Co. v. Atlas Van Lines Inc.*, 792 F.2d 210 (D.C. Cir. 1986); *Beatrice Foods Co. v. FTC*, 540 F.2d 303 (7th Cir. 1976)).

The FTC and the court could instead have chosen to frame the pricing evidence another way: as direct evidence of anticompetitive effect within a broader office supplies product market, not limited to the superstore distribution channel, in which the merging firms' market shares were low. Under this alternative description of the evidence on prices, the merger would represent an example of harmful unilateral competitive effects of a merger among sellers of differentiated products, reflecting a loss of localized competition within a broad market. This would have been a more difficult route for proving the case, however, because it would have required the court to conclude that the direct evidence from prices was more probative than the contrary implication of the market shares,[37] and because unilateral effects analysis, while well established at the antitrust enforcement agencies,[38] had only tentative acceptance in the courts.[39] An FTC victory on this basis, therefore, could have been more difficult to sustain on appeal than one based on a merger to monopoly within a narrow product market.

The FTC staff, comparing these alternatives, decided to challenge the merger within a narrow product market, rather than as leading to harmful unilateral effects within a broad product market. They argued the pricing evidence in terms of market definition, and prevailed on that basis. Some observers nevertheless view *Staples* as reflecting acceptance by the court of the unilateral competitive effects theory in the Horizontal Merger Guidelines. George Cary, the FTC's lead attorney, put it this way:

> "I do think of *Staples* as a unilateral effects case. . . . Ultimately, I think it has to be viewed as a unilateral effects case because the proof that was put forward in defining the product market was the closeness of competition between Staples and Office Depot and the effect of that competition on prices, without regard to competition from other firms."[40]

---

[37] In a broader market, market concentration and its increase would have been much lower, possibly so low as to place the merger within the safe harbors for concentration set forth in the government's Horizontal Merger Guidelines. Although a number of economists have argued that this should not matter if unilateral effects of a merger among sellers of differentiated products can be established through direct evidence, the low Herfindahl–Hirschman Index (HHI) statistics resulting from defining a broad product market would have presented another litigation challenge for the government had the case been framed this way.

[38] This unilateral effects theory had been introduced into the government's Horizontal Merger Guidelines in 1992, and was routinely employed in the internal review of mergers by both the FTC and the Justice Department.

[39] In *New York v. Kraft General Foods, Inc.*, 926 F. Supp. 321 (S.D.N.Y. 1995), Judge Kimba Wood had accepted the theory "arguendo."

[40] Roundtable Discussion: Unilateral Effects Analysis After *Oracle*, 19 Antitrust 8, 9 (Spring 2005).

From this perspective, the narrow market definition adopted for the purpose of litigation operated as a vehicle for recognizing unilateral effects in an uncertain legal environment.[41]

b. Efficiencies. Defendants had submitted an "Efficiencies Analysis" predicting that the combined company would achieve savings of between 4.9 and 6.5 billion over the five years following the merger, and that two-thirds of those savings would be passed on to consumers. They claimed that these cost savings would outweigh any possible anticompetitive effect from merger.[42]

This claim drew the court into an exceptionally ambiguous area of antitrust. The Supreme Court in 1967 had announced that "[p]ossible economies cannot be used as a defense to illegality in Section 7 merger case."[43] On the other hand a significant number of lower courts had disregarded the Supreme Court directive and recognized the defense,[44] and the Department of Justice–FTC Horizontal Merger Guidelines had been revised earlier in the year, just before the *Staples* case was argued, to incorporate an efficiency defense where the claimed efficiencies were significant, credible, verified and likely to outweigh any anticompetitive effect.[45] Judge Hogan acknowledged the uncertainty of the issue as a matter of law but was willing to assume efficiencies could be a viable defense. He concluded, however, that the defendants' efficiencies evidence was inadequate to sustain their position.[46]

---

[41] *See generally*, Jonathan B. Baker, Stepping Out in an Old *Brown Shoe*: In Qualified Praise of Submarkets, 68 Antitrust L. J. 203, 209–17 (2000). Not every unilateral effects case will be amenable to reframing as alleging a merger to monopoly within a narrow product market, however, as some narrow markets look more gerrymandered than others. *See United States v. Oracle Corp.*, 331 F.Supp.2d 1098 (N.D.Cal.2004) (unilateral effects allegation was unsuccessful because the government did not prove a narrow product market within which the merger would create a near-monopoly).

[42] *Staples*, 970 F. Supp. at 1089–1090.

[43] *FTC v. Procter & Gamble Co.*, 386 U.S. 568, 579 (1967).

[44] *See FTC v. University Health, Inc.*, 938 F.2d 1206, 1222 (11th Cir. 1991) (acknowledging that claims of efficiency can rebut the government's prima facie case, but finding insufficient evidence in record); *United States v. Country Lake Foods, Inc.*, 754 F. Supp. 669, 680 (D. Minn. 1990) (efficiency evidence relevant but not necessary because proposed transaction raised no anticompetitive threat); *United States v. Rockford Memorial Corp.*, 717 F. Supp. 1251, 1289–91 (N.D. Ill. 1989), *aff'd*, 898 F.2d 1278 (7th Cir.), cert. denied, 498 U.S. 920 (1990) (efficiency evidence introduced, but violation nevertheless found because efficiencies may not have been unique to merger and in any event were not sufficiently substantial to overcome anticompetitive effects).

[45] 1992 U.S. Department of Justice and Federal Trade Commission Horizontal Merger Guidelines § 4 (Revised April 8, 1997), *available at* http://www.usdoj.gov/atr/public/guidelines/hmg.htm (last visited June 29, 2006).

[46] *Staples*, 970 F. Supp. at 1089–1090.

As we noted earlier, Judge Hogan credited the testimony of Commission expert David Painter over the testimony of defendants' efficiency witnesses.[47] As to the claim of cost savings of $4.9 billion over five years, the court observed that this amount was five times greater than the figures presented to the two boards of directors of the merging companies when their boards approved the transaction. The claim was also far greater than the numbers submitted to the Securities and Exchange Commission. The court also noted that the savings were largely unverified and that much of the total could have been achieved by either company absent a merger. Finally, the court expressed extreme skepticism over the claim that two-thirds of the savings would be passed through to consumers in light of evidence that showed, historically, that Staples had passed through 15–17% in the past.[48] The bottom line for Judge Hogan was that the efficiency claims offered an inaccurate prediction of the proposed acquisitions' probable effect.

Based on his review of the evidence, the Judge granted the Commission's request for a preliminary injunction and shortly thereafter Staples and Office Depot dropped the deal.[49]

10. Future Impact: Why the *Staples* Case was a Turning Point in Merger Enforcement

One significant impact of the FTC's victory in *Staples* was to demonstrate the agency's willingness to litigate with the necessary resources, even if it meant short-changing other portions of agency activity. A leading investment banker described the FTC's victory in *Staples* as "a particularly dramatic show-stopper, a sign of the [government's] new assertive posture and of the courts' willingness to block a deal."[50] In the years following the *Staples* decision, the FTC found itself in court several times advancing antitrust challenges to mergers: successfully blocking two simultaneous mergers among drug wholesalers that would have reduced the number of major firms from four to two;[51] stopping the merger of Beech–Nut and Heinz in the baby food market (a deal that would have reduced the number of baby food suppliers in the

---

[47] *Id.* at 1089.

[48] *Id.* at 1089–1090.

[49] *See* Richard Tomkins, *U.S. Court Upholds Ban On Staples Merger*, The Financial Times (London), July 1, 1997, at 32.

[50] Bruce Wasserstein, Big Deal: The Battle for Control of America's Leading Corporations, 148 (1998). Perhaps the arbitrageurs who spent unprecedented sums on the Staples case—first betting that the FTC would not bring the case and, second, that the agency would lose in court—will become more cautious in betting against the government. By one estimate, the "arbs" lost approximately $150 million by guessing wrong on both results. Wall Street Journal, C–2 (July 2, 1997).

[51] *FTC v. Cardinal Health, Inc.*, 12 F. Supp. 2d 34, 68 (D.D.C. 1998).

United States from three to two);[52] and challenging the proposed acquisition by British Petroleum of ARCO which would have consolidated major oil-producing assets in Alaska. When BP agreed to divest the overlapping Alaskan assets, the rest of the deal was allowed to proceed.[53] The agency still allowed the vast majority (perhaps 97%) of mergers to go through without serious investigation, but clearly was ready to litigate if that was the right thing to do.

One result of energizing government enforcement of antitrust was that the agencies were taken more seriously as litigation opponents, and there was a recognition by the private bar that clients could expect extensive data requests and careful data analysis. Incidentally, the Department of Justice's Antitrust Division enjoyed a similar change in attitudes as a result of its successful challenge to business tactics by Microsoft, including respect for the quality of government litigation.

The *Staples* litigation also illustrated the increasing importance of economics to merger analysis since the Warren Court era, when the government seemingly needed only to show up in court to win. The Commission's case in Staples was based almost entirely on documents (it called only three fact witnesses) and focused on a single issue: the effect of the proposed merger on prices. The agency's economic presentation, primarily through the testimony of two economic experts and an accounting expert on the Commission's staff, was sophisticated and in the end persuasive.[54] Judge Richard Posner, one of the major figures in introducing economic analysis into antitrust, and into law generally, stated at the conclusion of his review of the FTC's performance in

---

[52] *FTC v. H.J. Heinz Co.*, 246 F.3d 708 (D.C. Cir. 2001), *rev'g* 116 F. Supp. 2d 190 (D.D.C. 2000). The present authors had different views on the wisdom of this case, Pitofsky as Chairman of the agency that successfully challenged the merger and Baker as economic expert for the merging firms. For two perspectives, see Thomas B. Leary, An Inside Look at the *Heinz* Case, 16 Antitrust, No. 2 at 32 (Spring 2002) (views of Commissioner Leary) and Jonathan B. Baker, Efficiencies and High Concentration: Heinz Proposes to Acquire Beech–Nut (2001), in John E. Kwoka, Jr. and Lawrence J. White, eds., The Antitrust Revolution 150 (4th ed. 2004).

[53] In the Matter of The British Petroleum Co. p.l.c., 127 F.T.C. 515 (1999) (consent order). Other Commission victories included *FTC v. Swedish* Match, 131 F. Supp. 2d 151 (D.D.C. 2000). While the Commission's winning record in antitrust challenges after *Staples* was impressive, the FTC did occasionally lose a case, and had particular difficulty in court prevailing in its efforts to block mergers of hospitals in local communities. For example, see *Federal Trade Commission v. Tenet Health Care*, 186 F.3d 1045 (8th Cir. 1999).

[54] Cooperation among lawyers and economists at the Commission had in the past been uneven and at times less than constructive. The *Staples* trial was a different matter. Leading figures in both the Bureau of Economics and Bureau of Competition strongly supported the case and the cooperation between the two groups of staff was as good as it is ever likely to be.

Staples that "[e]conomic analysis of mergers had come of age."[55]

In addition, the *Staples* opinion solidified the view that antitrust theory grew primarily from initiatives of the enforcement agencies (guidelines and cases) and cases in the lower courts, largely because the Supreme Court had not reviewed a merger case on the merits since 1974.[56] Hopefully that will change in the next few years.

For most of its history, a succession of independent scholars and other analysts have consistently found the FTC wanting in the performance of its duties. It was often referred to as "The Little Old Lady of Pennsylvania Avenue." One courtroom victory does not justify the existence of an agency, but the staff's performance against outstanding and experienced antitrust lawyers in *Staples* was admirable.[57] In a subsequent case, the next major merger challenged in court by the FTC, Judge Stanley Sporkin, a prominent figure in the world of business and regulatory law, noted the fine performance of the FTC in court and described the agency as revitalized.[58]

---

[55] Richard A. Posner, Antitrust Law 158 (2d ed. 2001).

[56] *United States v. General Dynamics*, 415 U.S. 486 (1974). Coincidentally, Donald Kempf, lead attorney for Staples, had represented General Dynamics in that case. The Supreme Court issued substantive antitrust merger decisions in three bank cases shortly after *General Dynamics*, but *General Dynamics* is generally considered the Court's most recent interpretation of Clayton Act § 7.

[57] By one report, "most people who packed in to hear the case every day agreed that the government out-lawyered the defense in the courtroom...." Amy Singer, Staple Removers, American Lawyer 46 (Oct. 1997).

[58] *FTC v. Cardinal Health, Inc.*, 12 F. Supp. 2d 34, 68 (D.D.C. 1998).

12

Eleanor M. Fox*

GE/Honeywell: The U.S. Merger that Europe Stopped—A Story of the Politics of Convergence

I. INTRODUCTION

One chilly day in late February [2001], John F. Welch Jr. flew into Brussels on a vital mission: General Electric Co.'s chairman and chief executive had come on his corporate jet to urge the European Union's top antitrust regulator to give GE's bid for Honeywell International Inc. a speedy blessing [as the American authorities had done].[1]

Mr. Welch was disappointed. The European Commission enjoined the merger, which would have been the largest industrial merger in the world's history, combining two American giants, General Electric Company, of jet engine fame, and Honeywell, with avionics expertise.

American officials were disappointed also. Treasury Secretary Paul O'Neil called the European prohibition "off the wall" and described the European Commission as "the closest thing you can find to an autocratic organization that can successfully impose their will on things that one

* Eleanor Fox is Walter J. Derenberg Professor of Trade Regulation at New York University School of Law. The author thanks Margaret Bloom, Christopher Cook, Daniel A. Crane, Carles Esteva–Mosso, Damien Gerard and John Vickers for their helpful comments. Filomen D'Agostino and Max E. Greenberg Foundation provided research support for this chapter.

[1] Philip Shishkin, Behind Mario Monti Is a Whole Posse of EU Merger Cops–Enrique Gonzalez–Diaz Is a Force to Be Reckoned With—'A Very Developed Sense of Public Interest,' Wall St. J. Europe, May 9, 2001, C 1.

would think are outside their scope of attention."[2] Senator Ernest Hollings, Chairman of the Senate Commerce Committee, accused the European Commission of "an apparent double standard by swiftly approving mergers involving European companies and holding up those of US groups." He said: "EU disapproval gives credence to those who suspect that the EU is using its merger review process as a tool to protect and promote European industry at the expense of its US competitors."[3]

U.S. antitrust authorities were also among the outraged. They gave the European authorities "an unprecedented and extraordinarily direct public scolding"[4] for mistaking an efficient merger for an anticompetitive one. Later, they would take credit for causing the EC law to look more American.[5]

Was the European prohibition against this largest-ever, pan-world merger really so extraordinary? What is the place of *GE/Honeywell* in the story of merger law? In the story of conglomerate mergers with leveraging effects that shift market share to powerful firms? What is its place in the puzzle of governance in the new world order in which law is national, transactions are international, more than a few jurisdictions claim the right to regulate the same transaction, and dominant players nudge other nations' laws to converge with theirs? *GE/Honeywell* is predominantly a story about sovereignty and the political dance of convergence. Nesting within this picture are nuts and bolts of conglomerate merger analysis,[6] and a small cast of characters that, in retrospect, seemed programmed to bring on a clash of cultures, to stake out claims of "right law" and "right economics," and then to return to the congenial mode of cooperation and business as usual.

The antitrust story of *GE/Honeywell* begins with GE's Jack Welch setting his sights on Honeywell. It proceeds to the U.S. antitrust clearance of the deal; to the European prohibition; to internal reform and

---

[2] Tom Brown, Update 2—U.S. Treasury Chief Slaps at Europe Over GE Deal, Reuters, June 27, 2001.

[3] Matt Murray, Phillip Shishkin, Bob Davis, and Anita Raghavan, Oceans Apart: As Honeywell Deal Goes Awry for GE, Fallout May Be Global—The U.S. Giant's Troubles In Europe Could Chill Mergers of Multinationals—Raining on Welch's Parade (*"Oceans Apart"*), Wall Street Journal, June 15, 2001, A1.

[4] William Kolasky, Narrowing, But Not Closing, The Gap, ANTITRUST, Spring 2006, 69 at 69.

[5] *Id.*

[6] The nuts and bolts are not always standardized.

The case concerned a number of other important issues as well as conglomerate issues, including how to determine whether a firm is dominant, but conglomerate effects was its lightning rod.

economic modernization within the European Commission's Competition Directorate,[7] and eventually to the European appellate court's judgment affirming the Commission's prohibition on narrow horizontal grounds, while disclaiming any duty of deference to the United States. *GE/Honeywell* is a story of six years in the life of convergence.

To set the stage, I give a short background of the not-always-parallel development of U.S. and EC merger law, and especially the law governing major firms' uses of leverage and other strategic practices such as bundling to shift market share to themselves. I then recount the evolution of the case. Finally, I comment on the case's implications for the law of leveraging and bundling by dominant firms, and I explore the politics of antitrust interdependence in a globalized world.

II. BACKGROUND OF THE LAW: SEEDS OF DIVERGENCE BUT ALSO CONVERGENCE

The European Economic Community was founded in 1957 with the Treaty of Rome. The Treaty of Rome was intended to create one economic market among the Member States, which at first numbered six and, by the time of the proposed GE/Honeywell merger, numbered 15. While economics was the original and main tool to establish the European Economic Community, the main motivation and hope was peace among the nations of Europe. The concept of one common market required free movement of goods, services, capital, business, and workers. The competition articles were directed against distortions of competition that could, among other things, resurrect the internal barriers to trade; and abuses of a dominant position that could, among other things, "unlevel" the playing field. The Treaty of Rome contained no merger control. Mergers were not a problem in Europe in the years following World War II. Rather, the problem was that Europe was Balkanized. Each nation maintained high barriers, including tariffs and quotas, keeping markets too small. Businesses were below efficient scale. The Treaty prohibited the building of barriers between the member nations. Economic policy encouraged mergers, especially cross-border mergers, to help integrate the common market and increase the competitiveness of European firms.[8]

---

[7] Economic reform started before the *GE/Honeywell* case. See Margaret Bloom, The Great Reformer: Mario Monti's Legacy in Article 81 and Cartel Policy, 1 Competition Policy International 55 (spring 2005); Nicholas Levy, Mario Monti's Legacy in EC Merger Control, 1 Competition Policy International 99 (spring 2005).

[8] E. Fox, THE COMPETITION LAW OF THE EUROPEAN UNION, Cases And Materials, 941 (offprint, West 2002).

Europe still uses competition policy to encourage cross-border mergers in sectors that are still more national than European, such as energy. *See* E.ON/MOL, COMP/M 3696,

Only years later, Europe began to experience the problem of too much industrial concentration through mergers, and the European Commission launched a proposal for a merger regulation. The proposal pended for many years before adoption; it was opposed by France, which wanted to keep control of "its" mergers as a matter of industrial policy; Germany, which did not want to cede its rigorous merger control to a possibly laxer Community; and others, largely for reasons of national sovereignty. But at last the arguments for central merger control prevailed and, in 1989, Europe adopted its Merger Regulation, effective in 1990. Substantively, the Merger Regulation prohibited mergers that "create or strengthen a dominant position" constituting "a substantial impediment to effective competition."[9]

Thus, by the time the *GE/Honeywell* case arose, European merger control was only 11 years old. The European Commission had prohibited only 14 mergers, and had imposed conditions on many more. The prohibitions included horizontal, vertical and conglomerate mergers.

Horizontal mergers—mergers of competitors—are clearly the most likely to harm competition, for they may take an important competitor off the market, thereby deadening rivalry and raising prices. Conglomerate and vertical mergers raise concerns more rarely, but when they do, this is often on grounds that the merger creates a structure that invites harmful conduct; it may position a dominant firm to use its leverage in one market to get advantages in a related market, foreclosing rivals from a chance to contest an important segment of the market, and sometimes creating or increasing market power.

By the year 2000, a significant body of caselaw of the European Court of Justice—the highest court of the European Union—had already developed in the area of abuse of dominance. The challenged conduct was usually exclusionary conduct, foreclosing rivals through leverage or strategic behavior. The cases broadly condemned a dominant firm's use of leverage and other exclusionary conduct because it "unleveled the playing field" and deprived rivals of a fair opportunity to compete.[10] These cases informed the Commission's decisions under the relatively

---

Commission decision of Dec. 21, 2005: DONG/Elsam, COMP/M 3868, Commission decision of March 14, 2006.

[9] Council Reg. 4064/89, O.J. L 395/1 (Dec. 30, 1989). The prohibition has since been broadened to apply to anticompetitive oligopoly as well as dominance. Council Reg. 139/2004, O.J. L24/1 (Jan. 20, 2004). Under the revised Merger Regulation, the test is whether the transaction "significantly impedes effective competition . . ., in particular as a result of the creation or strengthening of a dominant position."

[10] See, e.g., Hoffmann–LaRoche v. Commission, Case 85/76 [1979] ECR 461; NV Nederlandsche Banden–Industrie Michelin v. Commission (*Michelin I*), Case 322/81 [1983] ECR 3461.

new merger law. The Commission developed a "portfolio theory," holding that, when a dominant firm owning a cluster of products acquired a significant firm holding a complementary cluster of products (e.g. liquor brands), the merged firm would be incentivized to engage in package selling; this would shift market share from rivals to the dominant firm and increase its dominance.[11]

Meanwhile, especially since the early 1980s, the U.S. merger law had become focused on consumers and efficiency. Mergers were deemed lawful unless they harmed efficiency, usually as measured by lessened consumer welfare in terms of higher price and lower output. The 1980s developments were a reaction against caselaw of the 1960s and early 1970s that regarded significant foreclosures of competitors as harms to competition. Reformers of the 1980s feared that these earlier precedents protected inefficient competitors at the expense of consumers and at the expense of world competitiveness. "The law protects competition, not competitors" became a buzz phrase, despite its genealogy.[12] Conglomerate mergers could in theory, but very rarely did, raise prices to consumers. Vertical mergers usually created efficiencies; they also could but rarely would raise prices. The new antitrust conception dictated that enforcers should be especially careful not to condemn efficient mergers.[13]

To Americans, the Competition Directorate of the European Commission ("DG Competition") was seen as protecting competitors, not competition. It would intervene against acts and transactions of dominant firms that made life more difficult for rivals.[14] Perhaps the "wrongheaded" perspective of the European officials would not matter so much to Americans when Europe enjoined European mergers;[15] but it would

---

[11] See, e.g., Bayer/Aventis Crop Science, COMP/M 2547, Commission decision of April 17, 2002; Guinness/Grand Metropolitan, Case IV/M 938, Commission decision of Oct. 27, 1998.

[12] The phrase is taken from Brown Shoe Co. v. United States, 370 U.S. 294 (1962), and means, in context, that the law protects the competitive structure of the market. It favors a structure of "numerous independent units" to one of few firms with leverage advantages over the rest. *Id.* at 333. Congress regarded as a vice "foreclosing the competitors . . . from a segment of competition otherwise open to them . . . ." This "may act as a 'clog on competition,' . . . which 'deprive[s] rivals of a fair opportunity to compete.' " *Id.* at 324. See Edward T. Swaine, "Competition, Not Competitors," Nor Canards: Ways of Criticizing the Commission, 23 U. Pa. J. Int'l Econ. L. 597 (2002).

[13] E. Fox, What is Harm to Competition? Exclusionary Practices and Anticompetitive Effect, 70 Antitrust L.J. 371, 375–80 (2002).

[14] The European Commission, following procedures common in its original six member states, has an inquisitorial and not adversarial system. The case-handling team in DG Competition writes the first draft of the proposed Commission decision, which is then vetted by the Director General of Competition, by the Legal Service competition team, by a member state advisory committee, and by the Competition Commissioner.

[15] Most American officials seemed oblivious to European law until it restricted the conduct of American firms. Americans' attention was, of course, captured in the case of

matter a lot if Europe enjoined an American merger. And it did.

III. THE COMPANIES

GE was the world's largest producer of large and small jet engines for commercial and military aircraft. GE and a joint venture, CMFI, made more than 52% of all engines for large commercial jets. GE accounted for 60% to 70% of engines for large regional aircraft in production, 40% to 50% of engines in the installed bases of large regional aircraft, and 10% to 20% (in both categories) of engines for corporate jets. The engine market was highly concentrated. Pratt & Whitney and Rolls–Royce were the world's second and third largest producers, respectively. GE Capital Aviation Services ("GECAS") was one of the world's largest aircraft leasing companies and one of the largest buyers of airplanes. GECAS purchased about 10% of all aircraft. Along with its sister corporation, GE Capital, GECAS financed the purchase of airplanes and was an important airplane launch customer. GECAS provided equity seed financing to smaller buyers of planes that used GE engines, creating commonality advantages that often induced these airlines to select similar equipment in the future. Once an aircraft manufacturer chose to incorporate a particular supplier's engine and other elements, it tended to continue purchasing the same brand because of significant efficiencies such as the acquired knowledge, training, and the ability to use parts across a fleet. GECAS had a policy to buy only aircraft that incorporated GE engines.

Honeywell was a leading producer of aerospace products, including aviation equipment, non-avionic products, engines for corporate jets, and engine starters. Honeywell accounted for 50% to 60% of avionic products generally. It made 60% to 70% of engines installed in medium-sized corporate jets. For aerospace equipment other than engines, Honeywell was the largest worldwide supplier. BF Goodrich ranked second, United Technologies Corporation ("UTC") third, and Rockwell Collins fourth. UTC was Honeywell's principal competitor in the market for non-avionic products. Honeywell was the only equipment manufacturer that offered a complete range of avionics equipment. It was the leading supplier of engine controls to engine manufacturers and the largest supplier of engine starters.[16]

Boeing's acquisition of McDonnell Douglas. Boeing/McDonnell Douglas, Commission decision, Case IV/877 (Dec. 8, 1997) (a threatened prohibition was avoided; conditions were imposed). For the FTC's clearance of the merger, see Matter of Boeing Company/McDonnell Douglas Corp., Transfer Binder 1997–2001, CCH Trade Reg. Rep. ¶ 24,295 (July 1, 1997).

[16] See facts in the Commission decision and CFI judgment. General Electric/Honeywell, Commission Decision, Case COMP/M 2220 (July 3, 2001), action for annulment dismissed, General Electric Co. v. Commission, Case T–210/01 (CFI Dec. 14, 2005).

Honeywell had become an object of corporate attentions.

IV.   WELCH SETS HIS SIGHTS ON HONEYWELL

GE had an active program of acquisitions. It had looked at Honeywell in 1999–2000. The GE executives liked the fit of the products, but believed that the Honeywell stock was overpriced.

On Thursday, October 19, 2000, as Jack Welch tells the story in his book, *Jack: Straight from the Gut*,[17] Welch accompanied an old friend to the floor of the New York Stock Exchange. The friend was celebrating the listing of his company, Wipro, and was invited to ring the closing bell at 4:00 p.m. After the ringing of the bell, when Welch and his friend were on the exchange floor, a CNBC reporter turned to Welch and asked what he thought of the news that United Technologies was buying Honeywell. Welch says in his book: "I damn near fell on the floor.... The news ... came as a complete surprise—and it really grabbed me."[18]

Welch sprang into action. He assembled "teams of GE people" and advisers in New York early on Friday morning, October 20. They decided that GE could "make a more compelling case for Honeywell than UT."[19] Although Welch had been planning to retire the following April, he decided that if GE could acquire Honeywell he would postpone his retirement and see the acquisition through. "I couldn't sit on my hands and watch the biggest deal in GE history go by."[20]

About 10:30 a.m. on the same Friday morning, Welch called Honeywell's CEO, Michael Bonsignore, at Honeywell headquarters in Morristown, New Jersey. Bonsignore was meeting with his board of directors with a view to approving the United Technologies offer. Bonsignore came to the phone and said that his board "was five minutes away from closing the deal." Welch said: "Don't. I want to make you a better offer."[21] And he did.

The UT board had already approved the merger, and was to be sorely disappointed (and UT was to become a principal complainant against the GE deal). The Honeywell board recessed. The next day, Saturday, at the offices of Honeywell's counsel, Skadden, Arps, Slate, Meagher & Flom, Welch and Bonsignore shook hands on the deal—for which GE was to exchange GE stock worth just under $45 billion. On

---

[17] Jack Welch with John A. Byrne, JACK: STRAIGHT FROM THE GUT (*FROM THE GUT*), Chap. 23 (2001).

[18] *Id.* at 357.

[19] *Id.* at 359.

[20] *Id.*

[21] *Id.* at 360.

the next morning, Sunday, Welch and Bonsignore appeared on a tele-vised press conference. Welch said:

> When someone asked about getting approval from the regulatory agencies, I said there should be no problem at all. I predicted the deal would close sometime in February.
>
> "This is just the cleanest deal you'll ever see." (I still believe that, and so did just about everybody except the European Commission.)[22]

But Welch had not talked yet with his European antitrust lawyers.[23] If he had, he would have been told of the EC caselaw condemning leveraging and other exclusionary devices to get competitive advantages.[24] Not having done so, he feigned constant surprise at the Commission's positions on the law.

GE and Honeywell filed their merger notification with the U.S. authorities in October 2000. This was an election year in the United States. George W. Bush had been elected President. He would take office in January 2001, and would appoint a new head of the Antitrust Division of the Department of Justice, Charles James. But James was not to take office until mid June 2001—after the die was cast.

The team at the Antitrust Division of the Department of Justice (DOJ) that vetted the merger had only two antitrust concerns—overlapping business in military helicopter engines, and maintenance and servicing of small jet engines and auxiliary power units. In early May, the DOJ cleared the merger subject to divestitures of overlapping businesses in those fields.[25]

---

[22] *Id.* at 363.

[23] This "was GE's largest ever [acquisition], negotiated over a three-day weekend, too fast for the company even to consult its outside antitrust counsel." *Oceans Apart, supra* note 3.

[24] See *Hoffmann–La Roche* and *Michelin I, supra* note 10; and for mergers, see Aerospatiale–Alenia/de Havilland, Commission decision, Case 91/619 (Dec. 5, 1991); Guinness/Grand Metropolitan, *supra* note 11. Regarding the preexisting law on bundling, see Stefan Schmitz, The European Commission's Decision in *GE/Honeywell* and the Question of the Goals of Antitrust, 23 U. Pa. J. Int'l Econ. Law 539, 581–83 (2002) (re: bundling); Götz Drauz, Unbundling GE/Honeywell: The Assessment of Conglomerate Mergers Under EC Competition Law, Chapter 9 in 2001 Fordham Corp. L. Institute, International Antitrust Law and Policy (B. Hawk ed. 2002), 183, 185–90.

[25] Procedurally, this means only that the U.S. federal agencies will not sue to enjoin the transaction before it closes. "Clearance" does not preclude challenge by a private party, a state attorney general, or even one of the other two federal antitrust enforcement agencies after the closing. This procedure contrasts with the European procedure. When a merger is within the jurisdiction of the European Commission, there is a one-stop-shop. Only the Commission can clear the merger, and if it does, no later challenge by the Commission or a member state will lie.

In February, four months after the U.S. filing, the parties filed in Europe with the Merger Task Force of the Competition Directorate. The matter was assigned to a case team headed by Enrique Gonzalez–Diaz, described by one journalist as a "brilliant mathematician and lawyer, hardworking and intensely ambitious."[26] Gonzalez–Diaz and his team were visited by lawyers for United Technology, Rolls–Royce, and Rockwell Collins. At first, reportedly, he regarded them as merely whining competitors.[27] But as the facts developed (albeit with the aid of the competitors), the team at DG Competition developed concerns. The concerns were confirmed, after vetting through the usual internal channels,[28] and conveyed to the parties. In brief, they were:

1. Elimination of competition, beyond what the U.S. had identified as having antitrust significance. The merger would create a horizontal overlap in engines for large regional jets, engines for corporate jets, and small marine gas turbines, strengthening GE's already dominant positions.

2. Bundling. The merged firm, having a large line of complementary products, including products in which it was dominant or near-dominant, would have the incentive to engage in bundling, especially mixed-bundling (meaning the product would be available both in a bundle and separately). Having access to the enormous financial resources of GE Capital, the merged company would probably lower the price of the bundle while raising the stand-alone price of the individual items. The competitors, who would face higher costs of capital, would be unable to lower their prices to the same extent. They would lose market share and would not make the profits necessary to invest in research and development. This would eventually lead to their market exit or to their marginalization in key market segments. Eventually, the merged firm would raise its prices, creating or strengthening a dominant position in the manufacture of jet aircraft engines and in avionics and non-avionics products.

3. Vertical foreclosure of competing engine manufacturers. Honeywell was an important supplier of engine controls. It was the dominant supplier of engine starters—an essential input. Honeywell would probably delay or disrupt the supply of engine

---

[26] Michael Elliott, How Jack Fell Down: Inside the Collapse of the GE/Honeywell Deal—And What It Portends for Future Mergers ("*Jack Fell Down*"), Time, July 16, 2001, p. 40, 41.

[27] *Id.*

[28] See Dimitri Giotakos, GE/Honeywell: A Theoretic Bundle—Assessing Conglomerate Mergers Across the Atlantic, 23 U. Pa. J. INT'L ECON. L. 469, 507–09 (2002).

controls to its rivals, strengthening GE's dominant position in engines.

4. Use of financial leverage and vertical integration. GE Capital provided extensive financial support to its customers, the aircraft makers, and used its and GE's financial power to procure exclusive supply positions for the GE products. GECAS used its buying leverage and launching platform leverage to encourage aircraft makers to shift their engine purchases to GE. The merged firm would similarly use its financial strength, buying power, and leverage to benefit the Honeywell products. Since airlines are relatively indifferent to component selection, they would probably shift purchases of avionic and non-avionic products from Honeywell's rivals to the merged firm. Competitors would be progressively marginalized and might exit the market, creating, for the merged firm, a dominant position in avionic and non-avionic products.[29]

During the months of investigation, as the U.S. and the EU were accustomed to do, the American and European authorities consulted with one another and shared their analyses. They disagreed regarding the effects of the merger. European Competition Commissioner Mario Monti was later to remark that he was handicapped in his consultation with the American authorities because the Assistant Attorney General (Charles James) had not yet been confirmed by the U.S. Congress. It was "unfortunately impossible to have any discussions at all at the very highest policy level" before the Justice Department decision[30] and before Europe had proceeded most of the way down its own road.

On May 8, the European Commission issued its Statement of Objections (which is like a complaint but comes after much deeper investigation and reads more like a court opinion than a complaint), listing all of the concerns and, in effect, tentative findings. On May 29–30, there were two days of hearings, which included not only the merger parties but also concerned competitors, including Rolls–Royce, Rockwell Collins and UT, and a customer, Lockheed.

Pursuant to the required procedure, Competition Commissioner Monti invited GE to propose remedies that would cure the concerns. As for the conglomerate/bundling concerns, GE offered promises not to

---

[29] *See* Commission Press Release, March 1, 2001, IP/01/298 of March 2, 2001. *See also* Dimitri Giotakos, Laurent Petit, Gaelle Garnier and Peter De Luyck, General Electric/Honeywell—An insight into the Commission's investigation and decision, Competition Policy Newsletter 3/2001, p. 6, available at http://ec.europa.eu/comm/competition/speeches/text/sp2001_037_en.pdf.

[30] U.S. and EU Wrangle Over Enforcement at OECD's Global Forum on Competition, 81 BNA Antitrust & Trade Reg. Rep. 347, 348 (Oct. 19, 2001).

bundle, which the Commission rejected almost categorically. As for the vertical (GECAS) issue, Welch put successive proposals on the table for the spin-off of assets, the value of which eventually (before June 13) amounted to $2.2 billion. The latter offers did not sufficiently deal with the problem of GECAS's power to pressure buyers of avionic and non-avionic products to shift their business from the rivals to the merged firm, and on that point Monti wanted one thing more. He wanted to neutralize GE's control of GECAS. He wanted an agreement that GE would put GECAS, or a part of it, up for sale, or possibly a strong structural commitment to modify GECAS's behavior. This, Welch would not do.

The final meetings between Welch and Monti took place on June 13. There was a meeting in the morning, with the whole team present. Welch came alone. He sat across from Commissioner Monti, his aide Carles Esteva–Mosso, Director General Alexander Schaub, Merger Task Force Director Götz Drauz, team head Enrique Gonzalez–Diaz, and two others. They discussed Welch's proposals for conditions that might meet the Commission's concerns. Monti laid out the parameters of an acceptable offer. Welch, referring to his own proposals, said: "If you are not satisfied you can tell me: 'Go home, Jack!'" He explained that he was writing a book and that his experiences in Brussels would provide material for the last chapter. Schaub quipped: "That can be the title of your last chapter, Mr. Welch. 'Go home, Jack' is a perfect title."[31]

There was a final meeting that evening. Welch reported that he could not submit a remedies offer within the parameters that Monti had described.

Mr. Welch went home. He telephoned Andrew Card, chief of staff to President George W. Bush. The President was on a European tour. On June 14, when he met with European leaders, the President did not raise the matter. At a news conference in Warsaw on June 15, Bush came modestly to Welch's aid. He said:

> We brought up the proposed merger at the appropriate levels during this trip and before the trip. Our government looked at the merger and approved it. The Canadian government looked at the merger and approved it. And I am concerned that the Europeans have rejected it.[32]

Politicians weighed in. On June 20, Senator John D. Rockefeller IV, Chairman of the Subcommittee on Aviation, wrote to the Vice President

---

[31] This paragraph combines recollections of Alexander Schaub, Carles Esteva–Mosso, and Jack Welch. See FROM THE GUT, *supra* note 17, p. 370.

[32] Raf Casert, General Electric to EU 'Negotiations are over'—Bush couldn't sway Europe on Honeywell deal, Toronto Star, June 16, 2001, E 11.

of the European Commission that he was "deeply disturbed" by reports that the commission could block the deal.

Mr. Rockefeller said the history of the case as reported so far "will raise serious concerns among Americans about whether this review has been conducted with fairness and neutrality." He hinted that his subcommittee would re-examine standards for foreign aerospace companies doing U.S. business if it concluded that the European Commission was acting to protect European companies by blocking the GE–Honeywell merger.[33]

Rockefeller made "threats about blocking mergers sought by European companies."[34]

Senator Phil Gramm said on CNBC: "It's a very real question—what power the EU should have in dealing with two companies that are fundamentally American companies."[35]

Meanwhile, in Brussels, "The European capital then experienced the most intense politicking old hands there have seen."[36]

Most of the charges by the politicians were targeted at Competition Commissioner Mario Monti, a distinguished and revered economics professor who was a faithful advocate against industrial policy, against protecting national champions, and against political pressure. He knew his economics well. He was sympathetic to and surely not antithetical to America. Responding to the charges, he said: "I deplore attempts to misinform the public and to trigger political intervention."[37] He pointed out that the United States had opposed European deals that the Europeans had approved. Indeed, the Americans had pioneered the by-then

---

[33] Brandon Mitchener, If EU Axes the GE Deal, an Appeal is Not Very Appealing—Odds of Reversal Are Long, Effort and Cost Great; A Senator Weighs In, Wall St. J, June 21, 2001, A 15.

[34] Bob Davis and Anita Raghavan, Divergent Histories Helped to Scuttle GE–Honeywell Deal—Competitors vs. Customers: both EU, U.S. Show Biases—Could Augur a Hiatus for Megadeals, Asian W. St. J., July 5, 2001, p. 1.

In fact, there is no evidence of anti-American or anti-foreign bias by the European Commission, and analysis of the facts suggests that the charge is unsupported. More likely, if the GE/Honeywell intervention was overly aggressive, this is explainable by "bureaucratic capture" and an incorrect perception that the court would apply a broad-brush and deferent rather than a rigorous review. See Jeremy Grant and Damien J. Neven, The Attempted Merger Between General Electric and Honeywell: A Case Study of TransAtlantic Conflict, 1 J. Comp. L. & Econ. 595, 601, 630 (2005).

[35] Peter Ford, EU is blocking major U.S. merger—Unless either side relents in the next three weeks, the mega General Electric–Honeywell deal could be history (*"EU is blocking"*), Christian Science Monitor, June 21, 2001, p. 1.

[36] *Jack Fell Down*, *supra* note 26, p. 41.

[37] *EU is blocking*, *supra* note 35, p. 1.

well-accepted principle that a nation has jurisdiction to vet any merger, even an offshore merger, that harms its market (although "harm to a market," it would be seen, is not a scientific fact).

Despite the flood of charges from Welch and the American politicians, and despite repeated innuendos of the press—who knew little of the law—Monti would decide the case on what he understood were its merits: the law, the economics, and the record built up by his team.

V.   THE COMMISSION'S DECISION, AND THE FIERY AFTERMATH

From the time Mr. Welch went home, it was clear what decision the Commission would take, and what it would say. This is typical practice. Once the Commission decides that a merger is incompatible with the common market,[38] the question is one of remedy. The merging parties are obliged to propose conditions. If the conditions are not sufficient to cure the competition problems, the merger is prohibited. Usually, as in the United States, conditions, including spin-offs, are sufficient; but not always.

The Commission's prohibition decision issued on July 3, 2001.

Charles James, the U.S. Assistant Attorney General in Charge of Antitrust, immediately issued a press release disagreeing with the Commission's analysis and conclusions in no uncertain terms. He stated that the merger was "procompetitive and beneficial to consumers." He stated that the merger would have made GE a more effective competitor and that was apparently the very reason why the Commission prohibited it. He said U.S. antitrust laws "protect competition, not competitors. Today's EU decision reflects a significant point of divergence."[39]

U.S. protects competition and consumers. Europe protects competitors. The American press liked that theme, and was not kind to Europe.

Commissioner Monti responded in a speech in London the next week. He said:

> We have recently seen such a substantial amount of statements and press articles indicating that merger control in the EU is about the protection of competitors rather than consumers, that there is a risk that, by repetition, this becomes a widely accepted truth. I think it would be a pity that such a conclusion was reached without any

---

[38] Note that the Commissioner with the competition portfolio is very influential. It is his or her responsibility to make the judgment call as to whether the merger should be blocked. The draft decision he approves is circulated to all other Commissioners and their cabinets. They can, but seldom do, disagree with the decision.

[39] DOJ Press Release, July 3, 2001.

serious scrutiny or debate about the goals or track record of the Commission in this area.

Actually, the goal of competition policy, in all its respects, is to protect consumer welfare by maintaining a high degree of competition in the common market.

* * *

Let me be clear on this point, we are not against mergers that create more efficient firms. Such mergers tend to benefit consumers, even if competitors might suffer from increased competition. We are, however, against mergers that, without creating efficiencies, could raise barriers for competitors and lead, eventually, to reduced consumer welfare.[40]

No Competition Commissioner before Monti had publicly identified consumer welfare as *the* goal of competition policy. Quite the contrary, the competition officials had categorized the goals as "an open market economy with free competition,"[41] "the maintenance of competitive markets,"[42] and a policy integral with a large number of objectives set forth in the Treaty, including "harmonious and balanced development" and "a high level of employment and of social protection."[43]

The controversy simmered over the summer and into the fall. The OECD held its inaugural Global Forum on Competition in Paris in October. "The opening salvo came from [DOJ's] Kolasky"[44] (standing in for Assistant Attorney General Charles James), who said he had hoped that the tremendous investment in U.S./EU cooperation and coordination would have borne fruit, but instead the EU used an eccentric theory—portfolio or range effects—that "is neither soundly grounded in economic theory nor supported by empirical evidence, but is rather antithetical to the goals of sound antitrust enforcement."[45]

---

[40] Mario Monti, The Future for Competition Policy in the European Union, Merchant Taylor's Hall, London, July 9, 2001 (emphasis added), available at http://ec.europa.eu. comm/competition/speeches/index_2001.html. Click on 09 July.

GE claimed that elimination of duplication (presumably in horizontal aspects) would save costs. It did not provide "a clearly articulated and quantified defense in terms of efficiencies." Giotakos, *supra* note 28, at 500, 502. The Commission stated to the Court that "no appreciable efficiencies would result from the merger." Court judgment, *supra* note 16, para. 377. This seems not to have been contested. At least, efficiencies were not a battleground in the litigation.

[41] XXXth Report on [European] Competition Policy (2000).

[42] XXIXth Report on [European] Competition Policy (1999).

[43] XXVIth Report on [European] Competition Policy (1996).

[44] U.S. and EU Wrangle, *supra* note 30.

[45] *Id.*

Commissioner Monti was stunned by the attack on the integrity of the Commission. He retorted that the *GE/Honeywell* matter had been "marked by loud political pressures," which were "neither pleasant nor appropriate.... I bluntly reject [the charges of protecting business from market forces] as a gross misrepresentation of 40 years of EU competition policy...."[46]

Eventually, the protagonists softened their rhetoric. The DOJ highlighted—in every ensuing relevant speech and on power point slides everywhere—Monti's statement in his London speech that "the goal of competition policy ... is to protect consumer welfare...."[47] DG Competition was already in the throes of a modernization process that included more rigorous economic analysis and more oversight of the merger vetting process.

Then, for the European Commission, lightning struck three times. Three merger prohibitions were successively annulled by the Court of First Instance (CFI), the first-level appellate court.[48] In each of the three judgments, the Court held that the Commission had not mustered the necessary facts to support the conclusion that the merger would create or strengthen dominance. In two, the Court found, the Commission had also deprived the parties of rights of defense.[49]

One of the three mergers, and only one, was a conglomerate merger: *Tetra Laval/Sidel*.[50] The Commission had found that this combination of milk and juice carton containers with plastic containers created opportunities for the use of leverage, and predicted that Tetra Laval would use that leverage to disadvantage rivals. The Court of First Instance drew a distinction between harmful effects that depend upon subsequent conduct of the merged firm (conglomerate mergers), and harmful effects that flow from the merger itself (horizontal mergers, which take a competitor off the market). In the first case, the predicted behavior

---

[46] U.S. and EU Wrangle, *supra* note 30.

[47] The DOJ's quotes did not highlight the end of Commissioner Monti's sentence: "by maintaining a high degree of competition in the common market." This clause contains a nuance that is a key point of difference in U.S. and EC competition law. The United States seeks to prevent only certain inefficient outcomes. The EU also seeks to preserve the competitive structure of the market. See point II *supra*.

[48] Airtours v. Commission, Case T–342-99, [2002] ECR II–2585; Schneider Electric SA v. Commission, Cases T–310/01 and T–77/02 (*Schneider/Legrand*), [2002] ECR II–4201; and Tetra Laval BV v. Commission, Cases T–5/02 and T–80/02 (*Tetra Laval/Sidel*, or *Tetra*), [2002] ECR II–4381, *aff'd*, Cases C–12/03 P and C–13/03 P, ECJ 15 Feb. 2005.

The Commission decided *Airtours* before it decided *GE/Honeywell*. It decided *Schneider/Legrand* and *Tetra Laval/Sidel* a few months after it decided *GE/Honeywell*.

[49] *Airtours* and *Schneider*, *supra*.

[50] Note 49 *supra*.

might never happen. In some cases, the feared conduct might constitute an abuse of a dominant position in violation of Article 82 of the EC Treaty, and the very existence of Article 82 and the threat of its enforcement might deter the conduct. Moreover, the Court said, negative effects from conglomerate mergers are rare. Therefore, the Commission must prove its case by convincing evidence.[51]

The judgment in *Tetra* was not good news for the Commission and DG Competition, which had their eyes on the appeal of *GE/Honeywell*.

In the period immediately after the first of the three Court annulments, Competition Commissioner Mario Monti and DG Competition, under the stewardship of Director General Alexander Schaub, implemented and accelerated reforms. In 2002 the Directorate announced the creation of the position of chief economist. Lars–Hendrick Röller was appointed the first chief economist in July 2003. DG Competition organized devil's advocate panels to cross-examine the case-handling teams and test their conclusions. It created hands-on oversight within the Directorate.[52]

Meanwhile, Welch was not keen to appeal the Commission's rejection of his bid, for Honeywell had lost luster in the market. But he was not happy that the Commission had labeled GE a "dominant firm"—a label that would expose GE to greater scrutiny as it undertook future mergers, and Welch wanted to contest this finding. Moreover, Honeywell complained that GE was failing to use its best efforts to clear the regulatory hurdles, as it had contracted to do.[53] GE appealed. In fact, the deal was essentially dead. GE did not ask for a fast-track appeal, which might have reduced the waiting time from 3½ years to 9 months.

In the interim, commissioners' terms expired, and the constituency of the Commission changed. Mario Monti stepped down, and Neelie Kroes of the Netherlands was appointed to the Commission and given the competition portfolio. Madam Kroes gave one of her first major speeches at the annual Fordham international antitrust conference in September 2005. She said: "First, it is competition and not competitors that is to be protected. Second, ultimately the aim is to avoid consumers harm." She noted that, "[i]n days gone by, 'fairness' played a prominent role in Section 2 [Sherman Act] enforcement in a way that is no longer

---

[51] *Tetra*, CFI judgment (2002), *supra* note 49, para. 155.

[52] Regarding the economic reforms of DG Competition, see Margaret Bloom, *supra* note 7; Nicholas Levy, *supra* note 7.

[53] Deborah Hargreaves and Andrew Hill, How Monti turned GE–Honeywell into a flight of fancy (*Flight of Fancy*), Financial Times, July 6, 2001, p. 25.

the case." She said: "I don't see why a similar development could not take place in Europe."[54]

VI. THE COURT SPEAKS

There was a long wait to judgment. In the interim, the Commission had appealed the CFI judgment annulling the prohibition in *Tetra Laval/Sidel*. It was concerned that the *Tetra* judgment took the legs out from under conglomerate merger cases by requiring proof—which could almost never be amassed—that the predicted conduct would not be deterred by Article 82.

The Court of Justice decided the appeal in *Tetra Laval* in February 2005.[55] It upheld the CFI's annulment of the Commission's prohibition, but it softened the burden to prove the deterrent effect of Article 82. Nonetheless, the Court of Justice ruled that, in vetting a conglomerate merger, the Commission must take into account all evidence regarding the likelihood that the feared conduct would occur, including whether it would run afoul of Article 82 and if so whether Article 82 would deter it. Moreover, it affirmed the CFI ruling that a conglomerate merger requires "a precise examination, supported by convincing evidence" of anticompetitive effects in the relatively near future, since conglomerate mergers are usually neutral or beneficial.[56] Moreover, the need to consider the future and "the leveraging necessary to give rise to a significant impediment to effective competition mean that the chains of cause and effect are dimly discernible, uncertain and difficult to establish."[57]

After *Tetra Laval*, most experts predicted that the Commission would lose *GE/Honeywell*. Whether the predicted conduct would occur was at best speculative. Moreover, experts disagreed as to whether the conduct, if it occurred, would create or strengthen dominance. The questions—Was this merger efficient and good for consumers, and did the prohibition protect competitors?—lurked in the background. Another loss for the Commission—and especially in so high profile a case—would be devastating. It would chip away at the Commission's credibility.

In December 2005, the other shoe fell. The CFI handed down its judgment in *GE/Honeywell*.[58] To the surprise of many, the CFI upheld

---

[54] Neelie Kroes, Tackling exclusionary practices to avoid exploitation of market power; Some preliminary thoughts on the policy review of Article 82, Fordham, New York, 23 Sept. 2005, available at http://europa.eu/rapid/pressReleasesAction.do?reference=SPEECH/05/537&format=HTML&aged=0&language=EN&guiLanguage=en.

[55] *Tetra*, ECJ judgment (2005), *supra* note 4.

[56] *Tetra*, CFI judgment, para. 155.

[57] *Tetra*, ECJ judgment, para. 44.

[58] General Electric Co. v. Commission, Case T–210/01, (CFI Dec. 14, 2005) (not yet published).

the Commission's prohibition. But it found that the Commission had not proved the conglomerate and vertical claims. The Court affirmed the prohibition by upholding horizontal aspects in the three engine markets. With respect to those markets, the Court found for the Commission on each of the highly contested issues of dominance, market definition, and increase of dominance, and it found that the Commission acted within the bounds of its discretion in rejecting as inadequate GE's offers of spin-offs to alleviate each of these alleged overlaps.

Immediately, everyone claimed victory, and the sleeping dogs (e.g., how to analyze competitive harm caused by foreclosure; whether mergers of firms that sell complements deserve a presumption of efficiency; how to deal with divergent law and multiple cooks of the international broth) went back to sleep.

Why did the vertical and conglomerate aspects of the case fall short?

Each conglomerate and vertical claim had rested on a prediction of future conduct, and, according to the Court, the Commission had not proved that the conduct would probably occur.

Vertical effects—engine starters

The case against the merger on the basis of the engine starter claim was the strongest. After all, engines needed starters, Honeywell was in a position to control supply of engine starters to engine makers, and GE was dominant in engines. The Court found that the Commission was correct to find that Honeywell had more than a 50% share of starters, that its only significant competitor did not sell on the open market, that GE's big competitor Rolls–Royce would be dependent on the merged firm for its engine starters, that harming GE's engine competitors would have been in the merged firm's commercial interests, and that the merged firm would have an incentive to limit or disrupt supplies to its competitors. But deliberately disrupting its competitors' supplies would amount to a clear abuse of Article 82; and since the Commission had not examined the deterrent effect of Article 82, the Commission's conclusion was "vitiated by a manifest error of assessment."[59]

With this analysis, the CFI was especially hard on the Commission. GE's acquisition of the engine starter business would give GE unusual control over its competitors, who would have to rely on GE. Article 82 might have deterred outright refusals to deal and outright discrimination, but non-transparent jockeying would be easy to accomplish and would probably escape the Article 82 radar. The merger would create the negative incentives for just such non-transparent maneuvers. Merger prohibition would prevent their emergence. By giving credence to a sword-of-Damocles effect of Article 82, the European court was more

---

[59] *GE*, CFI judgment, para. 312.

American than America—where neither a Section 1 nor Section 2 deterrence effect has (yet) been a factor in merger control.

Conglomerate Effects

Financial strength and vertical integration

According to the Court, the Commission correctly held that GECAS and GE Capital had used their aircraft buying power and financial power in the past to strengthen GE's pre-merger dominance. They had a policy to buy only aircraft that included a GE engine. But the Commission had not proved that the merged firm could have and would have used the same leveraging practices to enhance its share of Honeywell's products. The customers may have had preferences for other manufacturers' products. They may have successfully resisted an attempt to use leverage. If they acceded to buying the Honeywell equipment, they would probably have demanded a discount. The Commission had failed to examine these costs.[60]

Bundling

GE had not argued that it would bundle GE engines with products of Honeywell. The Commission predicted it would do so, and argued that bundling would shift market share to the merged firm and create or strengthen dominance in several markets. The U.S. authorities argued that the merged firm should and would engage in mixed bundling. This, they said, would result in lower-priced packages and was therefore efficient.

The Court pointed out that bundling is not possible in a variety of circumstances. For example, pure bundling (where products are offered only as a bundle and not separately) is not possible where the customer that selects the engine and the customer that selects the avionics are not the same. Sometimes it is the airframe manufacturer that selects the avionics. Sometimes it is the airline.

According to the Court, the Commission had not proved that the merged firm would engage in pure bundling. The Commission had given only one hypothetical example: Honeywell could withhold one of the inexpensive but vital products it sold unless the customer agreed to purchase GE engines. The Court called this hypothetical conduct commercial blackmail. Customers might have resisted it; a point that the Commission had not explored. They might have preferred to use an inferior product rather than accept an engine not of their choice. Moreover, Article 82 might have deterred this conduct; a point that, again, the Commission had not explored.

---

[60] *Id.*, paras. 325–364.

Nor had the Commission proved that the merged firm could and would engage in mixed bundling. To argue that the merged firm would have the incentive to engage in mixed bundling, the Commission had relied on the Cournot effect: a firm that has a wide range of products, while its competitors do not, and that discounts all products in the range, sells more of all products.[61] Prediction of mixed bundling, and its effect to shift share and weaken the rivals by deflecting an important earnings stream, was initially based on an economic model prepared by a consultant to one of the complainants (Rolls Royce), Professor Jay Pil Choi. Choi had relied in part on research by Professor Barry Nalebuff. When the role of Choi became known to GE, GE retained Barry Nalebuff, who concluded that the Choi model did not fit the facts of the aerospace industry, wherein the prices of all components are individually negotiated. Bundles are not discounted; rather, individual components may be discounted.[62] The Commission itself was forced to recognize the weaknesses of the Choi model. In the end, it claimed it did not rely on the model, but did not abandon it. The Court concluded that whether the merged firm had the incentive to engage in mixed bundling was a matter of doubt.

It was not necessary (said the Court) to proceed to examine whether bundling would have foreclosed competitors, since the Commission's conclusions that bundling would occur were not established.[63]

In sum, the Commission had not proved that the feared practices would probably occur. The billion dollar questions—If the feared acts were probable, would they have harmed competition? Would mixed bundling have helped or hurt consumers?—were never answered.

Comity

At one point and only one point in its judgment did the Court refer to comity—possible deference to the U.S. analysis of the same issues. The issue was whether GE was a dominant firm in a jet engine market, and the sub-issue was whether a certain engine should have been

---

[61] *Id.*, para. 450.

More commonly, Cournot effect refers to the effect that occurs when two firms, producers of complements, each of which has economic power in its market, merge. The merged firm has the incentive to avoid double marginalization and is likely to charge less for the bundle of the two products than the sum of the prices charged by the unaffiliated firms before the merger. This was the iteration embraced by the U.S. Justice Department analysts, who predicted that the merger of GE and Honeywell would therefore be efficient. See address by U.S. Deputy Assistant Attorney General William J. Kolasky, George Mason University, Washington, November 9, 2001, available at http://www.usdoj.gov/atr/public/speeches/9536.htm.

[62] See Stefan Schmitz, *supra* note 24 at 578–583.

[63] *GE*, CFI Judgment, paras. 366–471.

included in the market. Exclusion of the engine, as the U.S. had done, would have reduced GE's market share below the dominance line. GE, of course, argued for exclusion. The Court rejected this tack, and in particular it rejected comity as a reason to take it. It said:

> The fact . . . that the United States Department of Justice apparently took [this] view . . . is irrelevant for the purposes of these proceedings. That the competent authorities of one or more non-member States determine an issue in a particular way for the purposes of their own proceedings does not suffice per se to undermine a different determination by the competent Community authorities. The matters and arguments advanced in the administrative procedure at Community level—and the applicable legal rules— are not necessarily the same as those taken into account by the authorities of the non-member States in question and the determinations made on either side may be different as a result. If one party considers the reasoning underpinning the conclusion of the authorities of a non-member State to be particularly relevant and equally applicable to a Community procedure, it can always raise it as a substantive argument, as the applicant has done in this instance; but such reasoning cannot be conclusive.[64]

And so, the European Court affirmed the prohibition of a U.S. merger (albeit one with a substantial European presence) that the U.S. authorities had approved. In doing so, it had not impeached the Commission's conglomerate theories that had so widely diverged from U.S. law,[65] but it had made conglomerate cases almost impossible to prove. It upheld the prohibition of the merger on safe (horizontal) grounds, which were universally accepted in law (although contestable on the facts). By raising the bar to any challenge of conglomerate mergers, it dissipated the firestorm on the proper analysis of conglomerate effects.

Had Europe been led by logic to approximate the American model (by treading cautiously on conglomerate effects)? Had it been browbeaten to do so? Or had the Court simply chosen not to rock the boat of transatlantic relations while not turning its back on the Commission?

VII.   FORECLOSURE ANALYSIS AND *GE/HONEYWELL*

Substantively, at the Commission level, *GE/Honeywell* was largely about foreclosure analysis. It centrally concerned the fencing out or disadvantaging of competitors by power, not merits. The most palpable

---

[64] *Id.*, para. 179.

[65] The court did say, however, in rejecting the bundling claim, that "the mere fact that the merged entity would have had a wider range of products than its competitors is not sufficient to justify the conclusion that dominant positions would have been created or strengthened for it on the different markets concerned." *Id.*, para. 470.

problem was, to the Commission in *GE/Honeywell*: GE had used the leverage of its financial, multi-product, vertically integrated enterprise in the past to preempt sales that it otherwise would not have made, and it threatened to do so again. This would increase the market share of the already dominant firm at the expense of firms without power. The merger would have put into GE's copious corporate lap an array of new leveraging and bundling prospects. Of course the competitors worried. And they convinced the European Commission that the merger would hurt the market.

Mergers that created just such opportunities once also violated U.S. antitrust law.[66] But this was before U.S. antitrust law shifted to an efficiency/consumer welfare paradigm; before it began to assume that mergers were efficient, and to discount competitors' complaints on grounds that competitors are motivated to complain about their rivals' *efficient* deals, and therefore siding with the rivals usually hurts consumers.

In Europe, like the United States, competition law was not originally designed merely as an instrument for efficiency. Europe developed a foreclosure analysis not unlike the earlier U.S. foreclosure analysis: it worried about the loss of competitors' opportunities, and equated hurdles erected by market power with market harm. As in the United States, errors were made. Sometimes applications of the law protected competitors from conduct that was responsive to the market; thus it protected competitors from competition itself. This was a problem that, at first, went almost unnoticed.

Then two things happened. First, in the 1990s, in the wake of globalization with its special call for competitiveness, Europe took on board modern economic analysis. It did so slowly, however, and selectively.

Second, as the European Commission began to bring proceedings against U.S. firms among others (following the lead of the United States to scrutinize harms to their market from whatever source), Americans awoke to the fact that Europe had a highly developed competition law. Americans expected EC competition law to be just like U.S. antitrust law. Most knew little or nothing of the European context and the fit of EC competition law within the larger context of the Treaty of Rome. They usually assumed that, if and where EC competition law deviated from U.S. law, the EC law had gone astray.

Americans began to argue for modifications of EC law in tune with the American perspective, which, they asserted, was much more ready to

---

[66] See FTC v. Consolidated Foods Corp., 380 U.S. 592 (1965). See also FTC v. Texaco, Inc., 393 U.S. 223 (1968) (a conduct case under the Federal Trade Commission Act).

assume competitive harm from loss of firm efficiencies (and to assume efficiencies) than it was to assume competitive harm from loss of market access and foreclosure.[67] This phenomenon played out in the immediate aftermath of the Commission decision in *GE/Honeywell*, in bi-lateral U.S./Europe meetings, in OECD workshops, and in high-level international conferences. It is playing out now in the context of the U.S., EU, and world debates about the proper standards for anticompetitive unilateral conduct with particular regard to exclusionary practices.[68]

To a large extent, the *rhetoric* of the antitrust experts of the United States and of the European Union has converged. On both sides of the ocean, and with regard to *GE/Honeywell* itself, experts repeat the mantra that the antitrust law is meant to enhance consumer welfare and (or) efficiency.[69] But even the experts do, as they must, make assumptions. Sometimes the assumptions are transparently heroic—as in the Commission's *GE/Honeywell* finding that bundling would cause the competitors to stop investing in the niches dominated by GE/Honeywell, prices would go down in the short term, but eventually prices would go up. Sometimes, the assumptions are much more credible but still arguable. For example, U.S. Department of Justice officials repeatedly said that because Honeywell's products were complements (aircraft framers needed both avionics and engines), the merger would eliminate double marginalization and prices would go down; and that this gargantuan merger was an efficient one.[70] Nonetheless, two points are germane. First, around the world and even in the United States, the unfairness of exclusions by

---

[67] Europeans, also, argued for a more economics-based law. *See, e.g.*, Jeremy Grant and Damien J. Neven, The Attempted Merger between General Electric and Honeywell—A Case Study of TransAtlantic Conflict, J. Competition Law & Econ. 595 (2005); John Vickers, Abuse of Market Power, Economic Journal 115, F244 (Oxford, June 2005); Eleanor J. Morgan and Steven McGuire, Transatlantic Divergence: GE–Honeywell and the EU's Merger Policy, 11 J. European Public Policy 39 (February 2004).

[68] In the United States, the DOJ and FTC launched hearings on the proper standards for unilateral conduct. *See* http://www.usdoj.gov/atr/public/hearings/single_firm/docs/218672.htm. In the European Union, the Competition Directorate launched a public discussion on Article 82 standards for exclusionary conduct. *See* http://ec.europa.eu/comm/competition/antitrust/others/article_82_review.html. In the International Competition Network, a Working Group has been formed to consider standards for unilateral conduct. www.internationalcompetitionnetwork.org.workinggroups.html.

[69] See Monti, *supra* note 40.

[70] GE argued that it would not be able to bundle. Moreover, even Welch got disenamored of the merger because Honeywell began performing badly, and he worried whether GE could digest Honeywell. The Financial Times reported: "At the Commission, officials believe that GE lost interest in acquiring Honeywell in early June—perhaps because it was aware that the industrial group's performance was deteriorating and that integration would be difficult." *See* Flight of Fancy, *supra* note 53.

dominant firms using tactics of bullying and leveraging still has reso-
nance and will not die.[71] Second, a dominant firm's use of power to shift
significant market share to itself and away from a deserving rival *may*
hurt the market and ultimately consumers,[72] even if a plaintiff cannot
prove that specified conduct would probably monopolize a market.[73]
Moreover, one may prefer to trust the impartial market rather than
trust the dominant firm.[74]

With the ascendant U.S. premise that helping foreclosed rivals is
likely to harm consumers,[75] foreclosure violations have a very small scope
under U.S. law in the 21st century. With the premise in European cases
that preserving openness of markets[76] is likely to help consumers,
foreclosure violations have a somewhat larger scope. But even so, after
Tetra Laval and *GE/Honeywell*, a merger challenge based on predicted

---

[71] *See, e.g.*, Conwood Co. v. United States Tobacco Co., 290 F.3d 768 (6th Cir. 2002),
cert. denied, 537 U.S. 1148 (2003).

Numerous press reports on the *Microsoft* antitrust cases noted Microsoft's repeated
unfair acts. E.g., Steve Lohr, The Prosecution Almost Rests, New York Times, Jan. 8. 1999,
C1.

Many antitrust laws include a "fairness" value. This is especially true in Asia, and in
developing countries in general, wherein distribution of the gains of trade is at least as
important as allocation of resources. See Symposium Issue, APEC Competition Policy and
Economic Development, 1 Washington University Global Studies Law Review 1 (2002).

[72] Barry Nalebuff, Exclusionary Bundling, 50 Antitrust Bulletin 321 (2005).

[73] *See* EU Microsoft case COMP/C–3/37.792 paras. 694–95, 783 (undercutting rivals'
incentive to invent). See also E. Fox, "We Protect Competition, You Protect Competitors,"
26 World Competition 149, 155–62 (2003).

In Verizon Communications Inc. v. Law Offices of Curtis V. Trinko, 540 U.S. 398
(2004), the brief for the States argued that the incumbent telephone services supplier,
which controlled the local loop and gave rivals less good access than it took for itself,
threatened "death by a thousand cuts." Id. at 414. *See* Brief for the States of New York et
al. as Amici Curiae in Support of Respondent, 2003 WL 21755944 text after note 11 (July
25, 2003). The Court of Appeals for the Second Circuit had no difficulty finding that the
monopolist's intentional disruption of service to rivals stated an antitrust claim, 305 F.3d
89, 108 (2d Cir. 2002), even though Verizon was not en route to monopolizing the local
market, which it was bound by statute to open. The Supreme Court was not impressed,
viewing the "thousand cuts" as a reason to withhold court intervention, not to invite it, on
grounds of the limits of the capabilities of courts. 540 U.S. at 414.

[74] See E. Fox, *supra*.

[75] This is a default presumption. It may be overcome. See United States v. Microsoft
Corp., 253 F.3d 34 (D.C. Cir.), cert. denied, 534 U.S. 952 (2001).

[76] This is sometimes articulated as freedom to contest markets. *See* A Bundeskartel-
lamt/Competition Law Forum Debate on Reform of Art. 82: A "Dialectic" on Competing
Approaches, 2 European Competition J. 211, 216 (special issue 2006). *See also* Stefan
Schmitz, How Dare They?, European Merger Control and the European Commission's
Blocking of the General Electric/Honeywell Merger ("*How Dare They?*"), 23 U. Pa. J. Intl
Econ. L. 539, 542 (2002).

foreclosing conduct is hard to mount and harder yet to win. This phenomenon represents a convergence—toward U.S. law.

VIII.   GLOBALIZATION, NATIONALISM, COSMOPOLITANISM, CONVERGENCE, AND *GE/HONEYWELL*

GE/Honeywell triggered a predictable scenario. Europe prohibited a merger of U.S. firms that America had cleared. American politicians responded: Take your hands off my merger. American antitrust authorities responded: Learn economics and adopt the efficiency goal. Europe acknowledged an efficiency goal. It ratcheted up the rigor of its economic analysis. Gradually, its vocabulary (how to talk about antitrust) began to sound more American.

The controversy died. The officials proclaimed the clash exceptional; a thing of the past; and they resumed the tasks of coordination of national law in a globalized world. Eventually, the court ruling came down in *GE/Honeywell*, and, although the Court upheld the prohibition, it did so on innocuous (horizontal) grounds. Besides, the merger was moot.

Coordination and cooperation are indeed robust. Jurisdictions cooperate in pursuing world cartels and they cooperate in vetting international mergers. In 99.9% of the cases, they see eye-to-eye on the outcomes of investigations, even if nuances of analysis differ. The authorities share their analyses, and they listen to the concerns of one another. If the merger is a merger of U.S. firms, European authorities sympathetically consider the United States position, and tend to adjust the European treatment to the U.S. treatment,[77] and vice versa.

Still, clashes happen. They tend to recur in the area of conduct that forecloses rivals. The EU continues to value market access, and the U.S. continues to value freedom of action of even dominant firms. The major current "battle" is *Microsoft*. The European Commission and other nations have prohibited exclusionary conduct of Microsoft[78] that U.S. law might allow.[79] The U.S. DOJ has come to the aid of Microsoft in declaring the foreign decisions bad law and bad economics,[80] while the

---

[77] See Oracle/PeopleSoft, Commission decision, Case COMP/M 3216, O.J. L 218/6 (Oct. 10, 2004), agreeing in outcome with United States v. Oracle Corp., 331 F. Supp. 2d 1098 (N.D. Cal. 2004). See Drautz, *supra* note 24, discussing, among other cases, *MCI/World-Com/Sprint* and *Alcoa/Reynolds*, regarding mergers prohibited or conditioned on both sides of the ocean.

[78] Microsoft Corp., COMP/C–3/37.792, Commission decision of March 24, 2004, appeal pending; Microsoft Corp. KFTC, decision of Dec. 7, 2005, appeal pending.

[79] Compare Massachusetts v. Microsoft Corp., 373 F.3d 1199 (D.C. Cir. 2004).

[80] See statement of Bruce McDonald, DOJ Press Release, Dec. 7, 2005, available at http://www.usdoj.gov/atr/public/press_releases/2005/213562.htm, stating: "The Antitrust

U.S. politicians continue to decry foreign interventions as an affront to American sovereignty.[81] And so it goes.

GE/Honeywell is an important case along the international road. *GE/Honeywell* inspires hypotheses and observations. Here are four:

1. Clashes diminish; convergence happens. So many large mergers are now international. They affect the citizens of many nations. Even when the effects are uniform throughout the world, as in *GE/Honeywell*, clashes happen. The range for clashes narrows, however, as the competition authorities of the various nations intensify their communications with one another, both regarding abstract principles (what the law is and ought to be), and regarding laws and analysis as applied to particular cases. The antitrust authorities of the various nations now have intense, sustained communications with one another. The channels for communication have been carefully laid and are constantly nurtured, both bi-laterally and multilaterally. It is a great virtue of the International Competition Network that it facilitates cross-fertilization and nurtures understanding. I would venture a guess that in no other field of national law with large international ramifications is communication so intense and so fruitful.

2. Firms do not belong to nations; but still, law is political. It is now well-recognized by antitrust authorities that firms and mergers do not "belong" to the nation of their principal establishment. Effects matter, not the location of establishment. If the effects of a merger will be felt throughout the world, the various nations of impact have a proper interest in vetting and controlling the merger. But this point of economics is not accepted by politicians, who still claim mergers as their own.[82] The politicians' cries are heard at the antitrust agencies; they could be influential at a margin. The politicians' message (don't stop our merger; don't burden our business) may coincide with an antitrust authority's professional inclinations to bless the conduct. Then, law and politics are synergistic. They appear to interact, however independent the agency.

3. "Anticompetitive" and "efficient" are not self-defining terms, and efficiency as a goal is an elastic concept. Nations do not agree on what is "anticompetitive." They do not agree on whether antitrust is only about efficiency; and they do not agree on how to "get to" efficiency by the vehicle of antitrust law. The largest point of disagreement is

---

Division believes that Korea's remedy goes beyond what is necessary or appropriate to protect consumers, as it requires the removal of products that consumers may prefer."

[81] See *U.S. Lawmakers Meddle in CNOOC's Unocal Bid*, China Daily, July 6, 2005; Edward M. Graham, op-ed, *No Reason to Block the Deal*, FAR EASTERN ECONOMIC REV. July/Aug. 2005 at 24; C. Fred Bergsten, *Avoiding Another Dubai*, WASHINGTON POST op-ed, Feb. 28, 2006 at A15.

[82] See *How Dare They?*, *supra* note 76, 23 U. Pa. Int'l Econ. L. at 539, 540.

whether efficiency should be seen in terms of an environment conducive to robust rivalry among firms sufficiently large to realize economies, or whether it should be regarded in terms of a rule of non-intervention unless a challenger can prove that the particular transaction will probably raise prices to consumers.[83] Advocates of both approaches claim that their concern is consumer welfare,[84] and each side can make this claim with as much legitimacy as the other. This—plus the vagaries of analysis (including foundational economic assumptions)—means that different jurisdictions might reach different conclusions on the effect of the same conduct or transaction even when the jurisdictions are identically affected.[85]

4. Convergence is not the paramount goal, but convergence can be helpful. On the one hand, if all mergers were either anticompetitive or not according to one universal standard,[86] the wheels of transactions would be greased and trillions of dollars in transactions costs would be saved. Some efficient mergers might be incentivized and others saved from a premature demise.

Perhaps more importantly, there is much to be said for the proposition that international transactions should be governed by one set of rules. Often, the market is the world. A universal rule would treat the whole world community seamlessly and the market actors therein non-discriminatorily, with no place for nationalism.[87]

On the other hand, a single standard—whether achieved through soft harmonization or world rules—has its costs. Uniform rules, if too specific, would constrain the adaptation of law to a changing world. Moreover, they would frustrate localities' efforts to frame their own law according to their specific, contextual needs.[88]

---

[83] *See* Bundeskartellamt/Competition Law Forum joint paper on Article 82, *supra* note 76, pp. 211, 216.

[84] Or, they may identify their concern as total welfare. The point is—almost all jurisdictions deny protecting competitors at the expense of consumers.

[85] This is also true of different courts or other bodies within the same jurisdiction.

[86] I assume here, for simplicity, that there is a world market and effects are uniform all over the world, as in *GE/Honeywell*. Many transactions create differential effects in various national markets, and nations are normally permitted to counteract effects in their markets.

[87] See E. Fox, International Antitrust and the Doha Dome, 43 Va. J. Int'l L. 911 (2003).

[88] If the standard is too general, it leaves much room for discretionary judgment. If enforcement is left to national courts and authorities, a vague universal norm will produce as much divergence as there is without world rules. If the enforcement or ultimate appeal lies with or to a central body, a uniform world jurisprudence could be developed; but important questions must be resolved, including who will be the decision-makers and how will their decisions be enforced?

As an alternative, there might be one standard for any given transaction or practice. The standard might be the law of the country with the most contacts. All other jurisdictions could be bound to defer. This possibility, which could operate somewhat like a conflicts-of-law rule, has many attractions,[89] but rules of deference are not simple.[90] Moreover, such a standard could invite protection of national champions;[91] and it would end up privileging the law of the two dominant-player jurisdictions in the world—the United States and the European Union, "home" to most multinationals—to the exclusion of the rest of the world.

Although there is much talk among antitrust authorities and the bar that convergence of the antitrust laws of the various jurisdictions is the principal goal of "international" antitrust, enthusiasm for the goal seems to diminish when convergence is taken to mean anything other than: "Converge to my way."[92]

CONCLUSION

During the five years of the pendency of the *GE/Honeywell* matter, a significant change in antitrust rhetoric and analysis came about in the European Union. Institutional changes were made. Economics was elevated to a place of greater importance. Rigor of economic analysis increased. Why? And why at this time?

---

[89] See the methodology proposed in E. Fox, Report to the Attorney General and Assistant Attorney General of the International Competition Policy Advisory Committee, Chap. 2, p. 64, n. 72. The rules of the home jurisdiction could be applied to take account of all harms to competition, wherever they occur.

[90] For example, if Europe and Korea must defer to the United States for antitrust "regulation" of Microsoft, would a rule of deference require them to refrain from challenging conduct subsequent to and different from conduct challenged in the United States? Would it matter whether U.S. law would probably (or might) treat such conduct as legal or even procompetitive? See Testimony of Eleanor M. Fox before the Antitrust Modernization Commission hearing on international issues, Feb. 15, 2006, as revised, March 2, 2006, available at http://www.AMC.gov.

[91] See Laura D'Andrea Tyson, "McBoeing" Should Be Cleared For Takeoff, Wall St. J. July 22, 1997, A14 (antitrust authorities should approve Boeing's acquisition of McDonnell Douglas even if it means that the price of airline seats will rise, because the merger is good for America).

[92] Many advocates of the convergence goal assume there is one universal right answer and that the right answer is "my way." This is not the case for procedure and process. For example, regarding rules on pre-merger notification, the choice of logistical rules, such as the earliest date on which a filing is accepted, are often arbitrary, and the advantages of commonality clearly outweigh national particularities. Convergence on this front has been accepted. *See* International Competition Network, merger working group, guiding principles and recommended practices for merger notification and review procedures, available at http://www.internationalcompetitionnetwork.org/mergers/guidingprinciples.html.

There are several causal factors to which the change can be ascribed.[93] The three annulment decisions of the Court of First Instance in the summer and fall of 2002 undoubtedly played a leading role. Some Americans speculate that the sometimes contentious transAtlantic dialog in the aftermath of the Commission's *GE/Honeywell* decision[94] played a role; that it moved Europe to embrace the American paradigm, at least in large part;[95] and that this was a felicitous result of a hard won campaign to get the Europeans to see it the American way.[96] The truth is, however, that an intra-European movement towards a more economic approach had been working its way into the European mainstream for some time[97] and finally took root in CFI judgments and DG Competition disciplines and decisions,[98] much like Chicago School insights and claims

---

[93] See part II *supra*. See Nicholas Levy, *supra* note 7 at 107.

[94] See part V *supra*.

[95] The European competition officials agreed that consumer welfare is the goal of antitrust, and that there is no efficiencies "offense" in merger cases. See Neelie Kroes, *supra* note 54.

[96] *See* Kolasky, *supra* note 4.

There are a number of articles on the GE/Honeywell merger, the actual and the "appropriate" economic analysis, the course of the proceedings from the U.S. clearance to the EC prohibition and, in some cases, to the European court's affirmance. One of the best of these articles is Jeremy Grant and Damien J. Neven, The Attempted Merger Between General Electric and Honeywell: A Case Study of TransAtlantic Conflict, 1 J. Competition Law & Econ. 595 (2005).

[97] *See, e.g.*, David Deacon, Vertical Restraints Under EU Competition Law: New Directions, Chap. 20 in 1995 Fordham Corp. L. Institute (B. Hawk ed. 1995) at 307; Valentine Korah, An Introductory Guide to EC Competition Law and Practice (1st ed. 1978, now in 8th ed. 2004). For later European scholarship, *see* note 67 *supra*.

[98] European Commission cases of the new era, which is principally reflected in a major elevation in the standard of proof required to prove a conglomerate effects case, include Johnson & Johnson/Guidant, Commission Decision, Case COMP/M3687 (Aug. 25, 2005); Pernod Ricard/Allied Domecq, Commission Decision, Case COMP/M3779 (June 24, 2005), GE/Amersham, Commission Decision, Case COMP/M 3304 (Jan. 21, 2004). In *GE/Amersham*, the Commission set a standard even higher than outlined by the court, holding:

> [F]or commercial bundling to result in foreclosure of competition it is necessary that the merged entity is able to leverage its pre-merger dominance in one product to another complementary product. In addition, for such strategy to be profitable, there must be a reasonable expectation that rivals will not be able to propose a competitive response, and that their resulting marginalisation will force them to exit the market. Finally, once rivals have exited the market, the merged firm must be able to implement unilateral price increases and such increases need to be sustainable in the long term, without being challenged by the likelihood of new rivals entering the market or previously marginalised ones re-entering the market. *Id.*, para. 37.

of the 1960s found their way into U.S. court decisions and agency initiatives in the 1980s and beyond.[99]

---

[99] *See* Herbert Hovenkamp, Post–Chicago Antitrust: A Review and Critique, 2001 Colum. Bus. L. Rev. 257 (2001).

13

Alvin K. Klevorick and Alan O. Sykes[*]

United States Courts and the Optimal Deterrence of International Cartels: A Welfarist Perspective on *Empagran*

Introduction

Globalization has captured the attention of policymakers, commentators, and the general public. Its specific characteristics vary from one context to another and from one observer to another, but at its core is the increasing economic interdependence of countries around the world. Although some economists argue that from a historical perspective the current period is not one of especially heightened interdependence, globalization remains a dominant theme in discussions of economics and legal policy. In the antitrust arena two important aspects of globalization are the increased cooperation of firms across national boundaries for both good and ill, and the spread of antitrust or competition policy regimes among countries though without convergence on a unitary approach.

These two facets of globalization came together in the case of *F. Hoffmann–La Roche Ltd. v. Empagran S.A.*,[1] which was decided by the U.S. Supreme Court in June 2004. The case centered on the activity of a global price-fixing cartel in vitamins. The plaintiffs were foreigners who

* Alvin K. Klevorick is the John Thomas Smith Professor of Law and Professor of Economics at Yale University, and Alan O. Sykes is Professor of Law at Stanford University. We thank Daniel A. Crane, Eleanor M. Fox, Oona A. Hathaway, and Lawrence T. Sorkin for helpful comments and Michelle Messer (Yale Law School Class of 2007) and Jonathan T. Schmidt (Yale Law School Class of 2006) for excellent research assistance.

1 542 U.S. 155 (2004).

purchased vitamins outside the United States and sought relief under U.S. antitrust law. The Court's decision was heavily influenced by the respect it held should be accorded other nations' competition laws and policies.

We shall use the *Empagran* case as a vehicle to examine the effects of globalization on U.S. antitrust law. In particular, how do some common themes of antitrust law take on a different shape or form in a world of greater economic interdependence? What should the form and substance of U.S. antitrust law and policy be in this globalized setting? We begin in Section I with a discussion of the *Empagran* case and its background. Then, in Section II, we offer a welfare-analytic perspective on the decision and the opinion's reasoning supporting it. In Section III, we draw out the legal implications of our analysis for the *Empagran* decision itself and for the Foreign Trade Antitrust Improvements Act (henceforth, "FTAIA"),[2] the interpretation of which was at the heart of the case. In the final section, we offer some concluding comments.

I. THE *EMPAGRAN* CASE

The *Empagran* matter began its journey to the Supreme Court in the District Court for the District of Columbia. The plaintiffs included foreign and domestic firms that had purchased vitamins for delivery outside the United States from the defendant vitamin manufacturers or their alleged co-conspirators. The plaintiffs, including corporations from Ecuador, Panama, Australia, Mexico, Belgium, the United Kingdom, Indonesia, and Ukraine as well as the United States, sought to bring a class action on behalf of all similarly situated foreign and domestic customers of the defendant members of the international vitamins cartel. For the cartel's alleged supracompetitive pricing, the *Empagran* plaintiffs asked both "damages and injunctive relief under the antitrust laws of the United States, the antitrust laws of the relevant foreign nations, and international law."[3]

A. *The Global Vitamins Cartel*

The global vitamins cartel, self-styled "Vitamins, Inc." by some of its members, actually comprised a set of overlapping cartels, each fixing prices and allocating markets for one or more vitamins. It consisted of "wheels within wheels," in one observer's characterization,[4] and included multinational corporations located in Belgium, France, Germany, Japan, the Netherlands, Switzerland, and the United States. The cartel

---

[2] 15 U.S.C. § 6a (2000).

[3] Empagran S.A. v. F. Hoffman–La Roche, Ltd., No. Civ. 001686TFH, 2001 WL 761360, at *1 (D.D.C. June 7, 2001).

[4] JOHN M. CONNOR, GLOBAL PRICE FIXING: OUR CUSTOMERS ARE THE ENEMY 305 (2001).

thrived during the 1990s and encompassed at least 16 products manufactured by at least 20 parent companies. The price fixing was more effective and lasted longer for some products than for others. An undertaking of that scale and scope required a complex organization, which the vitamins cartel had—a hierarchy of three management tiers running from regional managers, who met quarterly to make necessary price and quantity adjustments, to major policymakers, who met once a year. John M. Connor, a leading student of global price-fixing cartels, estimates that the international vitamins cartel affected over \$34 billion of commerce, measured by the sales revenues derived from the products during the price-fixing period.[5] He further estimates that on these sales the cartel members earned global monopoly profits of somewhere "between \$9 and \$13 billion, of which 15% accrued in the United States, 1% in Canada, 26% in the EU, and 58% in the rest of the world."[6]

The international vitamins cartel ended with the close of the twentieth century principally as the result of enforcement actions by the United States Department of Justice. Competition authorities in other jurisdictions, including Australia, Canada, the European Union, Japan, and South Korea, also imposed sanctions on cartel members, and enforcement actions were facilitated by the cooperation of authorities across national boundaries. The Department of Justice emphasized the importance to its success of its leniency program, which grants amnesty from criminal prosecution to potential antitrust defendants under specific conditions, and especially the cooperation elicited from Rhône–Poulenc. Other countries' competition authorities also stressed the central place of their amnesty programs in their actions against the global vitamins cartel, a point that will take on importance when we come to the Supreme Court's *Empagran* decision.

A large number of state attorneys general, who pursued *parens patriae* actions on behalf of their states and their states' residents as indirect buyers of vitamins and vitamin premixes, also played a role in the enforcement effort. Finally, private attorneys contributed to the cartel's demise as they brought class actions against members of the cartel in federal court on behalf of direct purchasers and in state courts on behalf of indirect buyers, where state indirect-purchaser statutes provided for such actions. The suits initiated by the private class-action lawyers and by the state attorneys general addressed the injuries inflicted on United States purchasers by sales of vitamins and vitamin products sold in the United States, which sharply distinguishes them from the harms for which the *Empagran* plaintiffs sought recovery.

---

[5] Brief Amici Curiae of Professors Darren Bush et al. in Support of Respondents at 11, *Empagran*, 542 U.S. 155 (No. 03–724), 2004 WL 533933.

[6] *Id.* at 15.

The corporate members of the international vitamins cartel and a significant number of their senior managers paid a very high price for their illegal activity. As reported in the government's amicus brief to the Supreme Court in the *Empagran* case in Spring 2004:

> To date, the investigation ... has resulted in plea agreements with twelve corporate defendants and thirteen individual defendants and the imposition of fines exceeding $900 million—including the largest criminal fine ($500 million) ever obtained by the Department of Justice under any statute.... Eleven of the thirteen individuals have received sentences resulting, in imprisonment, and an additional individual awaits a criminal trial. European Union, Canadian, Australian, and Korean authorities similarly have obtained record civil penalties exceeding € 855 million against the vitamin companies.

> In the wake of the government's investigations, domestic private parties sued the vitamin companies seeking treble damages and attorney's fees ... for overcharges that the domestic companies paid in United States commerce as a result of the price-fixing conspiracy. In settlement of suits by some United States purchasers, the vitamin companies paid amounts "exceeding $2 billion."[7]

The amicus brief submitted at the same time by Professor Connor and his colleagues characterized "[t]he vitamins cartel [as] the most harshly sanctioned conspiracy in antitrust history"[8] and reckoned the total financial antitrust fines and penalties imposed on the cartel at between $4.4 and $5.6 billion.[9] This included $907 million in criminal fines in the United States, $100 million in criminal fines paid in Canada, $759 million of administrative fines imposed by the European Union, a fine of $14 million ordered by Australia, and a $3 million fine charged by South Korea.[10] The damages and legal fees and costs recovered by direct buyers in the United States are difficult to calculate. While some of these sanctions are publicly known, as they resulted from resolved class actions in federal courts, the amounts paid to original class-action plaintiffs who opted out of the class to litigate on their own are not public information. Connor states that there were about 225 such opt-out plaintiffs, within a class originally established at above 4000, and they represented more than 75% of the purchases by class members.

---

[7] Brief for the United States as Amicus Curiae Supporting Petitioners at 2, *Empagran*, 542 U.S. 155 (No. 03–724), 2004 WL 234125.

[8] Brief Amici Curiae of Professors Darren Bush et al. in Support of Respondents, *supra* note 5, at 15.

[9] *Id.* at 21.

[10] *Id.* at 19.

"Assuming that they will settle for a somewhat larger percentage of affected sales than those buyers that remained in the class, amicus Connor estimates the total payout to be in the range of $1200 to $2400 million."[11]

B. The District Court Decision

The *Empagran* defendants moved to dismiss the complaint "for lack of subject matter jurisdiction and for failure to state a claim upon which relief may be granted."[12] The District Court deferred ruling on the motion with respect to the domestic plaintiffs' claims until they provided more specific factual allegations about how the defendants' conduct had injured those plaintiffs in United States commerce. In sharp contrast, Judge Hogan granted the defendants' motion with respect to the foreign plaintiffs. He dismissed the foreign purchasers' claims under federal antitrust law, the ones they pressed through supplemental jurisdiction under the competition laws of foreign nations, and their claims under the Alien Tort Claims Act for violations of customary international law proscribing the cartel's conduct. The District Court's dismissal of the foreign plaintiffs' federal antitrust claims shaped the question that came before the Supreme Court in *Empagran*. But the trial court's consideration of the other two claims, its finding that there is no customary international law of antitrust and its discussion of the multiplicity of foreign tribunals weighing foreign purchasers' claims against the vitamins cartel, highlight important aspects of the current context of antitrust policy and the background for the Supreme Court's decision.

In finding that it lacked subject matter jurisdiction over the *Empagran* plaintiffs' claims under federal antitrust law, the District Court characterized "[t]he critical question in this case [as] whether allegations of a global price fixing conspiracy that affects commerce both in the United States and in other countries gives persons injured abroad in transactions otherwise unconnected with the United States a remedy under our antitrust laws."[13] The answer to that question was to be found, the court said, in the FTAIA and its interpretation in the caselaw. That Act provides as follows:

> Sections 1 to 7 of this title shall not apply to conduct involving trade or commerce (other than import trade or import commerce) with foreign nations unless—
>
> **(1)** such conduct has a direct, substantial, and reasonably foreseeable effect—

---

[11] *Id.* at 20.

[12] Empagran S.A. v. F. Hoffman–La Roche, Ltd., No. Civ. 001686TFH, 2001 WL 761360, at *1 (D.D.C. June 7, 2001).

[13] *Id.* at *2.

(A) on trade or commerce which is not trade or commerce with foreign nations, or on import trade or import commerce with foreign nations; or

(B) on export trade or export commerce with foreign nations, of a person engaged in such trade or commerce in the United States; and

(2) such effect gives rise to a claim under the provisions of sections 1 to 7 of this title, other than this section.

If sections 1 to 7 of this title apply to such conduct only because of the operation of paragraph (1)(B), then sections 1 to 7 of this title shall apply to such conduct only for injury to export business in the United States.[14]

The FTAIA excludes from coverage under the Sherman Act conduct involving non-import trade or commerce with foreign nations unless it meets the two stipulated conditions. The District Court found that the *Empagran* plaintiffs' complaint satisfied what we shall call the "effects condition" in (1) because "plaintiffs generally allege that the defendants' price fixing behavior had direct, substantial, and reasonably foreseeable effects on U.S. commerce."[15] But Judge Hogan determined that the vitamins purchasers failed to meet condition (2), the "claim condition," because they did not allege that the *effects* on United States commerce that they had identified gave rise to the injury they suffered. The District Court emphasized the distinction between *conduct as the cause of harm* and *effects as the cause of harm*, which would be central to the Supreme Court's decision in the case. As Judge Hogan wrote, "Plaintiffs argue that the jurisdictional nexus is provided solely by the global nature of the defendants' conduct. In plaintiffs' view, the territorial effect of that conduct is irrelevant. However, the existing caselaw does not support plaintiffs' position."[16] Put another way, although the global cartel's activity may have caused injury to the plaintiffs and in United States commerce, the vitamin buyers before the court had "not alleged that the precise injuries for which they [sought] redress [had] the requisite domestic effects necessary to provide subject matter jurisdiction over [the] case."[17]

C.   The Court of Appeals Decision

The foreign purchasers appealed to the Court of Appeals for the District of Columbia Circuit. A divided court found, contrary to Judge Hogan, that the District Court had subject matter jurisdiction in the case

---

[14] 15 U.S.C. § 6a (2000).

[15] *Empagran*, 2001 WL 761360, at *3.

[16] *Id.*

[17] *Id.*

and the foreign plaintiffs had standing to press their claim under the federal antitrust laws. Consequently, the Court of Appeals reversed the District Court's decision, vacated its judgment, and remanded the case.[18] For the Court of Appeals, "The precise issue presented in this appeal [was] whether the 'gives rise to a claim' requirement under § 6a(2) of FTAIA authorizes subject matter jurisdiction where the defendant's conduct affects both domestic and foreign commerce, but the plaintiff's claim arises only from the conduct's foreign effect."[19] Could a plaintiff proceed with a Sherman Act action only if it could show that it was injured by "anticompetitive effects of the defendant's conduct on U.S. commerce," or did it suffice for the plaintiff to show that the defendant's conduct's anticompetitive effects on U.S. commerce "give rise to an antitrust claim under the Sherman Act by someone, even if not the plaintiff who is before the court"?[20]

Judge Edwards, writing for Judge Rogers and himself, answered this central question by examining the language, structure, and legislative history of the FTAIA, as well as the deterrence objective and effect of the antitrust laws. The court also weighed the conflicting interpretations of the FTAIA's claim condition given by the Second and Fifth Circuits. In *Den Norske Stats Oljeselskap As v. HeereMac Vof*, the Fifth Circuit had read the FTAIA as requiring that the plaintiff's injury must arise from the anticompetitive domestic effects of the defendant's conduct.[21] The effects of that conduct had to give rise to *the* claim made by the plaintiff. The Second Circuit, on the other hand, in *Kruman v. Christie's International PLC* had taken a much more relaxed interpretation of the FTAIA's Section 2.[22] It held that a plaintiff could bring an action under the federal antitrust laws, even if its injury did not arise from the domestic effects of the defendant's conduct so long as those domestic effects "violate the substantive provisions of the Sherman Act."[23] For the *Kruman* court, the FTAIA's claim condition required only proof of a violation of the substantive antitrust law, not a showing that the conduct's domestic effect caused an injury that would ground an action under the Clayton Act.

The *Empagran* Court of Appeals decision came to an interpretation of the FTAIA that "falls somewhere between the views of the Fifth and

---

[18] Empagran S.A. v. F. Hoffman–La Roche, Ltd., 315 F.3d 338, 360 (D.C. Cir. 2003).

[19] *Id.* at 344.

[20] *Id.*

[21] 241 F.3d 420, 427 (5th Cir. 2001).

[22] 284 F.3d 384 (2d Cir. 2002).

[23] *Id.* at 400.

Second Circuits, albeit somewhere closer to the latter."[24] The court went on,

> We hold that, where the anticompetitive conduct has the requisite effect on United States commerce, FTAIA permits suits by foreign plaintiffs who are injured solely by that conduct's effect on foreign commerce. The anticompetitive conduct itself must violate the Sherman Act and the conduct's harmful effect on United States commerce must give rise to "a claim" by someone, even if not the foreign plaintiff who is before the court. Thus, the conduct's domestic effect must do more than give rise to a government action for violation of the Sherman Act, but it need not necessarily give rise to the particular plaintiff's (private) claim.[25]

Because the foreign purchasers alleged that the international vitamins cartel had effects in United States commerce that gave rise to antitrust claims by parties who were injured in the United States as a result of such domestic transactions, the Court of Appeals found that the District Court had subject matter jurisdiction over the *Empagran* plaintiffs' claims.[26]

Judge Henderson dissented because she disagreed with the majority's interpretation of the FTAIA. She believed that the District Court's and the Fifth Circuit's *Den Norske* interpretation of the FTAIA was "[t]he more natural reading of the statutory language" and supported by its legislative history.[27] The dissent determined that "subsection (2) of the FTAIA expressly limits jurisdiction to a claim which *itself* arises from the domestic antitrust effect required under subsection (1) of the statute."[28]

The *Empagran* defendants requested a rehearing before the panel and then a rehearing en banc. Both petitions were denied.[29]

D.   The Supreme Court Decision

The Supreme Court granted the petition for certiorari by the defendant vitamin manufacturers and distributors. In a unanimous 8–0 judgment, with Justice O'Connor not participating, the Court vacated the judgment of the D.C. Circuit and remanded the case for proceedings

---

[24] *Empagran*, 315 F.3d at 350.

[25] *Id.*

[26] *Id.* at 341.

[27] *Id.* at 360 (Henderson, J., dissenting).

[28] *Id.* at 361–62 (emphasis added).

[29] *See* Empagran S.A. v. F. Hoffman–La Roche, Ltd., No. 01–7115, 2003 U.S. App. LEXIS 19021, at *1 (D.C. Cir. Sept. 11, 2003).

consistent with the opinion of the Court. That opinion, written by Justice Breyer, began by characterizing the *Empagran* facts in a way that sharply narrowed the question the Court faced and hence the scope of applicability of its decision. Specifically, the opinion of the Court states, "We here focus upon anticompetitive price-fixing activity that is in significant part foreign, that caused some domestic injury, and that *independently* caused separate foreign injury."[30] Although we add the emphasis in this quotation, that stress seems merited by the number of times the Court itself intones the independent character of the foreign effect. For example, just two paragraphs following this characterization, Justice Breyer writes, "To clarify: The issue before us concerns (1) significant foreign anticompetitive conduct with (2) an adverse domestic effect and (3) an independent foreign effect giving rise to the claim."[31]

The Court applies the FTAIA to this setting and reaches two principal conclusions about "the price-fixing conduct and the foreign injury that it causes."[32] First, that price-fixing conduct comes within the FTAIA's general exclusion of the Sherman Act's reach because it constitutes "conduct involving trade or commerce . . . with foreign nations," and second, that conduct does not fit within the FTAIA's "domestic-injury exception to the general rule . . . where the plaintiff's claim rests solely on the independent foreign harm."[33] As a result, in the case of the global vitamins cartel, "a purchaser in the United States could bring a Sherman Act claim under the FTAIA based on domestic injury, but a purchaser in Ecuador could not bring a Sherman Act claim based on foreign harm."[34] The same conclusions applied to the other remaining *Empagran* plaintiffs from Australia, Panama, and Ukraine, just as it would apply to any other foreign buyer who suffered only foreign harm.[35]

---

[30] F. Hoffmann–La Roche Ltd. v. Empagran S.A., 542 U.S. 155, 158 (2004) (emphasis added).

[31] *Id.* at 159.

[32] *Id.* at 158.

[33] *Id.* at 158–59.

[34] *Id.* at 159.

[35] Although the *Empagran* plaintiffs were drawn from eight foreign countries and the United States, by the time the case reached the Court of Appeals for the District of Columbia, the appellants, all foreign, were from only Australia, Ecuador, Panama, and Ukraine. The domestic plaintiffs, Procter & Gamble Manufacturing Company and The Procter & Gamble Company, were by then parties in the domestic litigation. The foreign plaintiffs no longer in the litigation—from Belgium, Indonesia, Mexico, and the United Kingdom—were all foreign affiliates of Procter & Gamble. *See* Brief for Appellants at i n.2, Empagran S.A. v. F. Hoffmann–La Roche, Ltd., 417 F.3d 1267 (D.C. Cir. 2005) (No. 01–7115). On June 7, 2001, Judge Hogan had decided in *In Re Vitamins Antitrust Litigation* that the jurisdiction of the court, responsible for the action by U.S. vitamins purchaser-plaintiffs, encompassed the direct purchase claims of foreign affiliates of a U.S. firm when those purchases were part of a coordinated procurement plan of the U.S. firm. *See In re*

Justice Breyer begins the Court's analysis by quickly disposing of the vitamin buyers' first argument that the FTAIA has no applicability to the case because its exclusionary rule extends only to conduct relating to exports. Citing the legislative history and referring more generally to careful consideration of "the amendment itself and the lack of any other plausible purpose," he concludes "that the FTAIA's general rule applies where the anticompetitive conduct at issue is foreign."[36] This cleared the way for consideration of "the basic question presented, that of the exception's application."[37] Since, as the opinion continued, "[t]he price-fixing conduct significantly and adversely affects both customers outside the United States and customers within the United States,"[38] the *Empagran* plaintiffs met the effects condition of the FTAIA. The only remaining question was whether their action satisfied the claim condition—condition (2)—of the FTAIA, and the Court's answer was no.

The Court gave two main reasons for its decision that the FTAIA exception, and hence the Sherman Act, did not apply to the *Empagran* situation. First, as a matter of "prescriptive comity," the Court "ordinarily construes ambiguous statutes to avoid unreasonable interference with the sovereign authority of other nations."[39] Applying this rule of statutory construction, which reflects principles of customary international law, courts "assume that legislators take account of the legitimate sovereign interests of other nations when they write American laws."[40] Of course, any application of U.S. antitrust law to foreign conduct can interfere with another country's capacity to regulate its economy. When the antitrust law is invoked to remedy domestic antitrust injury, the Court has found that interference reasonable. But the Court sharply distinguishes the situation, as in *Empagran*, where the injury is entirely foreign.

Vitamins Antitrust Litig., No. 99–197 (TFH), 2001 WL 755852 (D.D.C. June 7, 2001). As a result, Procter & Gamble's foreign affiliates also departed the *Empagran* litigation.

[36] *Id.* at 163.

[37] *Id.*

[38] *Id.* at 164.

[39] *Id.*

[40] *Id.*

Differences abound among countries' laws governing the substance of competition policy (what conduct is legal and what behavior is outside the bounds), the remedies for established injury (injunction or damages at what level), and the appropriate enforcement strategy (for example, an amnesty policy). Given the range of policy choices made by different countries, the Court deems it unreasonable to interfere with foreign countries' sovereign authority by applying United States antitrust law to foreign conduct to remedy private plaintiffs' independent purely foreign injury. Such a case presents the same "serious risk of interference with a foreign nation's ability independently to regulate its own commercial affairs" as there is when the injury suffered is domestic, but with independent foreign injury, "the justification for that interference seems insubstantial."[41] The Court goes on to reject as "too complex to prove workable" the *Empagran* plaintiffs' proposed resolution that comity considerations be applied on a case-by-case basis in circumstances like theirs of independent foreign injury.[42]

There is at least a bit of irony in the Court's characterization of what the principle of prescriptive comity helps to achieve. This rule, Justice Breyer writes, "helps the potentially conflicting laws of different nations work together in harmony—a harmony particularly needed in today's highly interdependent commercial world."[43] But the Court never pauses to ask whether that high degree of commercial interdependence has any implications for the premise that the harmful foreign effects of the global vitamins cartel were independent of the adverse domestic ones. It is precisely this assumption that the *Empagran* plaintiffs and *amici* writing in support of them questioned.

The second principal reason the Court provides for its finding the Sherman Act inapplicable in *Empagran* revolves around the Court's understanding of the FTAIA's purpose and the state of antitrust law when the FTAIA was enacted in 1982. Referring to the language and legislative history of the FTAIA, the Court finds that Congress intended the Act "to clarify, perhaps to limit, but not *to expand* in any significant way, the Sherman Act's scope as applied to foreign commerce."[44] Hence, the plaintiff vitamins buyers would be able to establish subject matter jurisdiction only if they could have done so prior to the passage of the FTAIA. The Solicitor General and the vitamin manufacturers and distributors reported that they found no such pre-FTAIA case in which a court applied the Sherman Act to the *Empagran* plaintiffs' type of claim.

---

[41] *Id.* at 165.

[42] *Id.* at 168.

[43] *Id.* at 164–65.

[44] *Id.* at 169.

The Court observes that the vitamins purchasers themselves had apparently conceded the point in a District Court hearing but that they noted for the Supreme Court six cases that they argued provided support for their position.[45]

After reviewing the six cases, three decided by the Supreme Court and three decided by lower courts, Justice Breyer concluded that "no pre–1982 case provides significant authority for application of the Sherman Act in the circumstances we here assume."[46] The three Supreme Court cases were distinguished from *Empagran* because in each of them the United States government was the plaintiff, and "a Government plaintiff has legal authority ... to carry out [its] mission" of "obtain[ing] the relief necessary to protect the public from further anticompetitive conduct and to redress anticompetitive harm."[47] Furthermore, in none of the three cases had the Court focused on relief for "independently caused foreign harm."[48] The absence of consideration of that type of injury, Justice Breyer finds, also rendered the three lower court cases cited by the *Empagran* plaintiffs incapable of supporting the proposition that before the FTAIA's enactment, the Sherman Act applied to a claim like theirs.

Having concluded from considerations of comity and history "that Congress would not have intended the FTAIA's exception to bring independently caused foreign injury within the Sherman Act's reach,"[49] the Court gives brief attention to the plaintiffs' linguistic and policy arguments. The former focused on the FTAIA's reference to "a claim" rather than "the plaintiff's claim" or "the claim at issue," while the latter emphasized the deterrence value of applying the Sherman Act to the vitamins purchasers' claim. The Court finds the empirical dispute between the appellants and respondents about deterrence "neither clear enough, nor of such likely empirical significance" to outweigh its concerns about comity and history.[50] And, although Justice Breyer recognizes that the plaintiffs' arguments from the statute's language "might show that [their] reading is the more natural" one, comity and history show that it is inconsistent with Congress's intent in passing the FTAIA.[51] "If the statute's language reasonably permits an interpretation

---

[45] *Id.* at 169–70.

[46] *Id.* at 173.

[47] *Id.* at 170.

[48] *Id.* at 171.

[49] *Id.* at 173.

[50] *Id.* at 174–75.

[51] *Id.* at 174.

consistent with that intent," as the Court believes it does, "we should adopt it."[52] This last point is emphasized in the concurring opinion that Justice Scalia writes for Justice Thomas and himself. He finds that the FTAIA is "readily susceptible" of the Court's interpretation and that only that interpretation is consistent with the principle of prescriptive comity.[53]

The Court concludes by remanding the case to the District of Columbia Court of Appeals after noting once again its central assumption "that the anticompetitive conduct here independently caused foreign injury" and remarking that the plaintiffs offer an alternative argument that their injury was not independent of the cartel's domestic effects.[54] This argument, which the Court of Appeals had not considered and hence the Supreme Court had elided, is that because of the fungibility and ready transportability of vitamins, the cartel could not have succeeded in raising prices in foreign markets without raising them in the United States. Hence, the buyers argued, they would not have incurred their foreign injury without there having been a harmful domestic effect, and the conduct of which they complain comes within the FTAIA's exception. Justice Breyer leaves it to the Court of Appeals to determine whether the buyers had preserved their alternative argument and, if they had, to consider and decide that claim.[55]

E. The Court of Appeals Decision on Remand

On remand, the Court of Appeals found that the plaintiffs had preserved for appeal their alternative argument that their injury was not independent of the vitamins cartel's domestic effects, but the court rejected their theory and concluded that the FTAIA does not afford it subject matter jurisdiction.[56] Writing for the same, but now unanimous, panel that heard the original appeal, Judge Henderson adopted Justice Breyer's "but-for" characterization of the buyers' alternative argument. Rooted in the defendants' need to eliminate arbitrage possibilities, the purchaser-plaintiffs' argument, she writes, offers "a plausible scenario under which maintaining super-competitive prices in the United States might well have been a 'but-for' cause of the appellants' foreign injury."[57] But that does not suffice to satisfy the FTAIA's statutory language "gives rise to a claim," which requires instead "a direct causal relation-

---

[52] Id.

[53] Id. at 176 (Scalia, J., concurring).

[54] Id. at 175 (majority opinion).

[55] Id.

[56] Empagran S.A. v. F. Hoffmann–La Roche, Ltd., 417 F.3d 1267, 1269 (D.C. Cir. 2005).

[57] Id. at 1270.

ship, that is, proximate causation."[58] Consequently, the higher prices the
vitamins cartel engendered in the United States market—the domestic
effect the *Empagran* plaintiffs marshaled—did not cause their harm in
the way required to bring their antitrust claim within the exception that
the FTAIA provides.

The District of Columbia Circuit rejected, in particular, the plaintiffs' argument that the vitamins cartel's global price-fixing conspiracy
caused the supracompetitive prices they paid and the similarly higher
prices in the United States, and thereby caused the vitamins buyers'
harm. To satisfy the FTAIA exception, the court says, the plaintiffs must
show that one set of effects of the conspiracy—the domestic effects—
caused the other—the supracompetitive foreign prices that injured the
plaintiffs. Showing that both sets of effects had a common cause, in the
global cartel's price fixing, does not establish "the kind of direct tie" the
court finds in two prior cases whose facts met the FTAIA's claim
condition.[59] The *Empagran* plaintiffs' injury as a result of Vitamins Inc.'s
conduct "was not 'inextricably bound up with . . . domestic restraints of
trade' " as had been true in those distinguishable cases.[60]

II. A WELFARIST PERSPECTIVE ON *EMPAGRAN*

Following the bulk of modern academic commentary on antitrust,
we posit that the primary goal of U.S. antitrust policy, if not the
exclusive goal, is the promotion of economic welfare. Accordingly, this
section offers a welfarist perspective on the issues raised by *Empagran*.
We begin with some background considerations relating to optimal
antitrust remedies against cartels in a closed economy, and then proceed
to consider the issues introduced by the fact that the vitamins cartel was
international in scope.

A. *Economic Background: Optimal Remedies for Cartel Practices in a Closed Economy*

Much of the academic writing on antitrust addresses the appropriate
policies for a "closed economy," by which we mean an economy in which
all of the firms and consumers who might be affected by anticompetitive
practices are domestic. From the closed economy perspective, economic
commentary is uniformly hostile to cartels. Cartels create the standard
deadweight loss of monopoly by raising price above marginal cost and
pricing some consumers out of the market. They also transfer substantial rents to themselves from the consumers who buy their goods and
services. Further, in contrast to other business practices that sometimes

---

[58] *Id.* at 1271.

[59] *Id.*

[60] *Id.*

run afoul of the antitrust laws such as mergers, exclusive dealing, or tying, it is difficult to imagine any significant business efficiencies associated with cartels. Indeed, cartel members will often expend significant resources to fix their prices, allocate their markets, and monitor and enforce the cartel, thus compounding the economic costs of monopoly pricing. For these reasons, a consensus exists that cartels reduce economic welfare in a closed economy and ought to be sharply discouraged.

To deter their formation, cartels must be made unprofitable from the perspective of their members—that is, the *ex ante* expected returns to the formation of a cartel must be negative (at least from the perspective of the individual decision makers who may induce their firms to join the cartel). This objective can be accomplished in various ways using criminal and civil penalties. Individuals who initiate or participate in the cartel can be incarcerated or fined, and the firms that participate in the cartel can be made to pay fines to the state or monetary penalties to private plaintiffs.

If, to achieve deterrence, enforcement authorities rely solely on monetary penalties against the firms that participate in cartels, mainstream economic analysis suggests that those penalties should equal, in expectation, the sum of the monopoly profits that the cartel can expect to earn *plus* the value of the deadweight losses caused by the cartel.[61] Such a penalty structure forces the cartel to "internalize" all of the harms that it imposes on others, and will more than suffice to render it unprofitable.

If criminal penalties against individuals are used in conjunction with monetary remedies against firms, the penalties imposed on the firms themselves can be reduced. In principle, criminal penalties against individuals might become high enough (imagine life imprisonment and total forfeiture of assets for individuals who participate in cartel formation and administration) that penalties against firms could become unnecessary. In general, however, both types of penalties will be valuable, and many combinations of them can achieve the desired deterrence.

Whatever mix of penalties is employed, one difficulty that enforcement authorities face is that cartel members generally expect and strive to operate without detection, at least with some substantial probability. This "underdetection problem," familiar in criminal law, necessitates an upward adjustment in penalties to ensure that the *expected* penalty is sufficient to deter. For example, if cartel members expect to be caught about one-third of the time, and firms can be taken to be risk neutral, the penalties that are appropriate for a cartel that will be detected with certainty need to be approximately tripled. (The analysis is more subtle

---

[61] *See* RICHARD A. POSNER, ECONOMIC ANALYSIS OF LAW § 10.12 (5th ed. 1998).

for criminal penalties against individuals.) This observation is sometimes invoked in defense of the treble damages remedy under U.S. law in private antitrust actions, although a routine trebling of damages in all cases across all business practices is surely no more than the crudest sort of adjustment for the underdetection problem. A more careful approach would take account of the mix of civil and criminal penalties available in each type of case, as well as the likelihood that the anticompetitive practice in question would escape detection.

A further complication arises because litigation against cartels, whether by public or private complainants, is costly. How best, then, to achieve appropriate levels of deterrence while reducing litigation and enforcement costs? It is plausible that more effort and cost are required to detect the existence of a cartel than to extract a stiffer penalty once it has been detected. Optimal enforcement policy under these conditions may then require that penalties be set at a very high level in cases where cartel behavior is detected, while enforcement efforts directed at the detection of cartels are curtailed to reduce the attendant costs.[62]

This last observation suggests one reason why public enforcement of laws against cartels may be superior to private enforcement. If penalties increase with private enforcement, the result will be to attract *more* lawsuits and increase the social costs of litigation. In deciding whether to proceed with an action, private plaintiffs will weigh their private benefits and costs, and those may well diverge from their social counterparts. With public enforcement, by contrast, penalties can be increased while efforts to investigate and identify possible cartel behavior are simultaneously curtailed, thereby lowering the costs of enforcement.

U.S. antitrust policy does not seem to take much account of these considerations. It relies heavily on private litigation for antitrust enforcement, and it makes that litigation quite attractive to plaintiffs in general by trebling their damages and enabling them to recover their litigation costs. The distinct possibility exists that greater reliance on public enforcement coupled with a curtailment of private litigation would achieve appropriate deterrence at lower cost. A possible counterargument, to be sure, is that generous private damage awards are valuable at inducing private parties to reveal information about cartel activity that they might not otherwise be inclined to provide.

In summary, to deter the formation of cartels, the total of all penalties, criminal and civil, discounted by the probability that the cartel will escape detection, must be large enough to render the formation of cartels unprofitable from the perspective of the individuals who decide whether to induce their firms to participate. This objective may be

---

[62] *See* Gary S. Becker, *Crime and Punishment: An Economic Approach*, 76 J. POL. ECON. 169 (1968).

achieved by ensuring that any firms participating in a cartel will earn negative expected profits, by targeting the individual actors who choose whether or not to join a cartel with criminal and civil penalties large enough to make participation unattractive to them, or by combining these two approaches. Adding considerations of litigation and enforcement costs to the mix reveals that public and private enforcement efforts are not simple substitutes for each other. Acceptable levels of deterrence may be obtained most cheaply by relying on public enforcement coupled with stiff penalties, but we cannot be sure.

B.   The International Dimension: Global versus National Welfare

The analysis of antitrust policy can change, perhaps in quite important ways, when anticompetitive practices arise in "open economies"— that is, in settings where affected firms and consumers are no longer all of the same nationality. A business practice that reduces welfare in a closed economy will, of course, also reduce global economic welfare because the global economy as a whole is a closed economy. But the welfare effects on individual countries can vary. For example, it is well known that a merger may enhance national welfare but lower global welfare or vice versa.[63] Likewise, although a cartel will lower global welfare for the same reasons that it reduces welfare in a closed economy, the cartel may well enhance the national welfare of countries whose nationals reap cartel profits. What constitutes the "optimal" enforcement policy in a given case can thus turn critically on the question of *whose* welfare is to be promoted by antitrust policy.

Our focus here is on U.S. policy. One possibility is that policy should promote the economic welfare of all individuals regardless of their nationality—a "global welfare" maximand. Another possibility is that U.S. policy should place exclusive emphasis on the welfare of domestic nationals—a "national welfare" maximand. Of course, many intermediate possibilities can be imagined.

If nations cooperate on antitrust policy, a strong argument can be made for the global welfare maximand. When nations jointly pursue global welfare-maximizing policies, global economic surplus will increase, and all nations can gain on average. In principle, winners could compensate losers so that all are better off. Such reasoning has led various commentators to encourage international agreements on competition policy aimed at the promotion of global welfare.[64]

---

[63] *See* Janusz A. Ordover & Alan O. Sykes, *The Antitrust Guidelines for International Operations: An Economic Critique, in* Annual Proceedings of the Fordham Corporate Law Institute: North American and Common Market Antitrust and Trade Laws 4–1 (Barry Hawk ed., 1988).

[64] *See, e.g.,* Eleanor M. Fox, *Competition Law and the Millennium Round*, 2 J. Int'l Econ. L. 665 (1999); Andrew T. Guzman, *Is International Antitrust Possible?*, 73 N.Y.U. L.

The United States is indeed a party to a handful of international agreements relating to antitrust, including bilateral agreements with Australia, Canada, the European Union, and Japan. These agreements oblige the United States to cooperate with foreign competition policy authorities along certain dimensions such as the exchange of information and the coordination of simultaneous investigations.[65] World Trade Organization (WTO) obligations also place some limited constraints on U.S. antitrust policy. A violation of the GATT national treatment obligation (a non-discrimination principle) would arise, for example, if U.S. antitrust law were to impose quadruple damages on foreign defendants but only treble damages on domestic defendants.

For the most part, however, substantive antitrust rules remain outside the domain of international agreements, in part because much disagreement exists on what constitutes an "optimal" antitrust policy. Even in the area of cartel practices, where substantial consensus exists on the evils of cartels, international cooperation has been limited. A recent initiative of the OECD aimed at stimulating cooperative efforts to attack "hard core cartel" practices,[66] for example, has so far yielded little beyond the sorts of bilateral agreements for procedural cooperation just noted. The international legal system's approach to competition policy remains highly decentralized.

As a consequence, the United States is largely free to shape its policy toward international cartels to promote the national interest. The question then becomes, what is the "national interest," and to what extent does it deviate from a policy aimed at global welfare maximization?

To answer this question, it is helpful to begin by considering what global welfare maximization would imply for policy toward cartels. We know that cartels are economically undesirable in a closed economy, and the global economy is assuredly closed. Thus, a global welfare-maximizing policy would be indifferent to the location of a cartel and its activities and to the identity of those who are harmed. The policy would seek to deter any cartel regardless of whose firms benefit from participation in the cartel and whose consumers suffer from it, subject only to the requirement that the costs of deterring cartels must also be considered. If the United States pursued global welfare faithfully, it might then take

---

REV. 1501 (1998); Alan O. Sykes, *Externalities in Open Economy Antitrust and Their Implications for International Competition Policy*, 23 HARV. J.L. & PUB. POL'Y 89 (1999).

[65] The texts of existing U.S. antitrust cooperation agreements may be found at http://www.ftc.gov/bc/international/coopagree.htm.

[66] *See* Org. for Econ. Co-operation & Dev. [OECD], *Recommendation of the Council Concerning Effective Action Against Hard Core Cartels*, C(98)35/FINAL (Mar. 25, 1998), *available at* http://webdomino1.oecd.org/horizontal/oecdacts.nsf/linkto/C(98)35.

jurisdiction freely over conduct abroad regardless of its impact on U.S. commerce whenever the remedy for cartel practices elsewhere failed to provide adequate deterrence, as long as a U.S. court could impose additional penalties effectively. The caveat is that the United States might decline to take jurisdiction if it believed that it would thereby stimulate greater foreign enforcement efforts when such foreign enforcement is more efficient, perhaps because foreign enforcers have better access to evidence or can more easily punish the cartel participants.

While the pursuit of global welfare in this fashion might seem commendably high-minded to some observers, it does not ineluctably follow that the United States should undertake to subsidize global enforcement efforts in this way, and indeed it is questionable whether the U.S. Congress would wish it or authorize it. The Webb–Pomerene Act,[67] for example, exempts from the antitrust laws "export cartels" created by or involving U.S. firms, so long as the conduct in question does not have adverse effects on U.S. consumers. It thus allows U.S. firms to participate in cartels and profit at the expense of foreign consumers even though such behavior reduces global welfare. Likewise, the amendments to the Sherman Act embodied in the FTAIA and at issue in *Empagran* make clear that U.S. courts do not have subject matter jurisdiction over conduct that does not have a "direct, substantial, and reasonably foreseeable effect" on U.S. consumers engaged in domestic or import commerce, or on firms in the U.S. engaged in export commerce.[68] Thus, jurisdiction is precluded unless the conduct in question has adverse effects on the welfare of U.S. consumers or firms. Both statutes suggest that Congress is more concerned with U.S. welfare than with global welfare, a posture that is hardly surprising.

Accordingly, we proceed here on the assumption that U.S. policy toward international cartels should emphasize the pursuit of national welfare over the pursuit of global welfare when the two conflict, at least barring any conflict with the language of the FTAIA or other pertinent provisions of the antitrust laws, or any conflict with international law. We now elaborate what the pursuit of national welfare implies for enforcement policy.

C. *International Cartel Practices and National Welfare*

The national welfare effects of international cartels and of enforcement policies against them are complex. These effects often turn on empirical issues that vary from case to case, and hence theory alone does not provide simple guidelines for antitrust policy in this area or for resolving the particular issues raised in *Empagran*.

---

[67] 15 U.S.C. §§ 61–66 (2000).

[68] 15 U.S.C. § 6a (2000).

We develop the analysis in several steps and begin with a narrow focus on the welfare of firms and consumers in the markets potentially affected by international cartels, blended with attention to enforcement costs. We then add a discussion of the relation between private enforcement actions and amnesty programs (an issue raised by some of the parties in *Empagran*) and a brief discussion of "comity" considerations.

1. Net Welfare Effects on Firms, Consumers, and Enforcers

As Arnold Harberger argued half a century ago, the deadweight costs of monopoly pricing in a closed economy need not be terribly large. Although subsequent writers took issue with his empirics, it is possible that the primary effect of a cartel in a closed economy is to effect transfers from consumers to producers, and that the value of the deadweight loss triangle is modest.[69]

The effects of an international cartel can differ dramatically, however, and can be either favorable or unfavorable from the perspective of the United States. For example, if the firms that participate in a cartel are foreign while the affected consumers are domestic (at least in part), the rent transfer from those consumers to the cartel members becomes pure deadweight loss from the national perspective. The welfare cost is no longer the deadweight loss triangle that was Harberger's focus, but that triangle *plus* the portion of the monopoly profit rectangle earned outside the United States. Depending on the circumstances, the costs to the U.S. economy could be enormous (think of OPEC).

By contrast, if at least some of the firms that participate in the cartel are domestic and the consumers who suffer from the cartel are principally foreign, the cartel may raise U.S. welfare (as we noted earlier with respect to the Webb–Pomerene Act). This can occur even if U.S. consumers are injured by cartel practices to some degree. What is required for U.S. welfare to increase is that the deadweight loss in the United States associated with consumers who are priced out of the market, plus the rent transfer from U.S. consumers to foreign cartel members, must be less than the cartel profits earned by U.S. firms.

These considerations lead to several observations about enforcement policy. First, the United States seemingly has a powerful stake in enforcement policies aimed at *foreign* cartels that earn their profits at the expense of *domestic* consumers. From a national welfare perspective, enforcement policies that deter the formation of such foreign cartels, or that transfer their profits back to the United States after they have been discovered, may be considerably more important than enforcement efforts against purely domestic cartels.

---

[69] *See* Arnold C. Harberger, *Monopoly and Resource Allocation*, 44 AM. ECON. REV. (PAPERS & PROCEEDINGS) 77 (1954). The early response to Harberger is well surveyed in F. M. SCHERER, INDUSTRIAL MARKET STRUCTURE AND ECONOMIC PERFORMANCE 461–65 (2d ed. 1980).

Second, it may or may not be in the interest of the United States to provide *foreign* consumers with the opportunity to pursue antitrust actions against *domestic* cartel members. Other things being equal, the United States gains when domestic firms earn cartel profits at the expense of foreign consumers, and the nation loses when it transfers those profits abroad as antitrust damages. Other things may not be equal, however, because actions by foreign consumers against domestic cartel members may help to deter the formation of international cartels that, on balance, cause a welfare loss for the United States.

Third, and similarly, from a strictly national-welfare perspective, it is not always in the interest of the United States to allow actions by *domestic* consumers against *domestic* firms that participate in international cartels. The net impact on U.S. welfare from such actions will depend on the circumstances. The possibility arises that U.S. firms will be dissuaded from participating in cartels that reduce U.S. welfare, but it is also possible that cartels will be discouraged that actually enhance U.S. welfare.

Finally, the United States may or may not have an interest in allowing actions by *foreign* consumers against *foreign* cartel members. Of particular pertinence to the issues in *Empagran*, allowing actions by foreign consumers may help to deter the formation of international cartels that cause a net welfare loss for the United States. Rather trivially, a welfare gain also arises to the degree that U.S. law firms may earn rents at the expense of foreign cartel members through their representation of foreign plaintiffs. But there are also some potential sources of offsetting losses. A welfare cost will occur to the degree that the United States confers a subsidy on foreign consumers by allowing them to use the U.S. court system and its enforcement mechanism.

In light of these observations, one might imagine an enforcement policy that sorted cases based on an initial appraisal of the welfare effects of a particular cartel. Cartels that have no impact on U.S. commerce could reasonably be ignored (as indeed is the law under the FTAIA). For example, there is no welfare loss for the United States from a foreign cartel selling a product that is not consumed by U.S. consumers, and whose price does not affect the prices of other products sold in the United States. Such cartels can be ignored, and U.S. courts could decline to hear foreign purchasers' complaints about them. Other cartels that enhance U.S. welfare might be allowed to operate unfettered, while those that reduce U.S. welfare might be subject to challenge. The Webb–Pomerene Act accomplishes this sorting in a crude and limited way by exempting cartels that do not sell to U.S. consumers. In principle, the law might engage in further classification by examining indicators such as the share of U.S. firms in cartel profits and the share of U.S. consumers in cartel purchases. Where the former share was considerably greater than the latter, a presumption of net benefit to the United States might arise, and enforcement actions might then be foreclosed.

Of course, U.S. law does not engage in this type of analysis (beyond Webb–Pomerene), and it is easy to imagine how such an enforcement strategy might run into difficulties. The information necessary to make a determination regarding the national welfare effects of a particular cartel (such as data on the profits of U.S. cartel members) may be quite difficult to obtain in practice. Indeed, the net welfare effects may not be stable over time. Further, such a transparent policy of promoting national welfare over global welfare would likely trigger unfortunate strategic reactions abroad, or even a WTO complaint predicated on violation of GATT nondiscrimination obligations. Finally, allowing cartels that enhance U.S. welfare to operate might somehow facilitate the operation of domestic cartels.

As an alternative to distinguishing among cartels based on their welfare effects, enforcement policy might instead attempt to promote national welfare by circumscribing the set of private plaintiffs who may bring cases or the subject matter of the claims they can pursue. This brings us to the sorts of issues that confronted the courts in *Empagran*. Congress has made a clear choice through the FTAIA to allow injured domestic consumers to pursue cases against all cartel members whenever a cartel has "substantial effects" on U.S. commerce. Such suits by domestic consumers may at times discourage the formation of cartels that benefit the United States, but at least the lawsuits themselves transfer rents to U.S. nationals.

Should the same rule apply to suits by foreign plaintiffs in a case such as *Empagran*? The *Empagran* plaintiffs would answer that question in the affirmative, as would a number of the *amici* in the case, particularly the economists who filed amicus briefs. They note that antitrust enforcement outside the United States is often lax, and that penalties are generally lower under foreign antitrust law. They also note that because of arbitrage possibilities, cartels most often must set high prices on a global basis. Unless the combination of trade barriers and transportation costs is high enough, a cartel may be able to reap its supracompetitive profit only if it charges a supracompetitive price in every market it serves. Consequently, a cartel may not be able to charge a competitive price in one market (say, the United States) and still maintain cartel prices elsewhere. For this reason, an international cartel may choose to charge an inflated price in the United States even if penalties under U.S. antitrust law are adequate to deter purely domestic cartels—the added profits on foreign sales can more than compensate for the expected losses on U.S. sales due to antitrust liability. Based on such analysis, the *amici* argue that the total penalties faced by international cartels are inadequate to deter them, and they urge the Court to allow suits by foreign plaintiffs such as those in *Empagran* to enhance the level of deterrence.[70] And the courts should do so, argue the *amici*, whenever the cartel in question has substantial effects on U.S. commerce, even if the harm suffered by the foreign plaintiffs arises from purchases abroad.

The analysis of the *amici* is correct as far as it goes. Allowing foreign plaintiffs to sue will enhance deterrence, other things being equal, and the suggestion that international cartels are not "adequately" deterred without such suits because of weaker antitrust remedies abroad seems plausibly correct. But there are other issues that the *amici* do not address at least in part because they argue from the premise of flat condemnation of the entire category of cartels.

For example, do the international cartels that would be deterred by such a policy generally reduce U.S. welfare? The answer to this question requires at least some analysis. Perhaps it might be argued that because cartels reduce global welfare, they reduce U.S. national welfare on average, but this claim is conjectural. Of course, if one counts only consumer surplus and ignores producer surplus in the welfare calculus, then any international cartel selling into the U.S. national market will necessarily reduce U.S. welfare so measured. But we see little reason for neglecting domestic producer surplus in formulating a national welfare-maximizing policy.

The economist *amici* also downplay the fact that a welfare cost arises for the United States to the degree that U.S. resources are expended on litigation brought by foreign plaintiffs. One might restate the position of these *amici* as follows: Because foreign governments have not done enough to address the problem of international cartels, the United States should shoulder the costs of remedying the situation, effectively providing the rest of the world free use of the U.S. judicial system. So restated, their argument plainly loses some of its force. The *amici* do, however, make the important point that in calculating the incremental costs of making U.S. courts available to foreign plaintiffs, the effect that the enhanced liability has in deterring cartel formation—and hence reducing the need for litigation—must be taken into account.[71]

Indeed, the enforcement policies of other nations may be endogenous to U.S. policy. If the United States lends its judicial system to the

---

[70] *See* Brief of Amici Curiae Economists Joseph E. Stiglitz and Peter R. Orszag in Support of Respondents, F. Hoffmann–La Roche Ltd. v. Empagran S.A., 542 U.S. 155 (2004) (No. 03–724), 2004 WL 533934; Brief for Certain Professors of Economics as Amici Curiae in Support of Respondents, *Empagran*, 542 U.S. 155 (No. 03–724), 2004 WL 533930.

[71] *See* Brief of Amici Curiae Economists Joseph E. Stiglitz and Peter R. Orszag in Support of Respondents, *supra* note 70, at 24–25; Brief for Certain Professors of Economics as Amici Curiae in Support of Respondents, *supra* note 70, at 23.

world to address the problem of global cartels, other nations may freely accept the gift. But if the United States limits its enforcement activity and impliedly insists that other nations contribute to the effort, they may eventually be induced to do so to a considerably greater extent.[72]

Moreover, even if for some reason it is necessary for the United States to shoulder the burden of enhancing deterrence, widening the scope for private suits by foreign plaintiffs is not the only option. Greater levels of public enforcement are a substitute to at least some degree, and one must inquire which option is cheaper and more effective.

Finally, the *amici* do not take account of the fact that a national welfare loss will occur, other things being equal, when litigation brought by foreign plaintiffs transfers rents to them from U.S. firms. This danger is all the more acute since foreign plaintiffs can bring suit in U.S. courts only against firms over which the courts can secure personal jurisdiction, and those plaintiffs can collect damages only from defendants over which the courts have enough leverage to coerce them to pay. The firms that best fit this description may often be U.S. firms, not their fellow cartel members based abroad. The existence of "clawback" statutes in some nations—an attempt to preclude the collection of treble damages from defendants based in such countries—further encourages plaintiffs to pursue U.S. firms. Also, cartel members are subject to joint and several liability under U.S. law.[73] Plaintiffs can thus collect their damages from any one or more of the defendants, and will tend to collect from the defendants from whom they can most cheaply secure payment. U.S. firms may once again be the easy targets. Finally, because contribution actions are not allowed in federal antitrust cases,[74] the distinct possibility arises that plaintiffs will not only tend to collect their damages from U.S. firms, but that those firms will be unable to shift any of their liability to other cartel members through a cross-claim.

Of course, U.S. firms may well anticipate this prospect, and therefore decline to participate in international cartels. If, as a consequence, the cartels never get off the ground or, having launched, fall apart, the *amici*'s objective of deterrence will have been achieved. But cartels may be able to survive and operate without the participation of U.S. firms, especially if U.S. producers have a relatively small market share. Perhaps the cartels most likely to be undermined by allowing plaintiffs such as those in *Empagran* to bring actions are the ones in which U.S. firms have a large portion of the global market and are essential participants—

---

[72] A similar point is made in Christopher Sprigman, *Fix Prices Globally, Get Sued Locally? U.S. Jurisdiction over International Cartels*, 72 U. CHI. L. REV. 265 (2005).

[73] *See* HERBERT HOVENKAMP, FEDERAL ANTITRUST POLICY: THE LAW OF COMPETITION AND ITS PRACTICE § 17.7 (3d ed. 2005).

[74] *Id.*

precisely the cartels that may be more likely to contribute to U.S. national welfare.

For these reasons, a careful, more complete analysis of the national interest leaves a more complicated picture than the economist *amici* in *Empagran* acknowledged. Their policy conclusion may be the right one, but only if one embraces certain empirical assumptions that require justification that the *amici* themselves do not provide, or if in formulating policy one ignores the surplus earned by U.S. producers.

2. The Amnesty Issue

Returning to the relation between public and private enforcement efforts, part of the dispute in *Empagran* centered on the claim that allowing private suits by foreign plaintiffs would undermine public enforcement. In particular, an *amicus* brief filed on behalf of the United States by the State Department Legal Adviser, the Acting General Counsel of the FTC, and the Acting Solicitor General argued that greater *civil* liability because of suits by foreign plaintiffs such as those in *Empagran* would discourage cartel members from participating in the existing *criminal* amnesty program. That amnesty program allows cartel members and their executives who reveal valuable enforcement information about cartel activities to the U.S. government to receive a substantial reduction in criminal penalties. The first cartel member to disclose information about the group's organization and activities is treated the most leniently. Succeeding confessor firms benefit only if they provide information of sufficient incremental value. Because, however, criminal amnesty does not foreclose civil liability, the U.S. government *amici* argued that an increase in civil liability would make potential amnesty program participants less likely to break ranks with the cartel.[75] The *amici* further argued that the amnesty program had been exceptionally effective at uncovering cartel behavior, and that it did far more to discourage cartels than would expanded civil liability. Consequently, to maintain the attractiveness of amnesty, they strongly favored a construction of the FTAIA that would bar suits by foreign plaintiffs such as those in *Empagran*.

The merits of this argument turn on careful empirical evaluation of alternative enforcement measures. Neither the required data nor the full specification of relevant counterfactuals was provided, and the *Empa-*

---

[75] *See* Brief for the United States as Amicus Curiae Supporting Petitioners, *supra* note 7, at 20–21; *see also* Brief of the Governments of the Federal Republic of Germany and Belgium as Amici Curiae in Support of Petitioners at 29–30, *Empagran*, 542 U.S. 155 (No. 03–724), 2004 WL 226388; Brief for the Government of Canada as Amicus Curiae Supporting Reversal at 13–14, *Empagran*, 542 U.S. 155 (No. 03–724), 2004 WL 226389; Brief of the United Kingdom of Great Britain and Northern Ireland et al. as Amici Curiae in Support of Petitioners at 11–13, *Empagran*, 542 U.S. 155 (No. 03–724), 2004 WL 226597.

gran court wisely declined to try to resolve this empirical debate. It is indeed possible that public enforcement is superior to private enforcement. Public enforcers have both the power and the inclination to pursue individual wrongdoers, and to punish them severely with penalties that private enforcers cannot utilize (for example, incarceration). They can also ratchet up the penalties for cartel activity and curtail costly detection efforts in line with the teachings of optimal deterrence theory. The U.S. government *amici's* argument goes a step further, however, by emphasizing that public enforcement can employ an additional policy instrument—the promise of amnesty—to induce cartel members to break ranks. These *amici* are right that the advantage of seeking amnesty is, other things being equal, smaller the greater is the residuum of prospective civil liability. How much the incentive to seek amnesty is blunted depends on the effect that residuum has at the margin on individual cartel members' calculations of the costs and benefits of staying in the cartel versus disclosing its activities.[76] That calculus may entail weighing complex strategic interactions among the cartel members. If the adverse effect of greater civil liability on the incentives to seek amnesty is great enough, the net impact on deterrence may be adverse.

But if this is true, it is a generic problem and not one limited to suits by foreign plaintiffs against international cartels. As the economist *amici* argued in response to the United States, the interpretation of the FTAIA favored by the *Empagran* plaintiffs would expose participants in international cartels affecting the U.S. market to the same potential civil liability that the participants in purely domestic cartels already face. All victims of cartel activity would be allowed to sue in U.S. courts. In fact, foreign cartel participants likely would still face somewhat less liability than domestic cartel participants because foreign cartel members may have the capacity to ignore U.S. judgments, or may be protected by clawback statutes that reduce their liability. Hence, if allowing suits by the foreign plaintiffs in *Empagran* would undermine the amnesty program with respect to foreign cartels, the adverse effects of civil liability on the amnesty program would seem to be even more acute for domestic cartels unless for some reason the expected penalties for domestic cartels are otherwise lower than for foreign cartels, a situation which seems unlikely.

An irony is that just as the United States was arguing against extending cartel members' civil liability to foreign plaintiffs because of the deleterious effect it would have on the amnesty program, Congress was debating a bill to reduce the civil liability that an amnesty program

---

[76] For a related discussion, see Jonathan T. Schmidt, Note, *Keeping U.S. Courts Open to Foreign Antitrust Plaintiffs: A Hybrid Approach to the Effective Deterrence of International Cartels*, 31 YALE J. INT'L L. 211, 246–47 (2006).

participant might face. That proposal, which allows potential detrebling of the private damages that a fully cooperating leniency-program participant might face, was supported by the Department of Justice. It became law in 2004 as part of the Antitrust Criminal Penalty Enhancement and Reform Act of 2004.[77] Consequently, the harmful impact that the U.S. *amici* argued would follow from a plaintiff's victory in *Empagran* was soon to be considerably diminished in any event.

The U.S. government *amici*'s point may nevertheless be recast as a second-best argument. If civil liability for cartel activity is presently so high that it undermines public enforcement efforts, at least the problem is diminished in the case of international cartels as long as foreign plaintiffs are limited in their capacity to bring claims. So restated, we cannot exclude the possibility that the argument is correct.

3. "Comity"

One other set of considerations warrants attention and was central to the Supreme Court's *Empagran* decision. When the United States takes jurisdiction over conduct abroad, and especially when it seeks to impose stiff penalties on foreign firms or individuals, it may tread on the interests and preferences of foreign governments. Such concerns do not arise with purely domestic antitrust enforcement. The courts have long recognized that antitrust enforcement directed at parties or activities outside the U.S. should be attentive to international relations and to the question of when and to what extent the United States should defer to other countries' choices about competition policy rules and remedies. This set of issues may be subsumed under the rubric of "comity."

The comity issues are perhaps somewhat easier in the case of cartels because there is now little international disagreement that cartels are detrimental to the global economy. The problems of international cooperation, and hence jurisdiction, are greater with respect to other offenses for which there is not a shared understanding of what should be sanctioned. But even with regard to cartels, differences of opinion remain with respect to the proper remedy. The divergence may relate to the different remedies and penalties that the United States and other nations have imposed. Alternatively, other countries with fledgling antitrust policies may have a more general concern about having a U.S. court determine the criminal and civil penalties that foreign nationals—individuals and businesses—would face, and instead wish to evolve their own systems of remedies.

As the economist *amici* point out in their analysis of why international cartels may not be adequately deterred, other nations often have considerably weaker criminal penalties than the United States does and

---

[77] *See* Pub. L. No. 108–237, § 213, 118 Stat. 661, 666–67 (2004).

limited or non-existent private enforcement. In nations where private enforcement exists, the damages are often limited to compensatory amounts (no trebling). The fact that other nations employ weaker remedies, however, does not necessarily imply that international relations will be undermined in any important way if the United States employs stiffer remedies. Foreign governments might be delighted to see the United States take on the costs of more vigorous cartel enforcement. In *Empagran,* however, numerous foreign governments intervened to argue against allowing the foreign plaintiffs to sue. The foreign government *amici* included the United Kingdom, Republic of Ireland, Federal Republic of Germany, Belgium, Canada, Japan and the Netherlands. All of them argued, at least implicitly, that considerations of comity should lead the United States to defer to foreign remedies.

The mere fact that foreign governments express preferences on an issue, while deserving careful consideration, does not establish that the United States should honor those preferences in the interests of comity. The idea of comity has a simple economic interpretation. It is a way of saying that nations may defer to the preferences of other nations at times because they expect to benefit on balance through some form of reciprocity, whether in the form of reciprocal deference or cooperation on some entirely unrelated matter. So understood, it is easy to see why, in principle, nations might at times wish to defer to others on grounds of comity. But it is exceedingly difficult to decide, as a practical matter, when to do that.

The dimensions of international relations that may be affected by matters before a court, and by decisions that foreign governments find objectionable, are vast. Courts have no direct way to obtain reliable information about them. Private litigants face much the same problem, and, in any event, their assessments are shaped by their interest in the case's outcome. As a result, courts are generally forced to rely on representations by various government *amici*. Yet, none of the *amici* has systematic incentives to offer advice that unbiasedly balances the relevant costs and benefits. Foreign governments have every incentive to overstate their interests and to ignore the U.S. domestic interest. The U.S. Executive Branch is no doubt somewhat more inclined to consider both sides of the ledger, but it too may be driven by excessive concern for one type of problem over another, or by political considerations that do not map well with the national interest. Nevertheless, the position taken by the Executive Branch may be the most reliable indicator of the national interest available notwithstanding its imperfections.

III. THE IMPLICATIONS OF THE WELFARIST PERSPECTIVE ON *EMPAGRAN*

In this section we explore the implications of our welfarist perspective on the Supreme Court's *Empagran* decision. We assess whether the

Court's decision advanced the development of antitrust law and policy in an increasingly interdependent world. In particular, we consider the Court's approach to comity and the role that it ought to play in deciding antitrust cases under U.S. law. Then, we examine the implications of the welfarist perspective for the statute at the center of the *Empagran* case, the FTAIA.

A. Comity and the "Independence" of the Plaintiff's Injury

In deciding *Empagran*, the Court could not undertake a welfare analysis from first principles as we and other commentators can. The Court needed to follow the canons of faithful statutory interpretation and decide the case as it had been precisely framed. When the statute at issue in an antitrust case is perceived to be ambiguous, as the Court regarded the FTAIA in this case, perhaps, however, the Court has more scope to shape the doctrine in a way that systematically promotes economic welfare. In any event, as an analytical matter, with regard to any antitrust case, we can ask whether the Court's approach and the factors it considered—not just the decision it reached—comports with welfarist analysis undertaken from either a global or a national perspective. In *Empagran* the Court's analysis did not proceed along that path.

The disjunction results, in large part, because of the central concept that drives the Court's analysis, its postulated "independence" of the effects that the global vitamins cartel's activities had on foreign consumers and domestic ones. Sometimes the effect of a cartel can be confined to one nation or one region, and sometimes high transportation costs, tariff barriers, or other national regulatory requirements may insulate the effects of a truly international cartel between countries or regions. But what meaning can the Court's hypothesized "independent effect" have in the case of a global price-fixing cartel that sets prices in many countries when traders can easily arbitrage price differences? The concept is difficult to fathom unless it is meant to be another (redundant) way of asking whether the conduct at issue harms U.S. nationals. That, however, is not what the Court seemed to be saying. The Court takes independent foreign injury to be an injury that the conduct's domestic effects did not help to create. It is difficult to understand what this concept means when maintenance of the cartel's price in one location requires its maintenance wherever it is sold because arbitrage can successfully overcome price differences.

The Court's causation language is distinctly unhelpful, and it created further problems when the *Empagran* case returned on remand to the D.C. Circuit, which said that the effect of the cartel in the U.S. market was a but-for cause but not a proximate cause of the plaintiffs' harm. There is need for a change in thinking and language about the appropriate concept of causation. The cartel's *activity* gives rise to a *set of effects* in different countries. No one of those effects is causally related to the others. Unless trade between the countries is impeded and arbitrage ineffective, the international worldwide action has international, world-wide effects. A welfarist-based policy that aims to deter the formation and activities of detrimental cartels must take account of the full set of effects such cartels engender.

The "independent" character of the *Empagran* plaintiffs' injury plays an important role in the Court's application of prescriptive comity. "[W]hy is it reasonable," Justice Breyer asks, "to apply [America's antitrust] laws to foreign conduct *insofar as that conduct causes indepen-dent foreign harm and that foreign harm alone gives rise to the plaintiff's claim?*"[78] It is the independence and purely foreign character of the injury that renders "insubstantial" the gains from interference with foreign countries' regulation of their own commercial affairs. With respect to comity, *Empagran* takes a step away from the Court's ap-proach in *Hartford Fire Insurance Co. v. California.*[79] It follows much more closely Justice Scalia's dissent in *Hartford Fire,* a case concerning *foreign* conduct causing *domestic* effects and *domestic* harm, than it does the majority opinion in that case. The *Empagran* Court's approach represents a revival of prescriptive comity analysis as it proceeds along the lines of Justice Scalia's *Hartford Fire* dissent to consider the reach of U.S. law to foreign behavior and conduct, and as it rejects the case-by-case interest-balancing approach of *Timberlane.*[80]

Considering Justice Breyer's question, suppose that the foreign plaintiff's domicile does not provide any remedy for the supracompetitive prices it pays as a result of the cartel's price fixing. Would prescriptive comity require that U.S. courts defer and not allow suit under U.S. antitrust law? The penalty imposed for international price-fixing cartel behavior then might be less than required for optimal deterrence, even from a national welfare perspective. To paraphrase Justice Breyer, Why would that be reasonable? Why ignore this problem of inadequate deterrence? By contrast, if the potential plaintiff's home country does provide adequate remedy, then there is little reason for the U.S. court to accept the case, and the directive of prescriptive comity would be well-aligned with the theory of optimal deterrence. This analysis suggests that comity considerations alone should not be determinative, but merely one factor to consider along with others, including the adequacy of deterrence from the U.S. perspective and the likely impact on U.S firms of allowing the suit to proceed (as discussed in our section on welfare issues).

---

[78] *Empagran,* 542 U.S. at 165.

[79] 509 U.S. 764 (1993).

[80] Timberlane Lumber Co. v. Bank of Am., N.T. & S.A., 549 F.2d 597 (9th Cir. 1976).

In addition, while discussing considerations of prescriptive comity, the Court sharply distinguishes between private and public enforcement of the antitrust laws. This distinction is, of course, important in purely domestic actions as well, especially in the context of an action brought by a firm's competitor. There is always the concern that private interests may motivate the filing of an action when the public enforcement agency would stay its hand. The antitrust injury doctrine emerged from just such concerns. But the *Empagran* Court's emphasis on the private-public distinction to explain why fewer questions would be raised by a public enforcement agency's claim than by a private party's in an *Empagran*-type setting reflects a new element injected by the international context. The Court correctly explains that in deciding whether to pursue a claim, public enforcement agencies weigh the international, diplomatic concerns while private parties have no incentive to do so. This is a variant of the point that with respect to questions of comity, reliance on the Executive is about the best we can do. The counterargument is that enforcement authorities face scarce resources and that U.S. antitrust enforcement has always relied heavily on private attorneys general. Inaction by the enforcement authorities does not provide conclusive evidence that concerns about an action's ramifications for international relations predominate.

Case-by-case application of comity can be difficult, as the *Empagran* Court argues, but that difficulty cannot completely determine how to proceed in such cases. What we are seeking is a second-best approach in the absence of shared international agreement about a global antitrust regime but in the presence of strong economic interdependence. When welfare effects are significant enough, careful examination of the substantive concerns traveling under the "comity" heading should be undertaken. In particular, as the *Empagran* plaintiffs argued,[81] it may be possible to identify categories of harmful behavior—for example, price fixing by cartels—on which there is sufficient international agreement that remaining inter-country differences pale in comparison with welfarist considerations.

B. *The Text of the Foreign Trade Antitrust Improvements Act*

Can the FTAIA be interpreted in a way that is consistent with a welfarist approach? The Act requires first that for the Sherman Act to apply to conduct involving non-import trade or commerce with foreign nations the activity must have a "direct, substantial, and reasonably foreseeable effect" on domestic commerce. This meshes with what our analysis sets as a necessary condition for U.S. courts to take jurisdiction over foreign plaintiffs' allegations that they have suffered anticompetitive harms.

---

[81] *See Empagran*, 542 U.S. at 168.

The central issue about the statute is the putative ambiguity of its language in speaking of "a claim." Justice Breyer recognizes the natural meaning of the text, but he says that it is not the only acceptable meaning. Justice Scalia, in his concurrence, emphasizes this possibility of other acceptable meanings. With "a claim" broadly construed, as the D.C. Circuit interpreted it in that court's original decision,[82] the FTAIA would permit *Empagran*-type claims in the circumstances in which we conclude jurisdiction should be granted.

The statute permits our preferred interpretation but apparently many others as well. Under the dictates of prescriptive comity, however, ambiguous statutes are ordinarily understood "to avoid unreasonable interference with the sovereign authority of other nations,"[83] and that might argue against reading the FTAIA to allow *Empagran*-type claims at least by nationals of countries that have effective competition policies of their own. In addition, the history of the FTAIA does not reveal any Congressional intent to extend the reach of the Sherman Act to foreign commerce. Quite to the contrary, the principal purpose of the FTAIA was to limit the antitrust exposure of U.S. exporters. Yet Congress rejected language proposed by business interests that would have prohibited suits by parties who were injured outside the U.S.[84]

The difficult questions are empirical in character: Is deterrence inadequate without a U.S. remedy? And what are the stakes in declining to exercise "comity"? These are not issues that can be neatly resolved by parsing the statutory language.

Conclusion

Empagran raises difficult issues for antitrust enforcement, as do global cartels more generally. We favor a welfarist approach to the issues here as elsewhere in antitrust, but that does not make the cases easy. The Supreme Court in *Empagran* does not follow any intelligible welfarist course, however, and instead confuses matters with a line of causal analysis that can promote public welfare only by coincidence.

The road forward is murky both as a legal matter and from an economic perspective. The government and economist *amici* in the case did a good job of identifying the stakes, but none of them provides a fully satisfactory framework for decisionmaking. The economists, who favored allowing the case to go forward, correctly emphasized the importance of adequate deterrence, but do not convince us that the United States should necessarily shoulder the burden in all of these cases, especially given the greater exposure that U.S. firms may face in U.S. courts as

---

[82] Empagran S.A. v. F. Hoffman–La Roche, Ltd., 315 F.3d 338, 350 (D.C. Cir. 2003).

[83] *Empagran*, 542 U.S. at 164.

[84] *See* Sprigman, *supra* note 72, at 278.

compared to their foreign competitors. The government's concern about negative effects on its amnesty program, offered in opposition to the action, seems to prove far too much. Finally, appeals to "comity" by various *amici*, and ultimately by the Supreme Court itself, are of at best modest utility, for the simple reason that the weightiness of comity considerations in the face of other welfarist concerns is extremely difficult to assess.

The *Empagran* Court did not provide much help with the difficult issues in play. And the approach of the D.C. Circuit on remand suggests that foreign plaintiffs will systematically be excluded from the opportunity to pursue remedies in U.S. courts against global cartels regardless of the implications for deterrence. It is possible that this is the right policy from a national welfare perspective, but the reasoning behind it is dubious at best. The case may indicate the need for further Congressional action with the Supreme Court's *Empagran* decision considered an invitation to Congress to clarify whether the FTAIA should allow such claims against international price-fixing cartels to go forward in U.S. courts. But, more important, the case highlights the potential value of deeper international agreements on competition policy.

*

Author Biographies

Donald Baker: Don Baker formerly served as Assistant Attorney General for Antitrust in the United States Department of Justice and as a law professor at the Cornell Law School. He is currently a partner in the Washington, D.C., firm of Baker & Miller, which specializes in antitrust and competition policy issues. Mr. Baker has published numerous writings on a broad range of antitrust and economic regulation topics and is co-author of two treatises, Baker & Brandel, THE LAW OF ELECTRONIC FUNDS TRANSFER SYSTEMS (3rd ed. 1996), and Rowley & Baker, INTERNATIONAL MERGERS—THE ANTITRUST PROCESS (2d ed. 1996).

Jonathan B. Baker: Jon Baker is Professor of Law at Washington College of Law, American University. Between 1995 and 1998, he was Director, Bureau of Economics, Federal Trade Commission, and between 1993 and 1995, he was Senior Economist, President's Council of Economic Advisers. Professor Baker has written extensively in the antitrust field, including *Mavericks, Mergers and Exclusion: Proving Coordinated Competitive Effects Under the Antitrust Laws*, 77 N.Y.U. L. Rev. 135 (2002), *The Case for Antitrust Enforcement*, 17 J. Econ. Perspectives 27 (2003), and ANTITRUST LAW IN PERSPECTIVE: CASES, CONCEPTS AND PROBLEMS IN COMPETITION POLICY (2002) (with Andrew I. Gavil & William E. Kovacic).

Stephen Calkins: Stephen Calkins is Professor of Law and Director of Graduate Studies at the Wayne State University Law School. Between 1995 and 1997, Professor Calkins served as General Counsel to the Federal Trade Commission. He consults with federal, state, and foreign governmental agencies, has testified before Congress and at national hearings, and has an extensive speaking program here and abroad. He is currently serving his third three-year term on the Council of the ABA Antitrust Section. He is the author of numerous publications on antitrust and trade regulation, including the co-authored Antitrust Law and Economics in a Nutshell (West 5th ed. 2004).

Peter C. Carstensen: Peter Carstensen is the George H. Young–Bascom Professor of Law at the University of Wisconsin School of Law. From 1968 to 1973, he was an attorney at the Antitrust Division of the United States Department of Justice assigned to the Evaluation Section, where one of his primary areas of work was on questions of relating competition policy and law to regulated industries. His scholarship and teaching have focused on antitrust law and competition policy issues and include *How to Assess the Impact of Antitrust on the American Economy: Examining History or Theorizing?*, 74 Iowa L. Rev. 1175 (1989).

Daniel A. Crane: Dan Crane is Associate Professor at the Benjamin N. Cardozo School of Law, Yeshiva University and counsel to Paul, Weiss, Rifkind, Wharton & Garrison LLP. He is the author of a number of works on exclusionary practices such as predatory pricing and bundled discounting. His antitrust scholarship includes *The Paradox of Predatory Pricing*, 91 Cornell L. Rev. 1 (2005) and *Multiproduct Discounting: A Myth of Non–Price Predation*, 72 U. Chi. L. Rev. 27 (2005).

Harry First: Harry First is the Charles L. Denison Professor of Law and Director of the Trade Regulation Program at the NYU School of Law. He is the co-author of casebooks on antitrust and on regulated industries, the author of a casebook on business crime, and the author of numerous articles involving antitrust law, including *Microsoft and the Evolution of the Intellectual Property Concept*, 2006 Wis. L. Rev. 1369, and *Re-framing Windows: The Durable Meaning of the Microsoft Antitrust Litigation*, 2006 Utah L. Rev. 641 (with Andrew I. Gavil). From 1999 to 2001 he served as Chief of the Antitrust Bureau of the Office of the Attorney General of the State of New York.

Eleanor M. Fox: Eleanor Fox is the Walter J. Derenberg Professor of Trade Regulation at NYU, where she has taught since 1976. Professor Fox is the author of numerous articles and books on antitrust law and trade regulation, including U.S. ANTITRUST IN GLOBAL CONTEXT, CASES AND MATERIALS, West, 2004 (with Lawrence A. Sullivan and Rudolph J.R. Peritz), EUROPEAN UNION LAW: CASES AND MATERIALS, West, 2002, Supp. 2004 (with George A. Bermann, William J. Davey and Roger J. Goebel), *Antitrust and Regulatory Federalism: Races Up, Down and Sideways*, 75 NYU L. Rev. 178 (2000), *International Antitrust and the Doha Dome*, 43 Va. J. Int'l Law 911 (2003); *What Is Harm to Competition?—Exclusionary Practices and Anticompetitive Effect*, 70 Antitrust L.J. 371 (2002).

Warren Grimes: Warren Grimes is Irving D. & Florence Rosenberg Professor of Law at Southwestern Law School. He has served as Attorney Advisor to the U.S. Department of Justice Office of Legal Counsel, representative of the FTC to the Organization for Economic Cooperation and Development, and chief counsel of the United States House of Representatives Judiciary Committee's Subcommittee on Monopolies and Commercial Law. His numerous antitrust publications include THE LAW OF ANTITRUST: AN INTEGRATED HANDBOOK (West 2d ed. 2006) (with Lawrence Sullivan) and *Antitrust and the Systemic Bias Against Small*

Business: Kodak, Strategic Conduct, and Leverage Theory, 52 Case Western Reserve Law Review 231 (2001).

Alvin Klevorick: Al Klevorick, an economist, is the John Thomas Smith Professor of Law, Professor of Economics, and the Director of the Division of the Social Sciences at Yale University. His subject areas are antitrust, economic regulation, law and economics, torts, and market organization. His publications include *A Framework for Analyzing Predatory Pricing Policy*, 89 Yale L.J. 213 (1979) (with Paul L. Joskow), *The Fractured Unity of Antitrust Law and the Antitrust Jurisprudence of Justice Stevens*, 27 Rutgers L. J. 637 (1996), and *The Oversight of Restructured Electricity Markets*, in James M. Griffin and Steven L. Puller, eds., ELECTRICITY DEREGULATION: CHOICES AND CHALLENGES, Univ. of Chicago Press, 2005.

Jonathan Lewinsohn: Jonathan Lewinsohn is a graduate of the Yale Law School and a law clerk to the Honorable Richard A. Posner, United States Court of Appeals for the Seventh Circuit.

James May: Jim May is Professor of Law at the Washington College of Law, American University, where he teaches both antitrust law and United States legal history. Prior to his entry into law teaching, he was an attorney in the Antitrust Division of the U.S. Department of Justice from 1976 to 1982 and Senior Staff Assistant, National Commission for the Review of Antitrust Laws and Procedures from 1978 to 1979. His publications on antitrust law and legal history include: Science, Politics, and the Evolution of Law and Neoclassical Economics, 15 Law & Hist. Rev. 333 (1997), *Antitrust in the Formative Era: Political and Economic Theory in Constitutional and Antitrust Analysis, 1880–1918*, 50 Ohio St. L. J. 257 (1989) and *Antitrust Practice and Procedure in the Formative Era: The Constitutional and Conceptual Reach of State Antitrust Law, 1880–1918*, 135 U. Pa. L. Rev. 495 (1987).

A. Douglas Melamed. Doug Melamed is co-chair of the Antitrust and Competition Department at Wilmer Cutler Pickering Hale & Dorr. Mr. Melamed served in the US Department of Justice from October 1996 to January 2001, first as Principal Deputy Assistant Attorney General and then as Acting Assistant Attorney General in charge of the Antitrust Division. He has been a visiting professor at Georgetown University Law Center and a frequent speaker on antitrust matters. He was co-author, with Guido Calabresi, of *Property Rules, Liability Rules, and Inalienability: One View of the Cathedral*, 85 Harv. L. Rev. 1089 (1972), one of the most-cited law review articles ever published.

Rudolph J.R. Peritz: Rudy Peritz is Professor of Law and Director of the IProgress Project at New York Law School. His critically acclaimed COMPETITION POLICY IN AMERICA: HISTORY, RHETORIC, LAW (Oxford University Press, 1996, rev. ed., 2001) traces the public discourse of free competition and the underlying tension between its two different visions—freedom not only from oppressive government, but also from private economic power. He is co-author with Eleanor Fox and Lawrence

Sullivan of U.S. ANTITRUST IN GLOBAL CONTEXT, CASES AND MATERIALS (West 2004) and a frequent author on antitrust matters, especially those at the interface of intellectual property, including *The Impact of Antitrust Law on Intellectual Property Rights in the United States*, in Steven J. Anderman, ed., THE COMPETITION–INTELLECTUAL PROPERTY INTERFACE: A COMPARATIVE PERSPECTIVE (Cambridge University Press, forthcoming 2007).

Robert Pitofsky: Professor Pitofsky is the Joseph and Madeline Sheehy Professor in Antitrust and Trade Regulation Law; Dean Emeritus at Georgetown University Law Center. Professor Pitofsky served as a commissioner and later chairman of the Federal Trade Commission, the director of the Bureau of Consumer Protection of the FTC, counsel to the American Bar Association Commission to Study the FTC, and chair of a Department of Defense Task Force on downsizing the Defense Industry. In addition, he is co-author of the text, CASES & MATERIALS ON ANTITRUST (Foundation Press, 5th ed. 2003) (with Harvey J. Goldschmid and Diane P. Wood) and numerous other antitrust writings. Professor Pitofsky served as Dean of the Georgetown Law School from 1983 to 1989, and has taught courses at the Law Center in Antitrust, Consumer Protection, Federal Courts, and Constitutional Law. He practices law as counsel to the D.C. firm of Arnold and Porter.

George Priest: George Priest is the John M. Olin Professor of Law and Economics at the Yale Law School. Professor Priest is a prolific author on law and economics and antitrust matters. His publications include *Antitrust Enforcement in the Information Age*, 4 Tex. Rev. L. & Pol. 141 (1999) and *The Antitrust Suits and the Public Understanding of Insurance*, 63 Tul. L. Rev. 999 (1989). Professor Priest has taken a leading role in public commentary on a number of high-profile antitrust matters, including the Department of Justice's lawsuit against Microsoft and the European Commission's disapproval of the GE/Honeywell merger.

Daniel L. Rubinfeld: Daniel Rubinfeld received his Ph.D. in economics from M.I.T. and is the Robert L. Bridges Professor of Law and Professor of Economics at the University of California, Berkeley and Visiting Professor of Law at NYU. In December 1998, he completed an 18–month term as Deputy Assistant Attorney General at the U.S. Department of Justice, Antitrust Division. His current research interests relate directly to issues of antitrust enforcement, competition policy, and intellectual property. In his academic career, Dr. Rubinfeld's research has spanned a broad range of subject matter, including the political economy of federalism, law and economics, and industrial organization and competition policy. He has published or edited 6 books and over 100 articles. He is, with Robert Pindyck, the author of one of the leading microeconomics textbooks, MICROECONOMICS (6th ed. 2005).

Alan O. Sykes: Alan Sykes received his Ph.D. in Economics from Yale University and is Professor of Law at Stanford Law School and a leading expert on international economic relations. His writing and teaching have encompassed international trade, torts, contracts, insurance, antitrust, and economic analysis of law. He has been a member of the executive committee and the board of the American Law and Economics Association, and currently serves as reporter for the American Law Institute Project on Principles of Trade Law: The World Trade Organization. Professor Sykes is associate editor of the Journal of International Economic Law, and a member of the board of editors of the World Trade Review. He served as Editor of the Journal of Law and Economics from 1991 to 2000 and as editor of the Journal of Legal Studies from 2000–2006.

Spencer Weber Waller: Spencer Weber Waller is Professor, Associate Dean for Research, and Director of the Institute for Consumer Antitrust Studies at Loyola University Chicago School of Law. Professor Waller worked for the U.S. Department of Justice, as a trial attorney in the Foreign Commerce Section of the Antitrust Division, then as a special attorney in the Chicago Strike Force of the Criminal Division and later in private practice in Chicago, Illinois before entering teaching. His many publications include ANTITRUST AND AMERICAN BUSINESS ABROAD (3rd ed., West Group, 1997 and annual supplements) and THURMAN ARNOLD: A BIOGRAPHY (NYU Press 2006).

†